Pandora Hearts

Jun Mochizuki

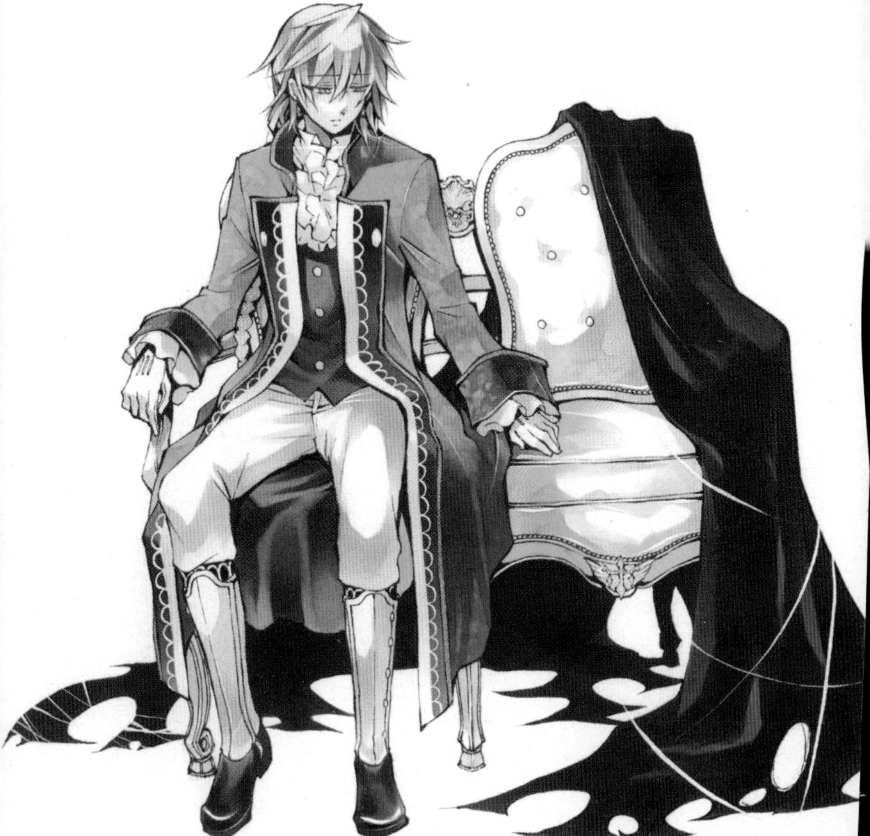

CONTENTS

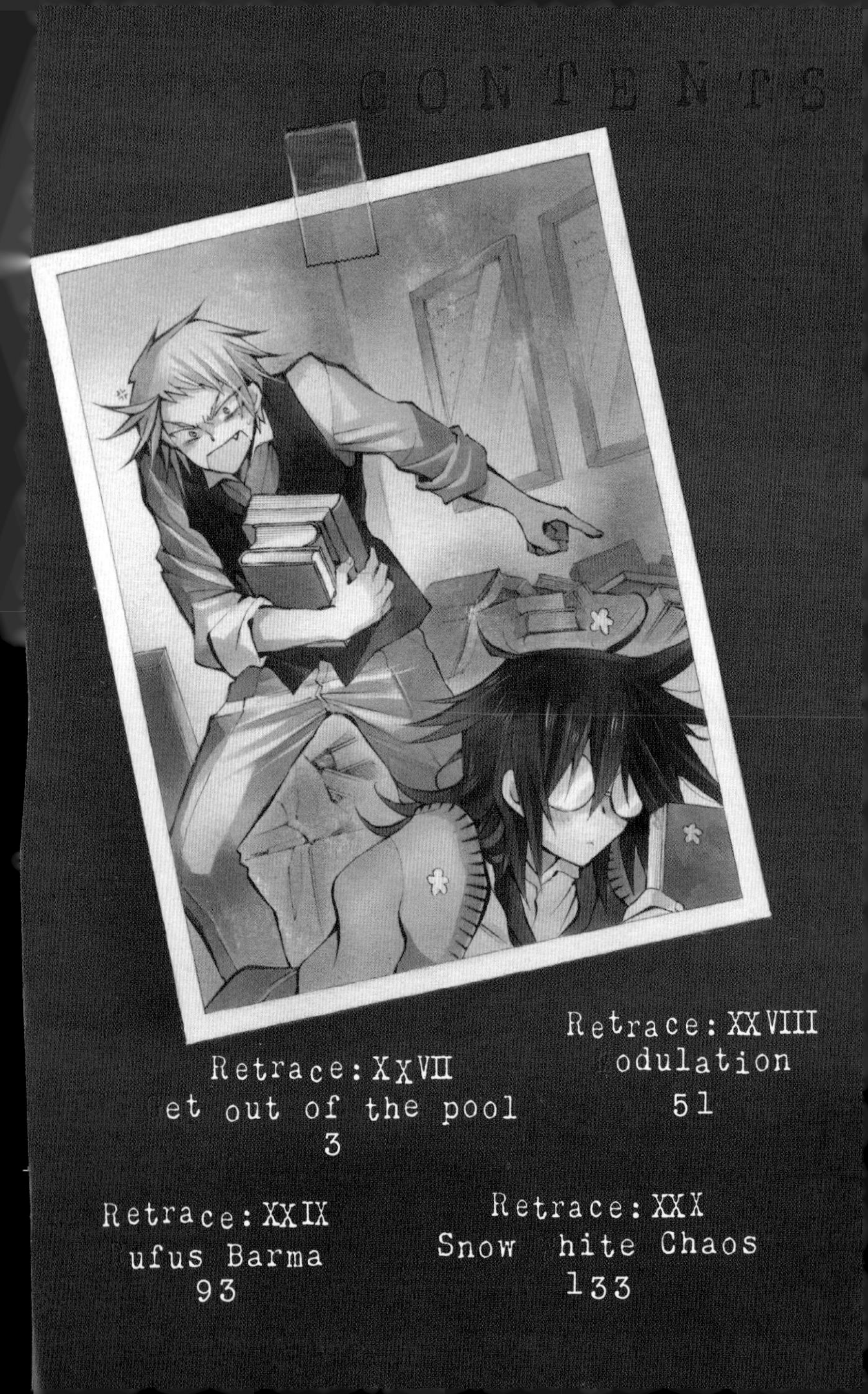

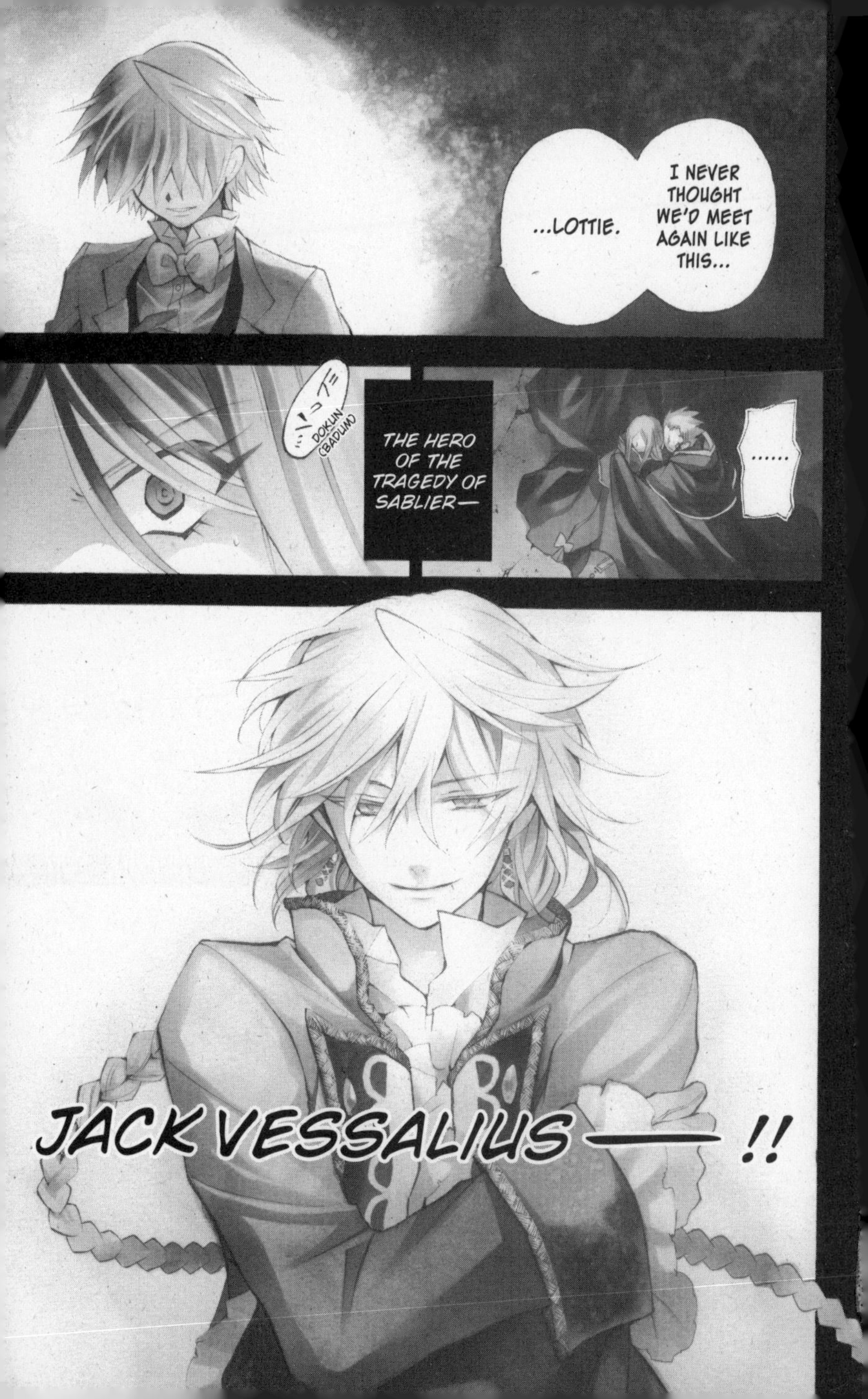
I NEVER THOUGHT WE'D MEET AGAIN LIKE THIS...
...LOTTIE.
......
THE HERO OF THE TRAGEDY OF SABLIER—
DOKUN (BADUM)
JACK VESSALIUS——!!

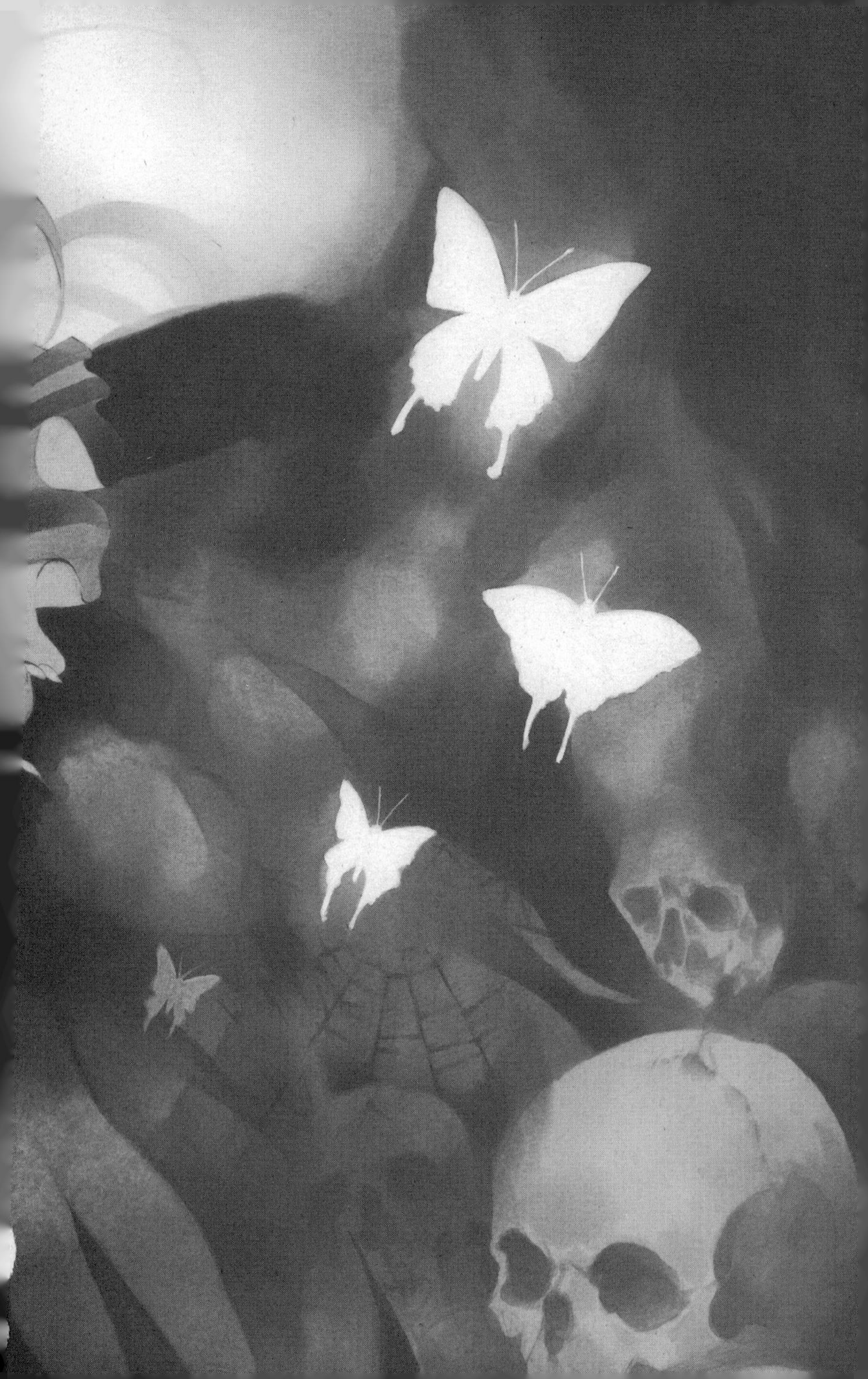

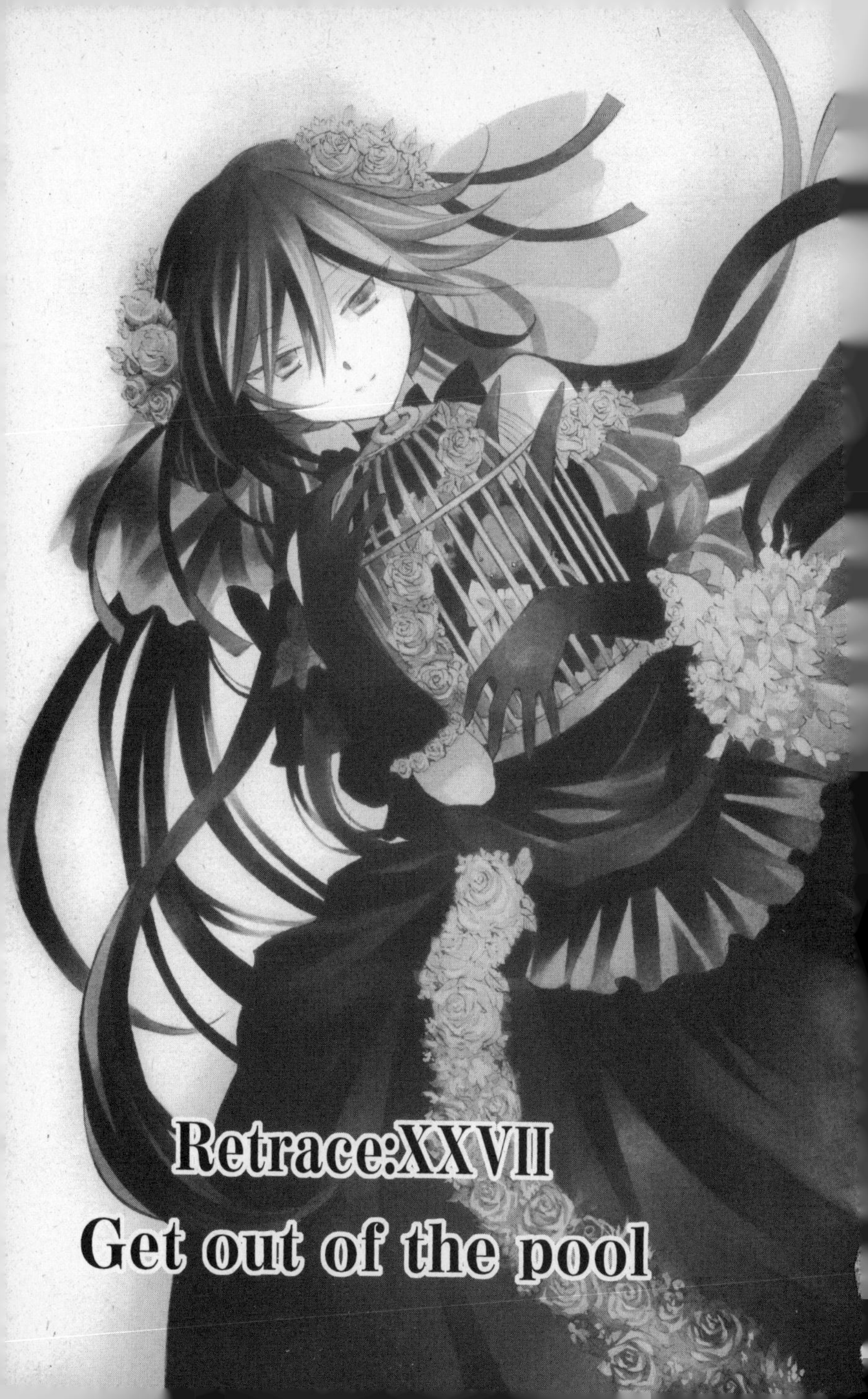
Retrace:XXVII
Get out of the pool

BONUS: "AND THUS THE READERS' EYESIGHT WAS PROTECTED"

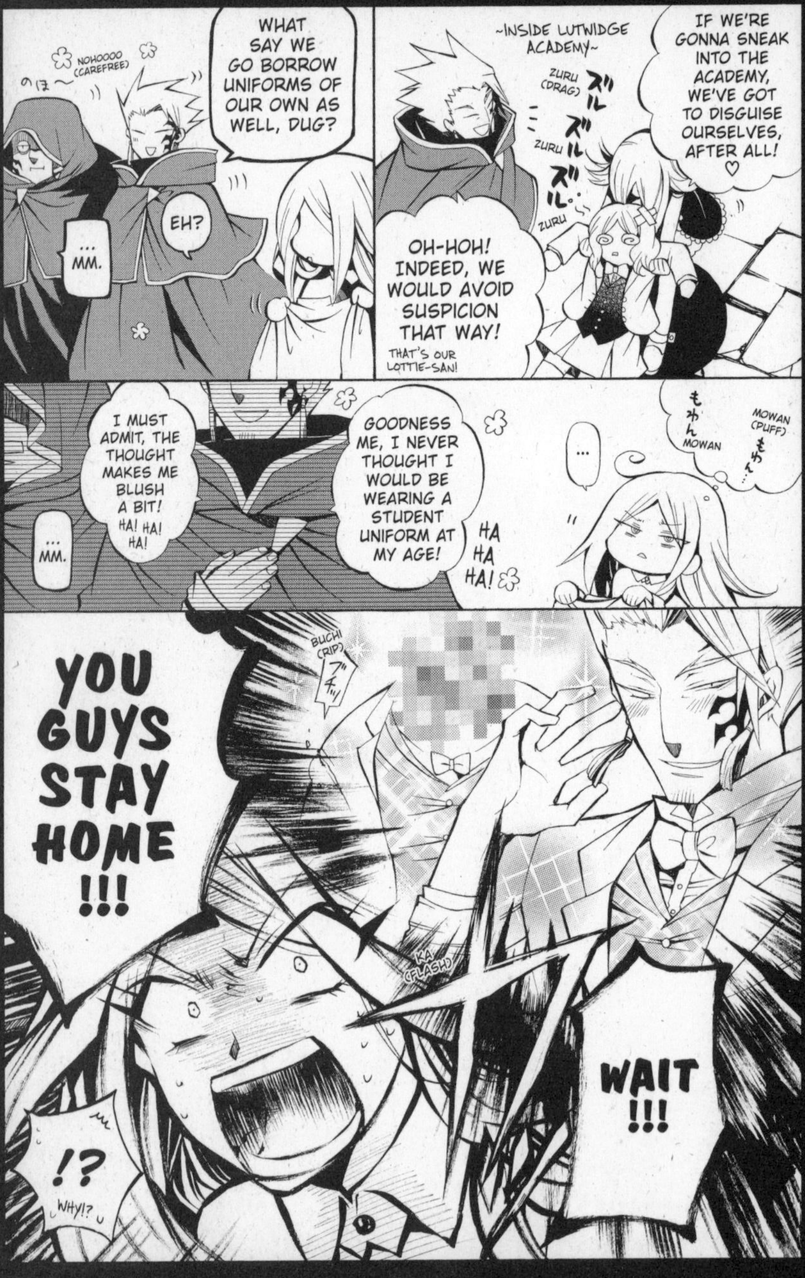
IF WE'RE GONNA SNEAK INTO THE ACADEMY, WE'VE GOT TO DISGUISE OURSELVES, AFTER ALL! ♡
~INSIDE LUTWIDGE ACADEMY~
ZURU (DRAG)
ZURU
ZURU
OH-HOH! INDEED, WE WOULD AVOID SUSPICION THAT WAY!
THAT'S OUR LOTTIE-SAN!
WHAT SAY WE GO BORROW UNIFORMS OF OUR OWN AS WELL, DUG?
NOHOOOO (CAREFREE)
EH?
... MM.
MOWAN (PUFF)
MOWAN
...
HA HA HA!
GOODNESS ME, I NEVER THOUGHT I WOULD BE WEARING A STUDENT UNIFORM AT MY AGE!
I MUST ADMIT, THE THOUGHT MAKES ME BLUSH A BIT! HA! HA! HA!
... MM.
BUCHI (RIP)
YOU GUYS STAY HOME!!!
KA (FLASH)
WAIT!!!
!?
WHY!?

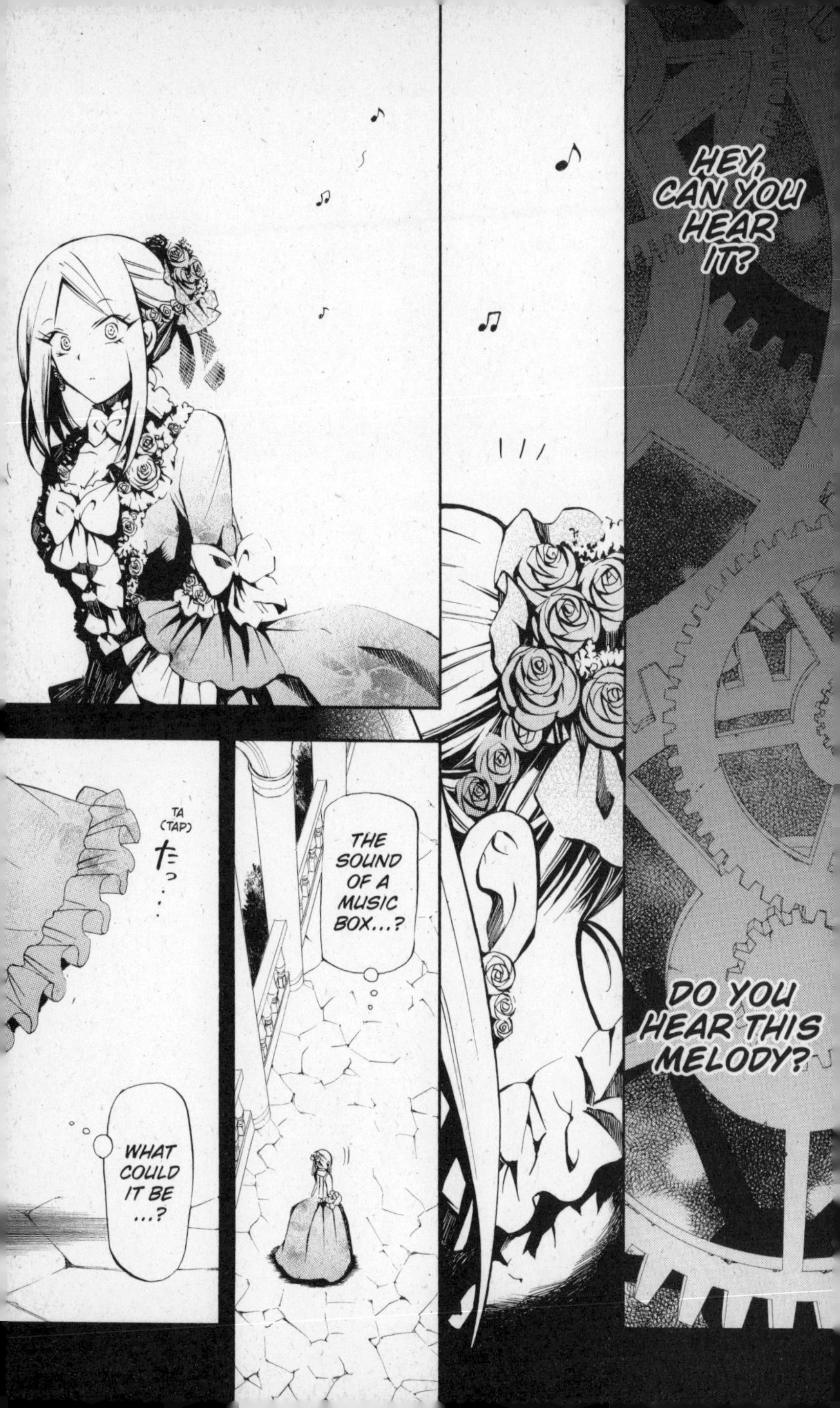
HEY, CAN YOU HEAR IT?
DO YOU HEAR THIS MELODY?
THE SOUND OF A MUSIC BOX...?
TA (TAP)
たっ
WHAT COULD IT BE ...?

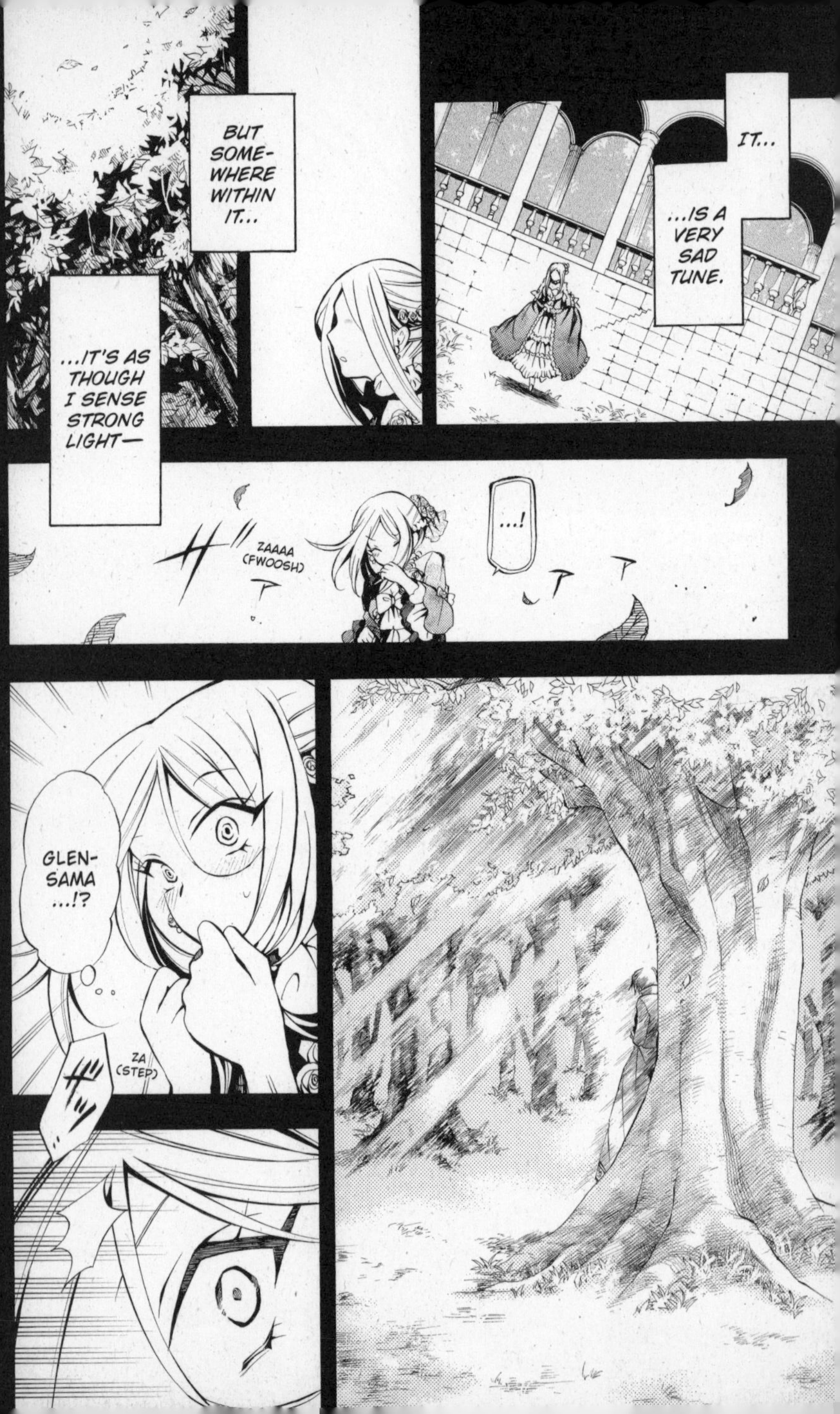
IT...
...IS A VERY SAD TUNE.
BUT SOMEWHERE WITHIN IT...
...IT'S AS THOUGH I SENSE STRONG LIGHT—
...!
ZAAAA (FWOOSH)
GLEN-SAMA ...!?
ZA (STEP)

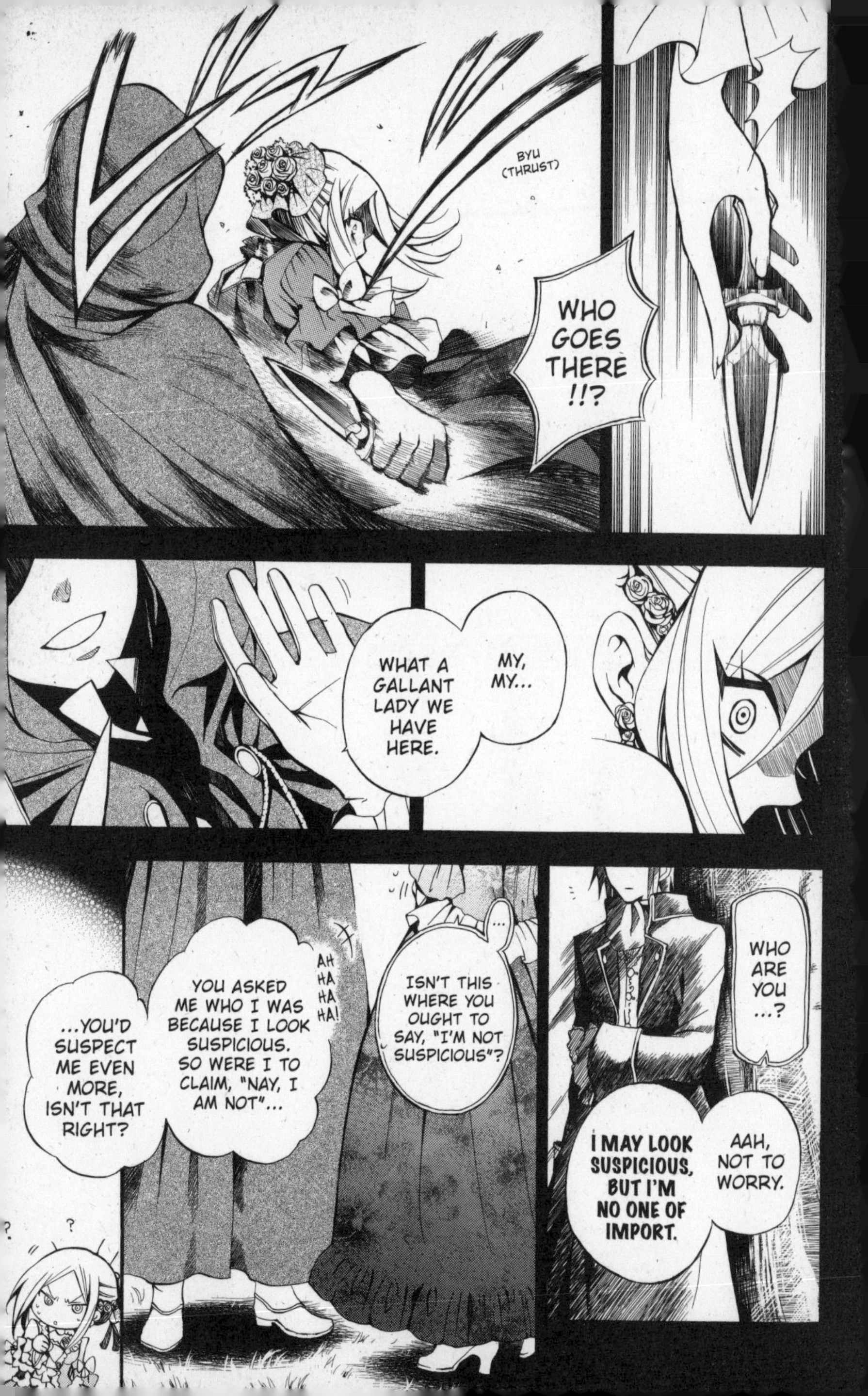
BYU (THRUST)
WHO GOES THERE!!?
MY, MY...
WHAT A GALLANT LADY WE HAVE HERE.
WHO ARE YOU...?
AAH, NOT TO WORRY.
I MAY LOOK SUSPICIOUS, BUT I'M NO ONE OF IMPORT.
...
ISN'T THIS WHERE YOU OUGHT TO SAY, "I'M NOT SUSPICIOUS"?
AH HA HA HA!
YOU ASKED ME WHO I WAS BECAUSE I LOOK SUSPICIOUS. SO WERE I TO CLAIM, "NAY, I AM NOT"...
...YOU'D SUSPECT ME EVEN MORE, ISN'T THAT RIGHT?
? ?

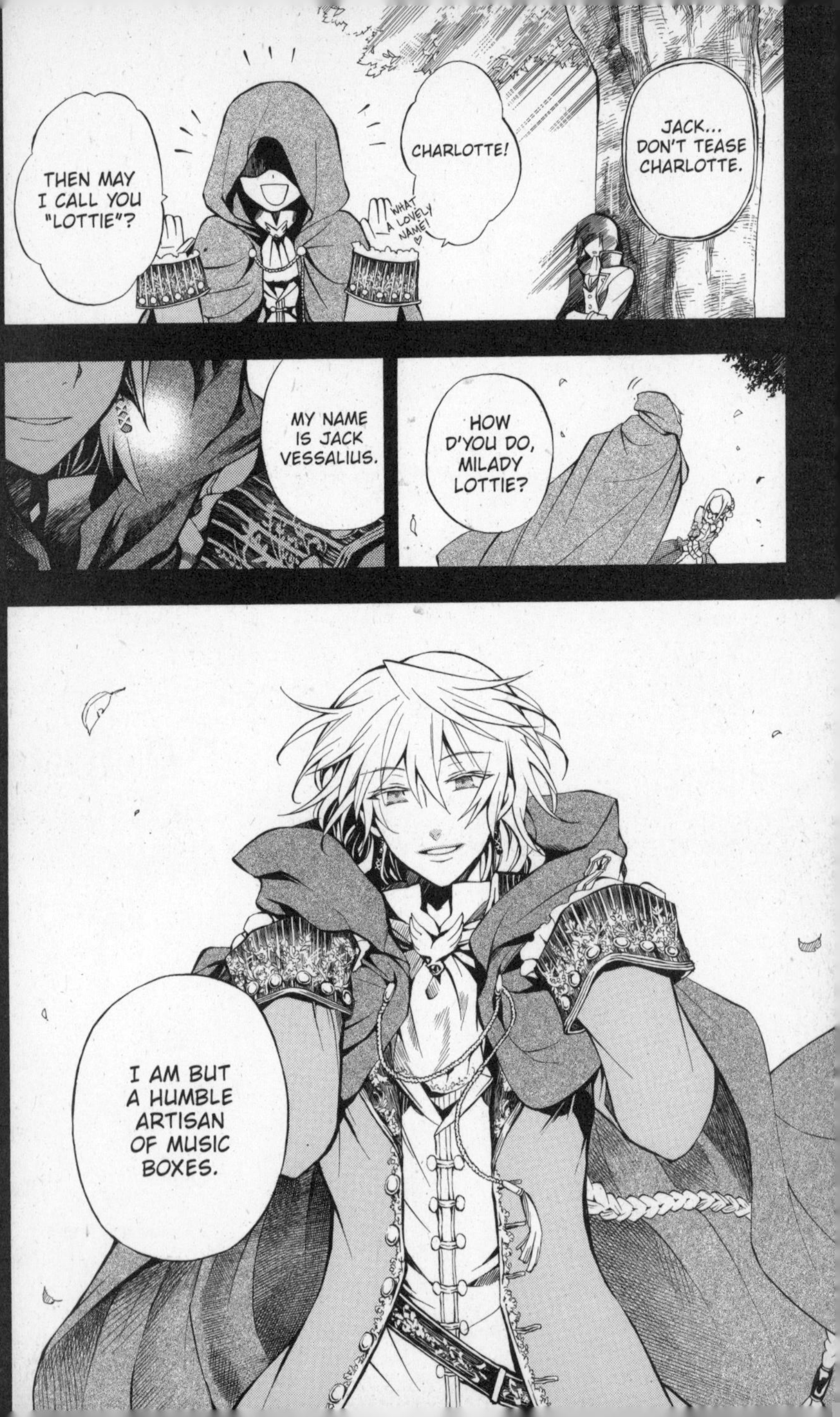
JACK... DON'T TEASE CHARLOTTE.
CHARLOTTE!
WHAT A LOVELY NAME! ♥
THEN MAY I CALL YOU "LOTTIE"?
HOW D'YOU DO, MILADY LOTTIE?
MY NAME IS JACK VESSALIUS.
I AM BUT A HUMBLE ARTISAN OF MUSIC BOXES.

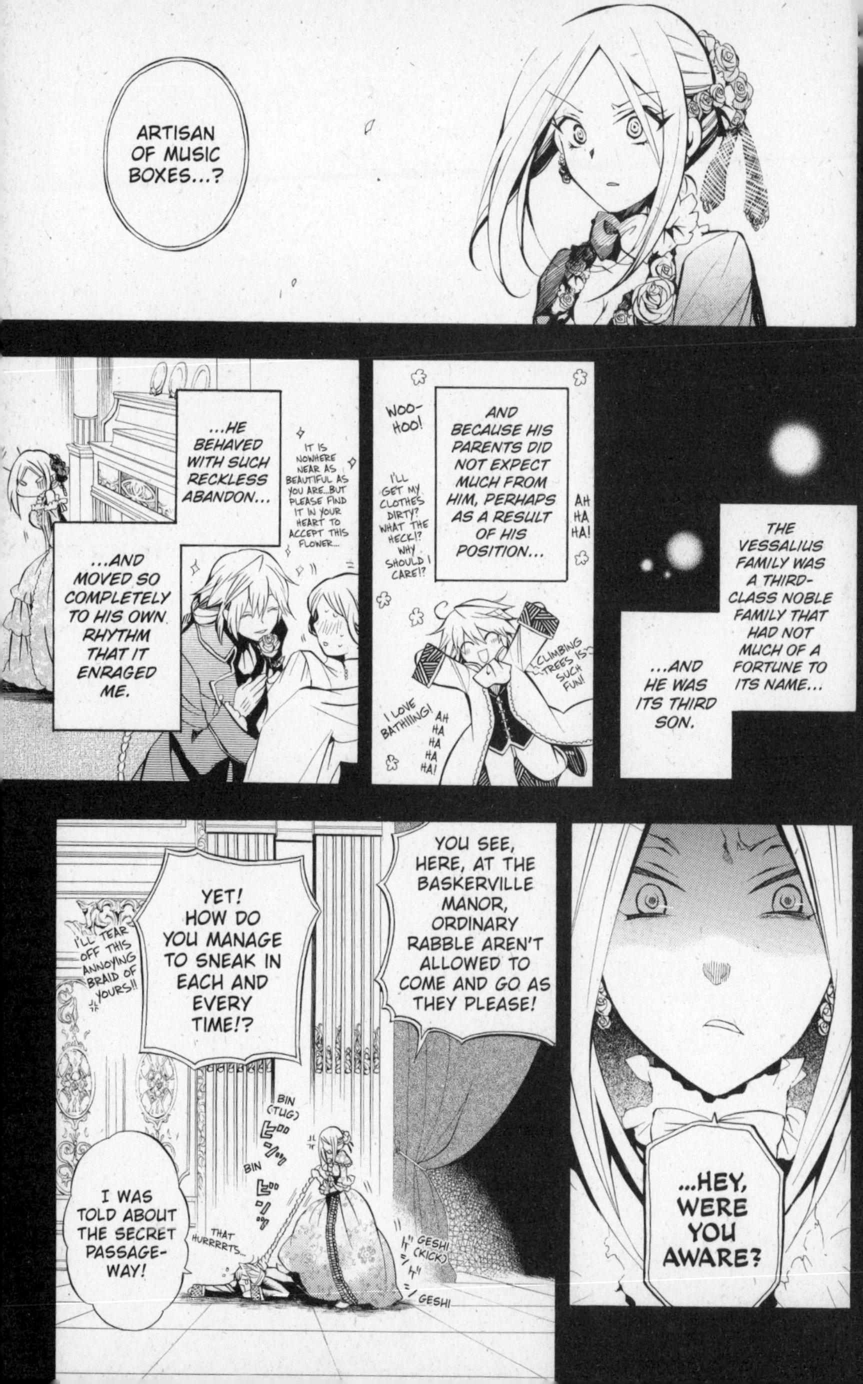
ARTISAN OF MUSIC BOXES...?
THE VESSALIUS FAMILY WAS A THIRD-CLASS NOBLE FAMILY THAT HAD NOT MUCH OF A FORTUNE TO ITS NAME...
...AND HE WAS ITS THIRD SON.
AND BECAUSE HIS PARENTS DID NOT EXPECT MUCH FROM HIM, PERHAPS AS A RESULT OF HIS POSITION...
AH HA HA!
WOO-HOO!
I'LL GET MY CLOTHES DIRTY? WHAT THE HECK!? WHY SHOULD I CARE!?
CLIMBING TREES IS SUCH FUN!
AH HA HA HA HA!
I LOVE BATHIIING!
...HE BEHAVED WITH SUCH RECKLESS ABANDON...
IT IS NOWHERE NEAR AS BEAUTIFUL AS YOU ARE...BUT PLEASE FIND IT IN YOUR HEART TO ACCEPT THIS FLOWER...
...AND MOVED SO COMPLETELY TO HIS OWN RHYTHM THAT IT ENRAGED ME.
...HEY, WERE YOU AWARE?
YOU SEE, HERE, AT THE BASKERVILLE MANOR, ORDINARY RABBLE AREN'T ALLOWED TO COME AND GO AS THEY PLEASE!
YET! HOW DO YOU MANAGE TO SNEAK IN EACH AND EVERY TIME!?
I'LL TEAR OFF THIS ANNOYING BRAID OF YOURS!!
BIN (TUG)
BIN
GESHI (KICK)
GESHI
THAT HURRRRTS...
I WAS TOLD ABOUT THE SECRET PASSAGE-WAY!

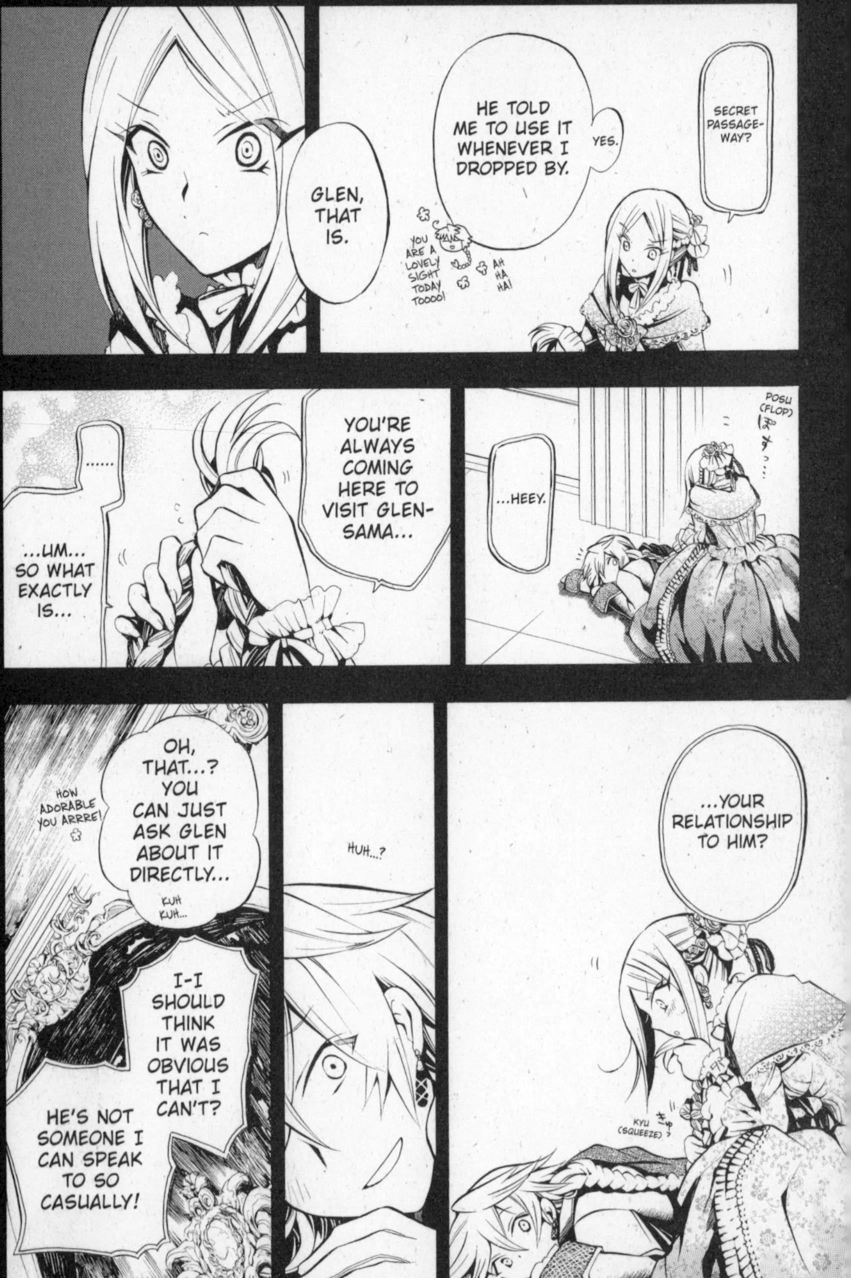
SECRET PASSAGE-WAY?
YES.
HE TOLD ME TO USE IT WHENEVER I DROPPED BY.
YOU ARE A LOVELY SIGHT TODAY TOOOO!
AH HA HA!
GLEN, THAT IS.
POSU (FLOP)
ぽす…
...HEEY.
YOU'RE ALWAYS COMING HERE TO VISIT GLEN-SAMA...
......
...UM... SO WHAT EXACTLY IS...
...YOUR RELATIONSHIP TO HIM?
KYU (SQUEEZE)
きゅ
HUH...?
OH, THAT...? YOU CAN JUST ASK GLEN ABOUT IT DIRECTLY...
HOW ADORABLE YOU ARRRE!
KUH KUH...
I-I SHOULD THINK IT WAS OBVIOUS THAT I CAN'T?
HE'S NOT SOMEONE I CAN SPEAK TO SO CASUALLY!

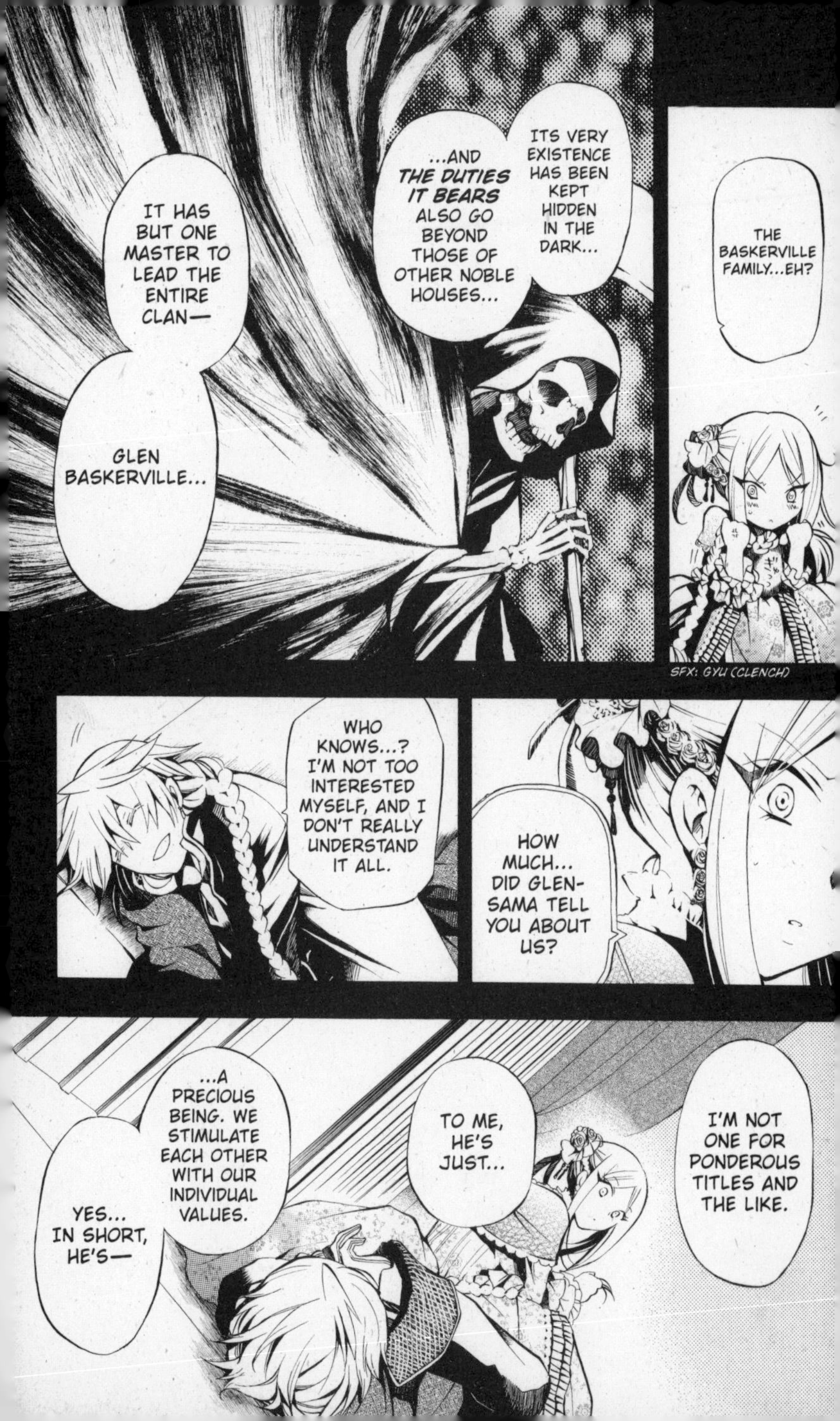
THE BASKERVILLE FAMILY...EH?
SFX: GYU (CLENCH)
ITS VERY EXISTENCE HAS BEEN KEPT HIDDEN IN THE DARK...
...AND ***THE DUTIES IT BEARS*** ALSO GO BEYOND THOSE OF OTHER NOBLE HOUSES...
IT HAS BUT ONE MASTER TO LEAD THE ENTIRE CLAN—
GLEN BASKERVILLE...
HOW MUCH... DID GLEN-SAMA TELL YOU ABOUT US?
WHO KNOWS...? I'M NOT TOO INTERESTED MYSELF, AND I DON'T REALLY UNDERSTAND IT ALL.
I'M NOT ONE FOR PONDEROUS TITLES AND THE LIKE.
TO ME, HE'S JUST...
...A PRECIOUS BEING. WE STIMULATE EACH OTHER WITH OUR INDIVIDUAL VALUES.
YES... IN SHORT, HE'S—

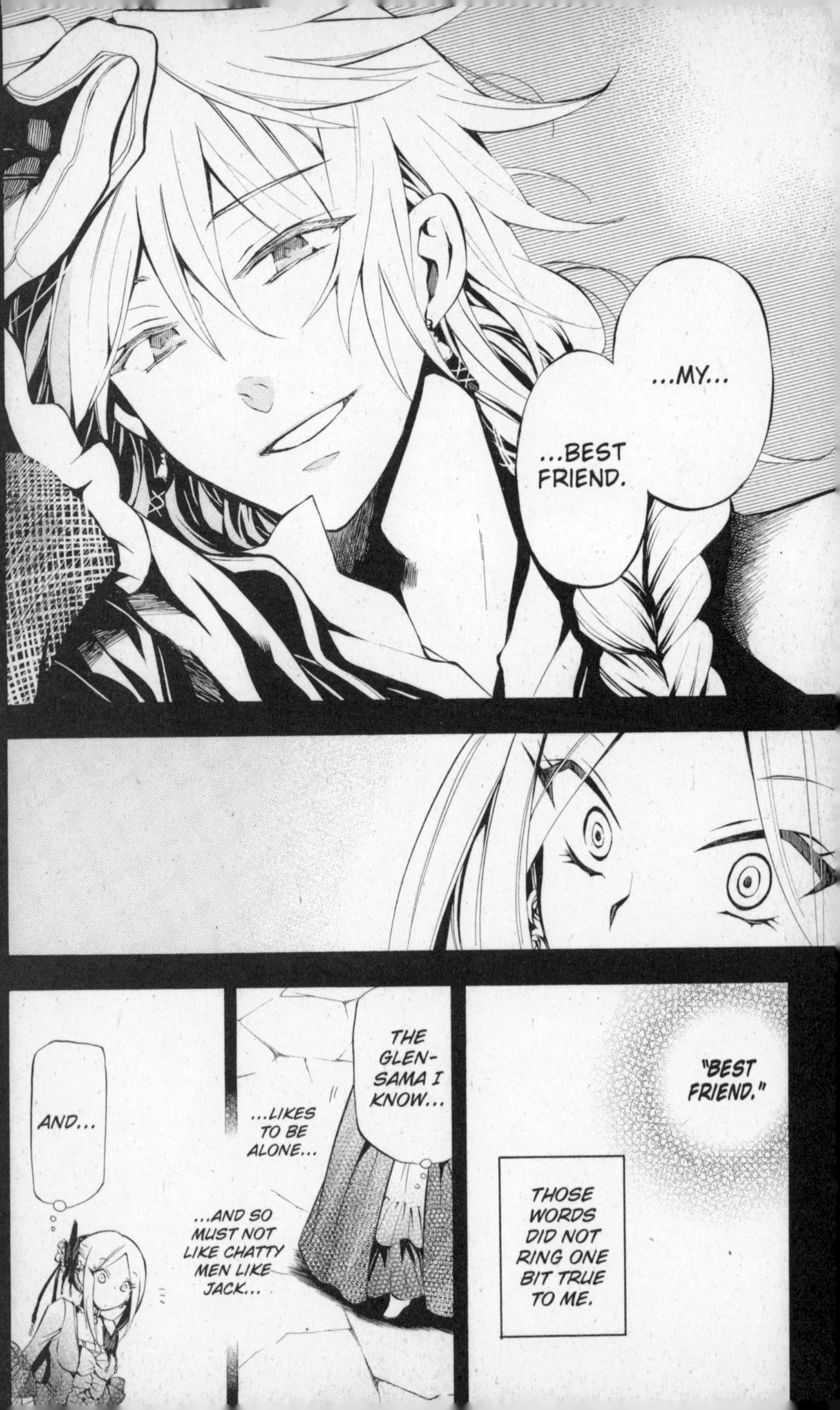
...MY...
...BEST FRIEND.
"BEST FRIEND."
THOSE WORDS DID NOT RING ONE BIT TRUE TO ME.
THE GLEN-SAMA I KNOW...
...LIKES TO BE ALONE...
...AND SO MUST NOT LIKE CHATTY MEN LIKE JACK...
AND...

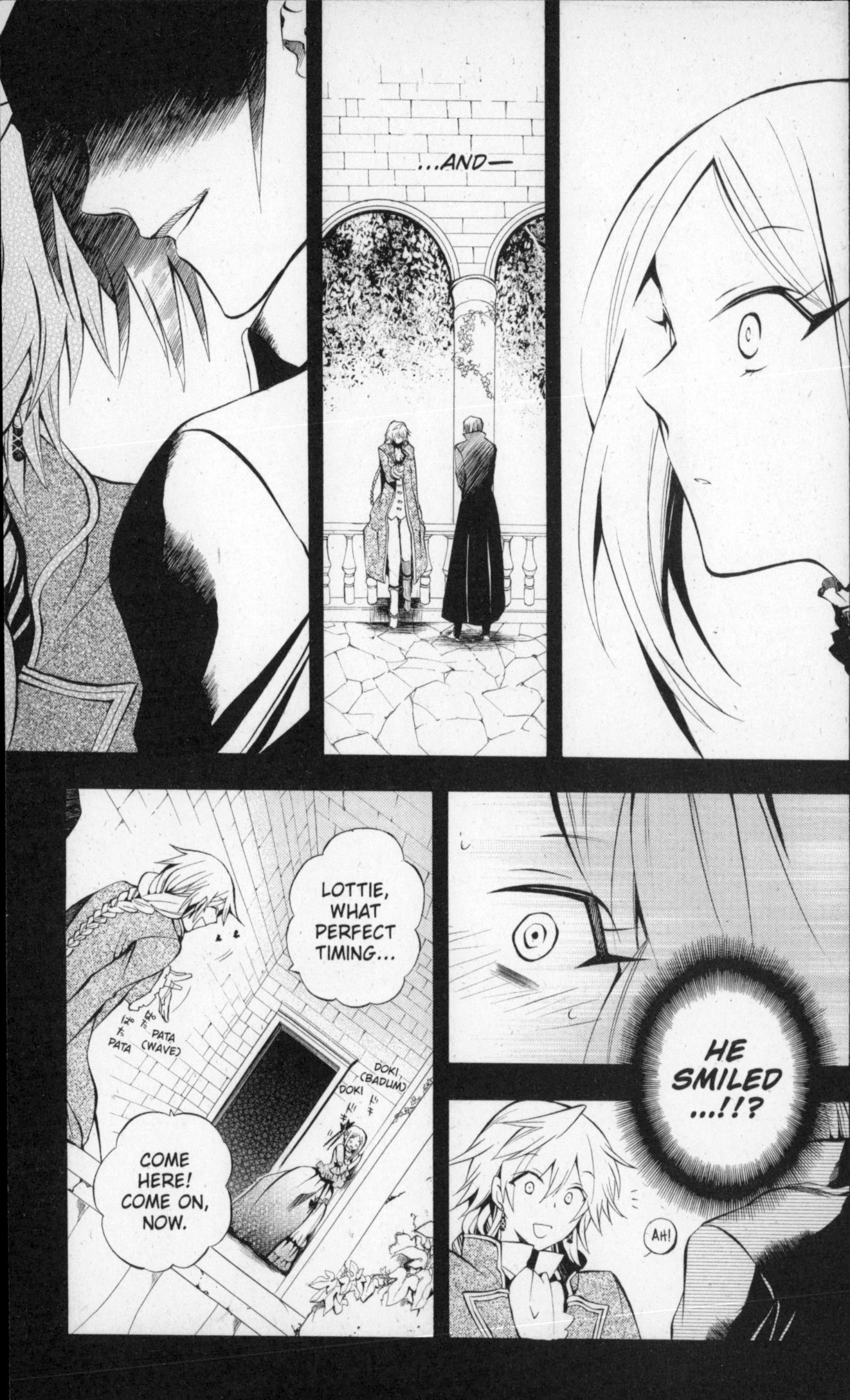
...AND—
HE SMILED ...!!?
AH!
LOTTIE, WHAT PERFECT TIMING...
PATA PATA (WAVE)
DOKI DOKI (BADUM)
COME HERE! COME ON, NOW.

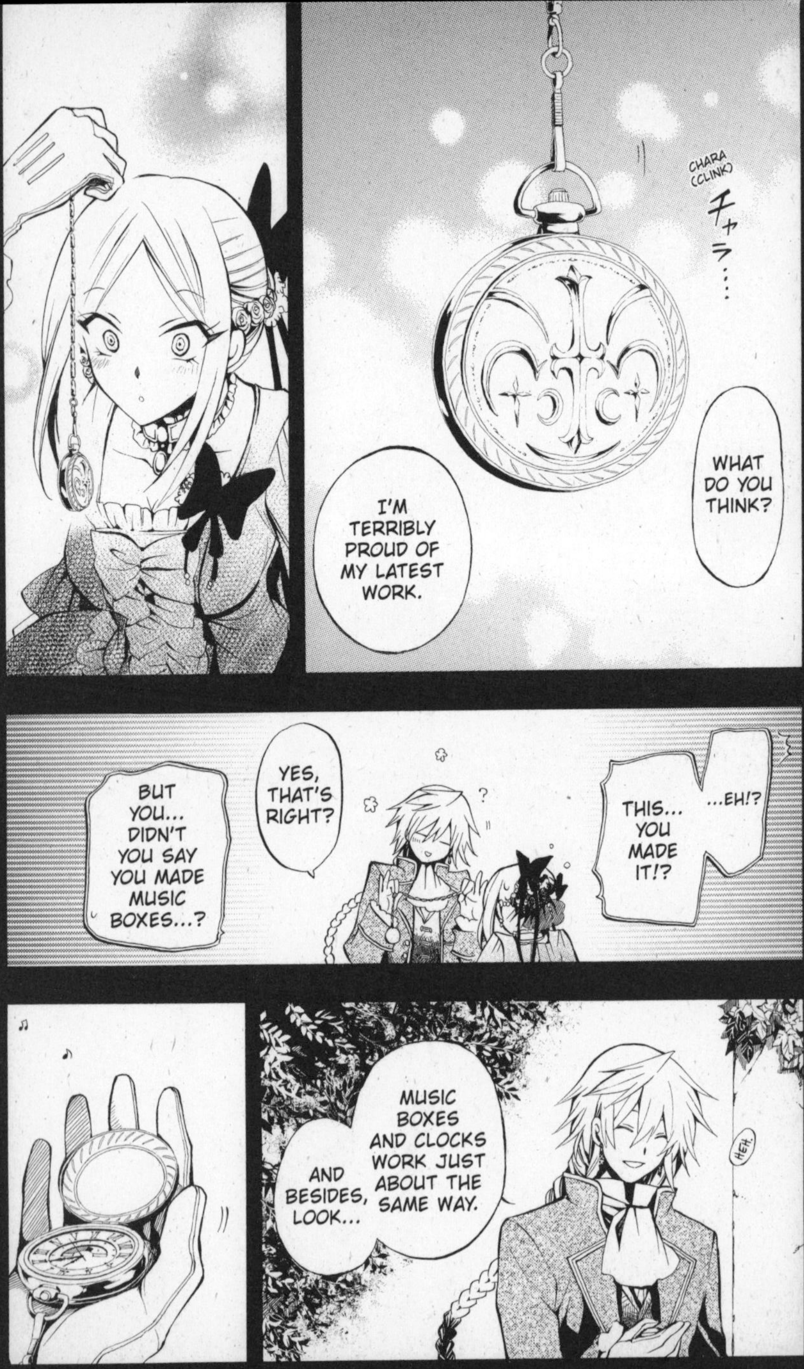
CHARA (CLINK)
チャラ…
WHAT DO YOU THINK?
I'M TERRIBLY PROUD OF MY LATEST WORK.
...EH!?
THIS... YOU MADE IT!?
YES, THAT'S RIGHT?
BUT YOU... DIDN'T YOU SAY YOU MADE MUSIC BOXES...?
HEH.
MUSIC BOXES AND CLOCKS WORK JUST ABOUT THE SAME WAY.
AND BESIDES, LOOK...

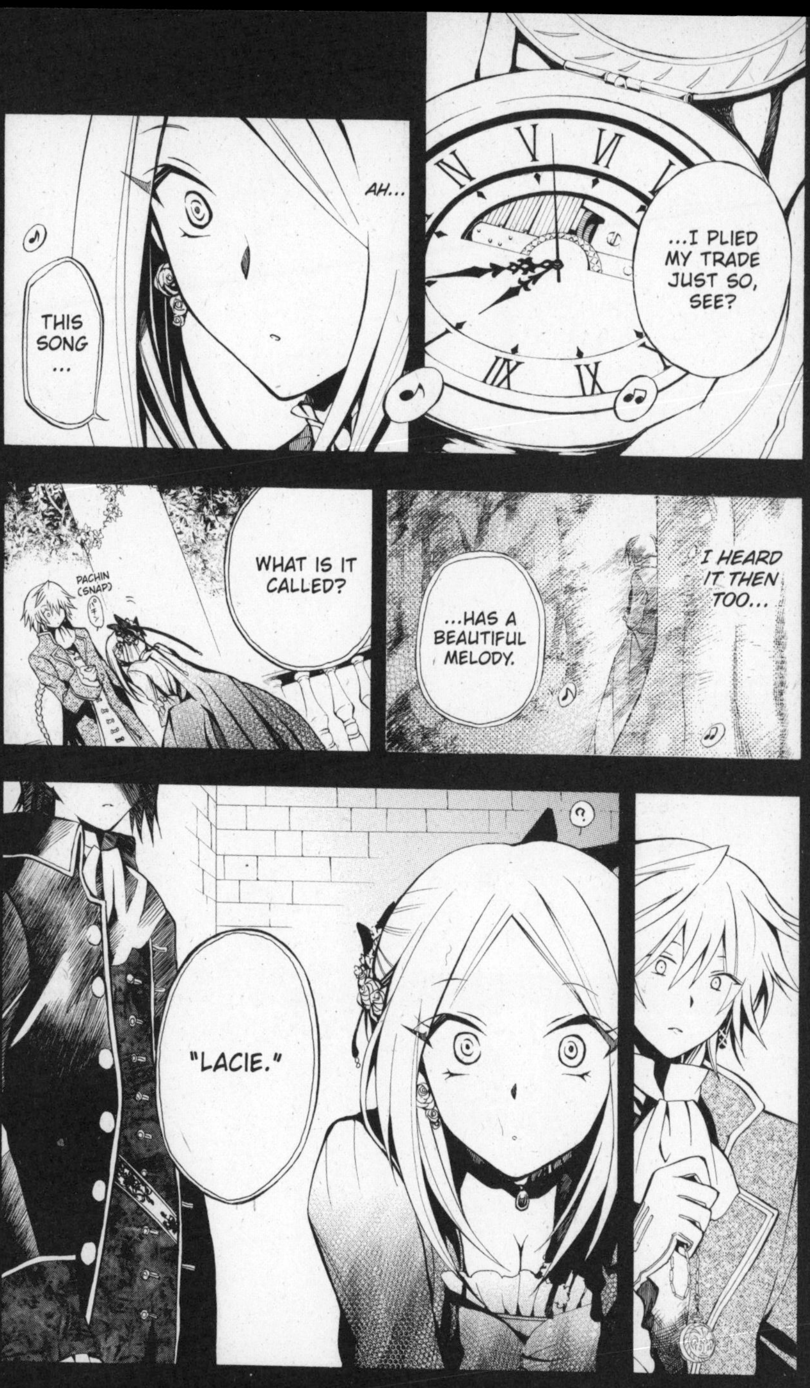
...I PLIED MY TRADE JUST SO, SEE?
AH...
THIS SONG ...
I HEARD IT THEN TOO...
...HAS A BEAUTIFUL MELODY.
WHAT IS IT CALLED?
PACHIN (SNAP)
?
"LACIE."

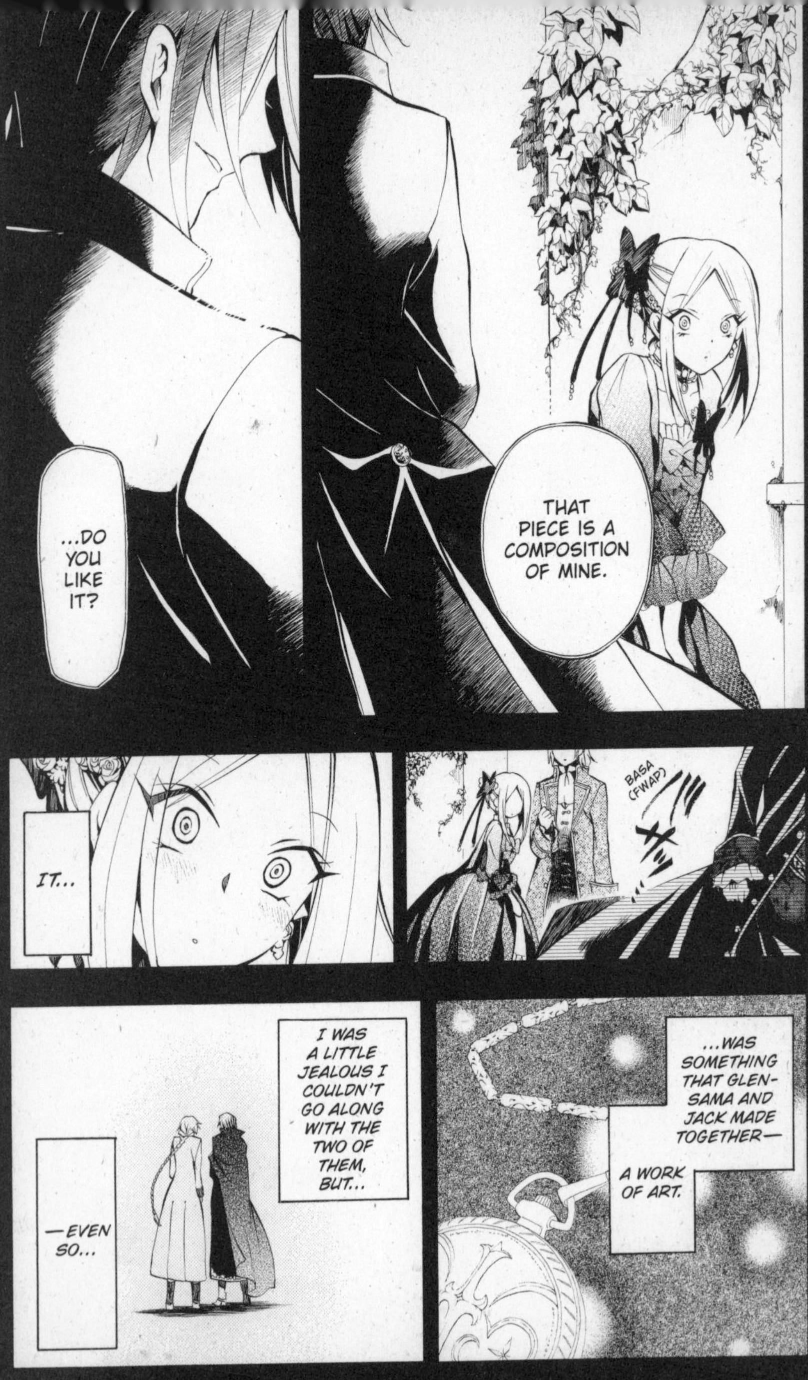
THAT PIECE IS A COMPOSITION OF MINE.
...DO YOU LIKE IT?
BASA (FWAP)
IT...
...WAS SOMETHING THAT GLEN-SAMA AND JACK MADE TOGETHER—
A WORK OF ART.
I WAS A LITTLE JEALOUS I COULDN'T GO ALONG WITH THE TWO OF THEM, BUT...
—EVEN SO...

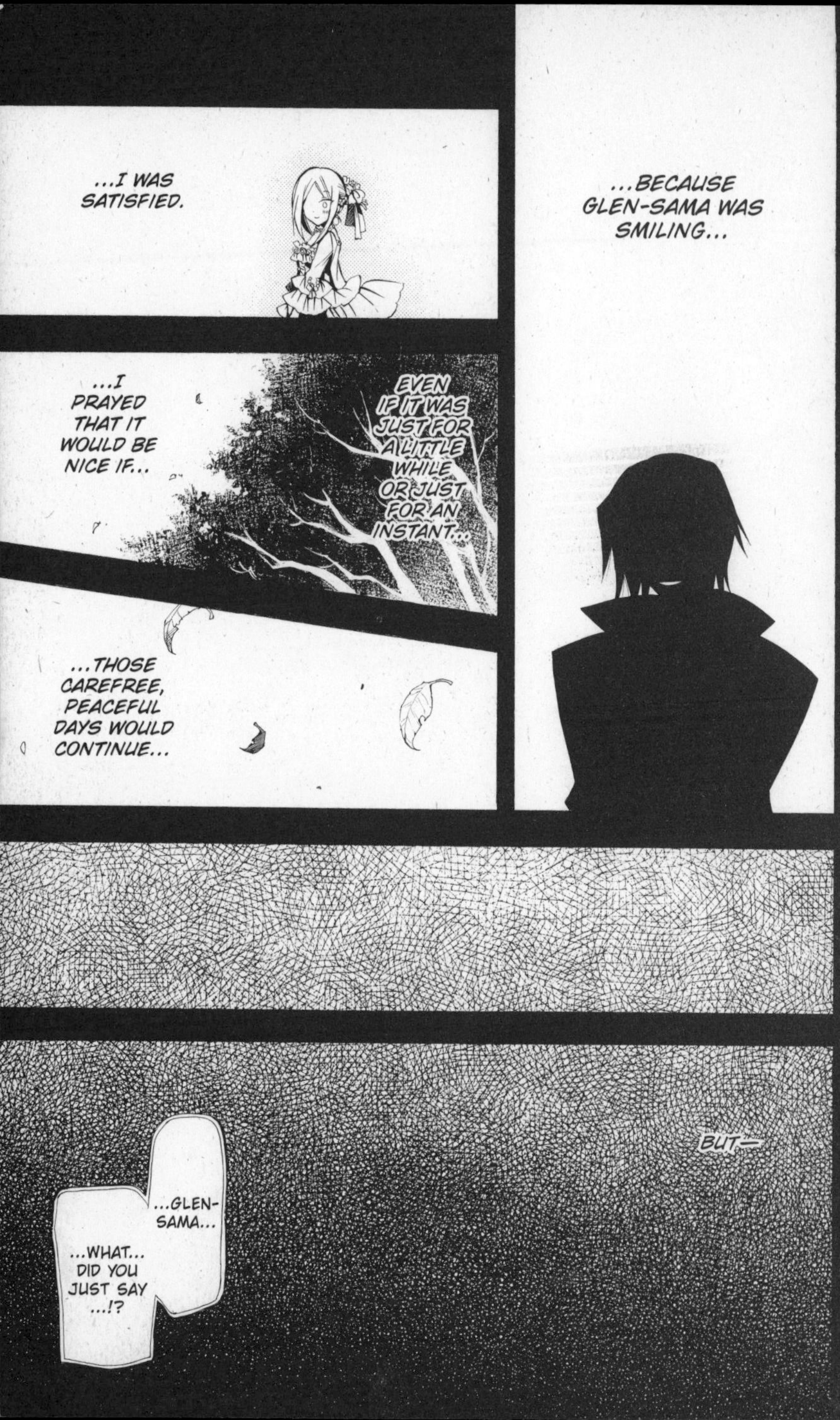
...BECAUSE GLEN-SAMA WAS SMILING...
...I WAS SATISFIED.
EVEN IF IT WAS JUST FOR A LITTLE WHILE OR JUST FOR AN INSTANT...
...I PRAYED THAT IT WOULD BE NICE IF...
...THOSE CAREFREE, PEACEFUL DAYS WOULD CONTINUE...
BUT—
...GLEN-SAMA...
...WHAT... DID YOU JUST SAY ...!?

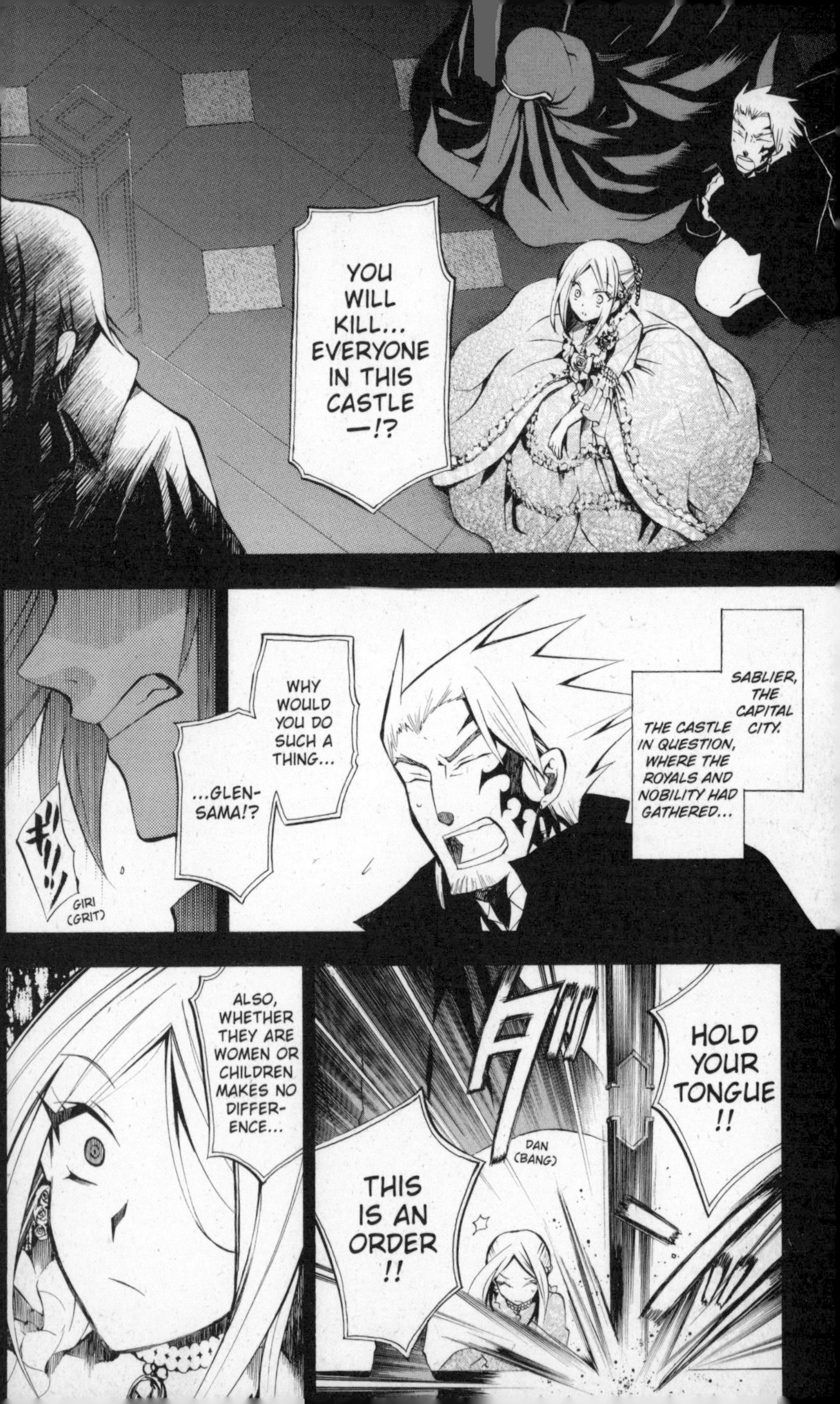
YOU WILL KILL... EVERYONE IN THIS CASTLE —!?
SABLIER, THE CAPITAL CITY.
THE CASTLE IN QUESTION, WHERE THE ROYALS AND NOBILITY HAD GATHERED...
WHY WOULD YOU DO SUCH A THING...
...GLEN-SAMA!?
GIRI (GRIT)
HOLD YOUR TONGUE!!
DAN (BANG)
THIS IS AN ORDER!!
ALSO, WHETHER THEY ARE WOMEN OR CHILDREN MAKES NO DIFFER-ENCE...

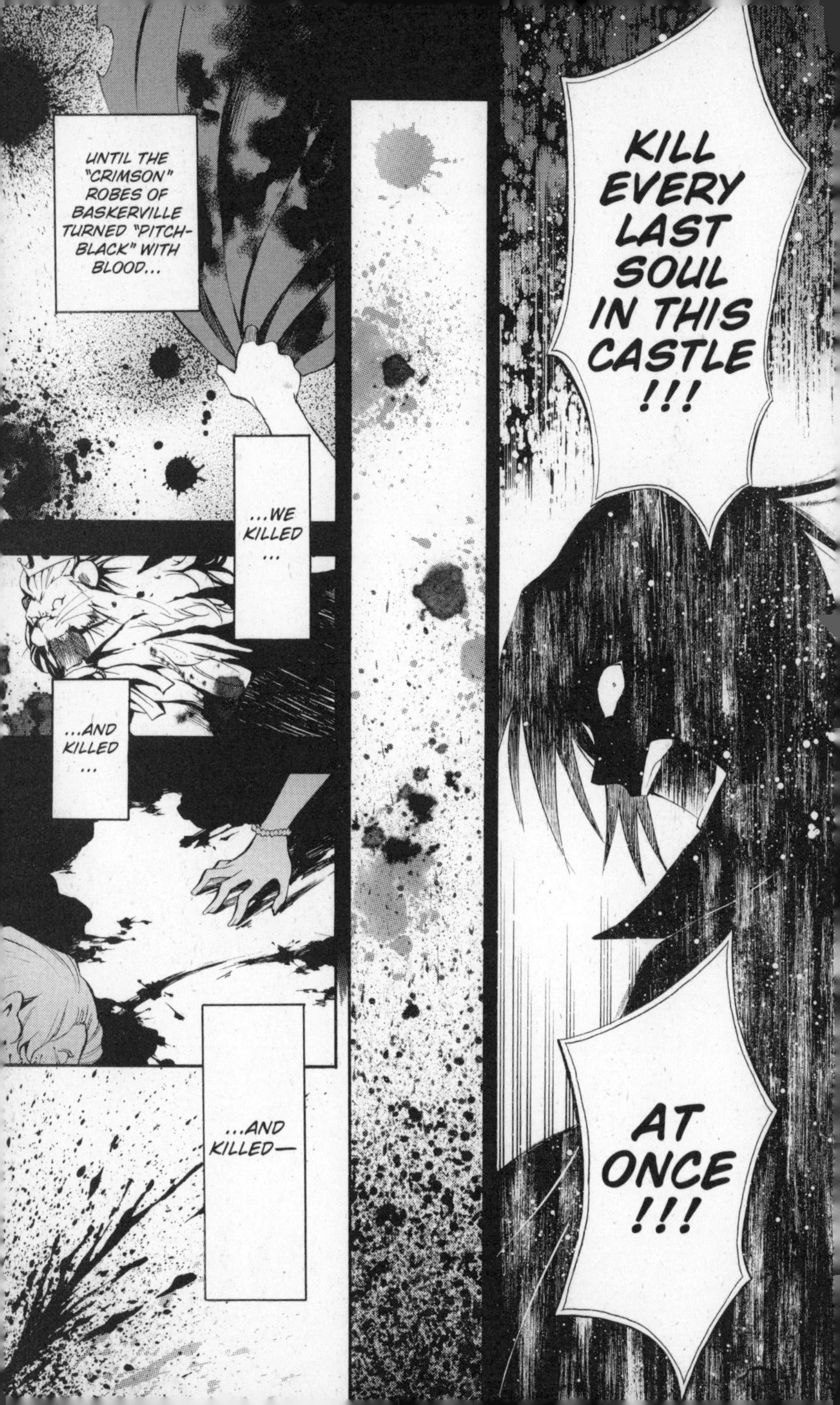
KILL EVERY LAST SOUL IN THIS CASTLE !!!
AT ONCE !!!
UNTIL THE "CRIMSON" ROBES OF BASKERVILLE TURNED "PITCH-BLACK" WITH BLOOD...
...WE KILLED ...
...AND KILLED ...
...AND KILLED—

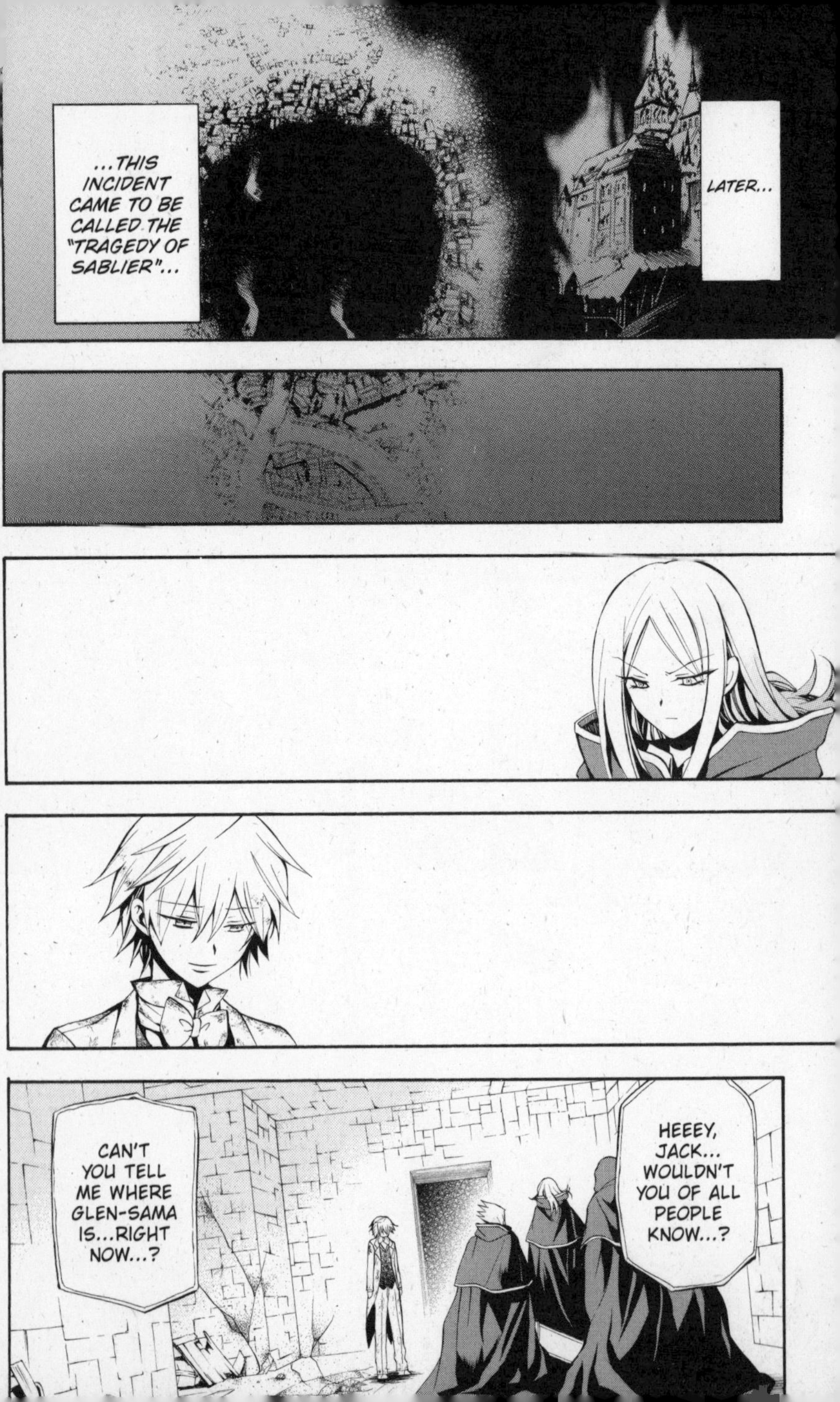
LATER...
...THIS INCIDENT CAME TO BE CALLED THE "TRAGEDY OF SABLIER"...
HEEEY, JACK... WOULDN'T YOU OF ALL PEOPLE KNOW...?
CAN'T YOU TELL ME WHERE GLEN-SAMA IS...RIGHT NOW...?

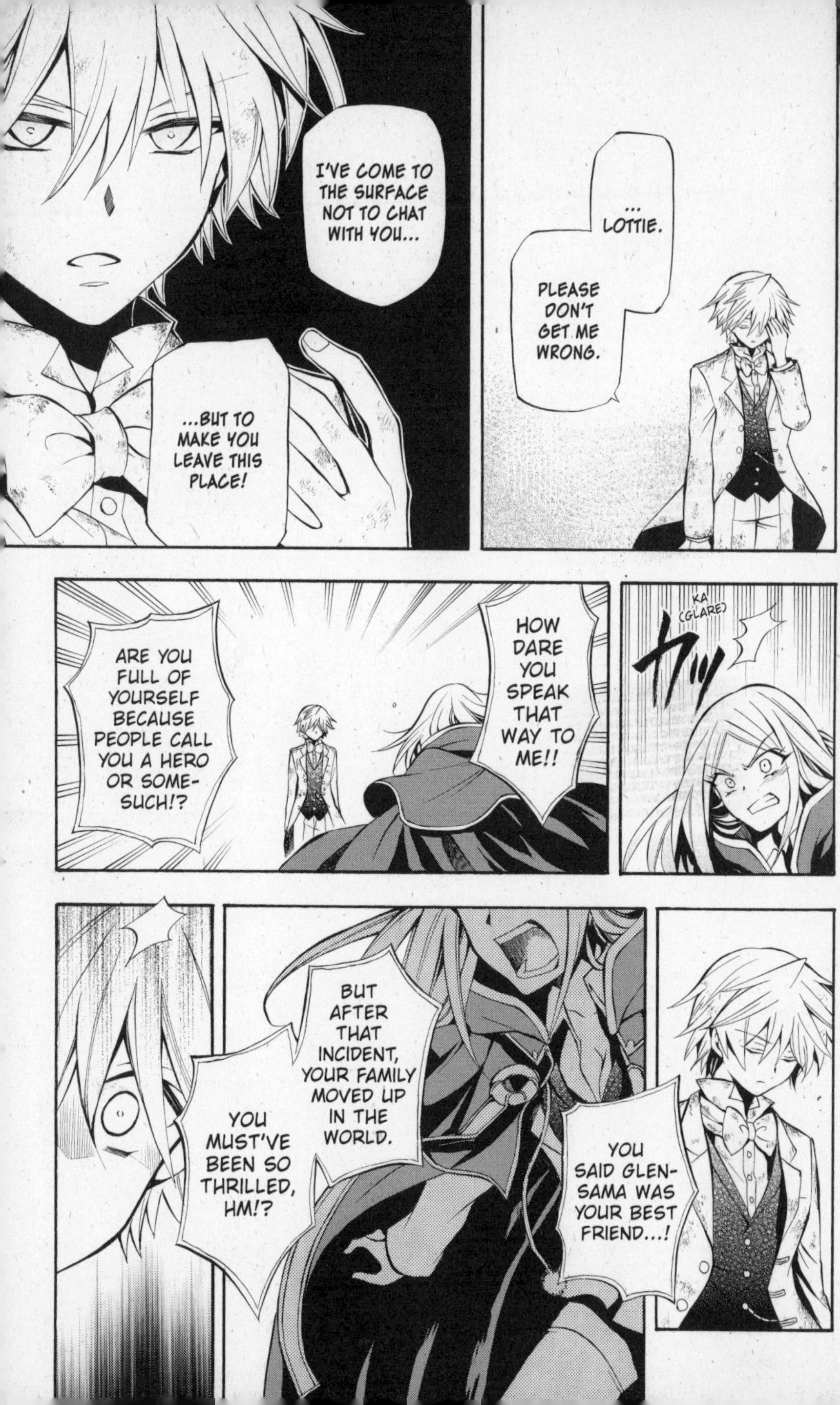
...LOTTIE.
PLEASE DON'T GET ME WRONG.
I'VE COME TO THE SURFACE NOT TO CHAT WITH YOU...
...BUT TO MAKE YOU LEAVE THIS PLACE!
KA (GLARE)
HOW DARE YOU SPEAK THAT WAY TO ME!!
ARE YOU FULL OF YOURSELF BECAUSE PEOPLE CALL YOU A HERO OR SOME-SUCH!?
YOU SAID GLEN-SAMA WAS YOUR BEST FRIEND...!
BUT AFTER THAT INCIDENT, YOUR FAMILY MOVED UP IN THE WORLD.
YOU MUST'VE BEEN SO THRILLED, HM!?

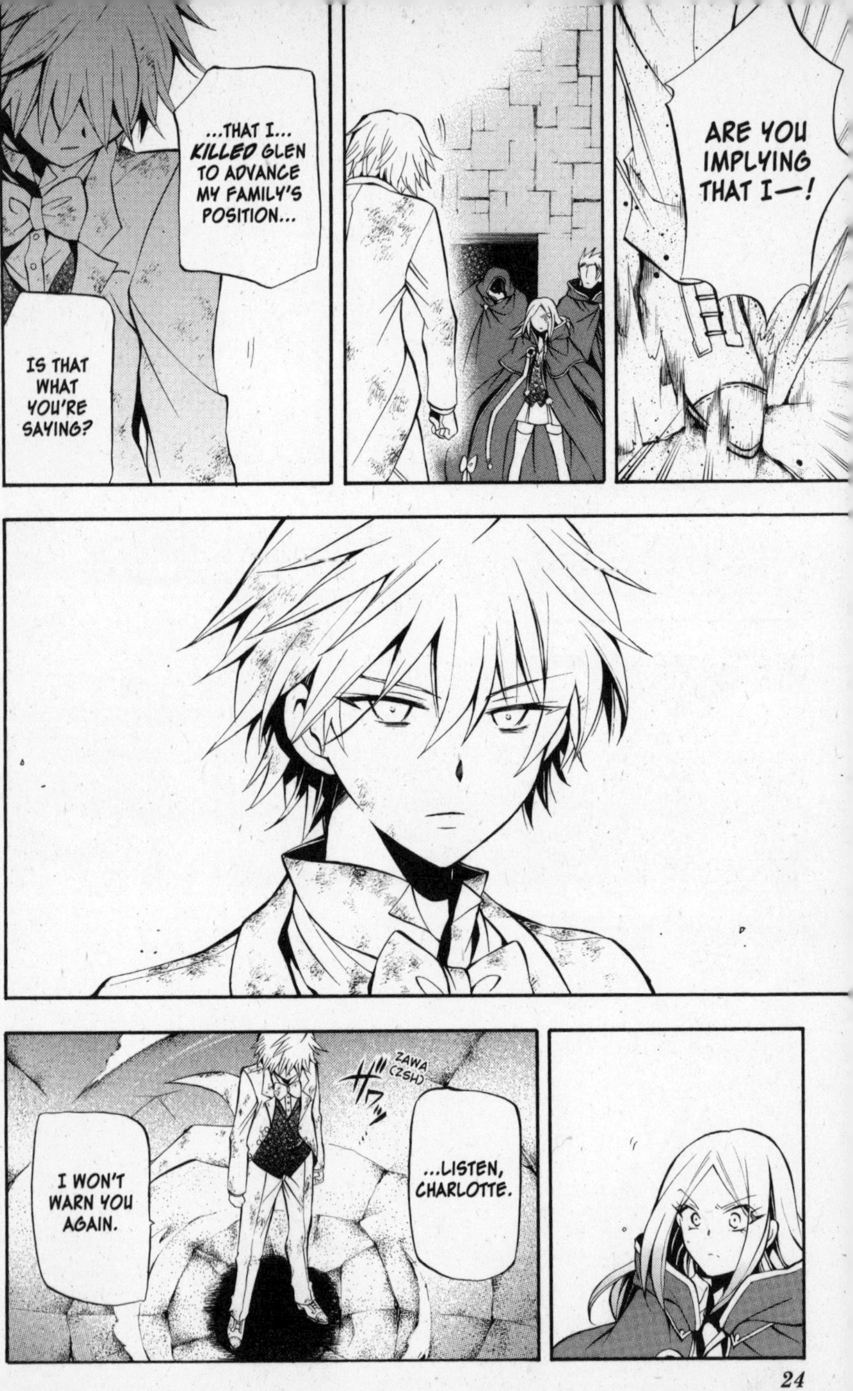
ARE YOU IMPLYING THAT I—!
...THAT I... KILLED GLEN TO ADVANCE MY FAMILY'S POSITION...
IS THAT WHAT YOU'RE SAYING?
ZAWA (ZSH)
...LISTEN, CHARLOTTE.
I WON'T WARN YOU AGAIN.

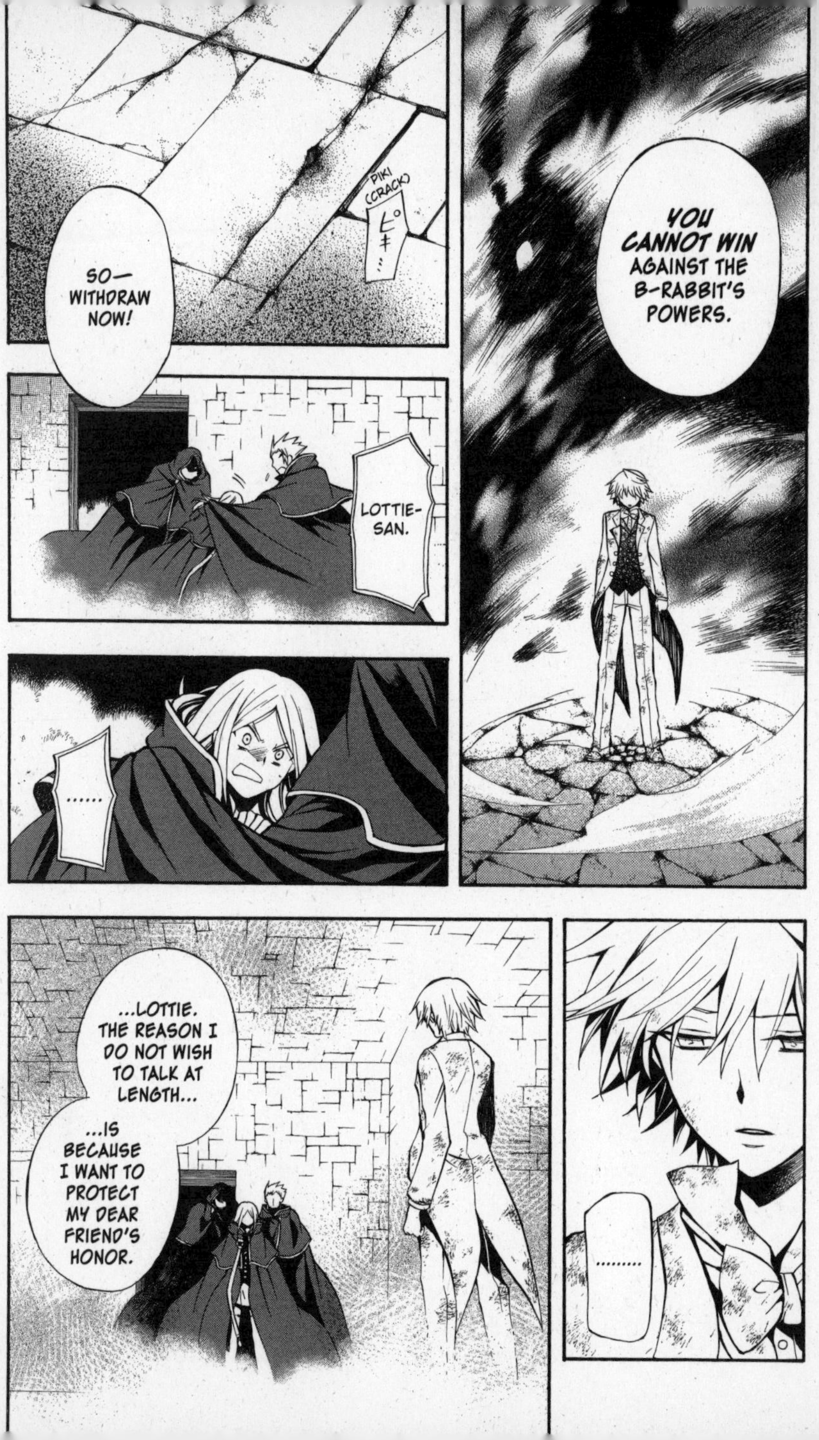
YOU CANNOT WIN AGAINST THE B-RABBIT'S POWERS.
PIKI (CRACK)
ピキ…
SO— WITHDRAW NOW!
LOTTIE-SAN.
......
....
...LOTTIE. THE REASON I DO NOT WISH TO TALK AT LENGTH...
...IS BECAUSE I WANT TO PROTECT MY DEAR FRIEND'S HONOR.

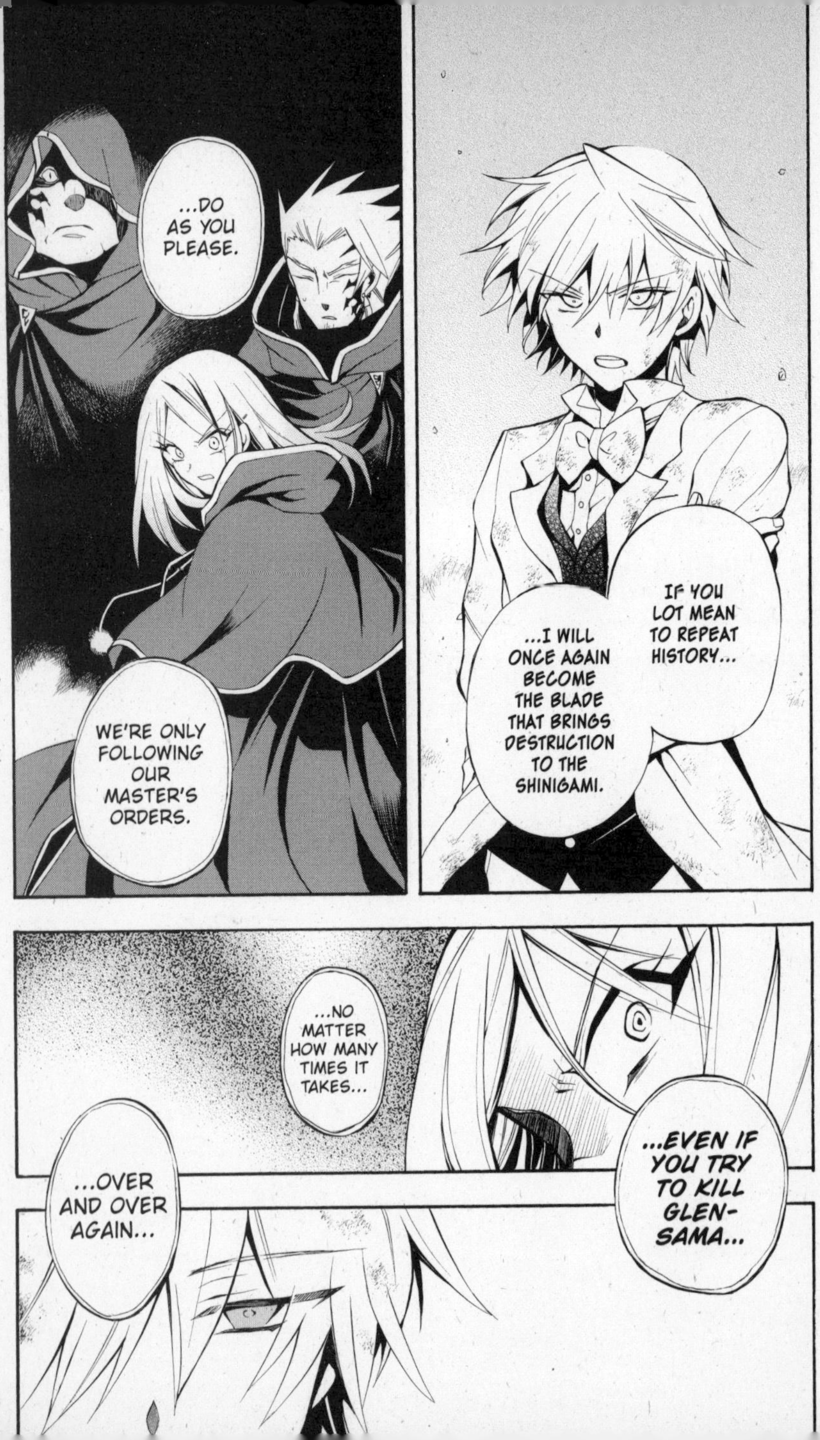
IF YOU LOT MEAN TO REPEAT HISTORY...
...I WILL ONCE AGAIN BECOME THE BLADE THAT BRINGS DESTRUCTION TO THE SHINIGAMI.
...DO AS YOU PLEASE.
WE'RE ONLY FOLLOWING OUR MASTER'S ORDERS.
...EVEN IF YOU TRY TO KILL GLEN-SAMA...
...NO MATTER HOW MANY TIMES IT TAKES...
...OVER AND OVER AGAIN...

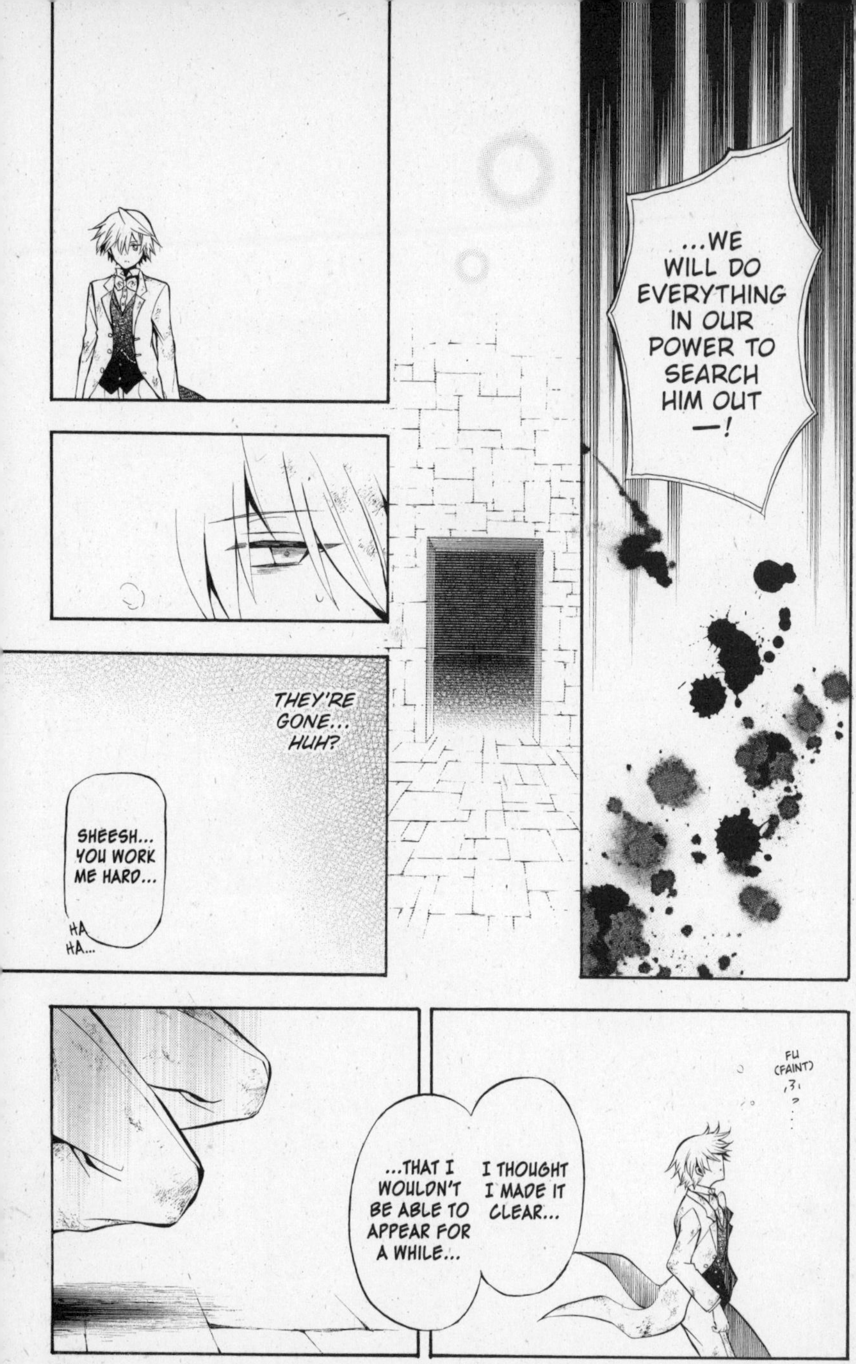
...WE WILL DO EVERYTHING IN OUR POWER TO SEARCH HIM OUT—!
THEY'RE GONE... HUH?
SHEESH... YOU WORK ME HARD...
HA HA...
FU (FAINT)
I THOUGHT I MADE IT CLEAR...
...THAT I WOULDN'T BE ABLE TO APPEAR FOR A WHILE...

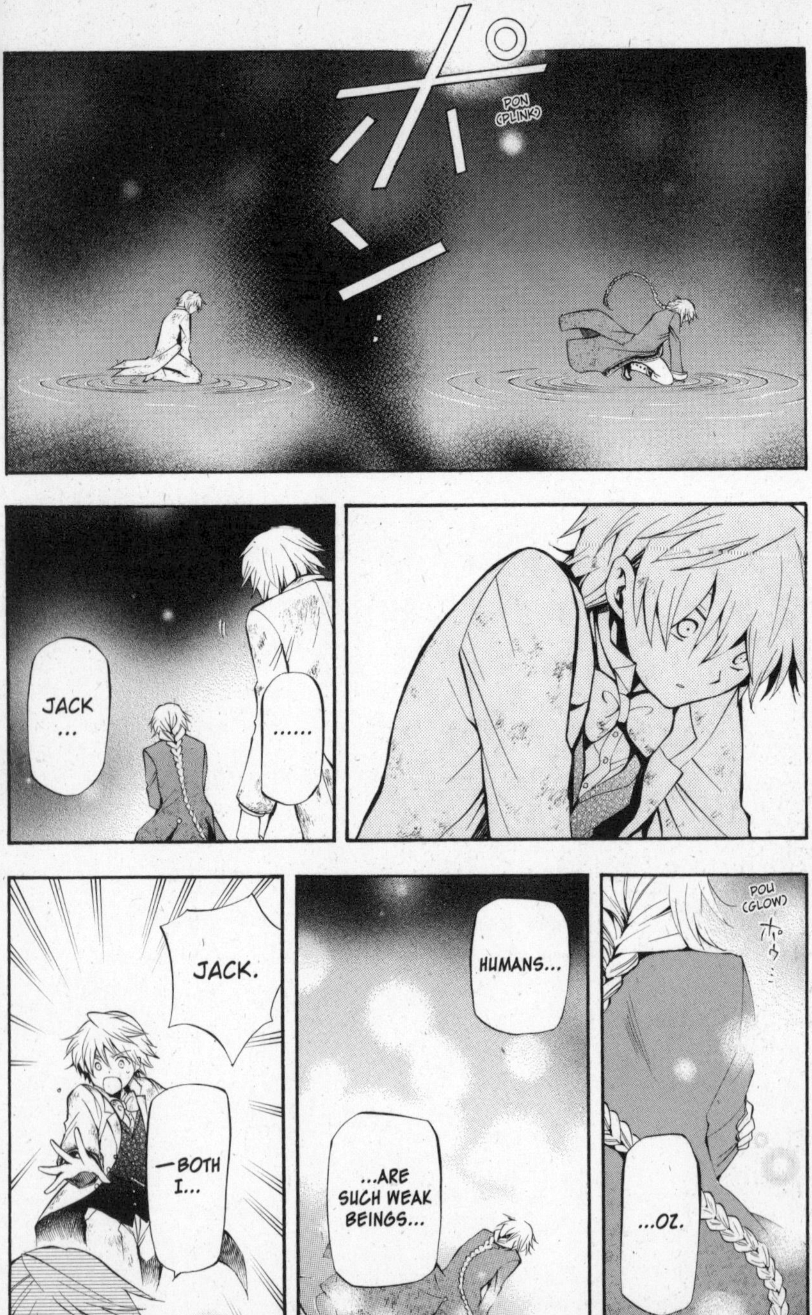

ポン
PON (PLINK)
......
JACK ...
POU (GLOW)
ぽう…
...OZ.
HUMANS...
...ARE SUCH WEAK BEINGS...
JACK.
—BOTH I...

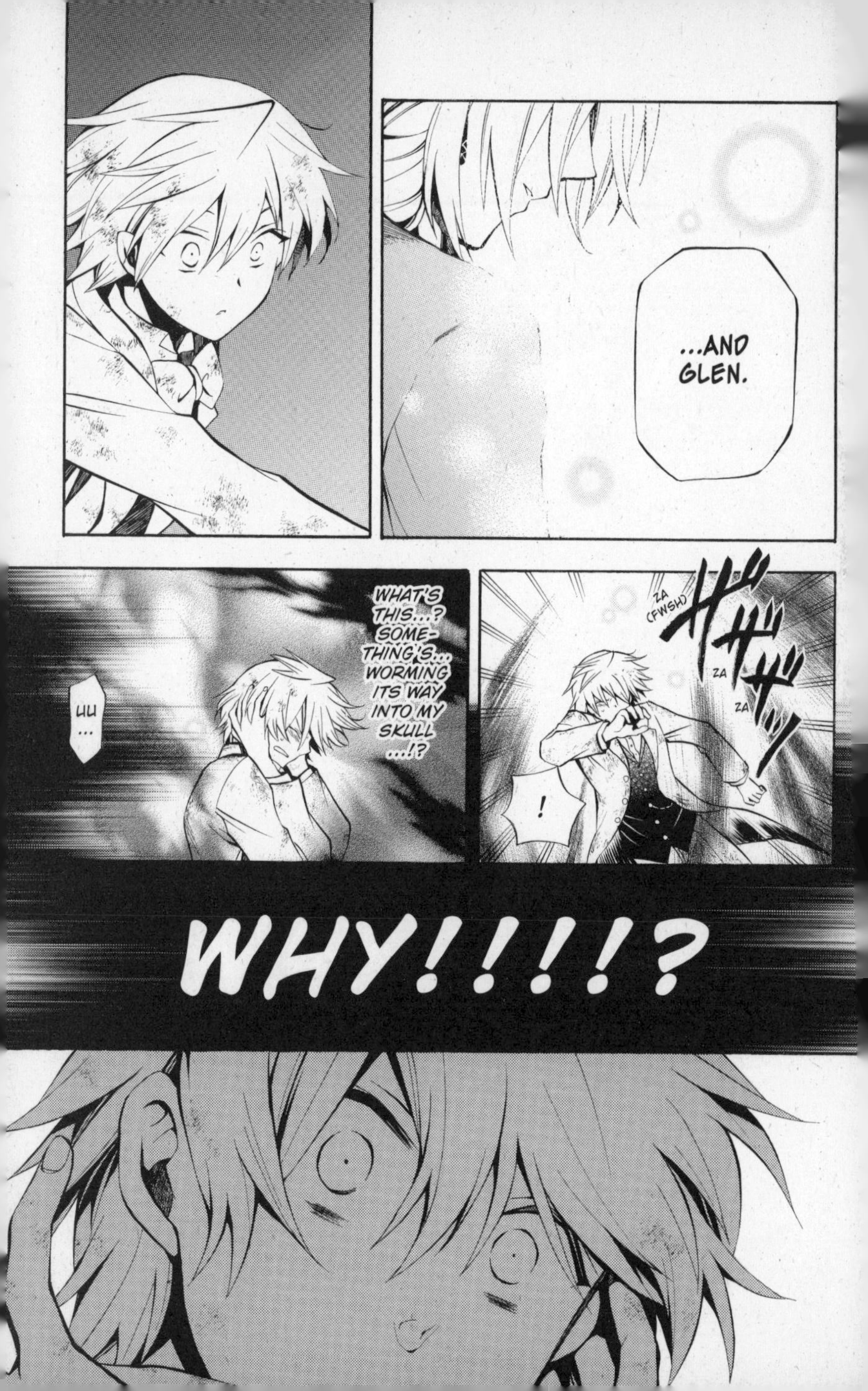
...AND GLEN.
ZA (FWSH)
ZA
ZA
!
WHAT'S THIS...? SOME-THING'S... WORMING ITS WAY INTO MY SKULL ...!?
UU ...
WHY!!!!?

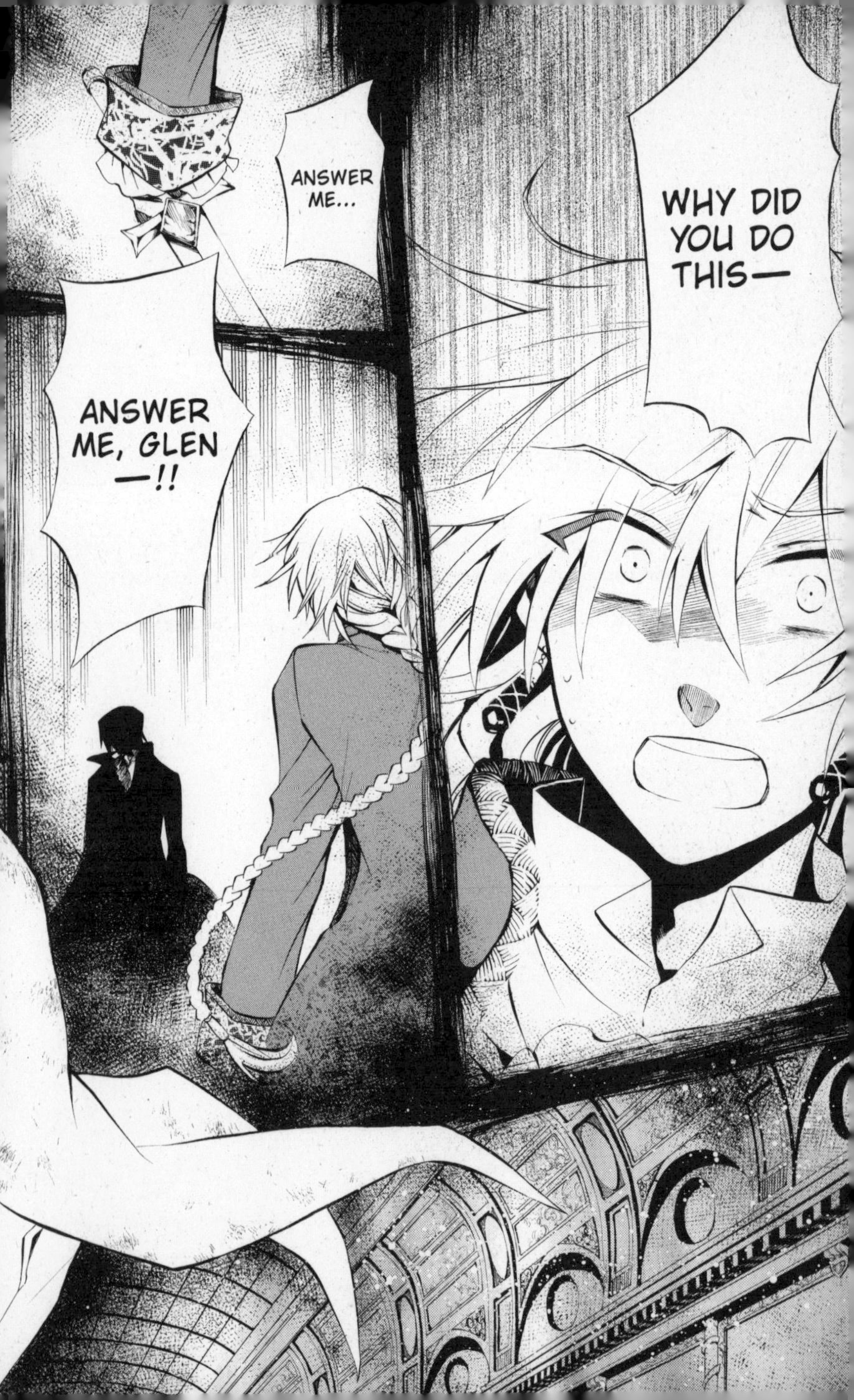
WHY DID YOU DO THIS—
ANSWER ME...
ANSWER ME, GLEN —!!

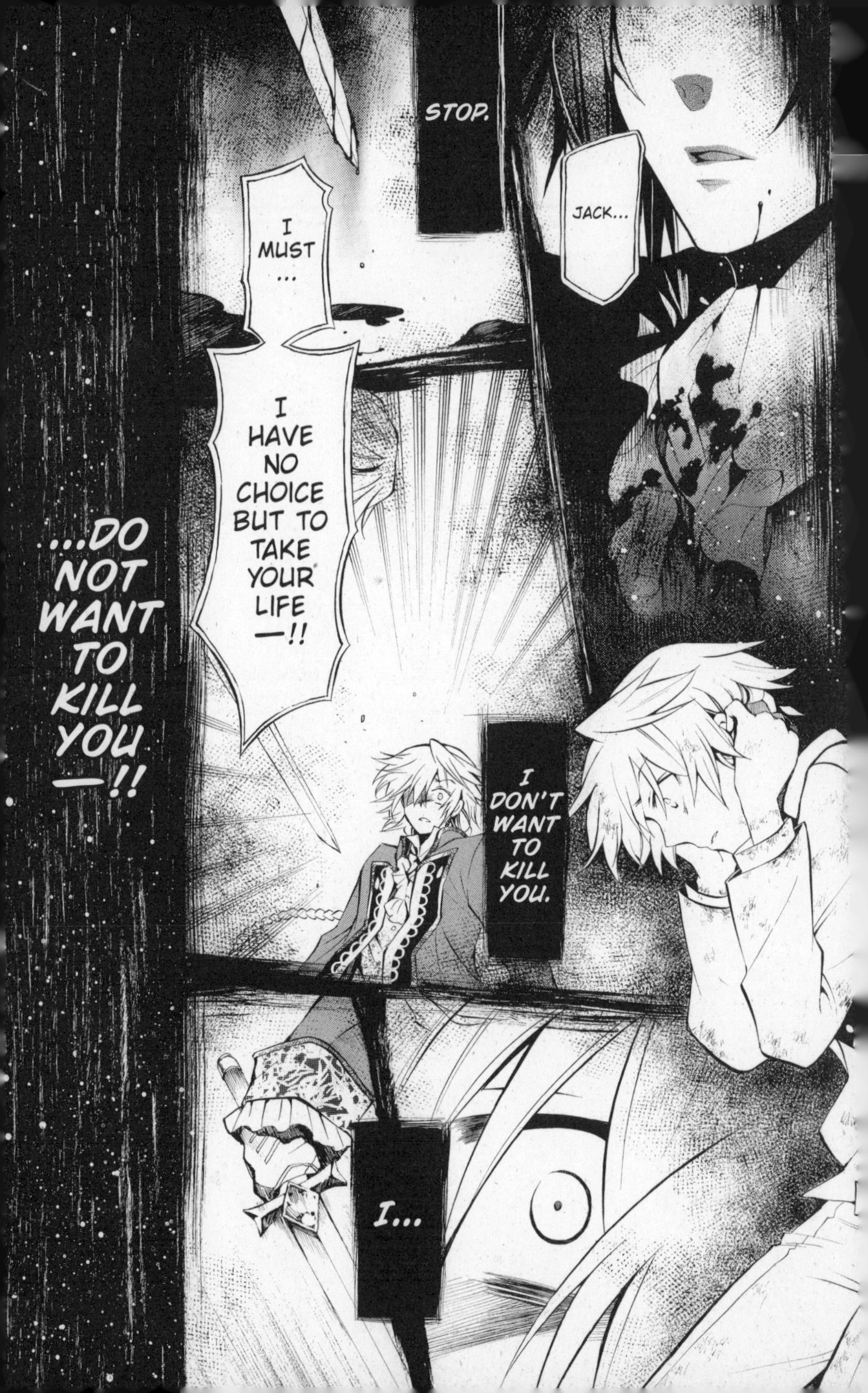
JACK...
STOP.
I MUST ...
I HAVE NO CHOICE BUT TO TAKE YOUR LIFE —!!
I DON'T WANT TO KILL YOU.
I...
...DO NOT WANT TO KILL YOU —!!

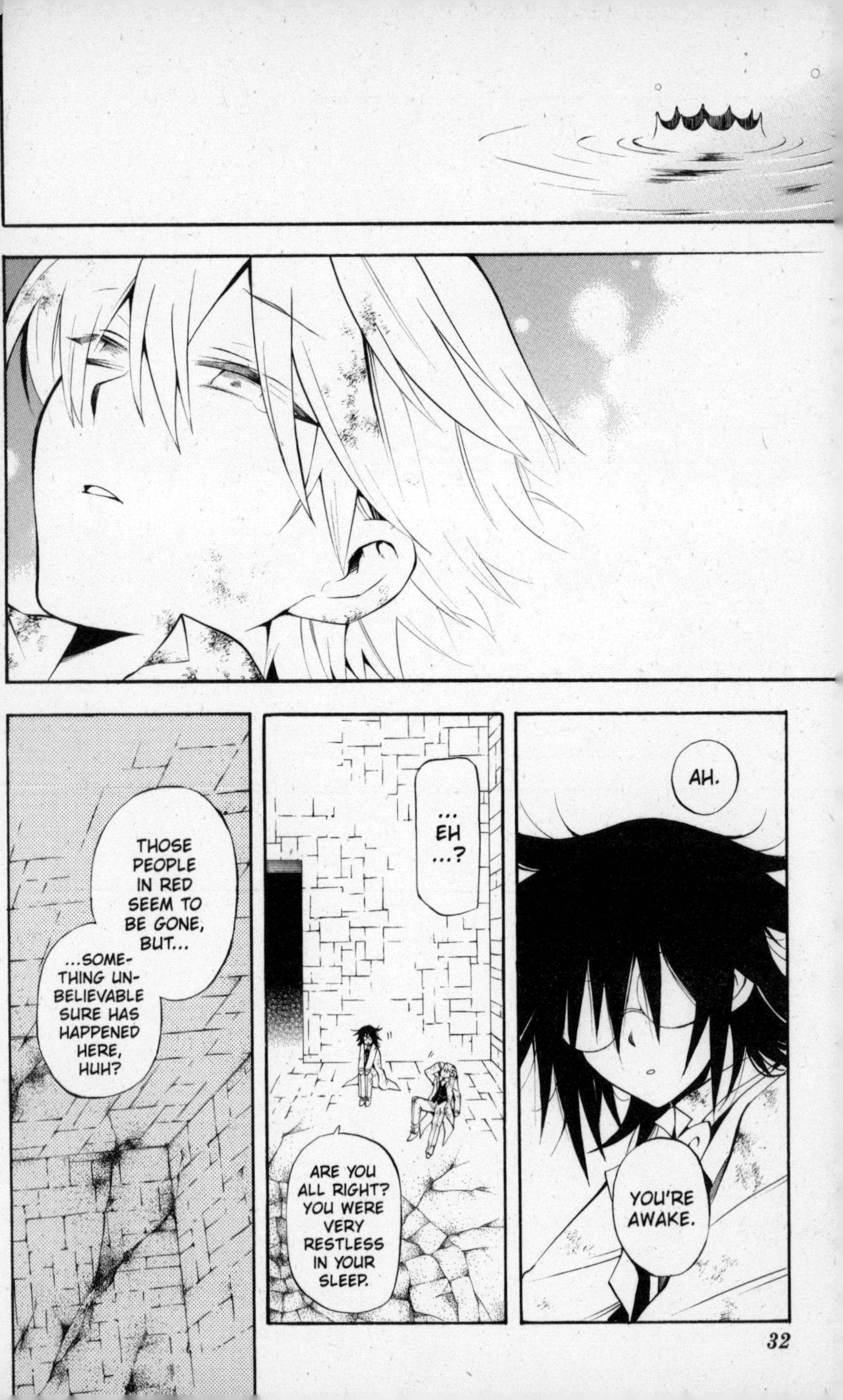
AH.
YOU'RE AWAKE.
...EH ...?
ARE YOU ALL RIGHT? YOU WERE VERY RESTLESS IN YOUR SLEEP.
THOSE PEOPLE IN RED SEEM TO BE GONE, BUT...
...SOME-THING UN-BELIEVABLE SURE HAS HAPPENED HERE, HUH?

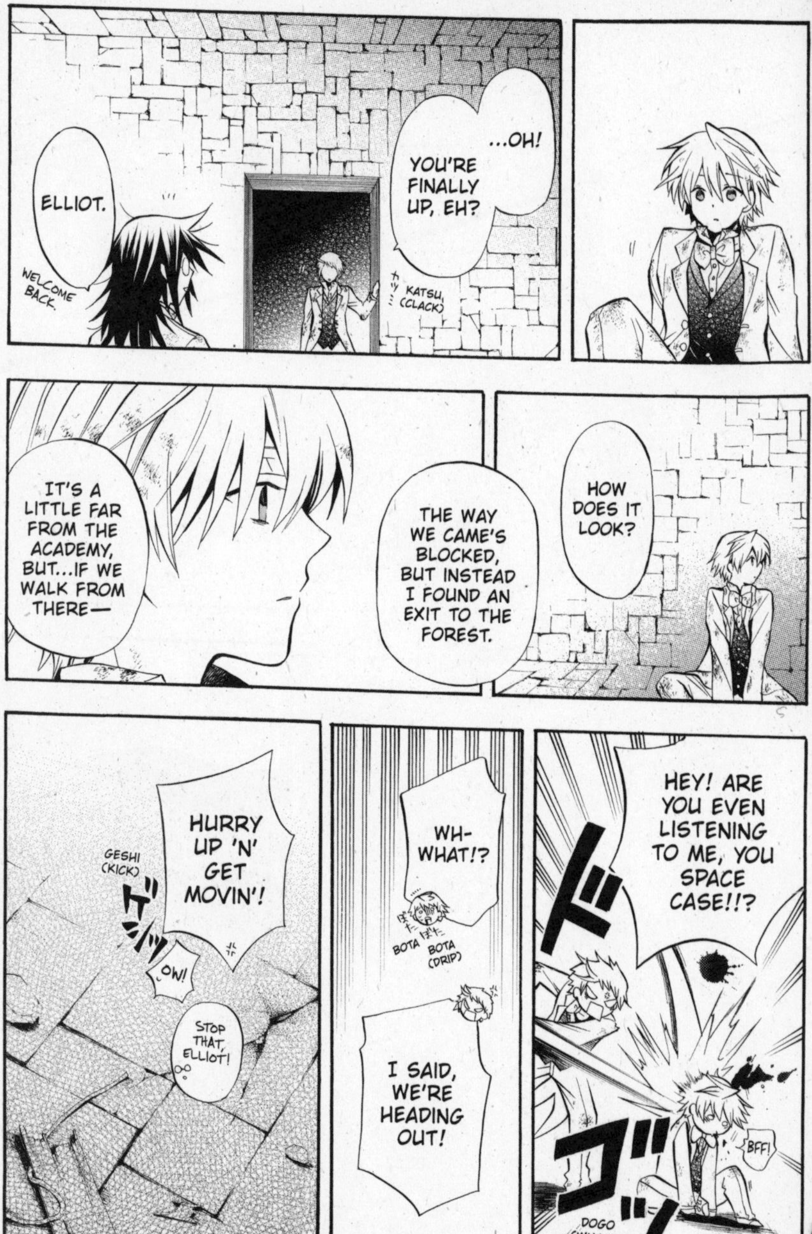
...OH!
YOU'RE FINALLY UP, EH?
KATSU (CLACK)
ELLIOT.
WELCOME BACK.
HOW DOES IT LOOK?
THE WAY WE CAME'S BLOCKED, BUT INSTEAD I FOUND AN EXIT TO THE FOREST.
IT'S A LITTLE FAR FROM THE ACADEMY, BUT...IF WE WALK FROM THERE—
HEY! ARE YOU EVEN LISTENING TO ME, YOU SPACE CASE!!?
BFF!
DOGO (WHACK)
WH-WHAT!?
BOTA BOTA (DRIP)
I SAID, WE'RE HEADING OUT!
HURRY UP 'N' GET MOVIN'!
GESHI (KICK)
OW!
STOP THAT, ELLIOT!

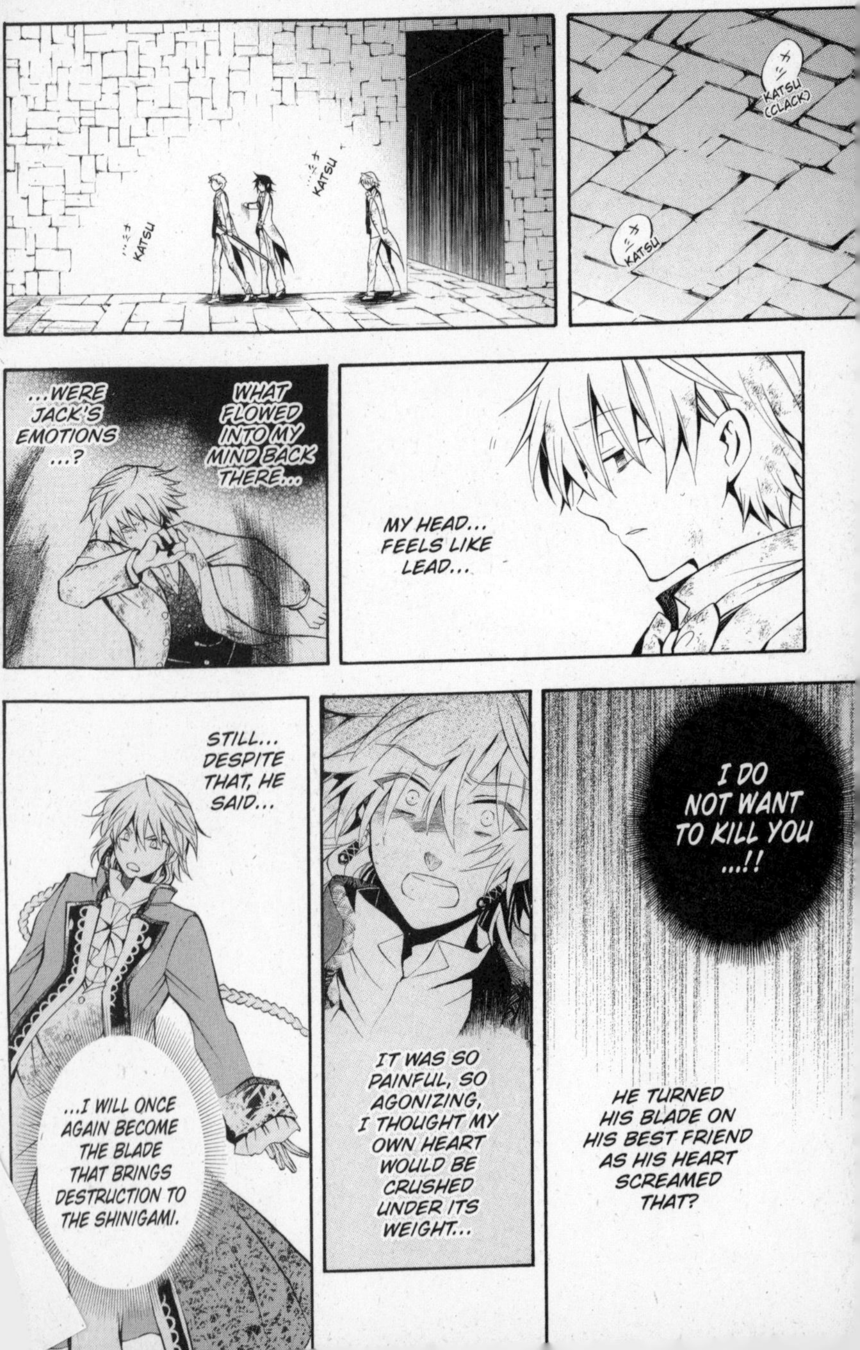
KATSU (CLACK)
KATSU
KATSU
KATSU
MY HEAD... FEELS LIKE LEAD...
WHAT FLOWED INTO MY MIND BACK THERE...
...WERE JACK'S EMOTIONS ...?
I DO NOT WANT TO KILL YOU ...!!
HE TURNED HIS BLADE ON HIS BEST FRIEND AS HIS HEART SCREAMED THAT?
IT WAS SO PAINFUL, SO AGONIZING, I THOUGHT MY OWN HEART WOULD BE CRUSHED UNDER ITS WEIGHT...
STILL... DESPITE THAT, HE SAID...
...I WILL ONCE AGAIN BECOME THE BLADE THAT BRINGS DESTRUCTION TO THE SHINIGAMI.

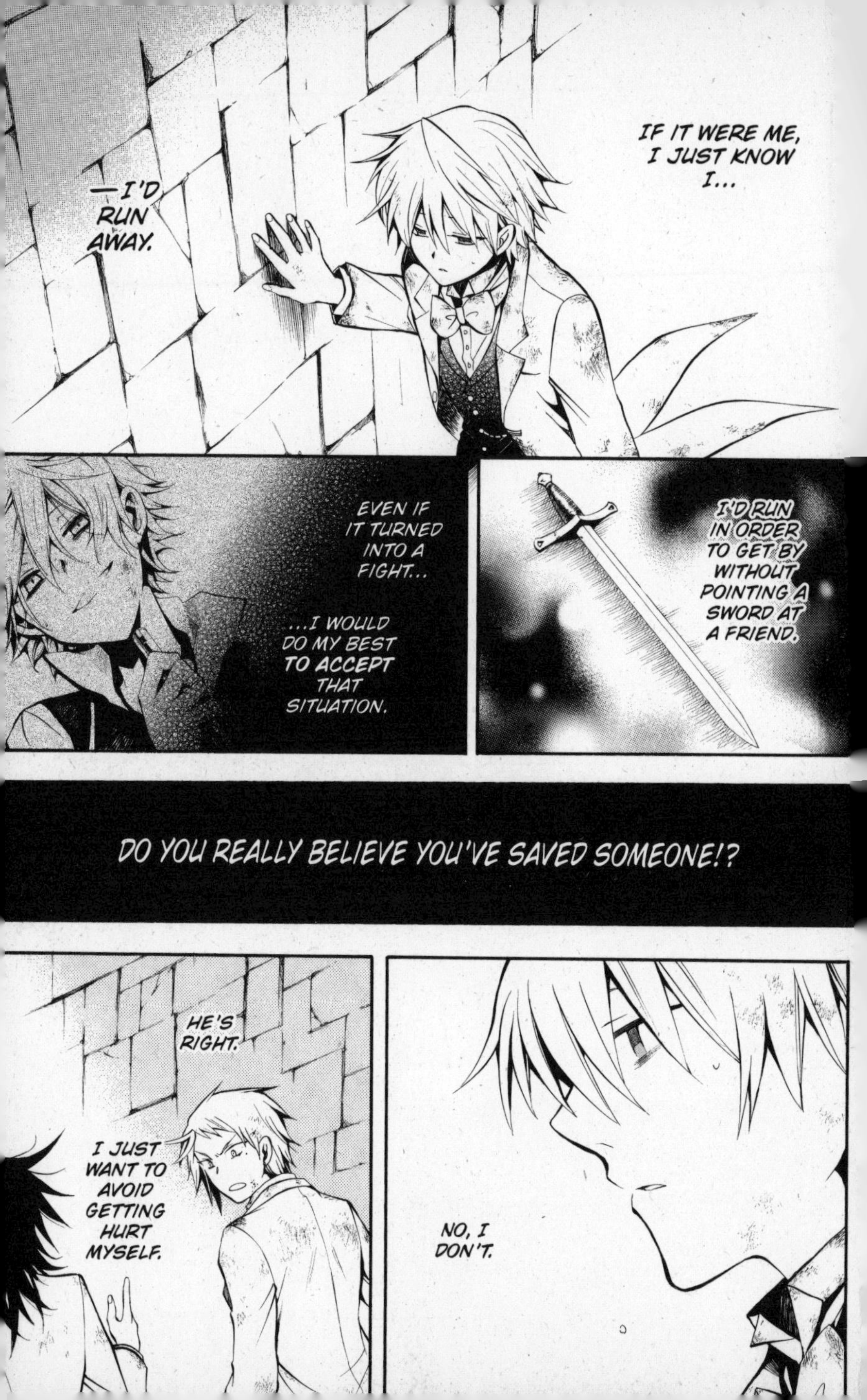
IF IT WERE ME, I JUST KNOW I...
—I'D RUN AWAY.
I'D RUN IN ORDER TO GET BY WITHOUT POINTING A SWORD AT A FRIEND.
EVEN IF IT TURNED INTO A FIGHT...
...I WOULD DO MY BEST TO ACCEPT THAT SITUATION.
DO YOU REALLY BELIEVE YOU'VE SAVED SOMEONE!?
NO, I DON'T.
HE'S RIGHT.
I JUST WANT TO AVOID GETTING HURT MYSELF.

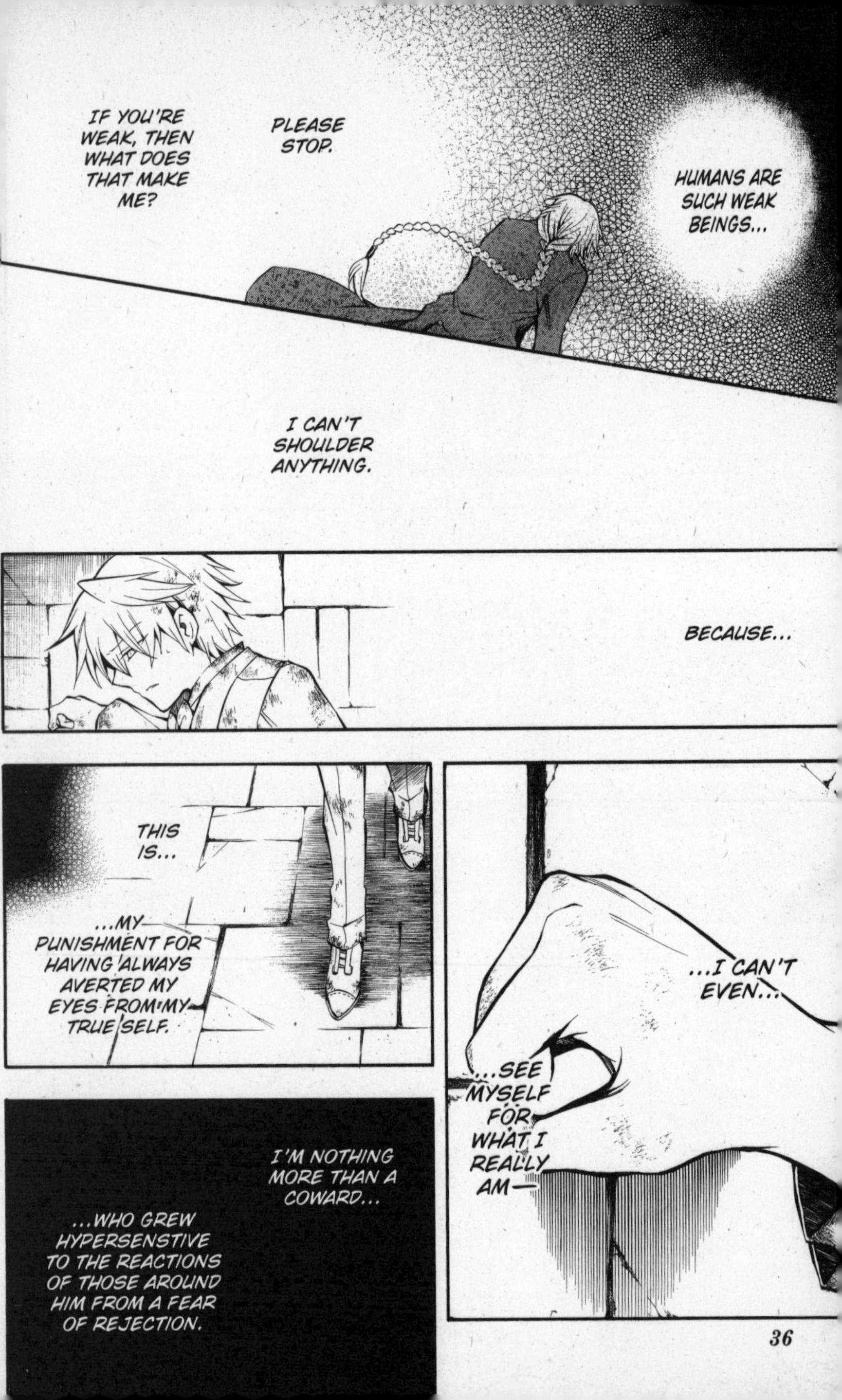
HUMANS ARE SUCH WEAK BEINGS...
PLEASE STOP.
IF YOU'RE WEAK, THEN WHAT DOES THAT MAKE ME?
I CAN'T SHOULDER ANYTHING.
BECAUSE...
...I CAN'T EVEN...
...SEE MYSELF FOR WHAT I REALLY AM—
THIS IS...
...MY PUNISHMENT FOR HAVING ALWAYS AVERTED MY EYES FROM MY TRUE SELF.
I'M NOTHING MORE THAN A COWARD...
...WHO GREW HYPERSENSTIVE TO THE REACTIONS OF THOSE AROUND HIM FROM A FEAR OF REJECTION.

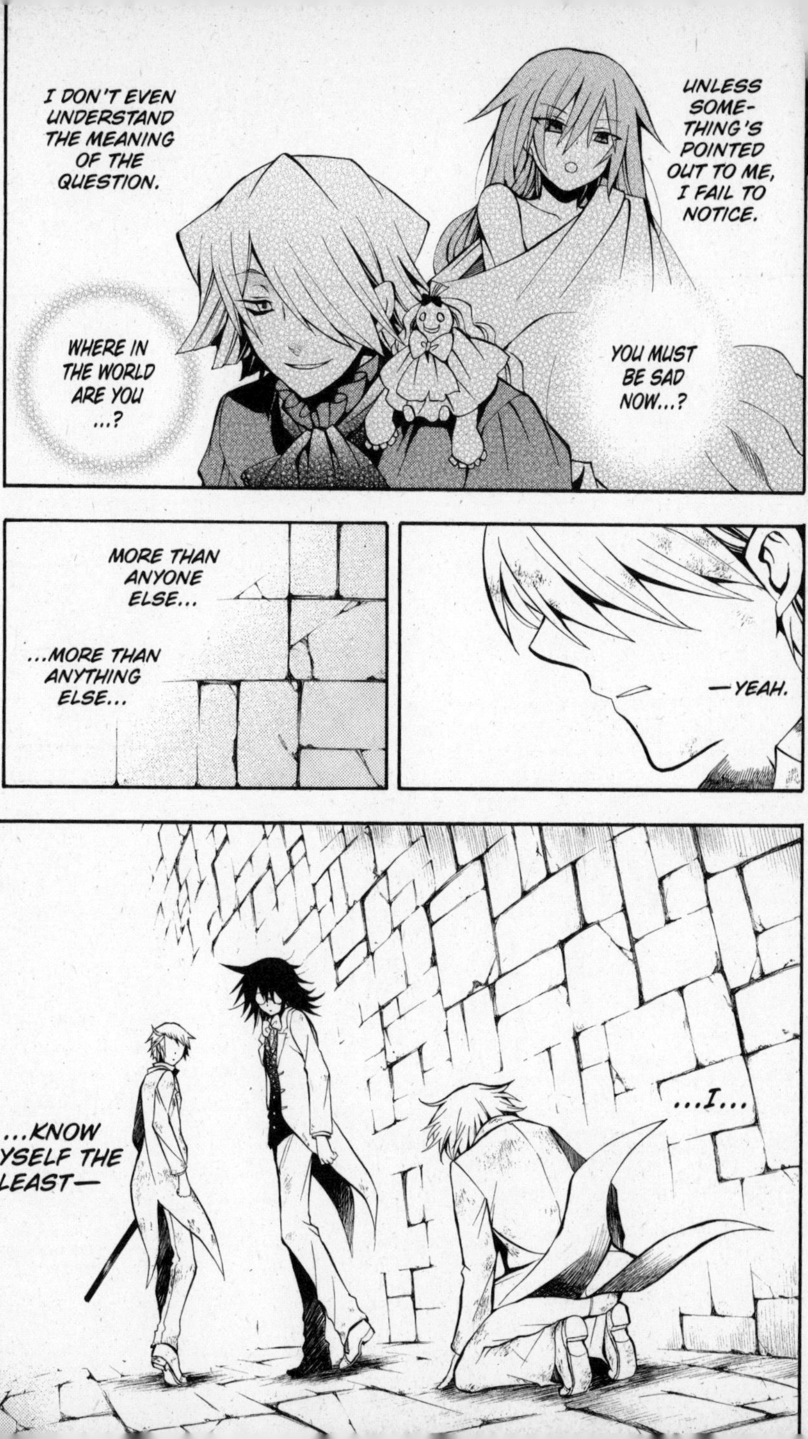
UNLESS SOME-THING'S POINTED OUT TO ME, I FAIL TO NOTICE.
I DON'T EVEN UNDERSTAND THE MEANING OF THE QUESTION.
YOU MUST BE SAD NOW...?
WHERE IN THE WORLD ARE YOU ...?
—YEAH.
MORE THAN ANYONE ELSE...
...MORE THAN ANYTHING ELSE...
...I...
...KNOW MYSELF THE LEAST—

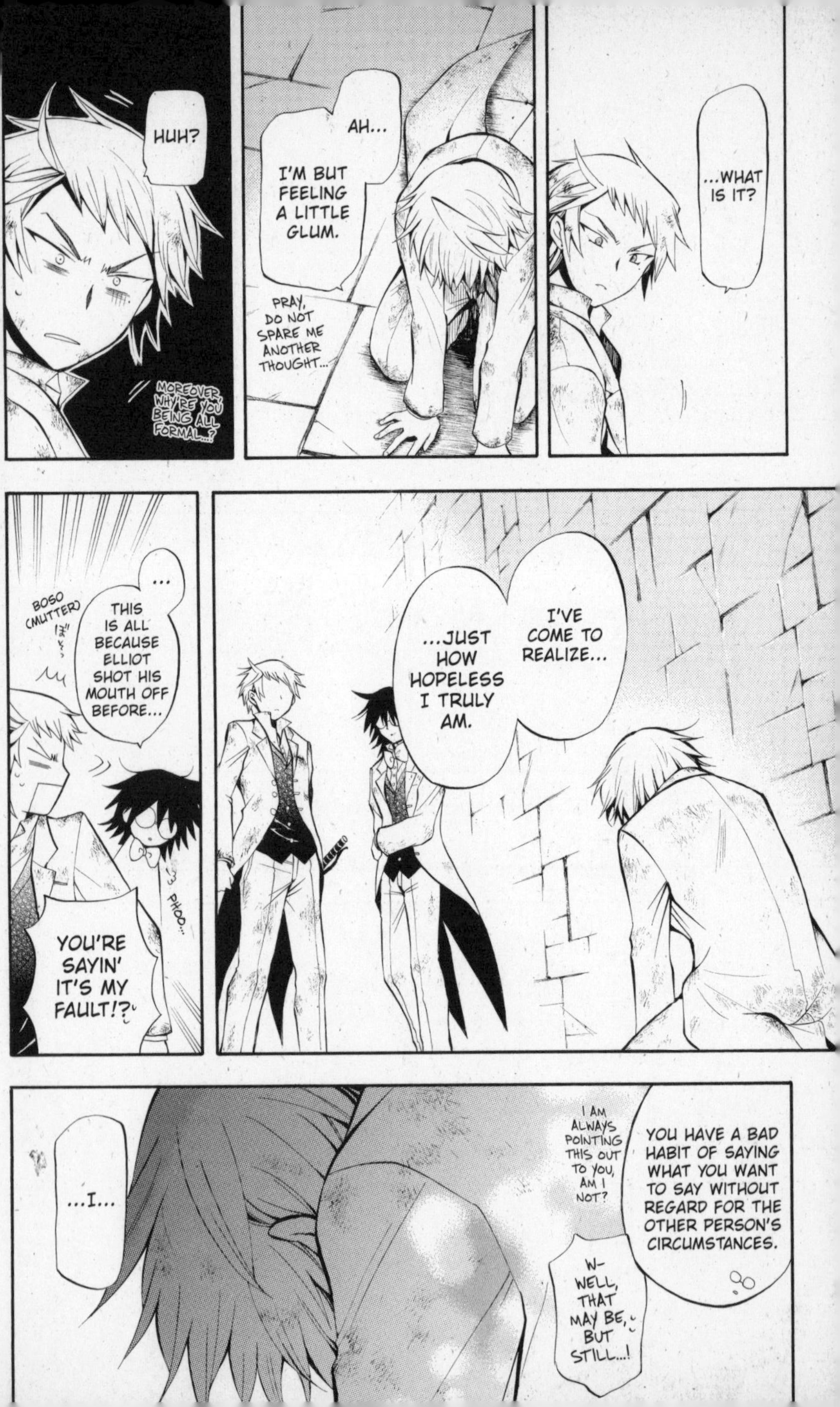
...WHAT IS IT?
AH...
I'M BUT FEELING A LITTLE GLUM.
PRAY, DO NOT SPARE ME ANOTHER THOUGHT...
HUH?
MOREOVER, WHY'RE YOU BEING ALL FORMAL...?
I'VE COME TO REALIZE...
...JUST HOW HOPELESS I TRULY AM.
...
THIS IS ALL BECAUSE ELLIOT SHOT HIS MOUTH OFF BEFORE...
BOSO (MUTTER)
PHOO...
YOU'RE SAYIN' IT'S MY FAULT!?
YOU HAVE A BAD HABIT OF SAYING WHAT YOU WANT TO SAY WITHOUT REGARD FOR THE OTHER PERSON'S CIRCUMSTANCES.
I AM ALWAYS POINTING THIS OUT TO YOU, AM I NOT?
W-WELL, THAT MAY BE, BUT STILL...!
...I...

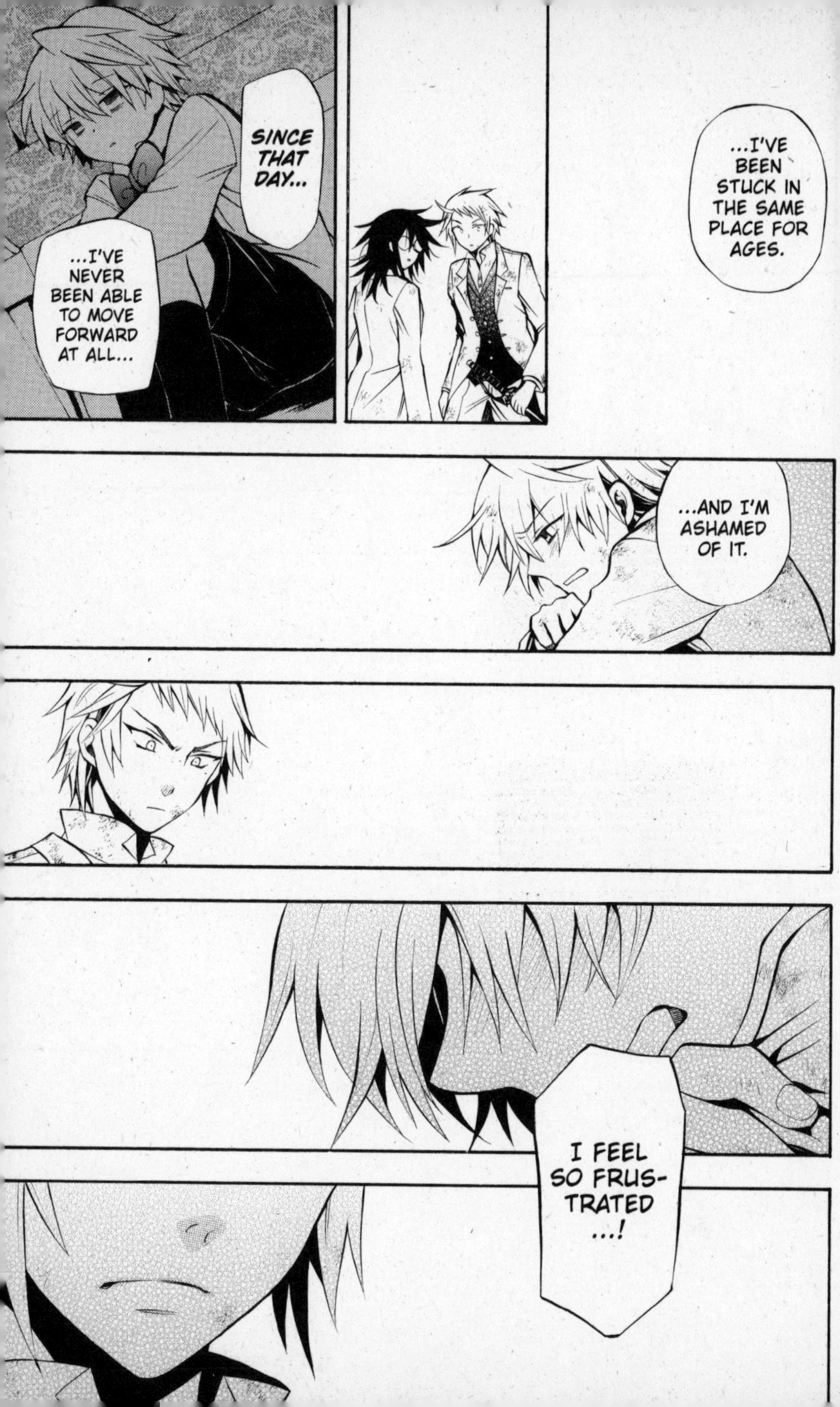
...I'VE BEEN STUCK IN THE SAME PLACE FOR AGES.
SINCE THAT DAY...
...I'VE NEVER BEEN ABLE TO MOVE FORWARD AT ALL...
...AND I'M ASHAMED OF IT.
I FEEL SO FRUS-TRATED ...!

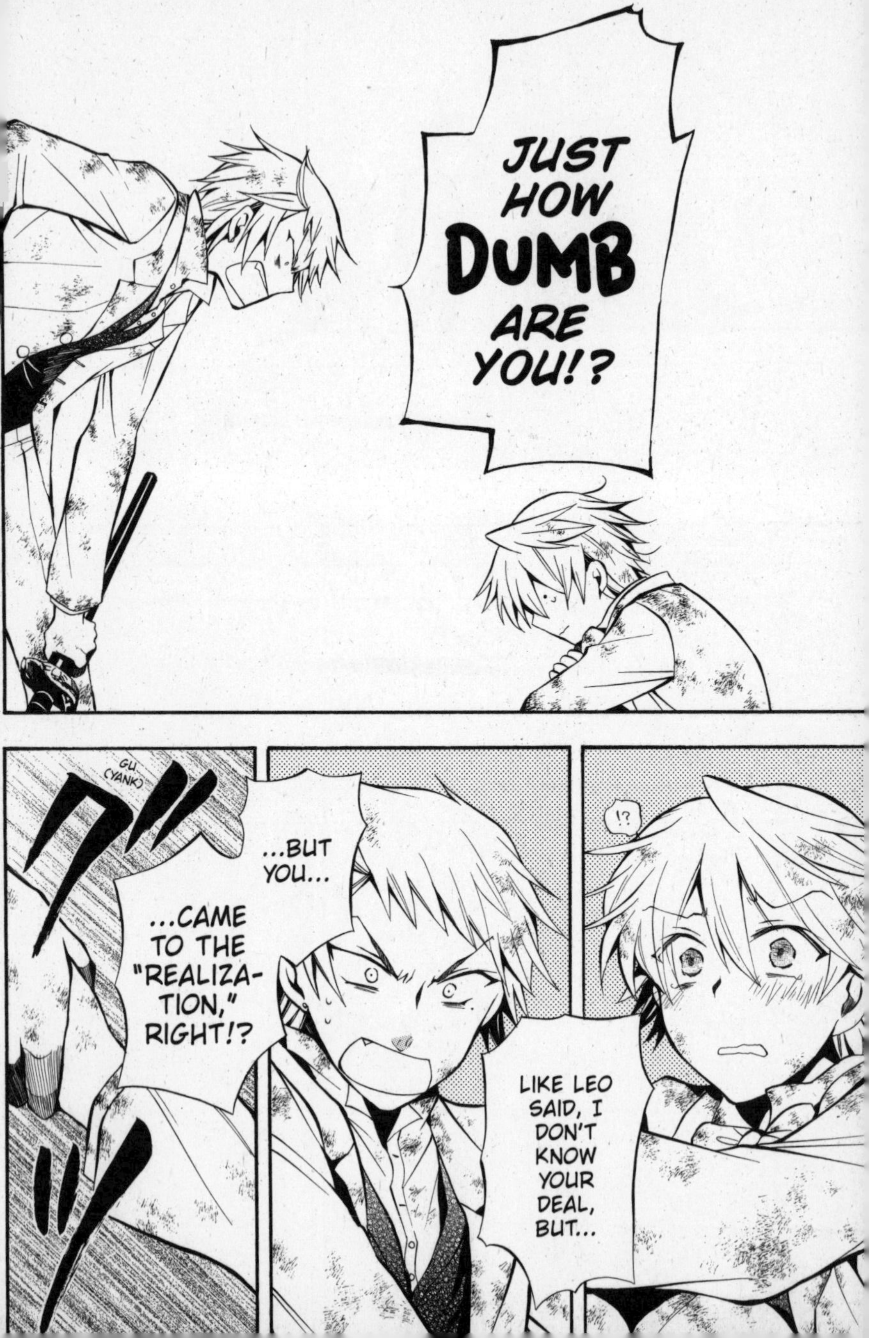
JUST HOW DUMB ARE YOU!?
!?
LIKE LEO SAID, I DON'T KNOW YOUR DEAL, BUT...
...BUT YOU...
...CAME TO THE "REALIZATION," RIGHT!?
GU (YANK)

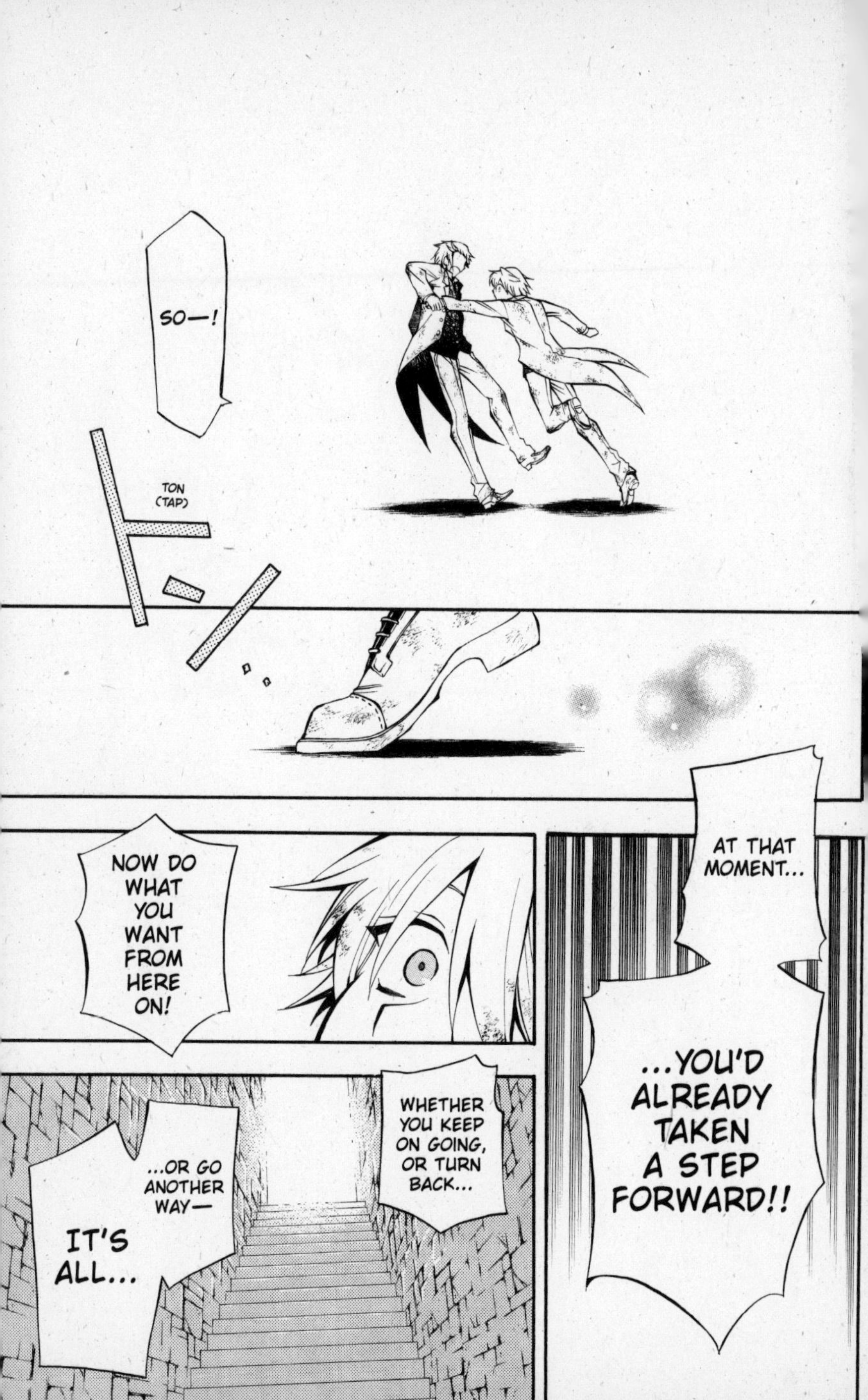
SO—!
TON (TAP)
AT THAT MOMENT...
...YOU'D ALREADY TAKEN A STEP FORWARD!!
NOW DO WHAT YOU WANT FROM HERE ON!
WHETHER YOU KEEP ON GOING, OR TURN BACK...
...OR GO ANOTHER WAY—
IT'S ALL...

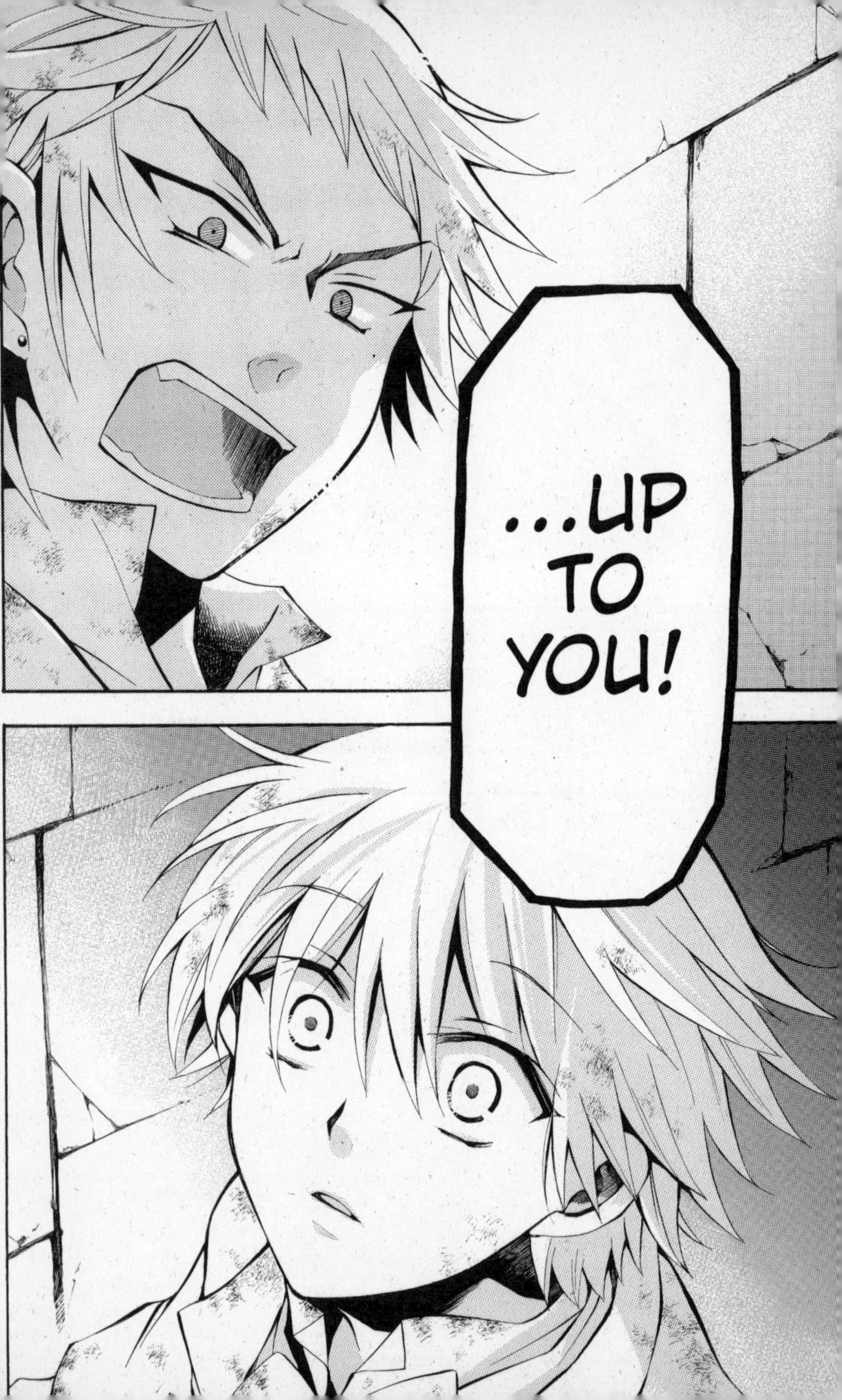
...UP TO YOU!

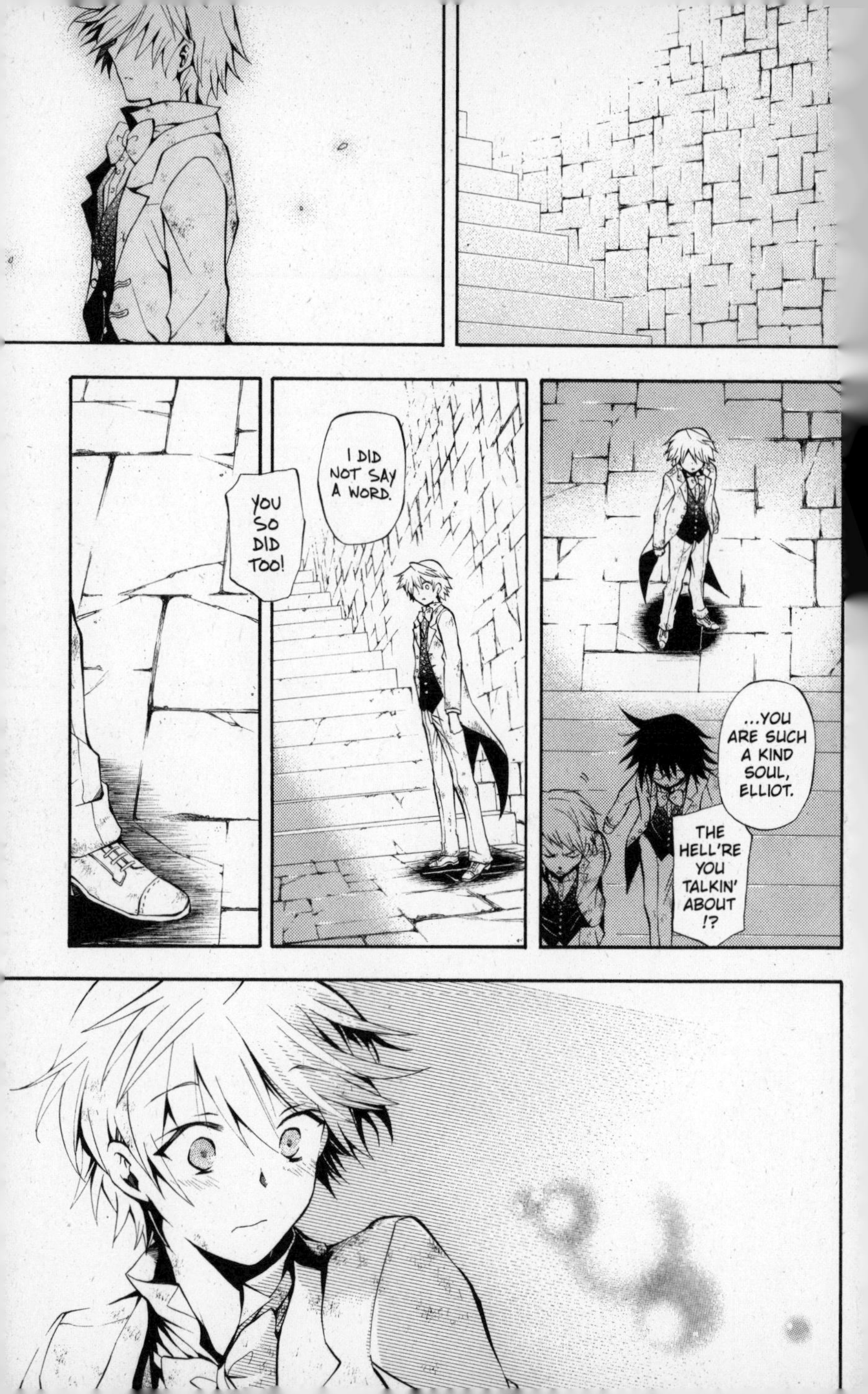
...YOU ARE SUCH A KIND SOUL, ELLIOT.
THE HELL'RE YOU TALKIN' ABOUT !?
I DID NOT SAY A WORD.
YOU SO DID TOO!

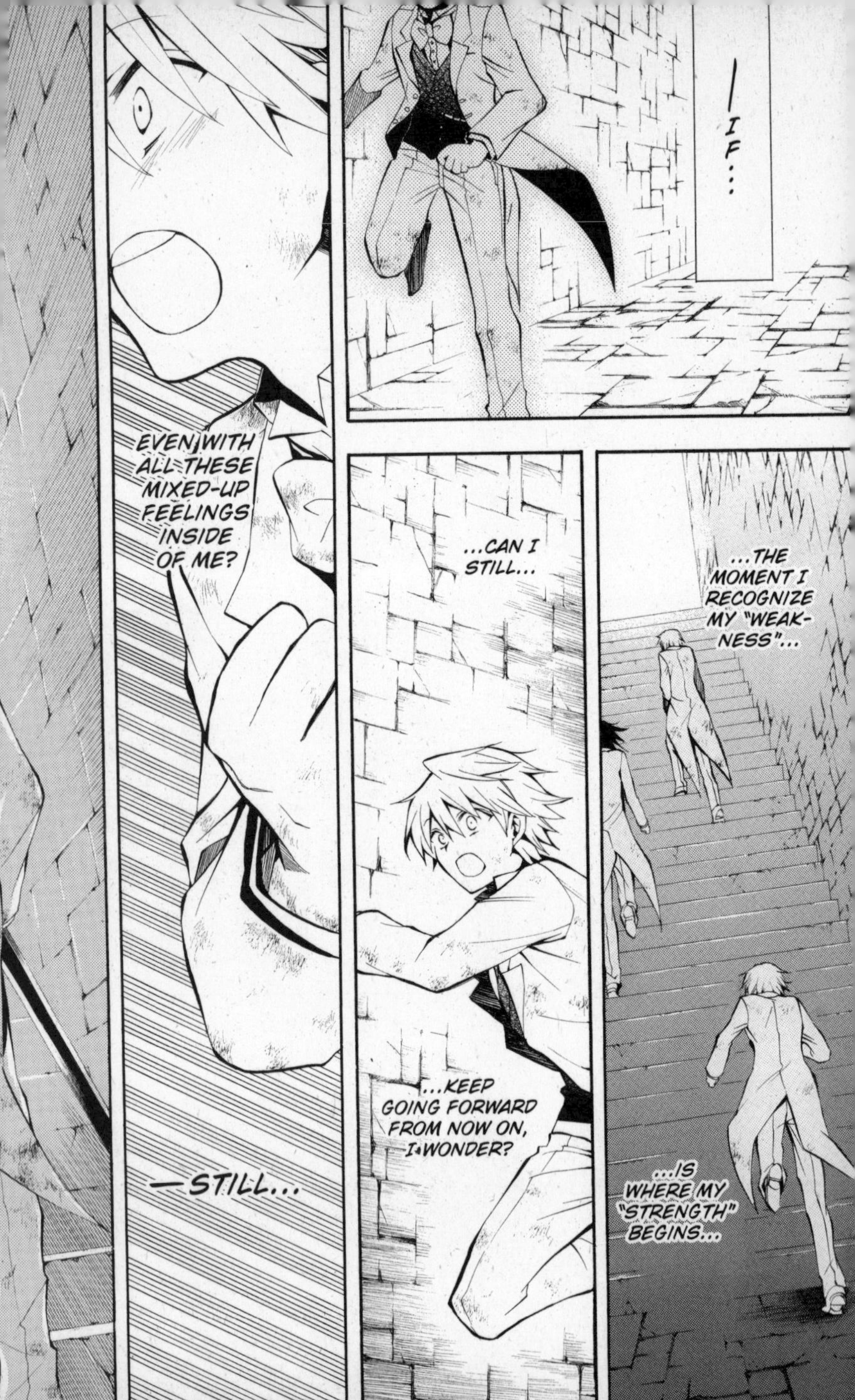
—IF...
...THE MOMENT I RECOGNIZE MY "WEAKNESS"...
...IS WHERE MY "STRENGTH" BEGINS...
...CAN I STILL...
...KEEP GOING FORWARD FROM NOW ON, I WONDER?
EVEN WITH ALL THESE MIXED-UP FEELINGS INSIDE OF ME?
—STILL...

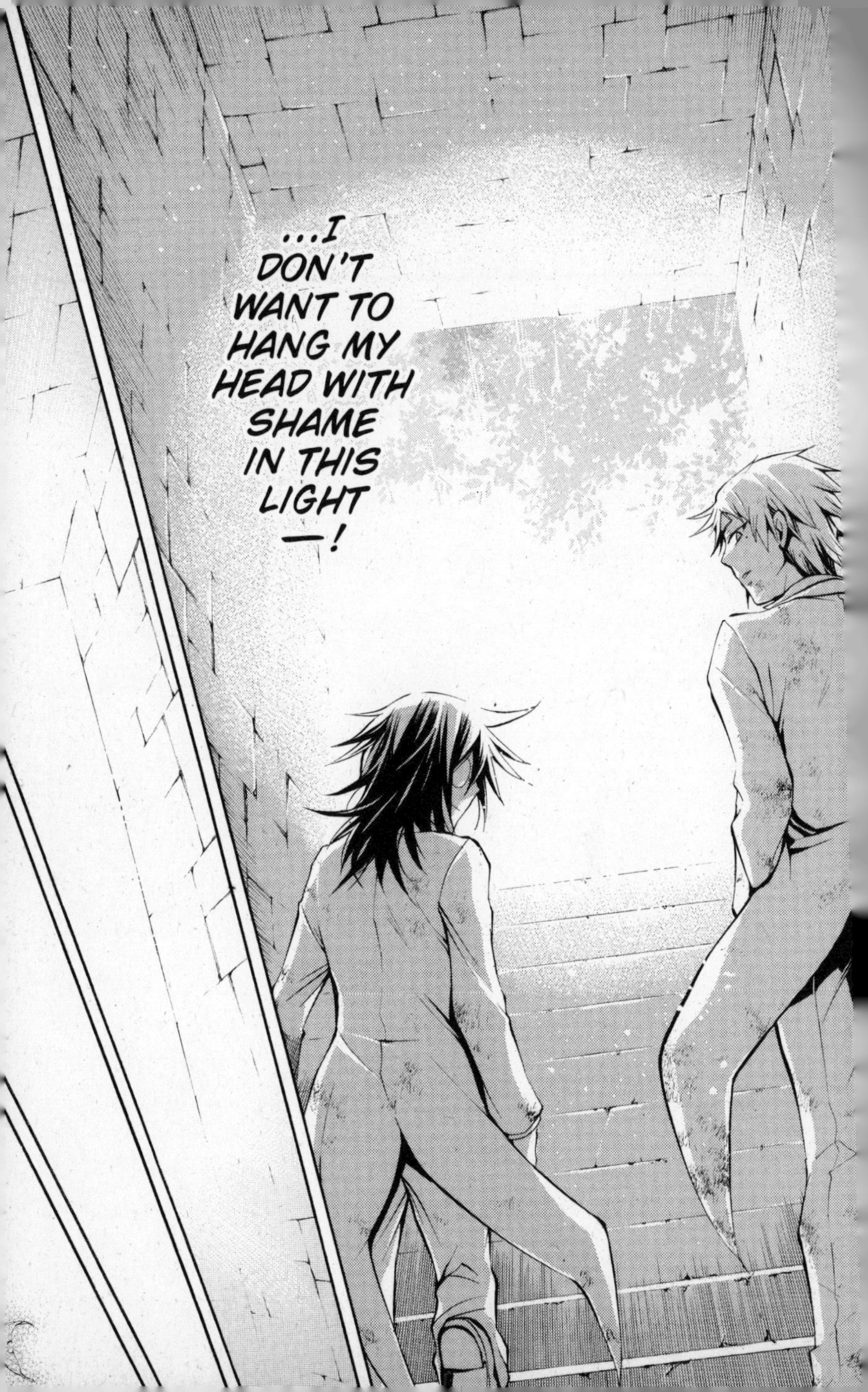
...I DON'T WANT TO HANG MY HEAD WITH SHAME IN THIS LIGHT—!

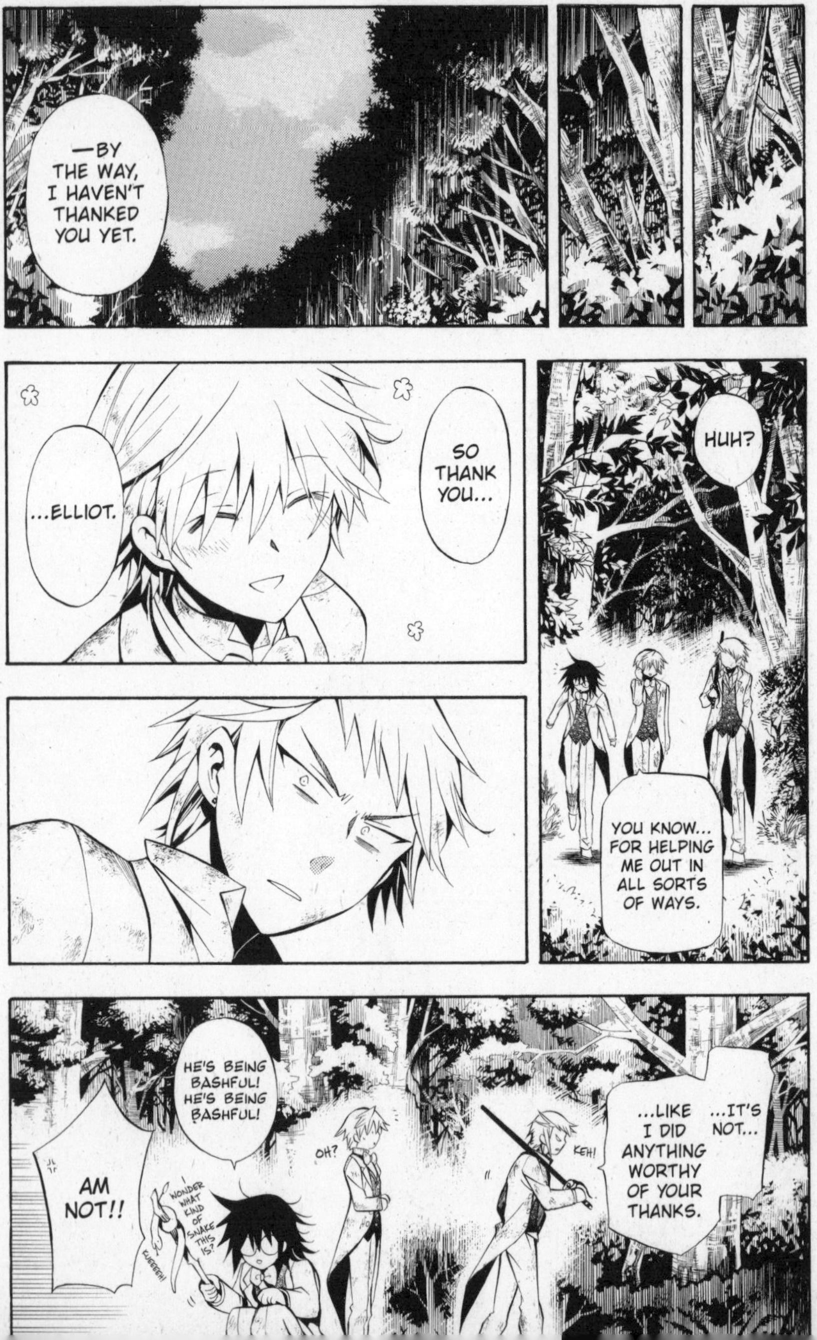
—BY THE WAY, I HAVEN'T THANKED YOU YET.
HUH?
YOU KNOW... FOR HELPING ME OUT IN ALL SORTS OF WAYS.
SO THANK YOU...
...ELLIOT.
...IT'S NOT...
...LIKE I DID ANYTHING WORTHY OF YOUR THANKS.
KEH!
OH?
HE'S BEING BASHFUL! HE'S BEING BASHFUL!
I WONDER WHAT KIND OF SNAKE THIS IS?
AM NOT!!

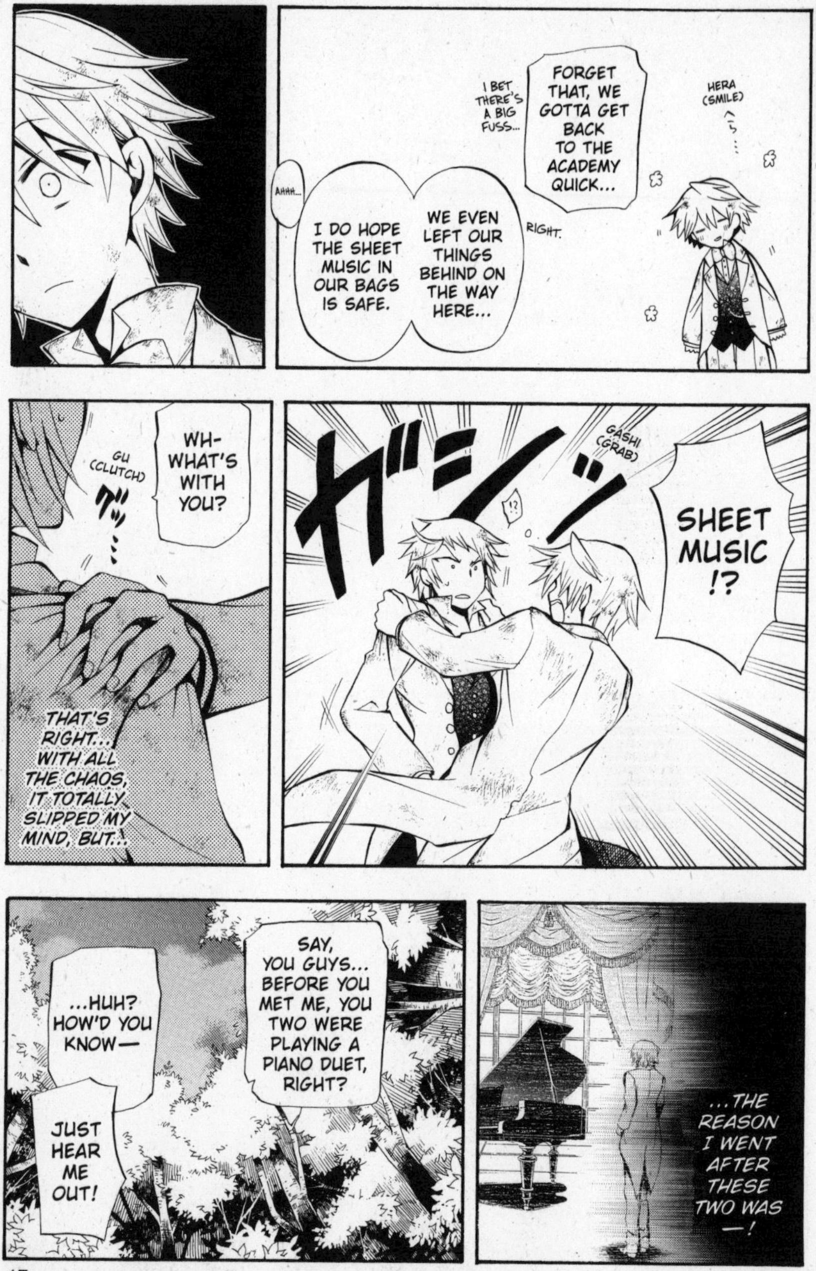
HERA (SMILE)
へら…
FORGET THAT, WE GOTTA GET BACK TO THE ACADEMY QUICK…
I BET THERE'S A BIG FUSS…
RIGHT.
WE EVEN LEFT OUR THINGS BEHIND ON THE WAY HERE…
I DO HOPE THE SHEET MUSIC IN OUR BAGS IS SAFE.
AHHH…
SHEET MUSIC !?
GASHI (GRAB)
ガシッ
!?
WH- WHAT'S WITH YOU?
GU (CLUTCH)
グッ…
THAT'S RIGHT... WITH ALL THE CHAOS, IT TOTALLY SLIPPED MY MIND, BUT...
...THE REASON I WENT AFTER THESE TWO WAS—!
SAY, YOU GUYS... BEFORE YOU MET ME, YOU TWO WERE PLAYING A PIANO DUET, RIGHT?
...HUH? HOW'D YOU KNOW—
JUST HEAR ME OUT!

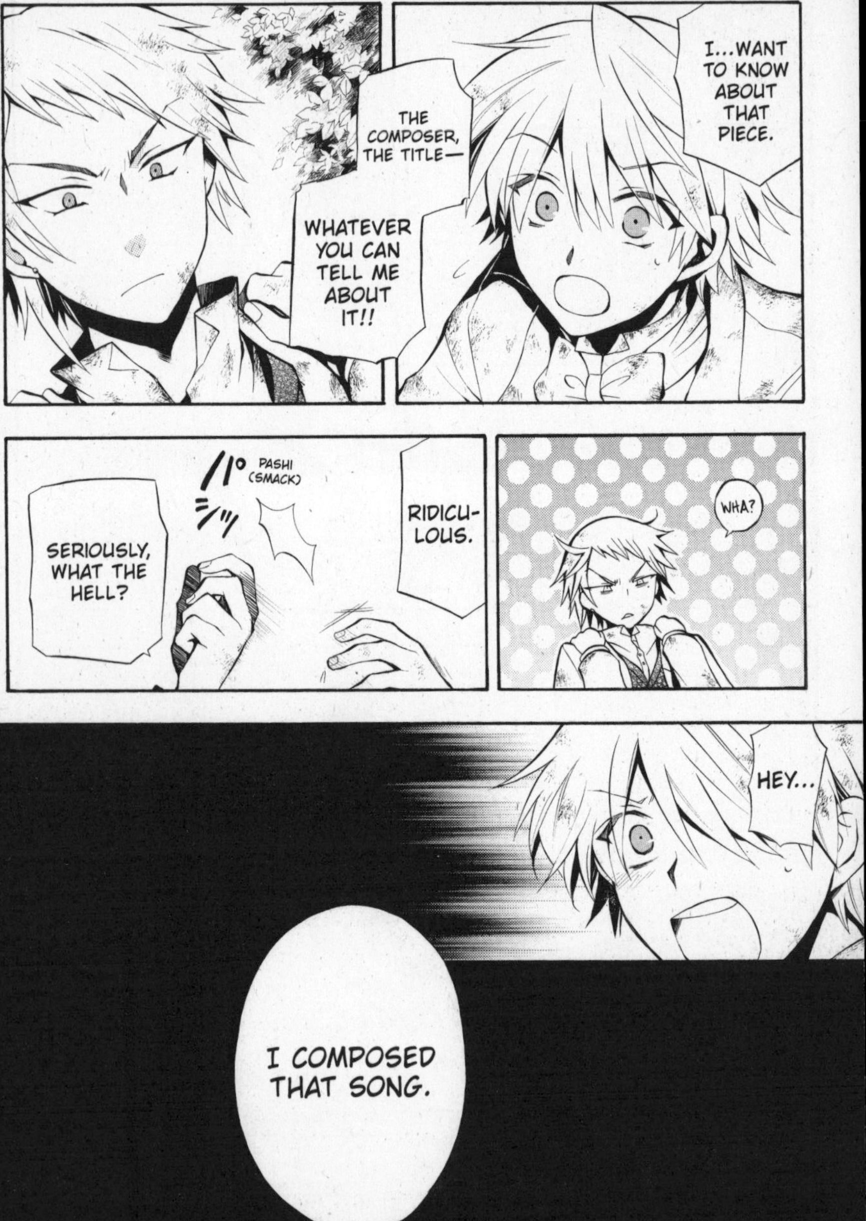

I...WANT TO KNOW ABOUT THAT PIECE.
THE COMPOSER, THE TITLE—
WHATEVER YOU CAN TELL ME ABOUT IT!!
WHA?
RIDICULOUS.
PASHI (SMACK)
SERIOUSLY, WHAT THE HELL?
HEY...
I COMPOSED THAT SONG.

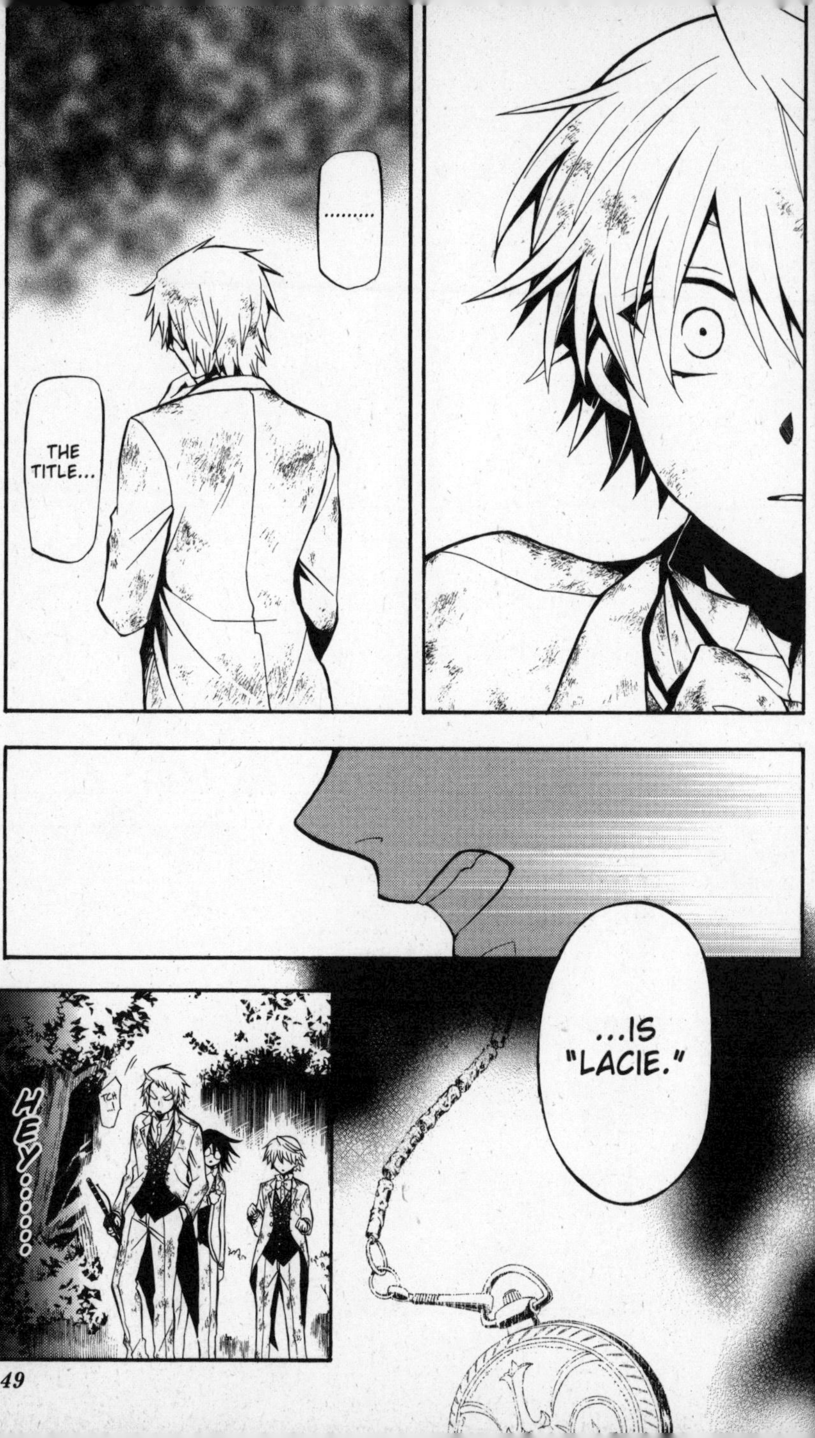

....
THE TITLE...
...IS "LACIE."
TCH ...!
HEYOOOOO

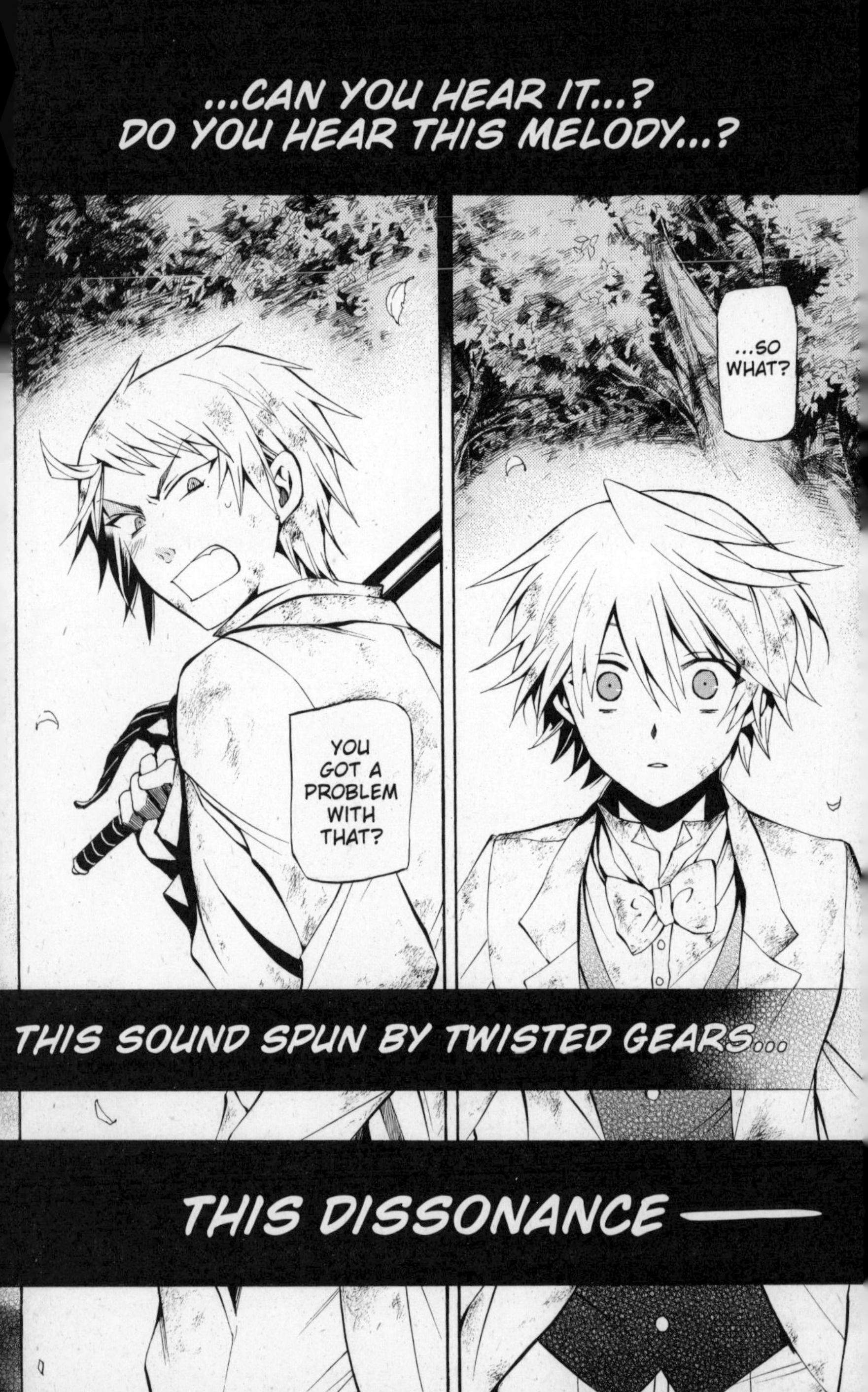
...CAN YOU HEAR IT...?
DO YOU HEAR THIS MELODY...?
...SO WHAT?
YOU GOT A PROBLEM WITH THAT?
THIS SOUND SPUN BY TWISTED GEARS...
THIS DISSONANCE —

Retrace:XXVIII Modulation

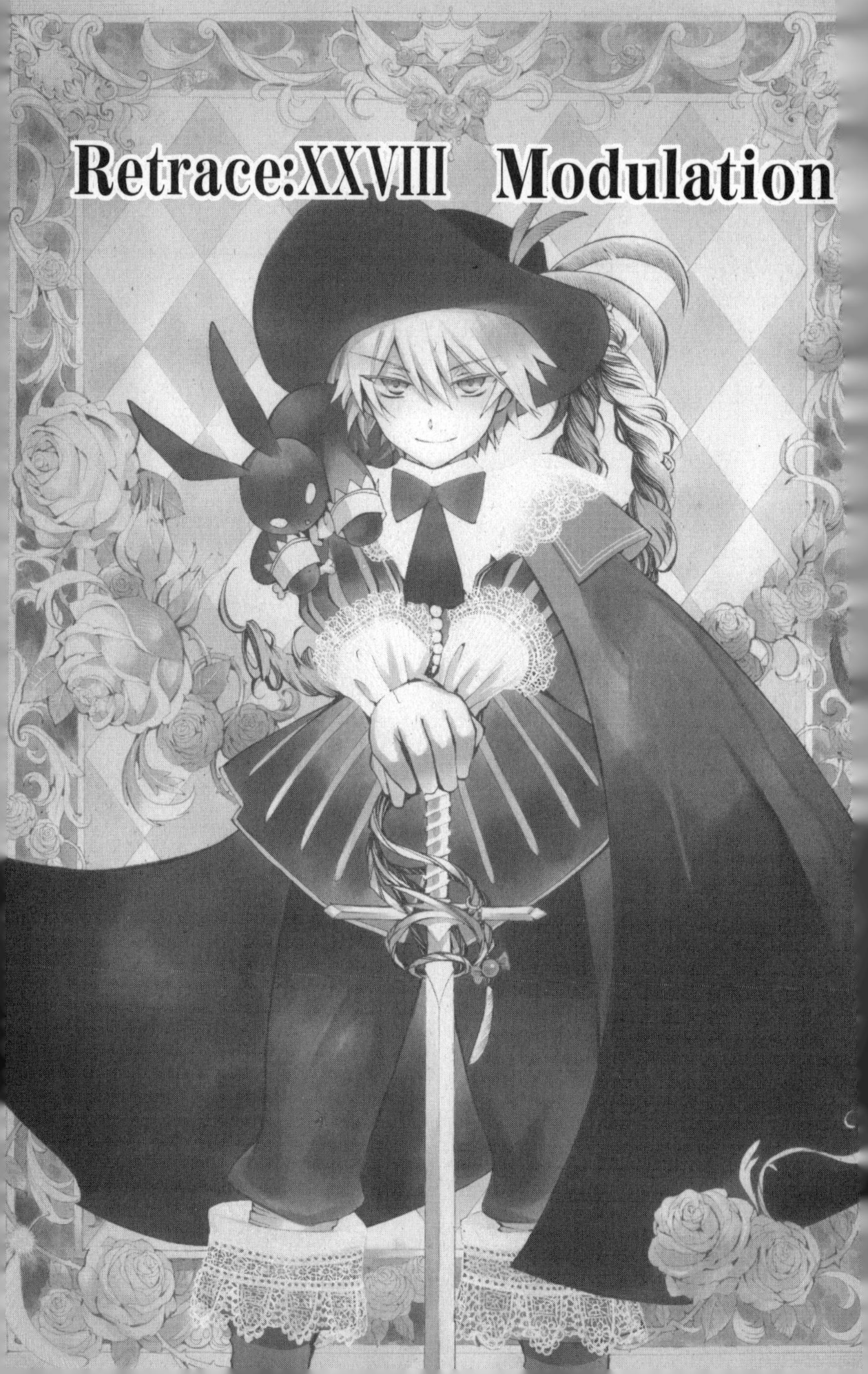

BONUS: "A MEETING OF BOOK OTAKU"

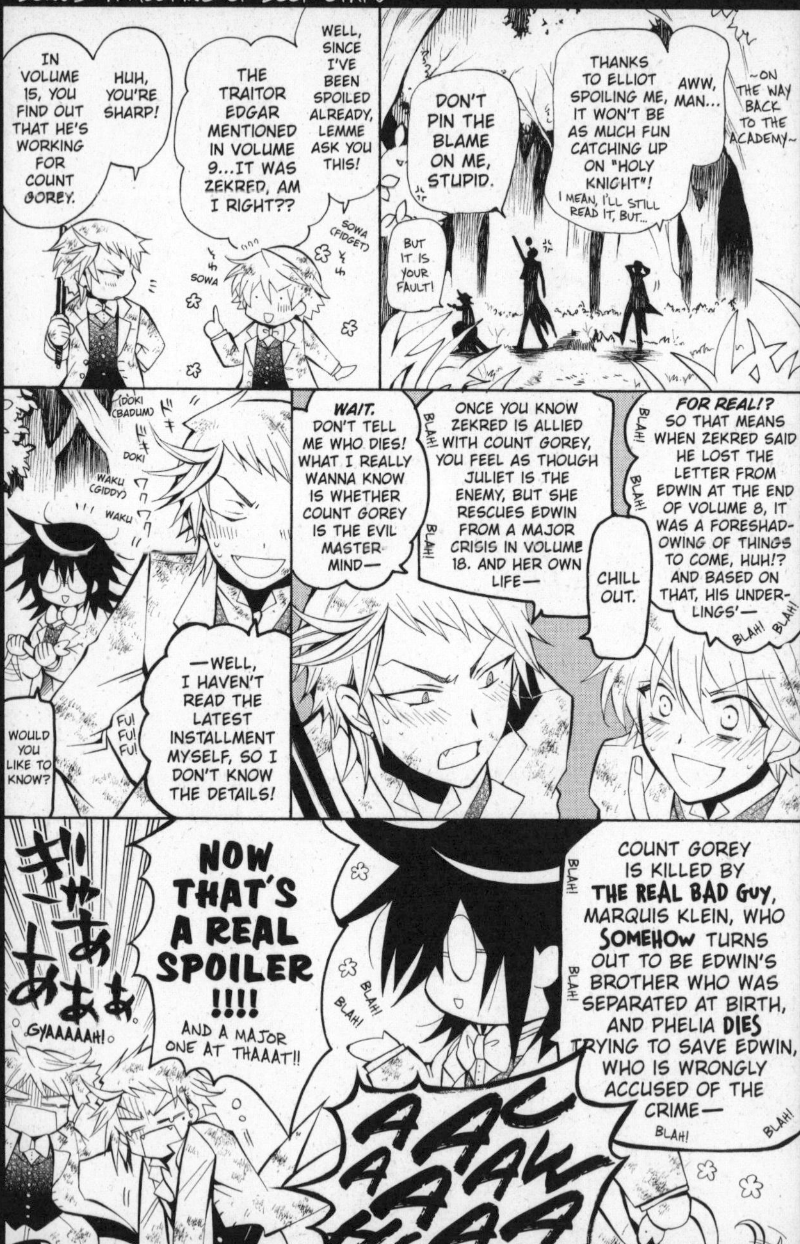
~ON THE WAY BACK TO THE ACADEMY~
AWW, MAN...
THANKS TO ELLIOT SPOILING ME, IT WON'T BE AS MUCH FUN CATCHING UP ON "HOLY KNIGHT"!
I MEAN, I'LL STILL READ IT, BUT...
DON'T PIN THE BLAME ON ME, STUPID.
BUT IT IS YOUR FAULT!
WELL, SINCE I'VE BEEN SPOILED ALREADY, LEMME ASK YOU THIS!
THE TRAITOR EDGAR MENTIONED IN VOLUME 9...IT WAS ZEKRED, AM I RIGHT??
SOWA (FIDGET)
SOWA
HUH, YOU'RE SHARP!
IN VOLUME 15, YOU FIND OUT THAT HE'S WORKING FOR COUNT GOREY.
FOR REAL!? SO THAT MEANS WHEN ZEKRED SAID HE LOST THE LETTER FROM EDWIN AT THE END OF VOLUME 8, IT WAS A FORESHADOWING OF THINGS TO COME, HUH!? AND BASED ON THAT, HIS UNDERLINGS'—
BLAH! BLAH!
CHILL OUT.
BLAH! BLAH!
ONCE YOU KNOW ZEKRED IS ALLIED WITH COUNT GOREY, YOU FEEL AS THOUGH JULIET IS THE ENEMY, BUT SHE RESCUES EDWIN FROM A MAJOR CRISIS IN VOLUME 18. AND HER OWN LIFE—
BLAH! BLAH!
WAIT. DON'T TELL ME WHO DIES! WHAT I REALLY WANNA KNOW IS WHETHER COUNT GOREY IS THE EVIL MASTERMIND—
DOKI (BADUM)
DOKI
WAKU (GIDDY)
WAKU
—WELL, I HAVEN'T READ THE LATEST INSTALLMENT MYSELF, SO I DON'T KNOW THE DETAILS!
FU! FU! FU!
WOULD YOU LIKE TO KNOW?
COUNT GOREY IS KILLED BY THE REAL BAD GUY, MARQUIS KLEIN, WHO SOMEHOW TURNS OUT TO BE EDWIN'S BROTHER WHO WAS SEPARATED AT BIRTH, AND PHELIA DIES TRYING TO SAVE EDWIN, WHO IS WRONGLY ACCUSED OF THE CRIME—
BLAH! BLAH! BLAH! BLAH!
BLAH! BLAH!
NOW THAT'S A REAL SPOILER!!!!
AND A MAJOR ONE AT THAAAT!!
ぎゃあーあああ。
GYAAAAAH!

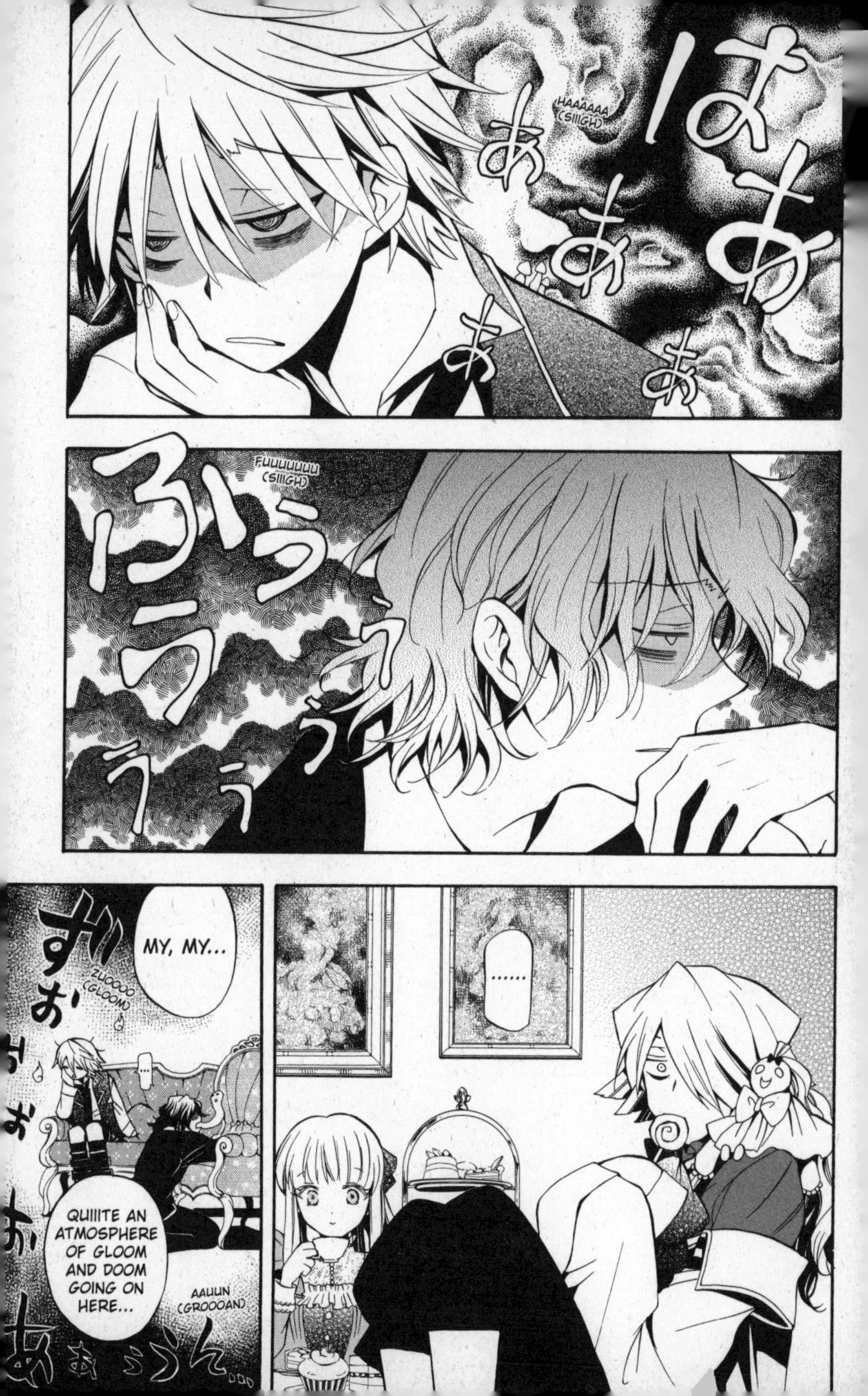
はあぁぁぁ
HAAAAAA (SIIIGH)
ふうぅぅぅ
FUUUUUUUU (SIIIGH)
......
MY, MY...
ずおぉぉぉ
ZUOOOO (GLOOM)
...
QUIIITE AN ATMOSPHERE OF GLOOM AND DOOM GOING ON HERE...
AAUUN (GROOOAN)
あぁうん

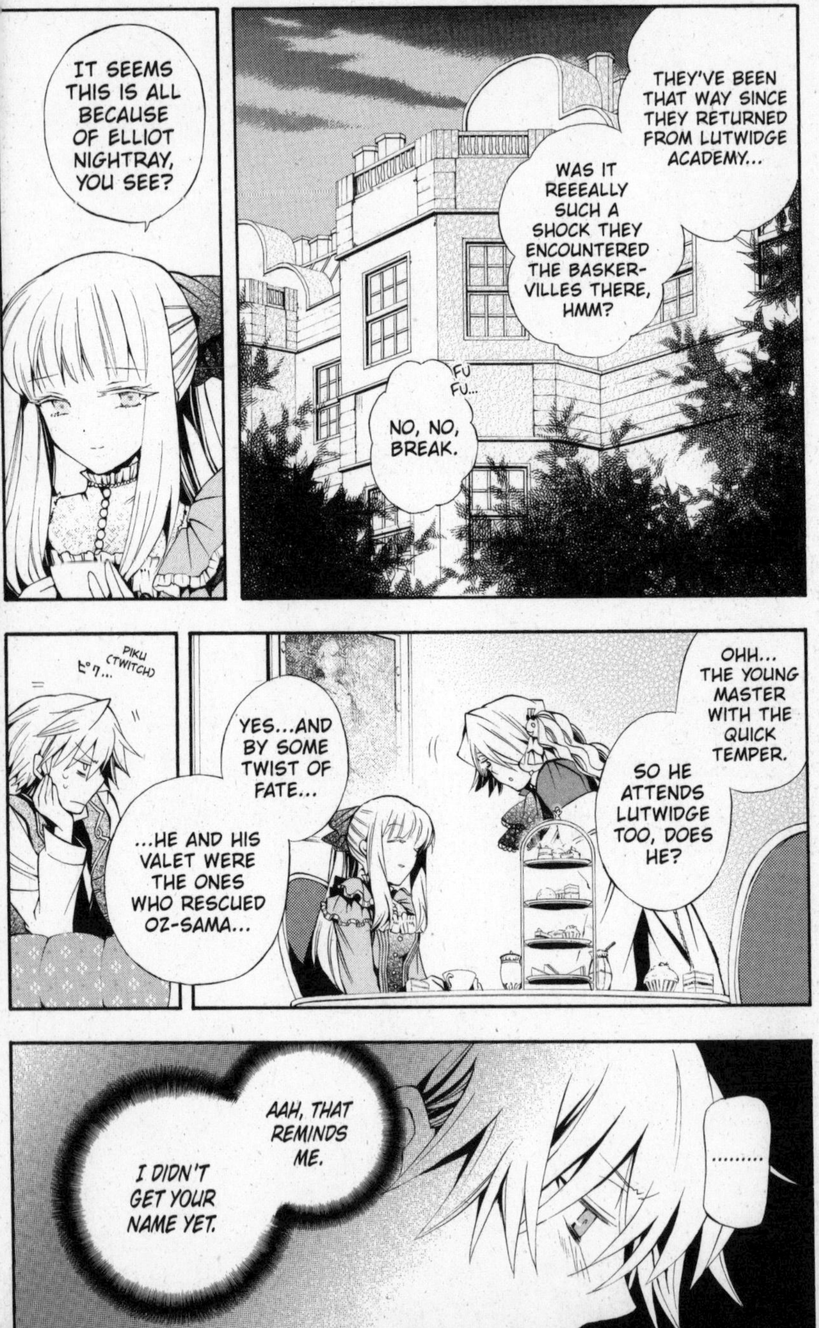
THEY'VE BEEN THAT WAY SINCE THEY RETURNED FROM LUTWIDGE ACADEMY...
WAS IT REEEALLY SUCH A SHOCK THEY ENCOUNTERED THE BASKER-VILLES THERE, HMM?
FU FU...
NO, NO, BREAK.
IT SEEMS THIS IS ALL BECAUSE OF ELLIOT NIGHTRAY, YOU SEE?
OHH... THE YOUNG MASTER WITH THE QUICK TEMPER.
SO HE ATTENDS LUTWIDGE TOO, DOES HE?
YES...AND BY SOME TWIST OF FATE...
...HE AND HIS VALET WERE THE ONES WHO RESCUED OZ-SAMA...
ピク... PIKU (TWITCH)
....
AAH, THAT REMINDS ME.
I DIDN'T GET YOUR NAME YET.

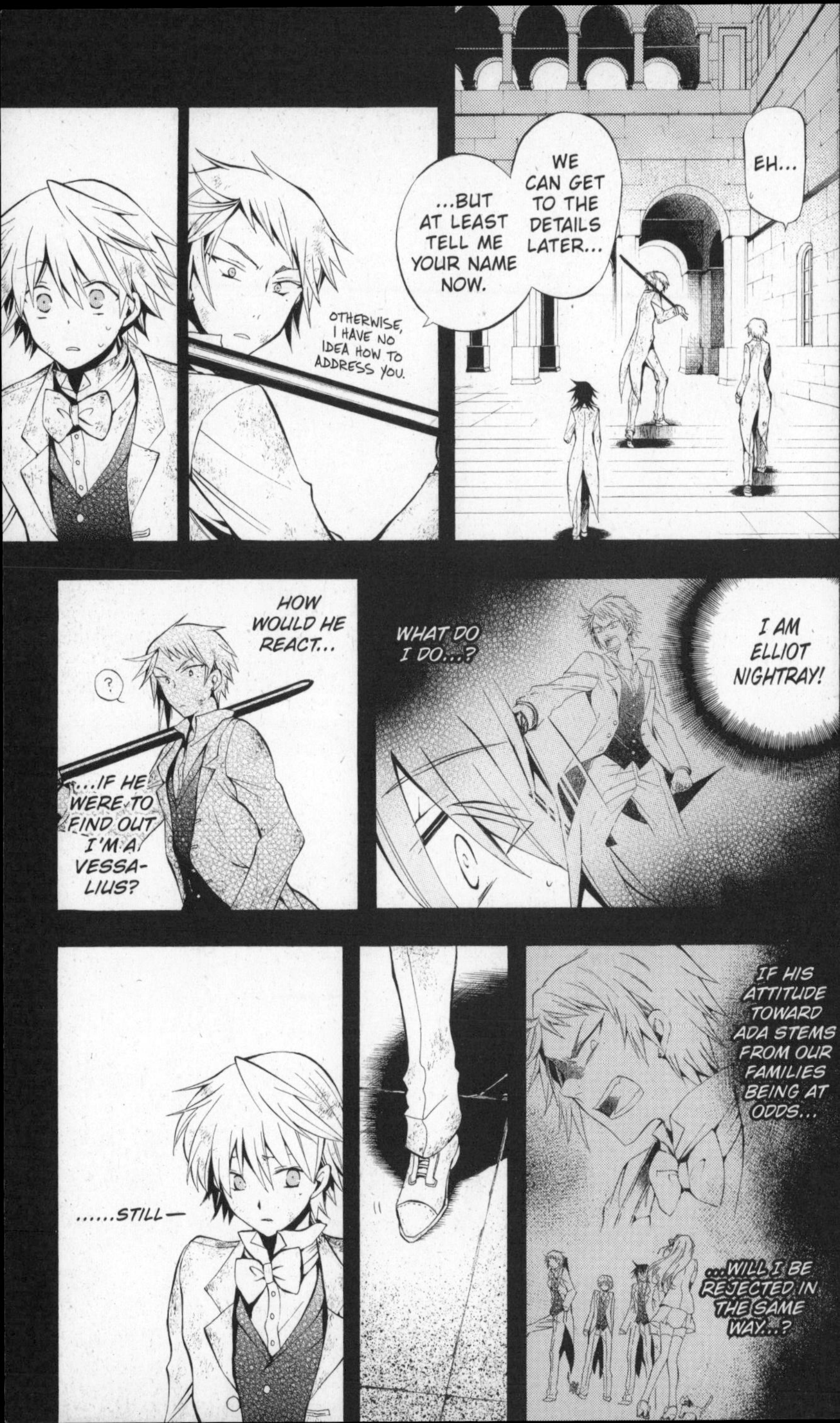
EH...
WE CAN GET TO THE DETAILS LATER...
...BUT AT LEAST TELL ME YOUR NAME NOW.
OTHERWISE, I HAVE NO IDEA HOW TO ADDRESS YOU.
I AM ELLIOT NIGHTRAY!
WHAT DO I DO...?
HOW WOULD HE REACT...
?
...IF HE WERE TO FIND OUT I'M A VESSA-LIUS?
IF HIS ATTITUDE TOWARD ADA STEMS FROM OUR FAMILIES BEING AT ODDS...
...WILL I BE REJECTED IN THE SAME WAY...?
......STILL—

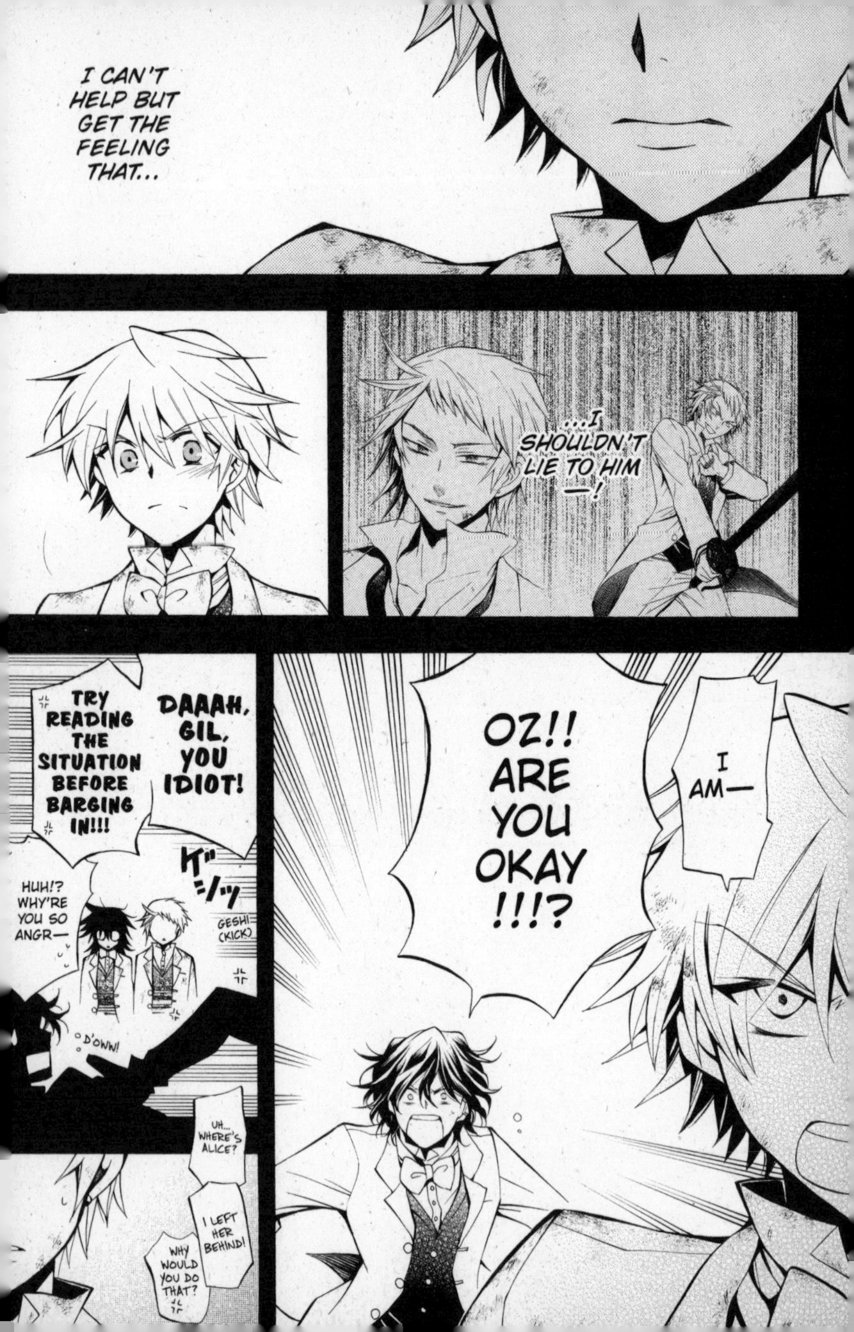
I CAN'T HELP BUT GET THE FEELING THAT...
...I SHOULDN'T LIE TO HIM—!
I AM—
OZ!! ARE YOU OKAY!!!?
DAAAH, GIL, YOU IDIOT!
TRY READING THE SITUATION BEFORE BARGING IN!!!
HUH!? WHY'RE YOU SO ANGR—
GESHI (KICK)
D'OWW!
UH... WHERE'S ALICE?
I LEFT HER BEHIND!
WHY WOULD YOU DO THAT?

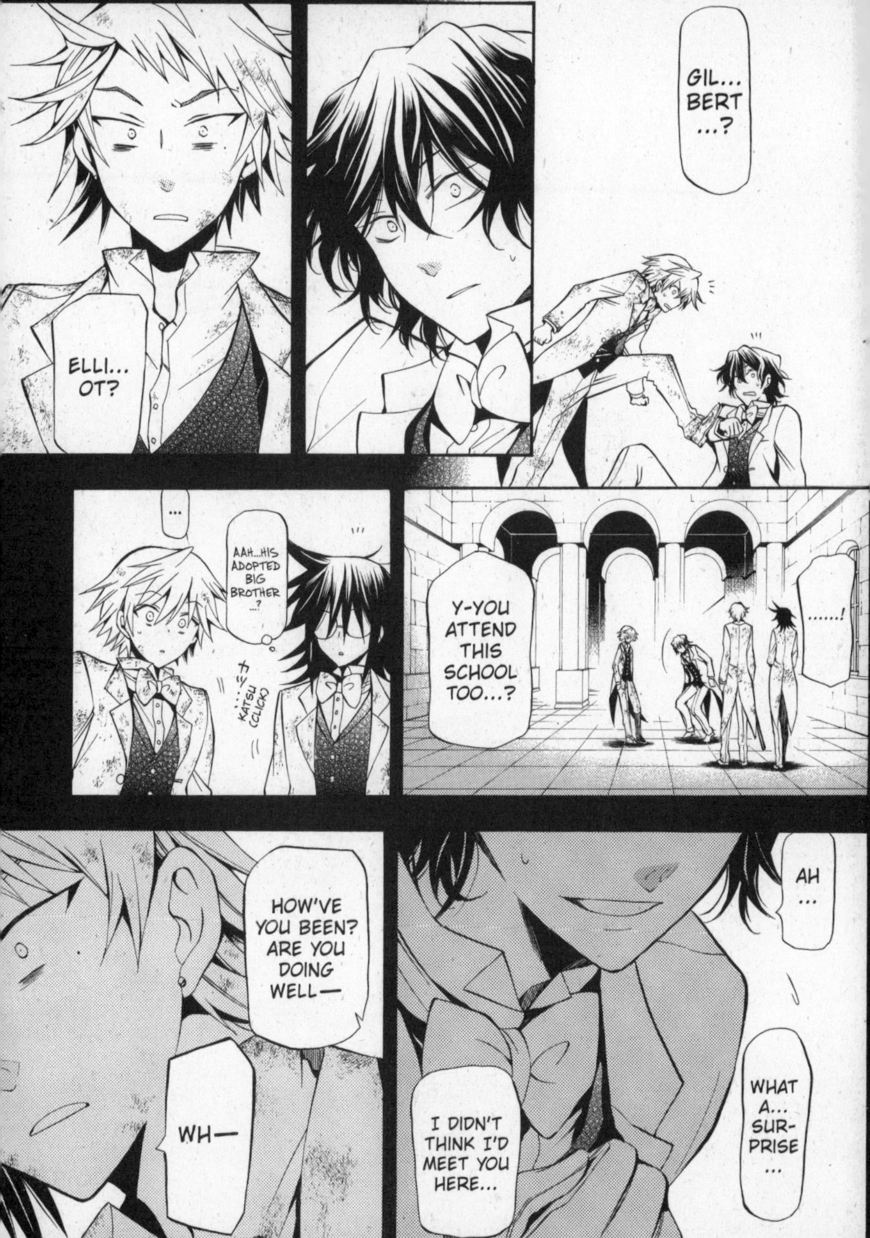
GIL... BERT ...?
ELLI... OT?
......!
Y-YOU ATTEND THIS SCHOOL TOO...?
...
AAH...HIS ADOPTED BIG BROTHER ...?
KATSU (CLICK)
AH ...
WHAT A... SUR-PRISE ...
I DIDN'T THINK I'D MEET YOU HERE...
HOW'VE YOU BEEN? ARE YOU DOING WELL—
WH—

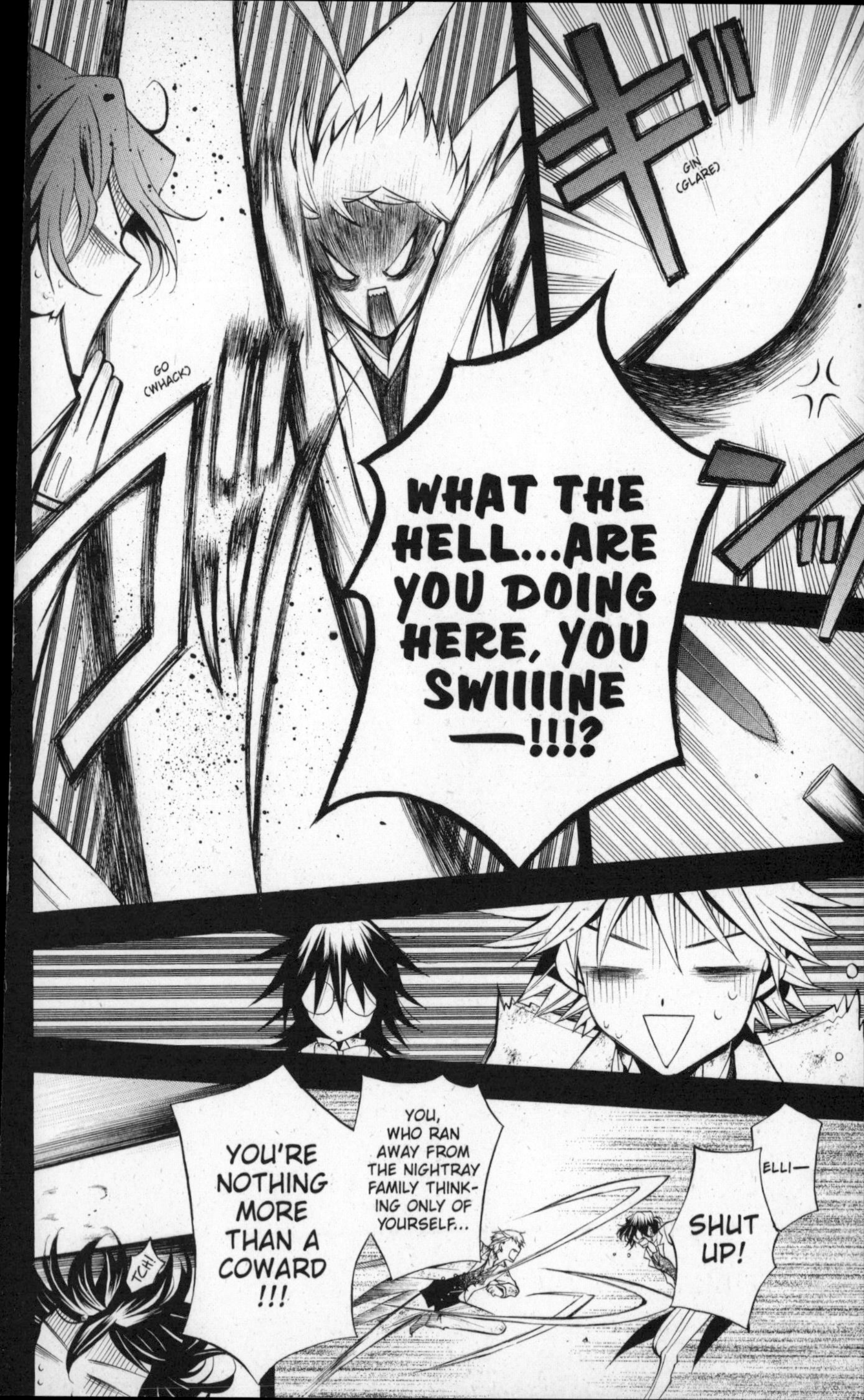
GIN (GLARE)
GO (WHACK)
WHAT THE HELL...ARE YOU DOING HERE, YOU SWIIIIINE—!!!?
ELLI—
SHUT UP!
YOU, WHO RAN AWAY FROM THE NIGHTRAY FAMILY THINK-ING ONLY OF YOURSELF...
YOU'RE NOTHING MORE THAN A COWARD!!!
TCH!

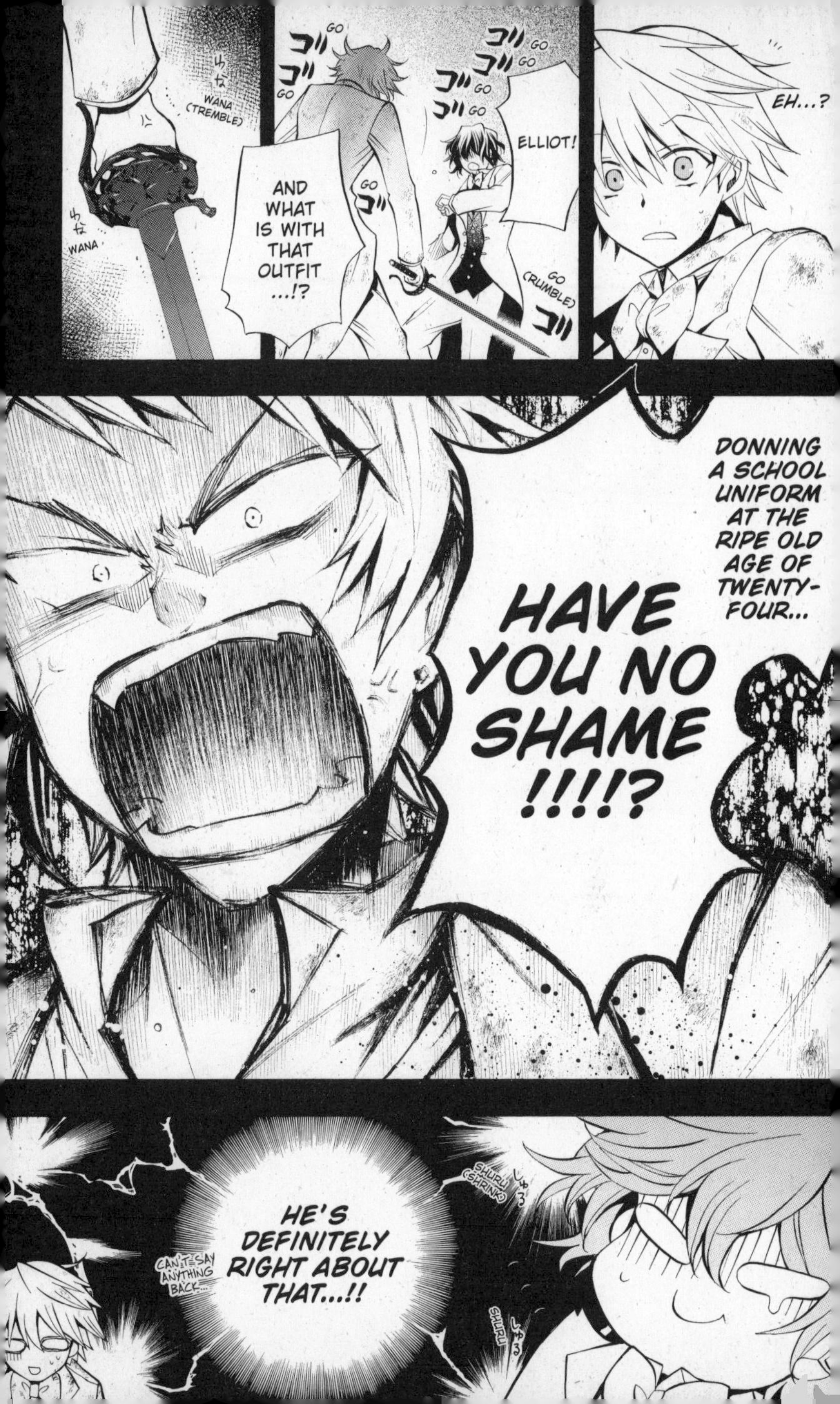

EH...?
GO GO GO GO GO GO
ELLIOT!
AND WHAT IS WITH THAT OUTFIT ...!?
GO
GO (RUMBLE)
WANA (TREMBLE)
WANA
DONNING A SCHOOL UNIFORM AT THE RIPE OLD AGE OF TWENTY-FOUR...
HAVE YOU NO SHAME !!!!?
SHURU (SHRINK)
HE'S DEFINITELY RIGHT ABOUT THAT...!!
CAN'T SAY ANYTHING BACK...
SHURU

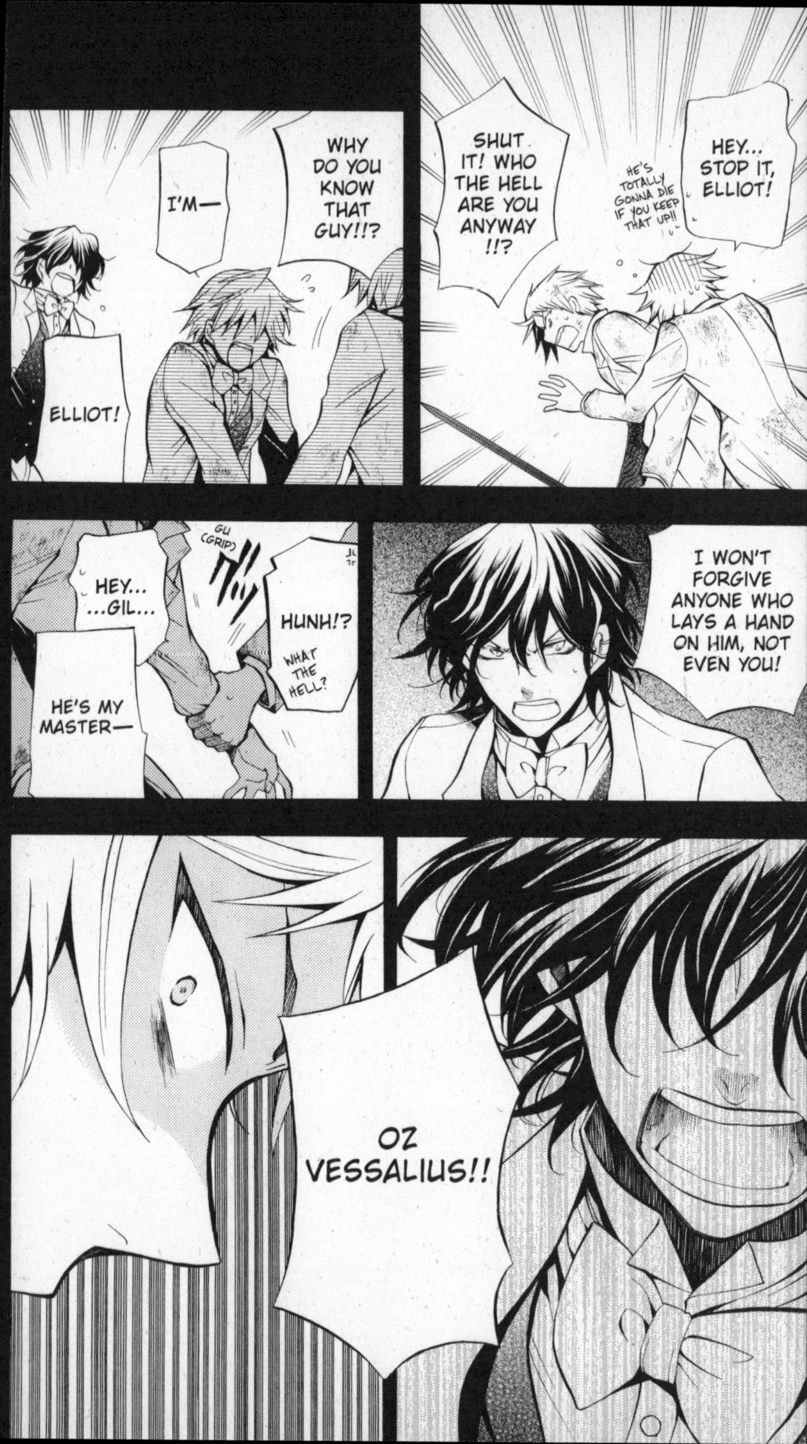
HEY... STOP IT, ELLIOT!
HE'S TOTALLY GONNA DIE IF YOU KEEP THAT UP!!
SHUT IT! WHO THE HELL ARE YOU ANYWAY !!?
WHY DO YOU KNOW THAT GUY!!?
I'M—
ELLIOT!
I WON'T FORGIVE ANYONE WHO LAYS A HAND ON HIM, NOT EVEN YOU!
HUNH!?
WHAT THE HELL?
GU (GRIP)
HEY... ...GIL...
HE'S MY MASTER—
OZ VESSALIUS!!

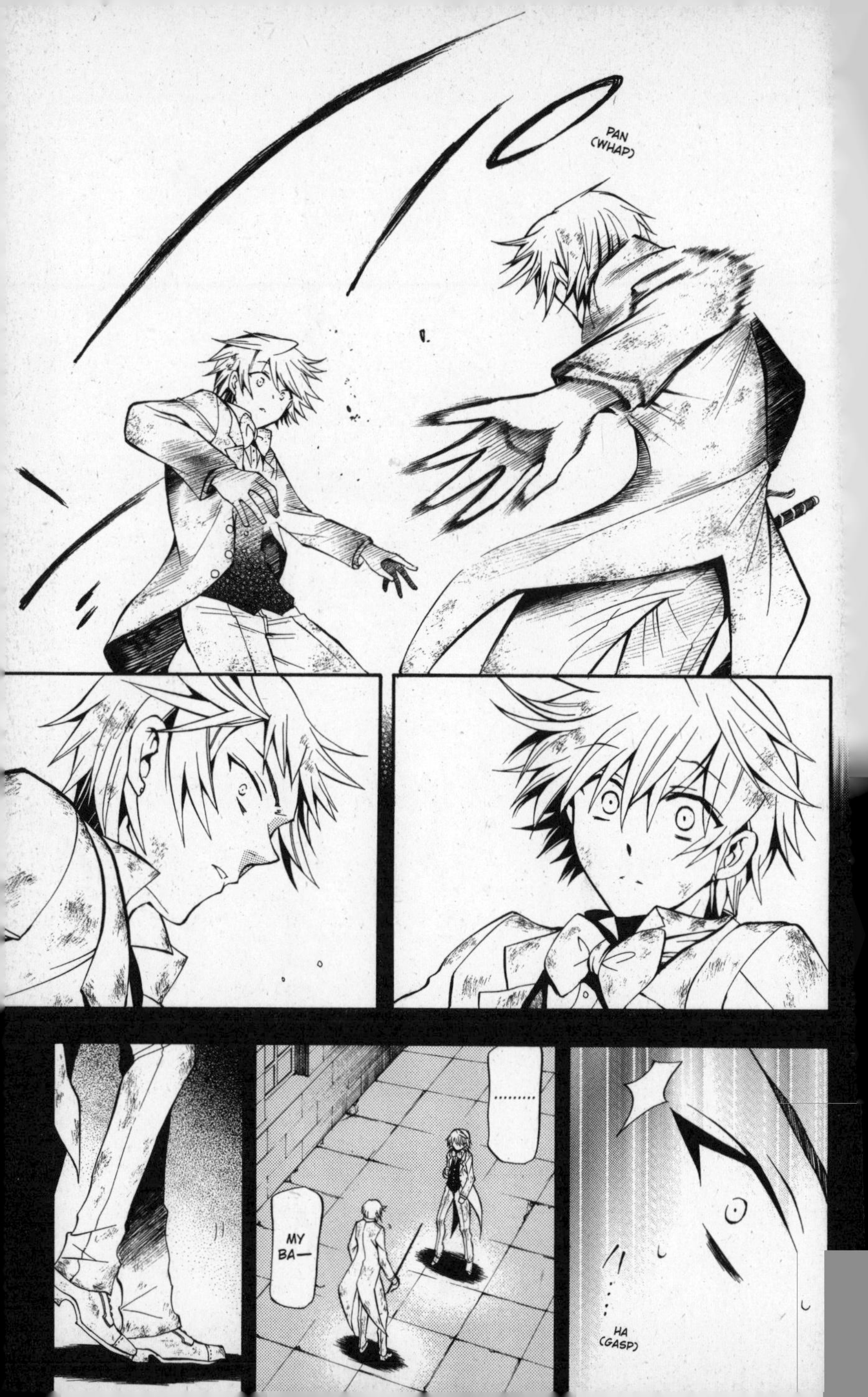
PAN
(WHAP)
HA
(GASP)
......
MY
BA—

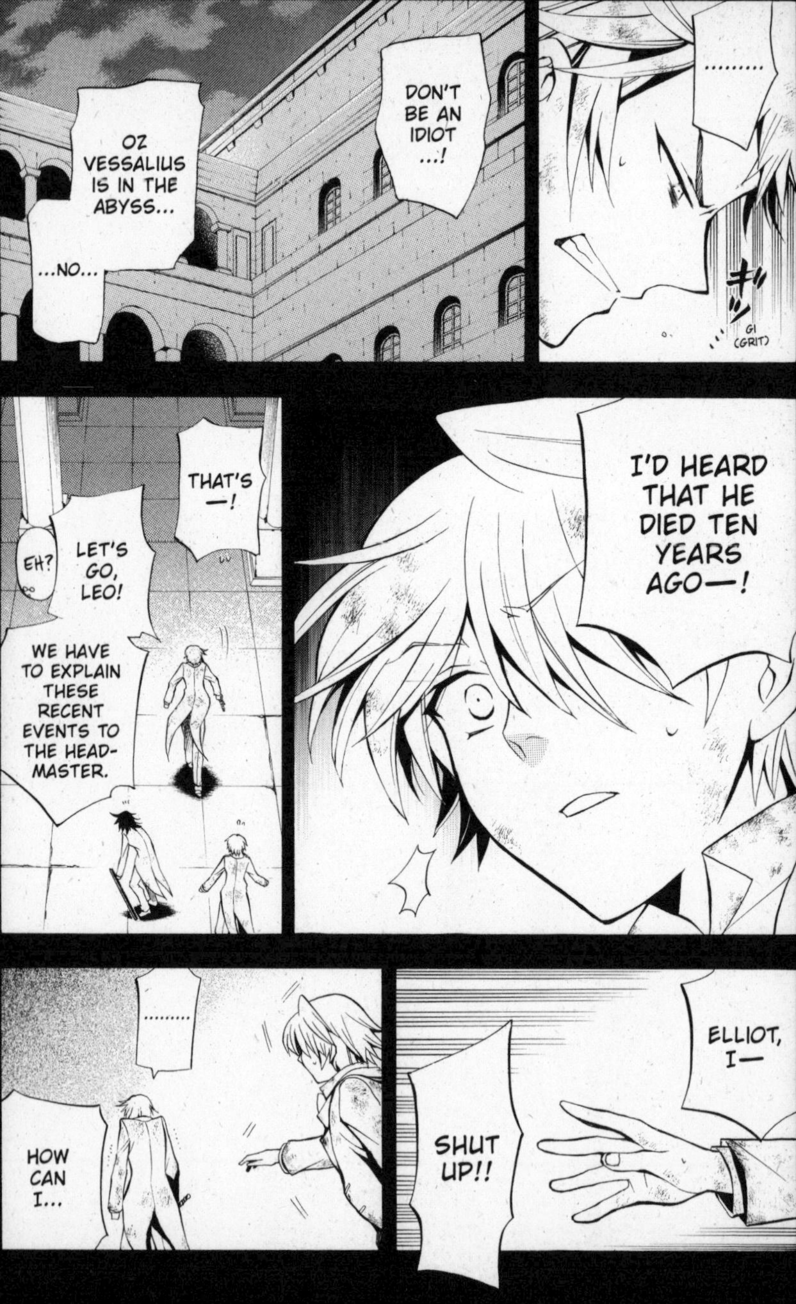
....
ギッ
GI (GRIT)
DON'T BE AN IDIOT ...!
OZ VESSALIUS IS IN THE ABYSS...
...NO...
I'D HEARD THAT HE DIED TEN YEARS AGO—!
THAT'S—!
LET'S GO, LEO!
EH?
WE HAVE TO EXPLAIN THESE RECENT EVENTS TO THE HEAD-MASTER.
ELLIOT, I—
SHUT UP!!
....
HOW CAN I...

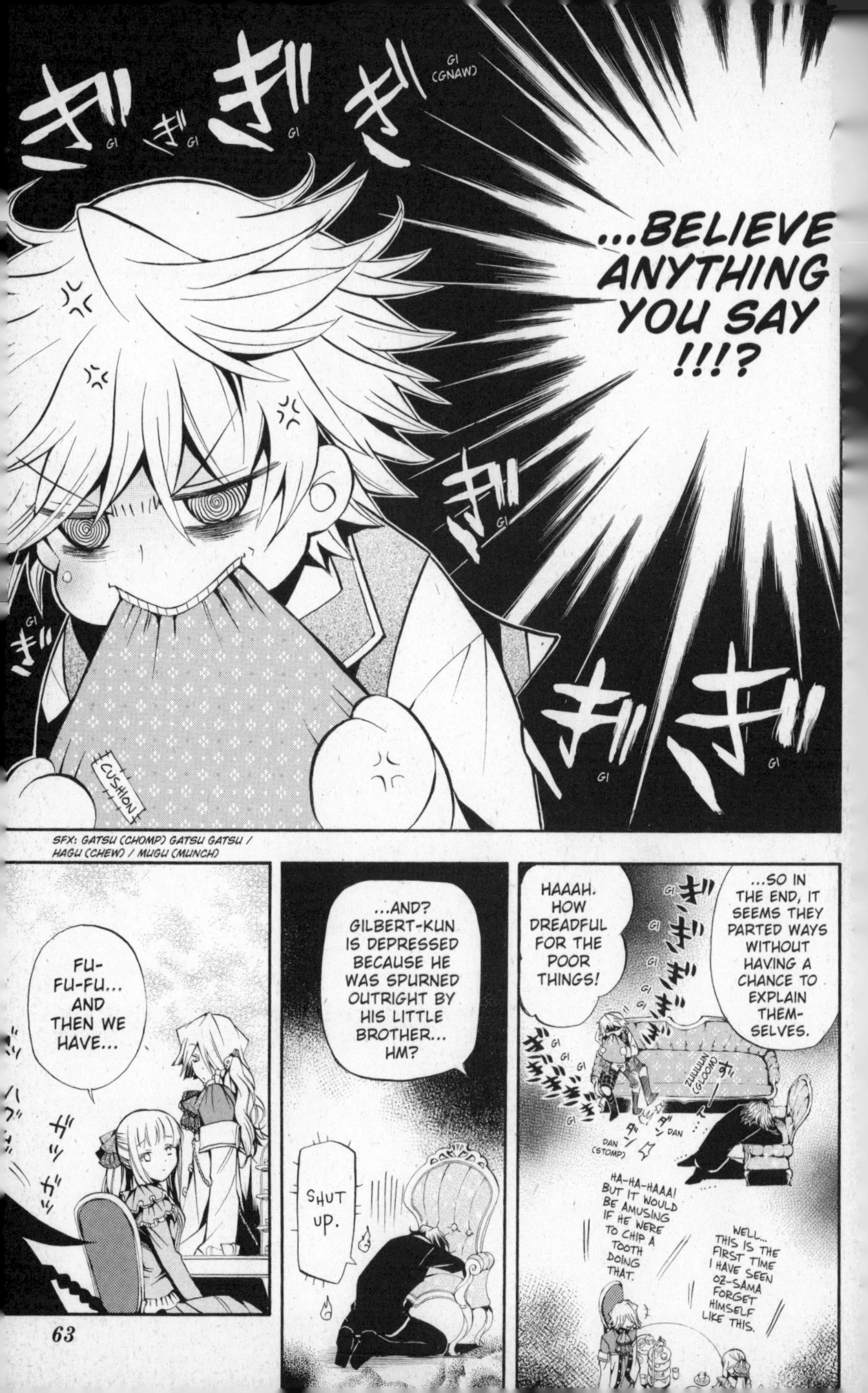
GI (GNAW)
GI
GI
GI
...BELIEVE ANYTHING YOU SAY !!!?
GI
GI
CUSHION
GI
GI
SFX: GATSU (CHOMP) GATSU GATSU / HAGU (CHEW) / MUGU (MUNCH)
...SO IN THE END, IT SEEMS THEY PARTED WAYS WITHOUT HAVING A CHANCE TO EXPLAIN THEM-SELVES.
HAAAH. HOW DREADFUL FOR THE POOR THINGS!
ZUUUN (GLOOM)
DAN (STOMP)
DAN
WELL... THIS IS THE FIRST TIME I HAVE SEEN OZ-SAMA FORGET HIMSELF LIKE THIS.
HA-HA-HAAA! BUT IT WOULD BE AMUSING IF HE WERE TO CHIP A TOOTH DOING THAT.
...AND? GILBERT-KUN IS DEPRESSED BECAUSE HE WAS SPURNED OUTRIGHT BY HIS LITTLE BROTHER... HM?
SHUT UP.
FU-FU-FU... AND THEN WE HAVE...

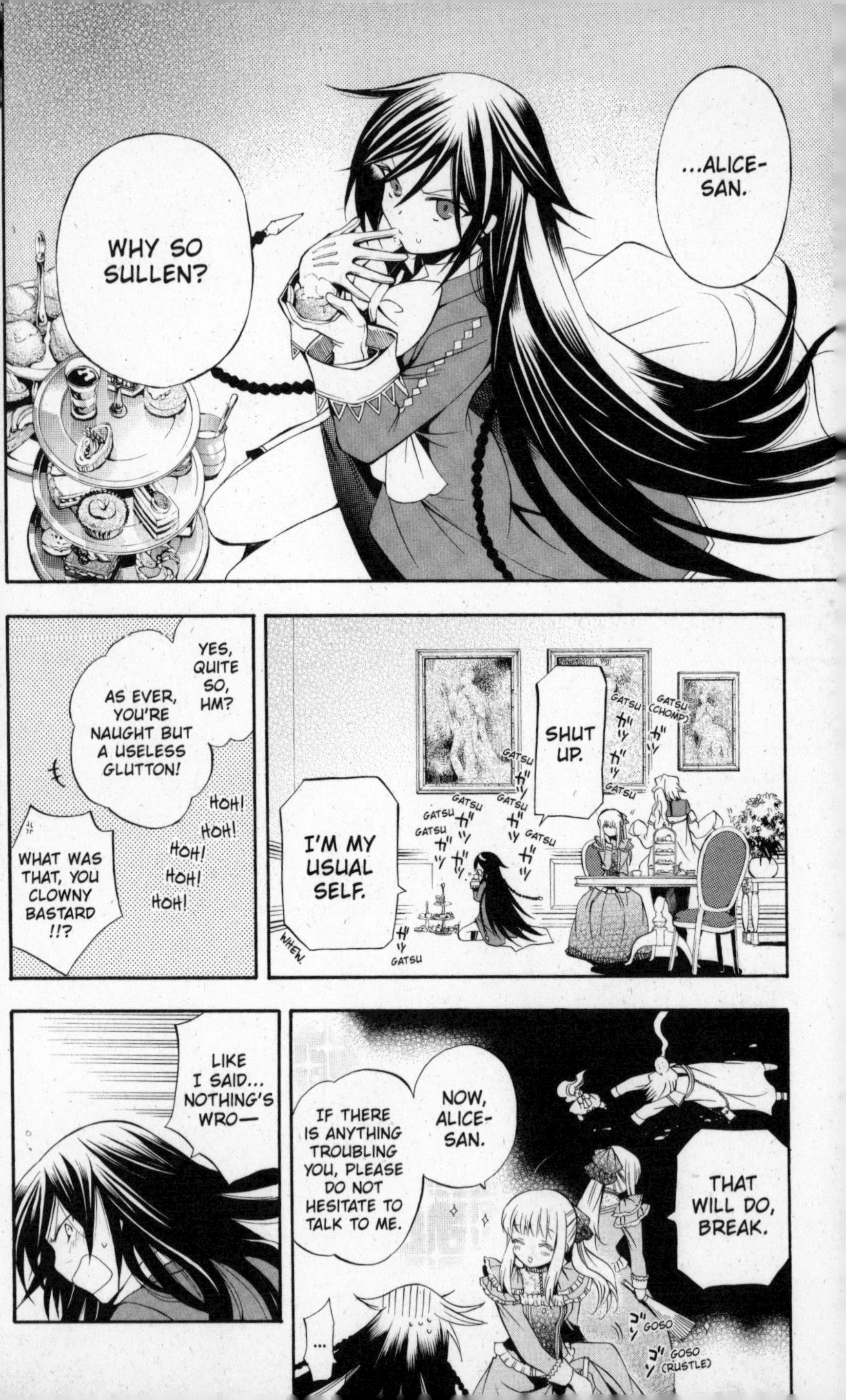
...ALICE-SAN.
WHY SO SULLEN?
SHUT UP.
GATSU (CHOMP)
GATSU
GATSU
GATSU
GATSU
GATSU
GATSU
GATSU
I'M MY USUAL SELF.
WHEW.
GATSU
YES, QUITE SO, HM?
AS EVER, YOU'RE NAUGHT BUT A USELESS GLUTTON!
HOH! HOH! HOH! HOH! HOH!
WHAT WAS THAT, YOU CLOWNY BASTARD !!?
THAT WILL DO, BREAK.
NOW, ALICE-SAN.
IF THERE IS ANYTHING TROUBLING YOU, PLEASE DO NOT HESITATE TO TALK TO ME.
GOSO
GOSO (RUSTLE)
...
LIKE I SAID... NOTHING'S WRO—

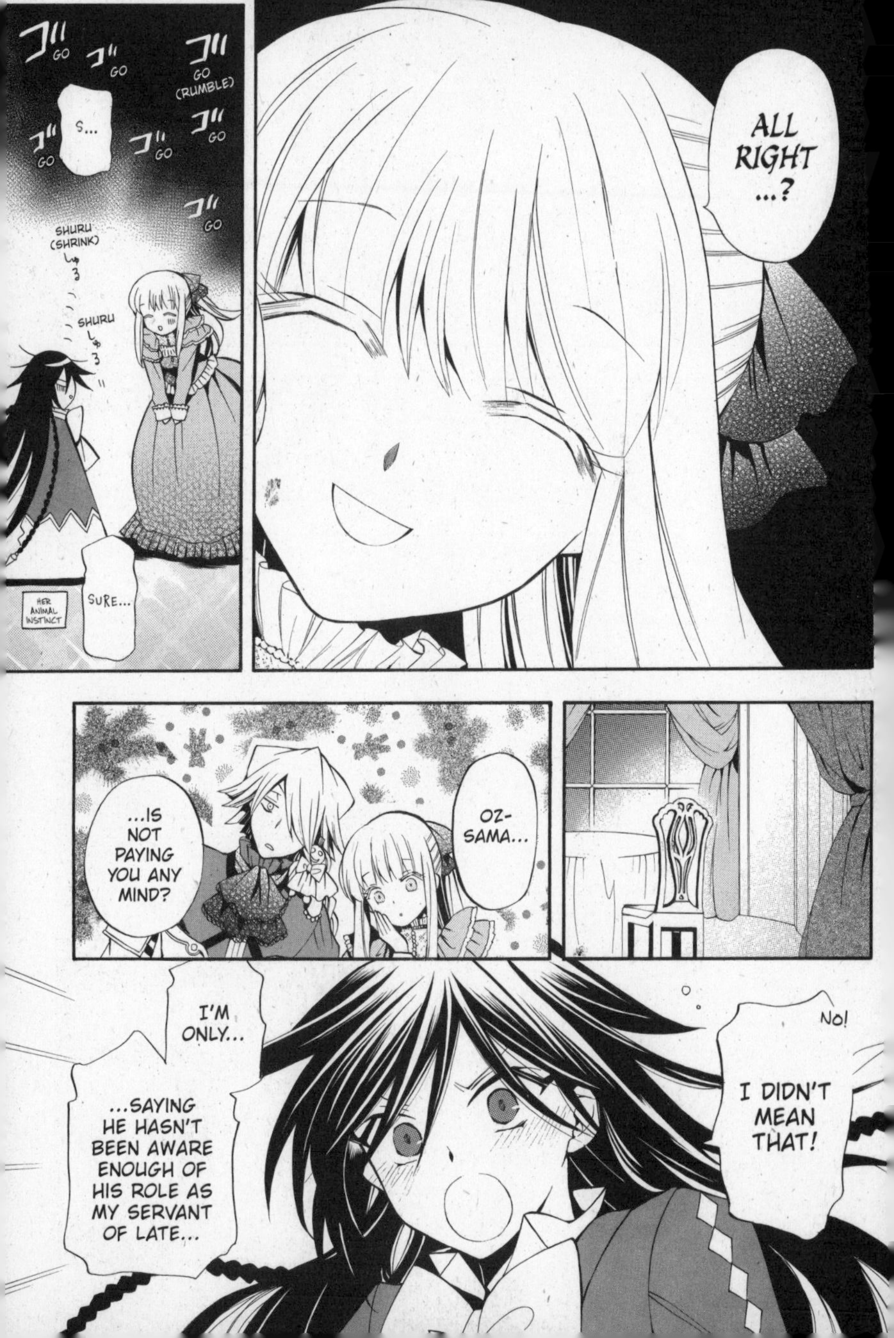
ALL RIGHT ...?
ゴ GO (RUMBLE)
ゴ GO
ゴ GO
S...
ゴ GO
ゴ GO
ゴ GO
ゴ GO
SHURU (SHRINK) しゅる
SHURU しゅる
SURE...
HER ANIMAL INSTINCT
OZ-SAMA...
...IS NOT PAYING YOU ANY MIND?
NO!
I DIDN'T MEAN THAT!
I'M ONLY...
...SAYING HE HASN'T BEEN AWARE ENOUGH OF HIS ROLE AS MY SERVANT OF LATE...

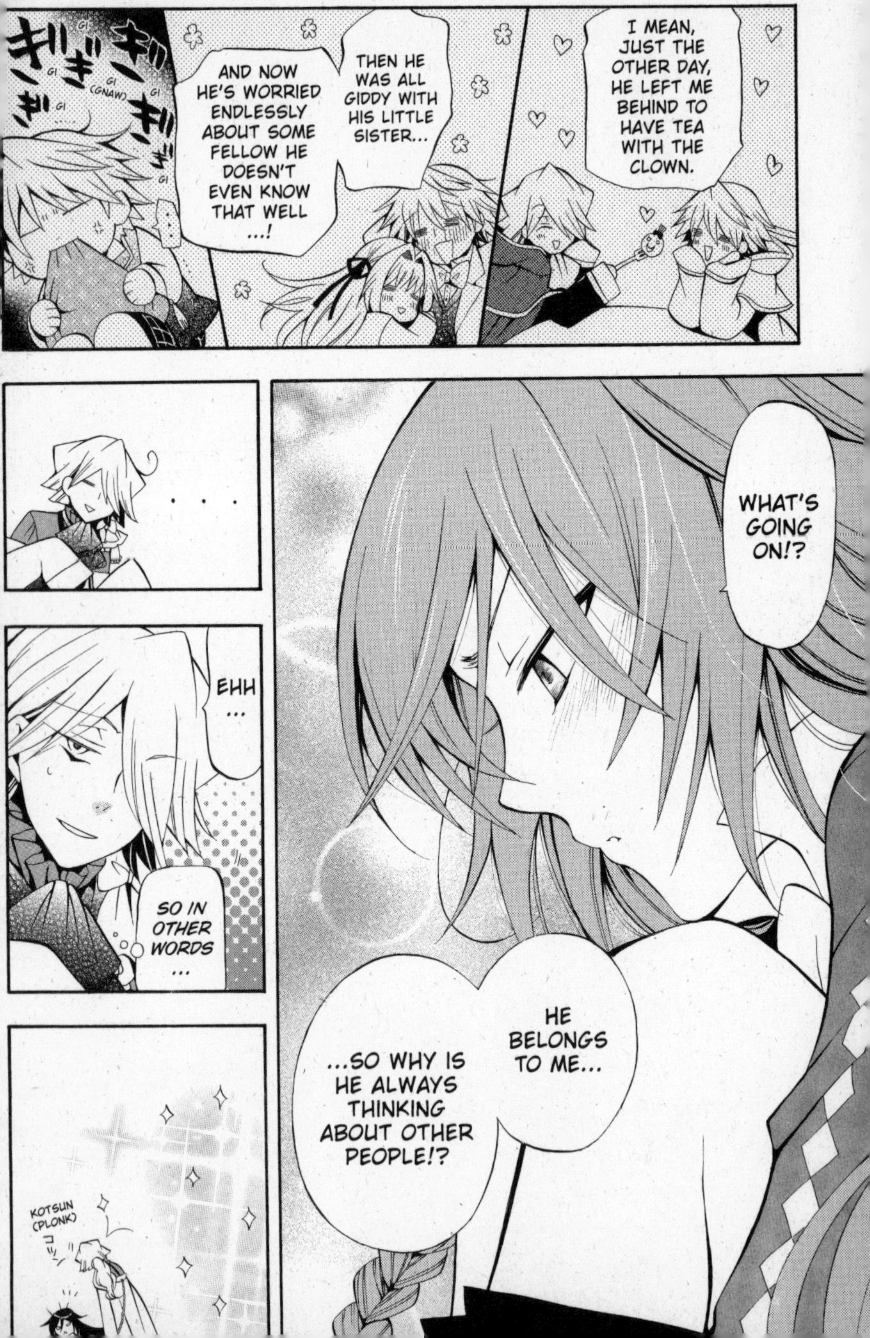
I MEAN, JUST THE OTHER DAY, HE LEFT ME BEHIND TO HAVE TEA WITH THE CLOWN.
THEN HE WAS ALL GIDDY WITH HIS LITTLE SISTER...
AND NOW HE'S WORRIED ENDLESSLY ABOUT SOME FELLOW HE DOESN'T EVEN KNOW THAT WELL ...!
GI GI GI GI GI (GNAW) GI
WHAT'S GOING ON!?
HE BELONGS TO ME...
...SO WHY IS HE ALWAYS THINKING ABOUT OTHER PEOPLE!?
. . .
EHH ...
SO IN OTHER WORDS ...
KOTSUN (PLONK)

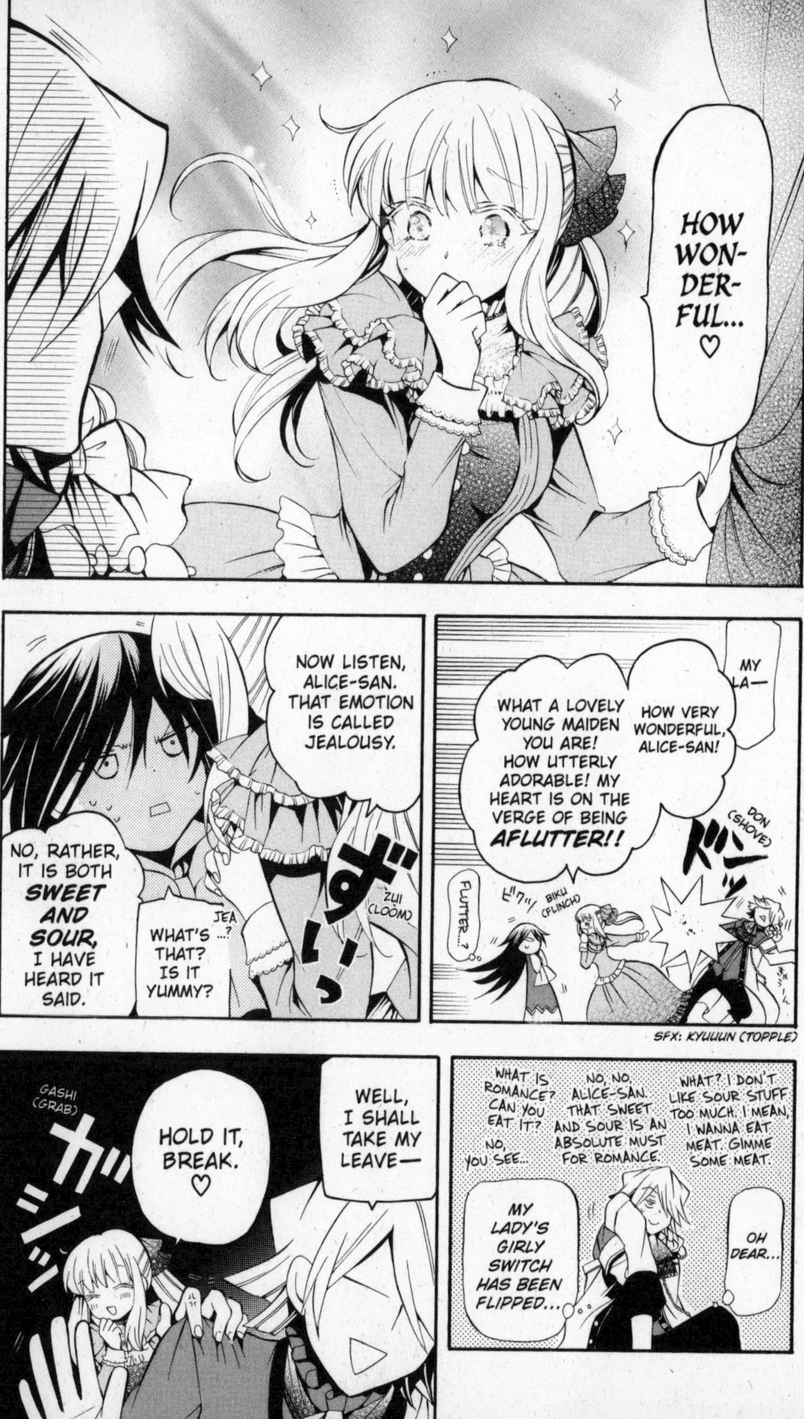
HOW WON-DER-FUL... ♡
MY LA—
HOW VERY WONDERFUL, ALICE-SAN!
WHAT A LOVELY YOUNG MAIDEN YOU ARE! HOW UTTERLY ADORABLE! MY HEART IS ON THE VERGE OF BEING **AFLUTTER!!**
DON (SHOVE)
BIKU (FLINCH)
FLUTTER...?
NOW LISTEN, ALICE-SAN. THAT EMOTION IS CALLED JEALOUSY.
NO, RATHER, IT IS BOTH **SWEET AND SOUR,** I HAVE HEARD IT SAID.
ZUI (LOOM)
JEA ...?
WHAT'S THAT? IS IT YUMMY?
SFX: KYUUUN (TOPPLE)
WHAT? I DON'T LIKE SOUR STUFF TOO MUCH. I MEAN, I WANNA EAT MEAT. GIMME SOME MEAT.
NO, NO, ALICE-SAN. THAT SWEET AND SOUR IS AN ABSOLUTE MUST FOR ROMANCE.
WHAT IS ROMANCE? CAN YOU EAT IT?
NO, YOU SEE...
OH DEAR...
MY LADY'S GIRLY SWITCH HAS BEEN FLIPPED...
WELL, I SHALL TAKE MY LEAVE—
HOLD IT, BREAK. ♡
GASHI (GRAB)

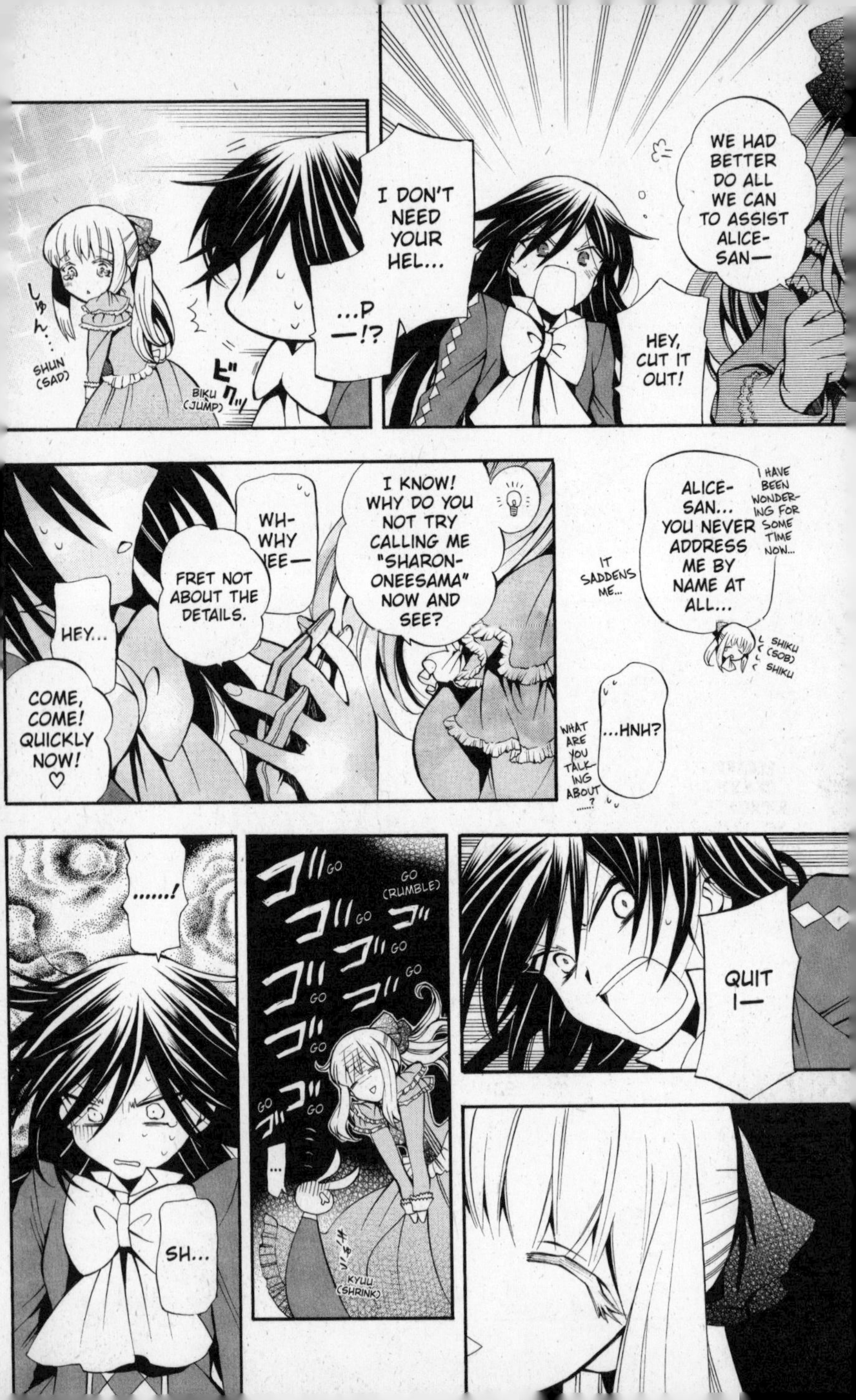
WE HAD BETTER DO ALL WE CAN TO ASSIST ALICE-SAN—
HEY, CUT IT OUT!
I DON'T NEED YOUR HEL...
...P —!?
BIKU (JUMP)
SHUN (SAD)
ALICE-SAN... YOU NEVER ADDRESS ME BY NAME AT ALL...
I HAVE BEEN WONDERING FOR SOME TIME NOW...
IT SADDENS ME...
SHIKU (SOB) SHIKU
...HNH?
WHAT ARE YOU TALKING ABOUT......?
I KNOW! WHY DO YOU NOT TRY CALLING ME "SHARON-ONEESAMA" NOW AND SEE?
WH-WHY NEE—
FRET NOT ABOUT THE DETAILS.
HEY...
COME, COME! QUICKLY NOW! ♡
QUIT I—
GO (RUMBLE)
GO GO GO GO GO GO GO GO GO
...
KYUU (SHRINK)
......!
SH...

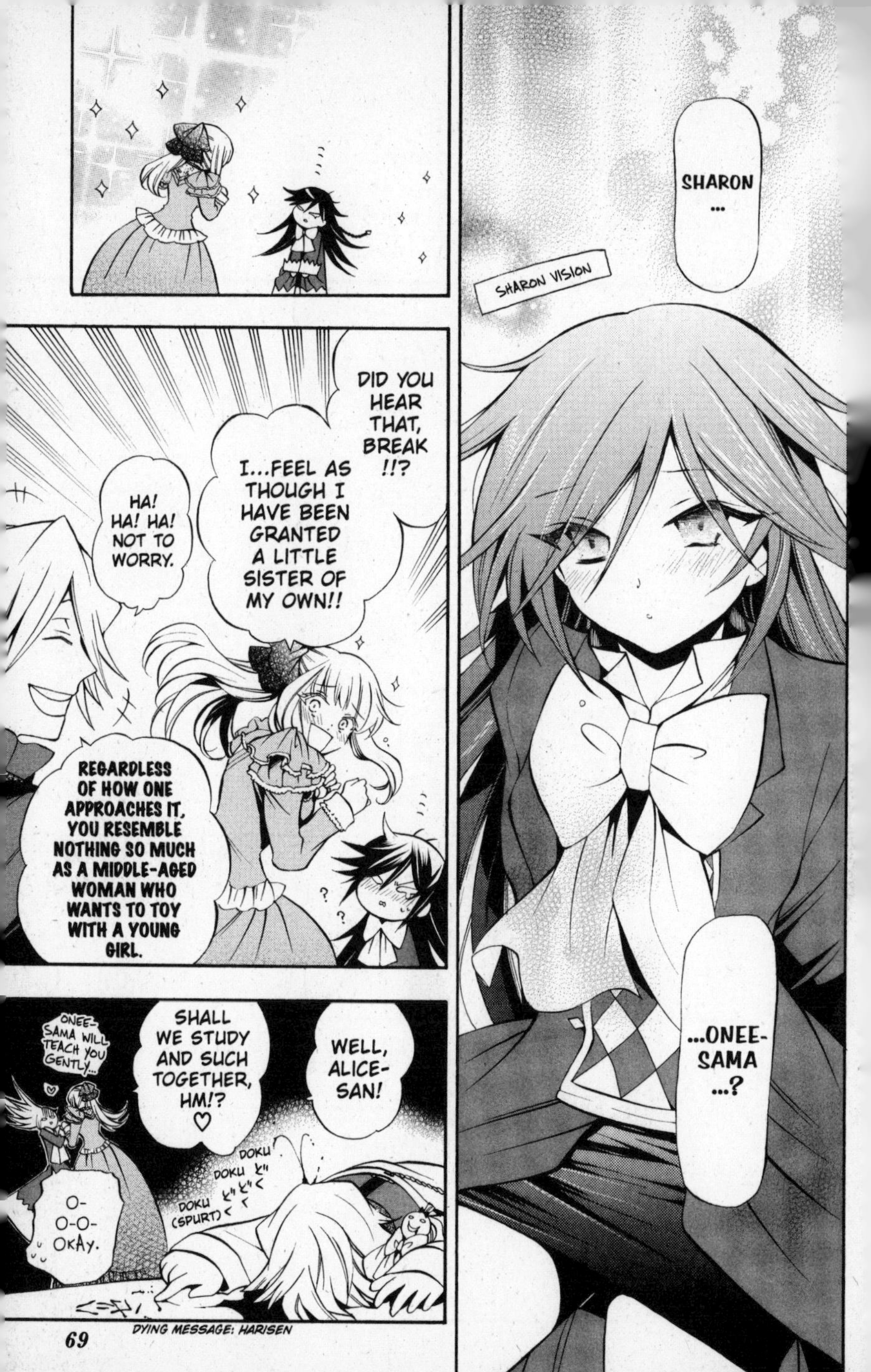
SHARON ...
SHARON VISION
...ONEE-SAMA ...?
DID YOU HEAR THAT, BREAK !!?
I...FEEL AS THOUGH I HAVE BEEN GRANTED A LITTLE SISTER OF MY OWN!!
HA! HA! HA! NOT TO WORRY.
REGARDLESS OF HOW ONE APPROACHES IT, YOU RESEMBLE NOTHING SO MUCH AS A MIDDLE-AGED WOMAN WHO WANTS TO TOY WITH A YOUNG GIRL.
WELL, ALICE-SAN!
SHALL WE STUDY AND SUCH TOGETHER, HM!? ♡
DOKU DOKU DOKU (SPURT)
ONEE-SAMA WILL TEACH YOU GENTLY...
O-O-O-OKAY.

DYING MESSAGE: HARISEN

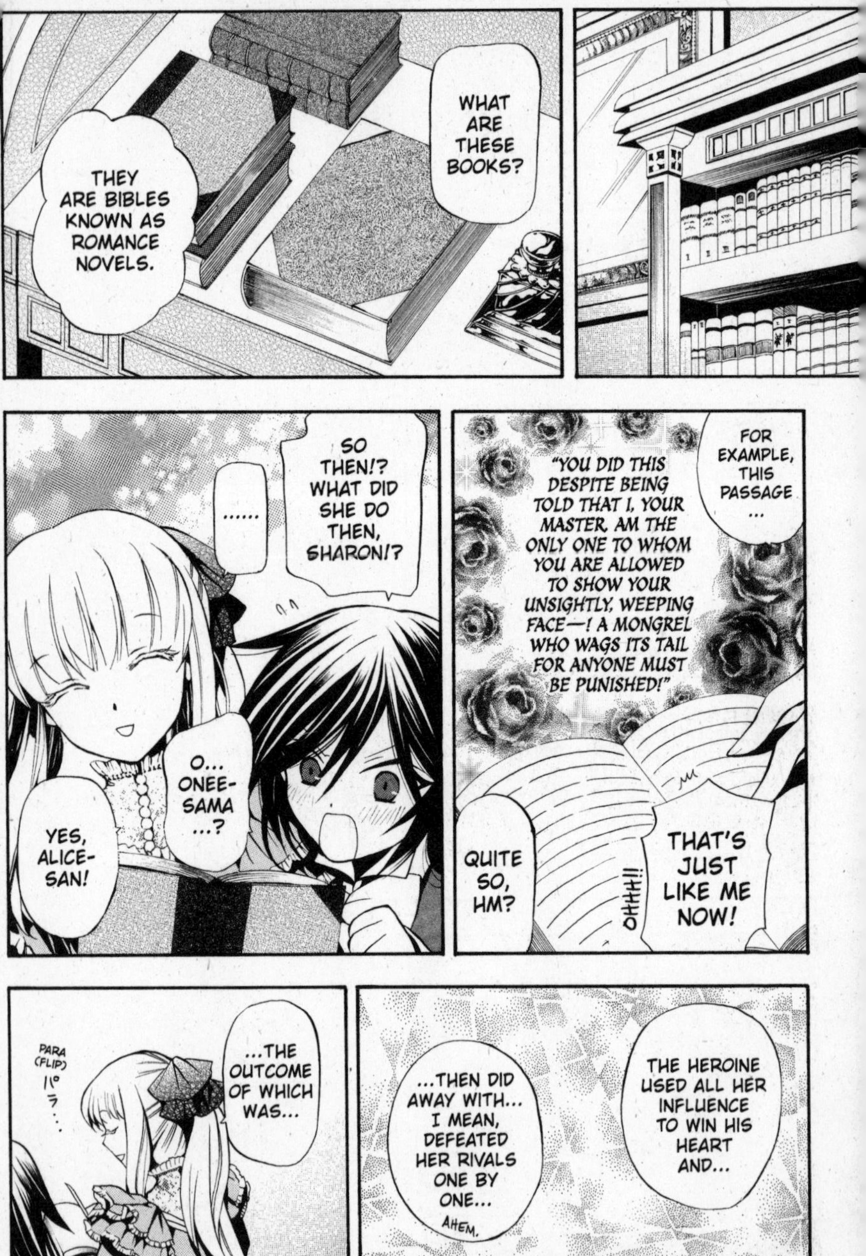

WHAT ARE THESE BOOKS?
THEY ARE BIBLES KNOWN AS ROMANCE NOVELS.
FOR EXAMPLE, THIS PASSAGE...
"YOU DID THIS DESPITE BEING TOLD THAT I, YOUR MASTER, AM THE ONLY ONE TO WHOM YOU ARE ALLOWED TO SHOW YOUR UNSIGHTLY, WEEPING FACE—! A MONGREL WHO WAGS ITS TAIL FOR ANYONE MUST BE PUNISHED!"
THAT'S JUST LIKE ME NOW!
OHHH!!
QUITE SO, HM?
SO THEN!? WHAT DID SHE DO THEN, SHARON!?
......
O... ONEE-SAMA...?
YES, ALICE-SAN!
THE HEROINE USED ALL HER INFLUENCE TO WIN HIS HEART AND...
...THEN DID AWAY WITH... I MEAN, DEFEATED HER RIVALS ONE BY ONE...
AHEM.
...THE OUTCOME OF WHICH WAS...
PARA (FLIP)

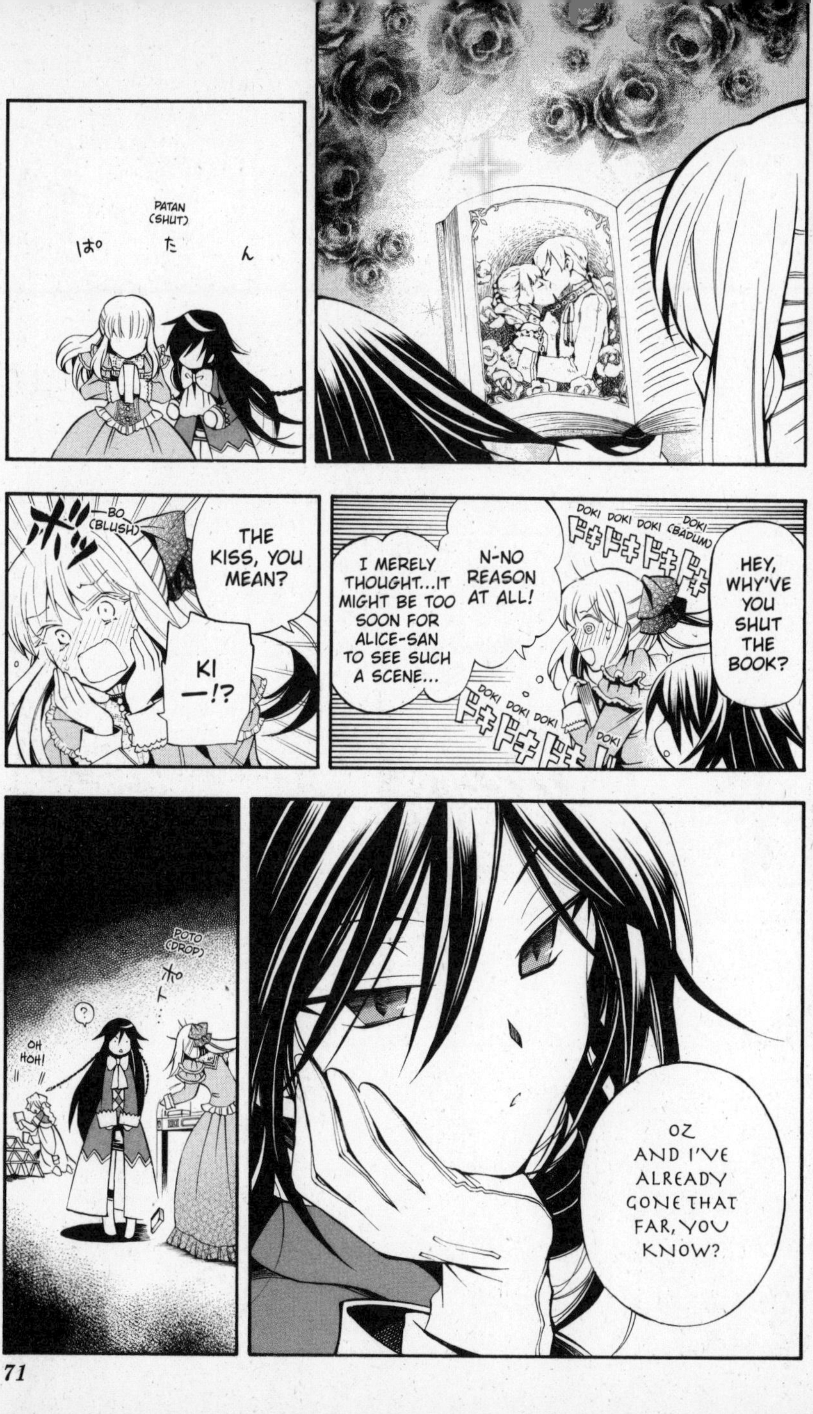
PATAN (SHUT)
ぱたん
HEY, WHY'VE YOU SHUT THE BOOK?
DOKI DOKI DOKI DOKI (BADUM)
ドキドキドキドキ
N-NO REASON AT ALL!
I MERELY THOUGHT...IT MIGHT BE TOO SOON FOR ALICE-SAN TO SEE SUCH A SCENE...
DOKI DOKI DOKI DOKI
ドキドキドキ
THE KISS, YOU MEAN?
BO (BLUSH)
ボッ
KI—!?
OZ AND I'VE ALREADY GONE THAT FAR, YOU KNOW?
POTO (DROP)
ポト...
?
OH HOH!

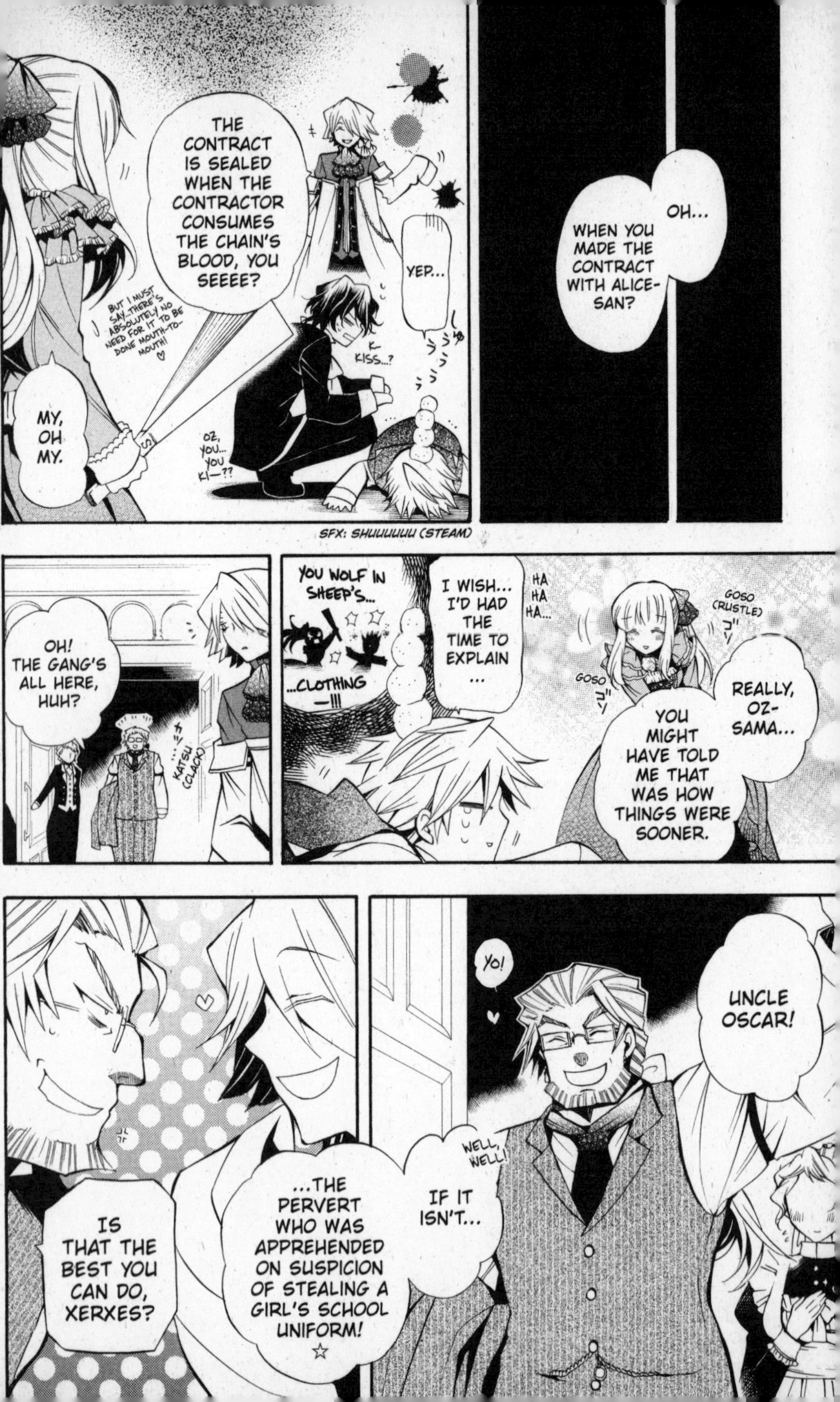
OH...
WHEN YOU MADE THE CONTRACT WITH ALICE-SAN?
YEP...
K-KISS...?
THE CONTRACT IS SEALED WHEN THE CONTRACTOR CONSUMES THE CHAIN'S BLOOD, YOU SEEEE?
BUT I MUST SAY...THERE'S ABSOLUTELY NO NEED FOR IT TO BE DONE MOUTH-TO-MOUTH! ♡
OZ, YOU... YOU KI—??
MY, OH MY.
SFX: SHUUUUUU (STEAM)
HA HA HA...
GOSO (RUSTLE)
I WISH... I'D HAD THE TIME TO EXPLAIN...
REALLY, OZ-SAMA...
YOU MIGHT HAVE TOLD ME THAT WAS HOW THINGS WERE SOONER.
GOSO
YOU WOLF IN SHEEP'S...
...CLOTHING—!!!
KATSU (CLACK)
OH! THE GANG'S ALL HERE, HUH?
UNCLE OSCAR!
Yo!
WELL, WELL!
IF IT ISN'T...
...THE PERVERT WHO WAS APPREHENDED ON SUSPICION OF STEALING A GIRL'S SCHOOL UNIFORM! ☆
IS THAT THE BEST YOU CAN DO, XERXES?

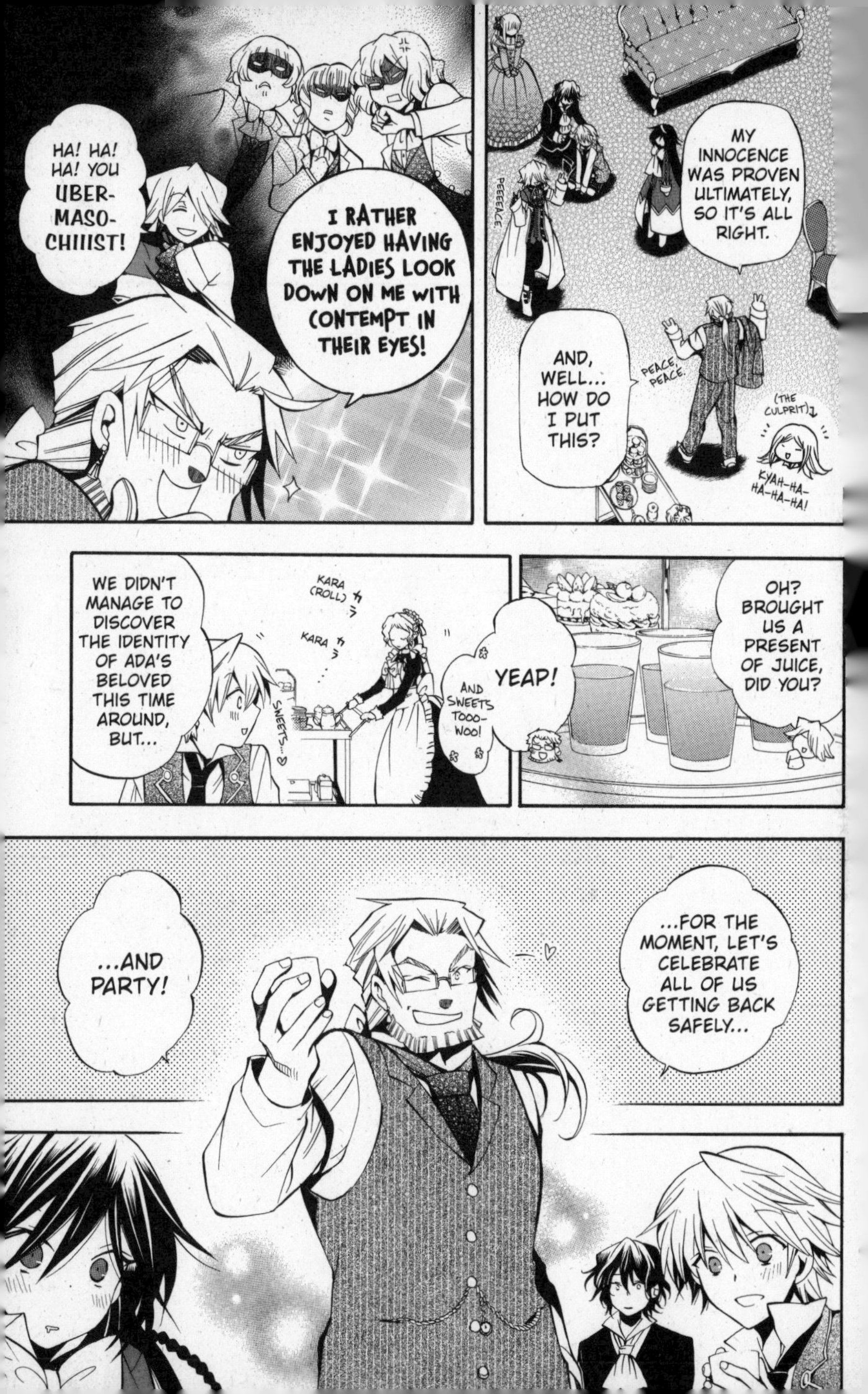
MY INNOCENCE WAS PROVEN ULTIMATELY, SO IT'S ALL RIGHT.
PEEEEACE
PEACE, PEACE.
AND, WELL... HOW DO I PUT THIS?
(THE CULPRIT)
KYAH-HA-HA-HA-HA!
I RATHER ENJOYED HAVING THE LADIES LOOK DOWN ON ME WITH CONTEMPT IN THEIR EYES!
HA! HA! HA! YOU UBER-MASO-CHIIIST!
OH? BROUGHT US A PRESENT OF JUICE, DID YOU?
YEAP!
AND SWEETS TOOO-WOO!
KARA (ROLL)
KARA
SWEETS...♥
WE DIDN'T MANAGE TO DISCOVER THE IDENTITY OF ADA'S BELOVED THIS TIME AROUND, BUT...
...FOR THE MOMENT, LET'S CELEBRATE ALL OF US GETTING BACK SAFELY...
...AND PARTY!

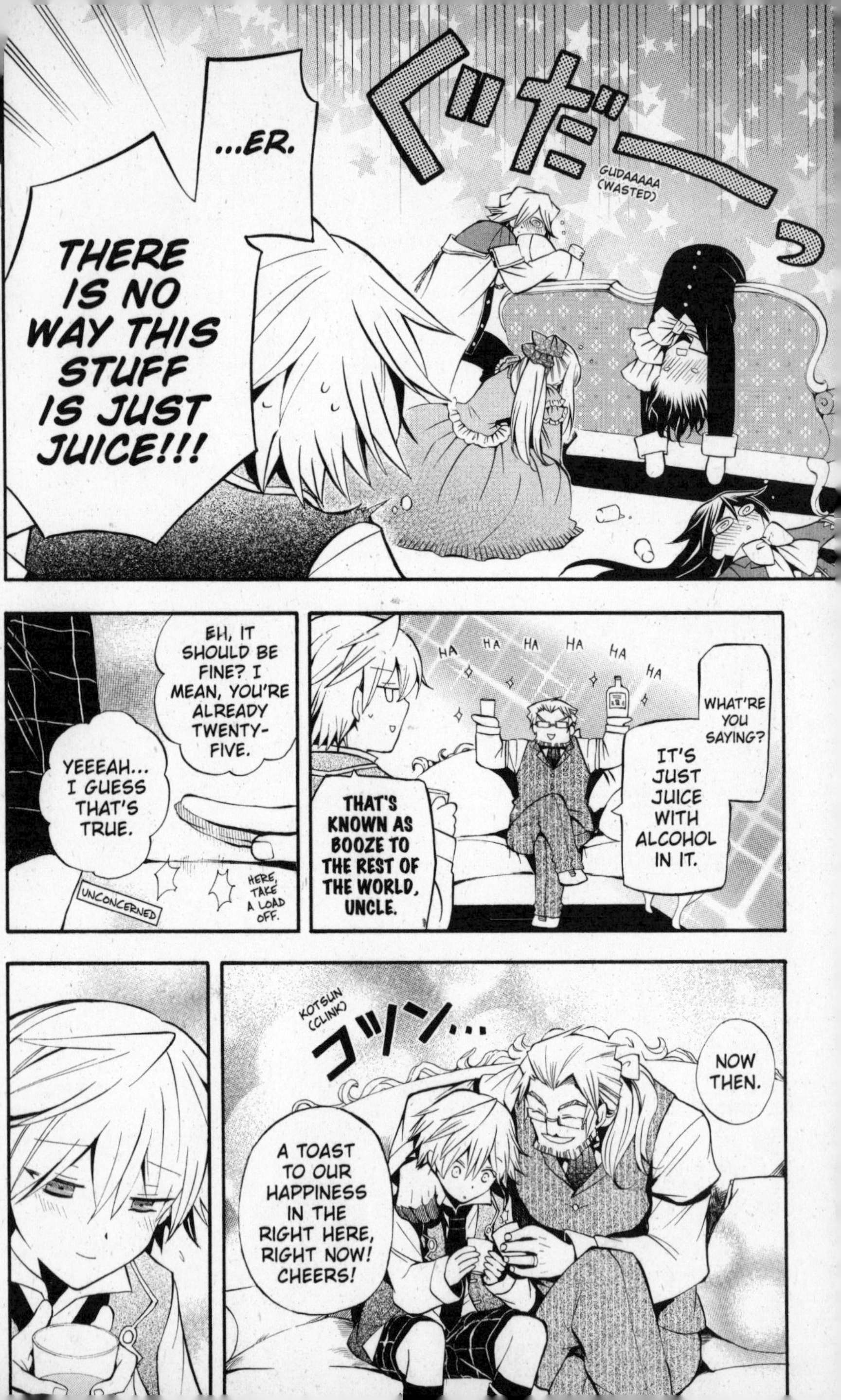
ぐだーっ
GUDAAAAA (WASTED)
...ER.
THERE IS NO WAY THIS STUFF IS JUST JUICE!!!
WHAT'RE YOU SAYING?
IT'S JUST JUICE WITH ALCOHOL IN IT.
HA HA HA HA HA HA
THAT'S KNOWN AS BOOZE TO THE REST OF THE WORLD, UNCLE.
EH, IT SHOULD BE FINE? I MEAN, YOU'RE ALREADY TWENTY-FIVE.
YEEEAH... I GUESS THAT'S TRUE.
HERE, TAKE A LOAD OFF.
UNCONCERNED
NOW THEN.
KOTSUN (CLINK)
コツン…
A TOAST TO OUR HAPPINESS IN THE RIGHT HERE, RIGHT NOW! CHEERS!

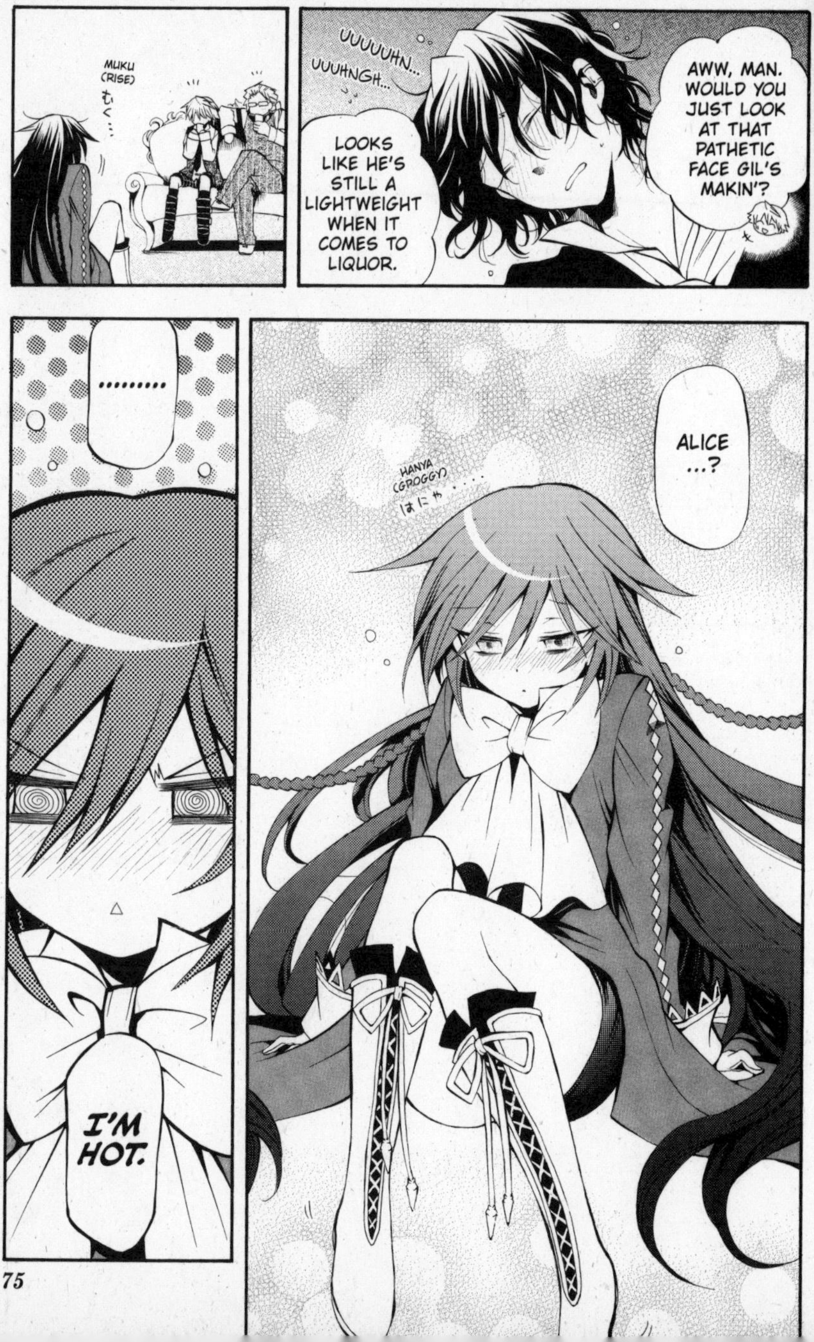
UUUUUHN...
UUUHNGH...
AWW, MAN. WOULD YOU JUST LOOK AT THAT PATHETIC FACE GIL'S MAKIN'?
LOOKS LIKE HE'S STILL A LIGHTWEIGHT WHEN IT COMES TO LIQUOR.
MUKU (RISE)
むく...
ALICE ...?
HANYA (GROGGY)
はにゃ....
....
I'M HOT.

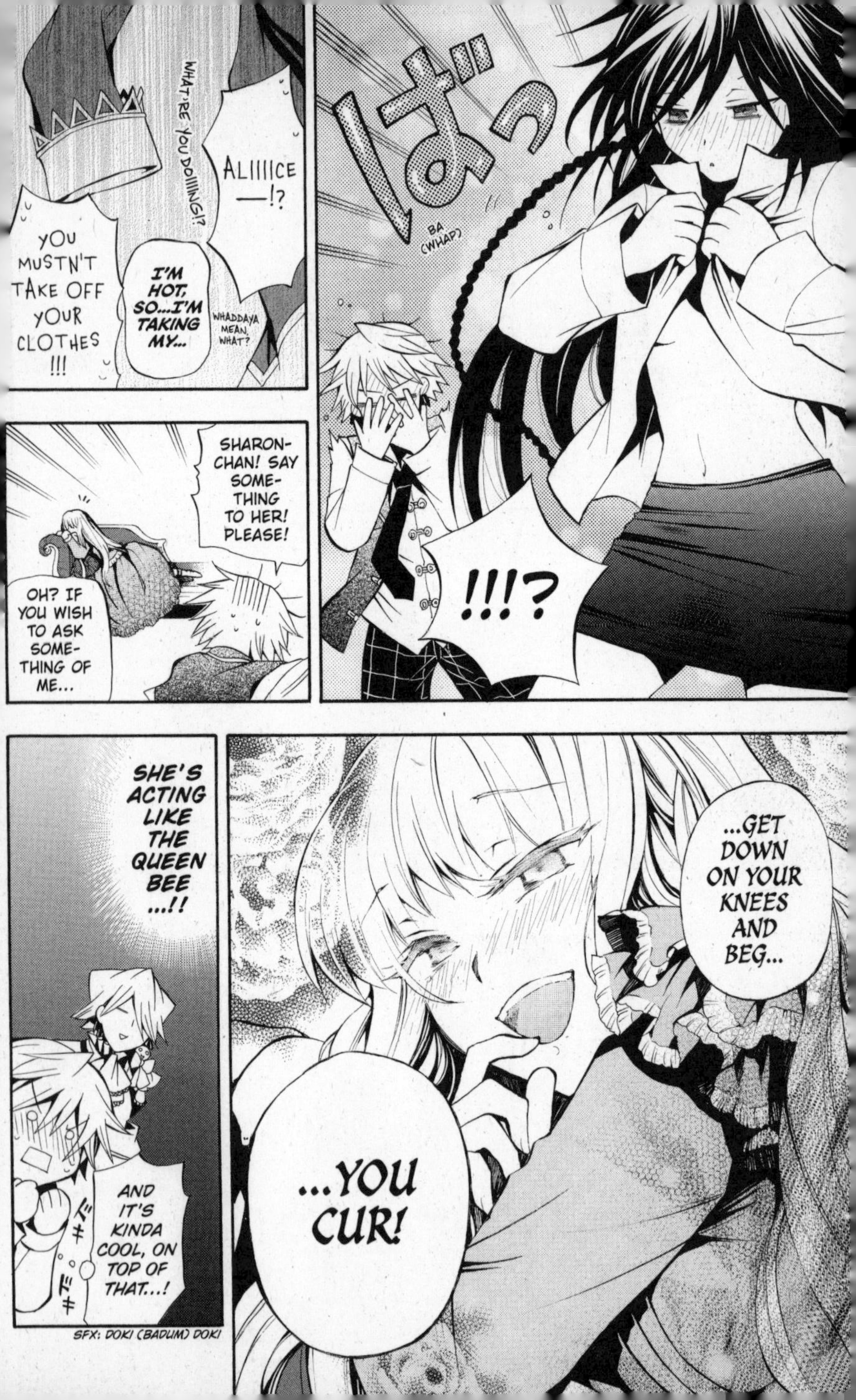
ばっ
BA (WHAP)
!!!?
ALIIIIICE—!?
WHAT'RE YOU DOIIIING!?
I'M HOT, SO...I'M TAKING MY...
WHADDAYA MEAN, WHAT?
YOU MUSTN'T TAKE OFF YOUR CLOTHES !!!
SHARON-CHAN! SAY SOMETHING TO HER! PLEASE!
OH? IF YOU WISH TO ASK SOMETHING OF ME...
...GET DOWN ON YOUR KNEES AND BEG...
...YOU CUR!
SHE'S ACTING LIKE THE QUEEN BEE ...!!
AND IT'S KINDA COOL, ON TOP OF THAT...!
ドキ
ドキ
SFX: DOKI (BADUM) DOKI

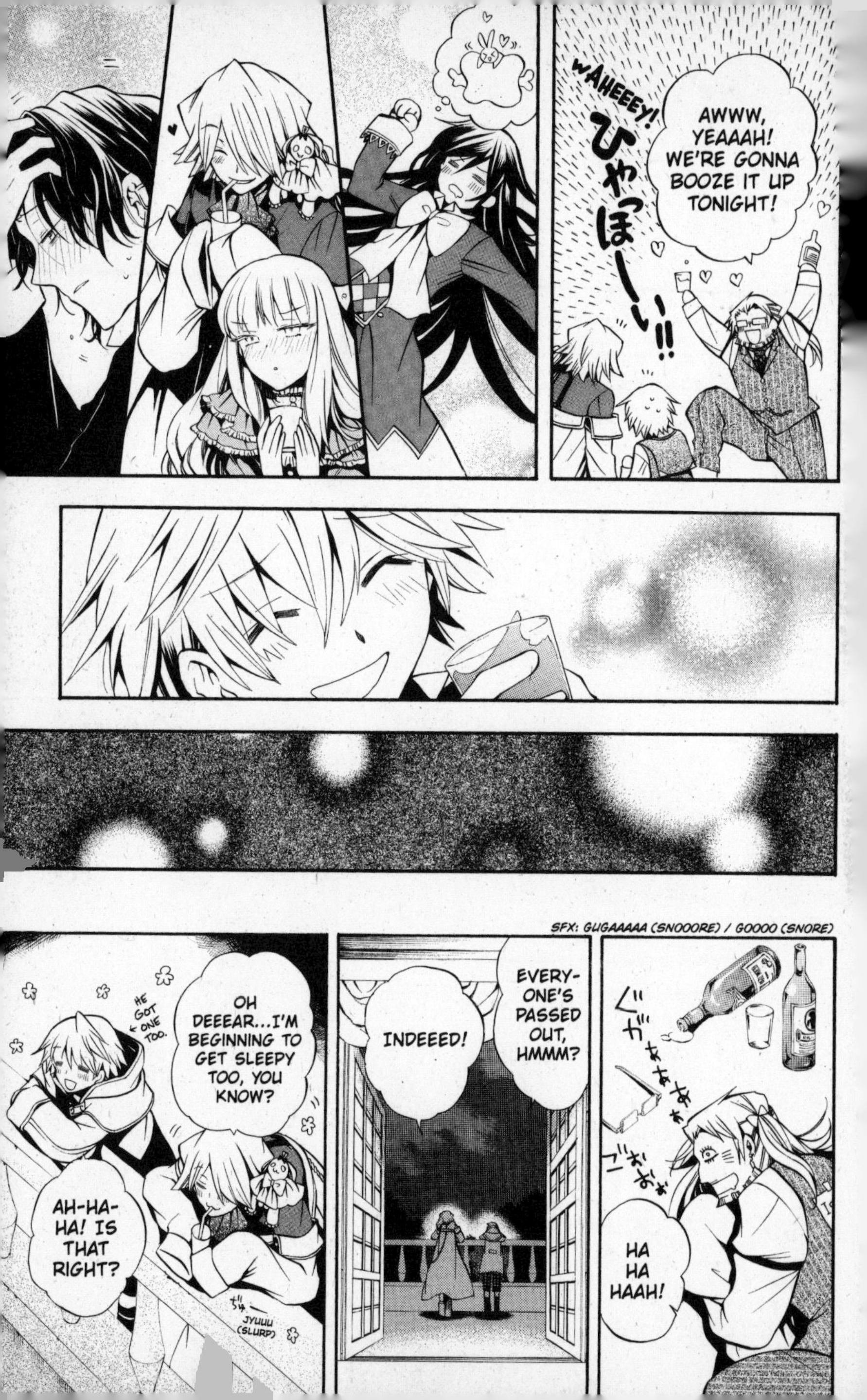
wAHEEEY!
ひゃっほーい!!
AWWW, YEAAAH! WE'RE GONNA BOOZE IT UP TONIGHT!
SFX: GUGAAAAA (SNOOORE) / GOOOO (SNORE)
HA HA HAAH!
EVERY-ONE'S PASSED OUT, HMMM?
INDEEED!
OH DEEEAR...I'M BEGINNING TO GET SLEEPY TOO, YOU KNOW?
HE GOT ONE TOO.
AH-HA-HA! IS THAT RIGHT?
JYUUU (SLURP)

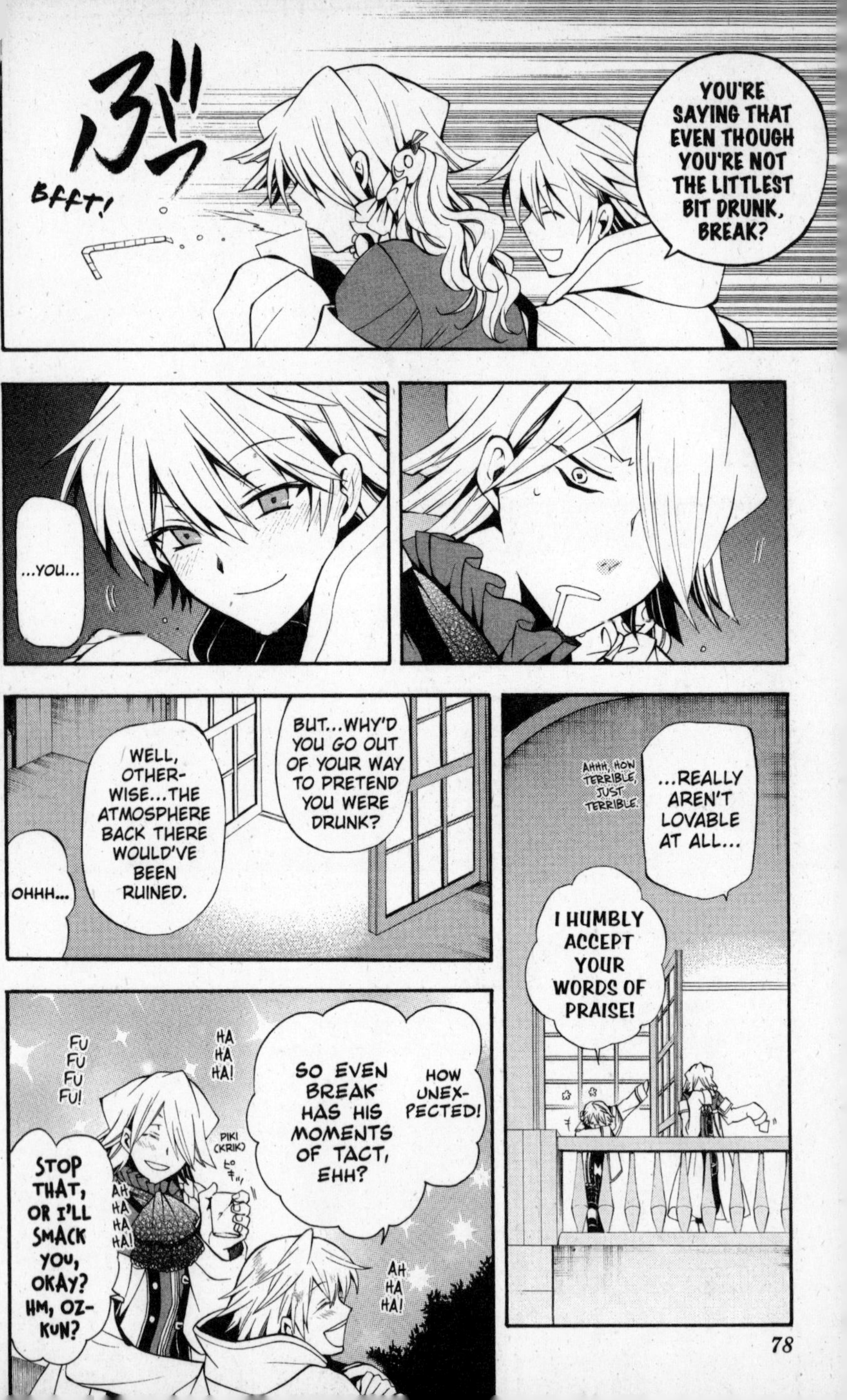

YOU'RE SAYING THAT EVEN THOUGH YOU'RE NOT THE LITTLEST BIT DRUNK, BREAK?
BFFFT!
...YOU...
...REALLY AREN'T LOVABLE AT ALL...
AHHH, HOW TERRIBLE, JUST TERRIBLE.
I HUMBLY ACCEPT YOUR WORDS OF PRAISE!
BUT...WHY'D YOU GO OUT OF YOUR WAY TO PRETEND YOU WERE DRUNK?
WELL, OTHER-WISE...THE ATMOSPHERE BACK THERE WOULD'VE BEEN RUINED.
OHHH...
HOW UNEX-PECTED!
SO EVEN BREAK HAS HIS MOMENTS OF TACT, EHH?
HA HA HA!
FU FU FU FU!
PIKI (KRIK)
STOP THAT, OR I'LL SMACK YOU, OKAY? HM, OZ-KUN?
AH HA HA HA!
AH HA HA!

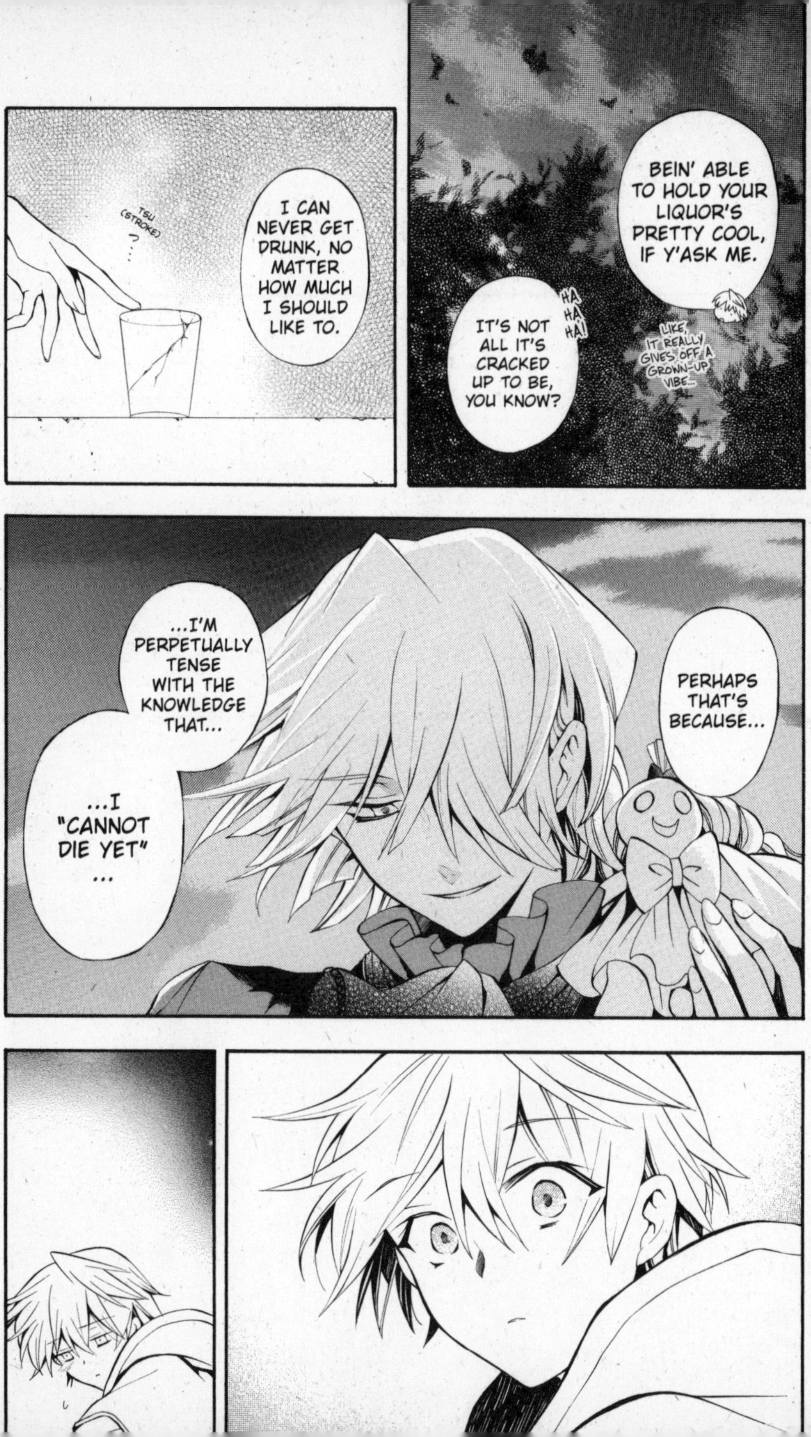
BEIN' ABLE TO HOLD YOUR LIQUOR'S PRETTY COOL, IF Y'ASK ME.
LIKE, IT REALLY GIVES OFF A GROWN-UP VIBE...
HA HA HA!
IT'S NOT ALL IT'S CRACKED UP TO BE, YOU KNOW?
TSU (STROKE)
?
...
I CAN NEVER GET DRUNK, NO MATTER HOW MUCH I SHOULD LIKE TO.
PERHAPS THAT'S BECAUSE...
...I'M PERPETUALLY TENSE WITH THE KNOWLEDGE THAT...
...I "CANNOT DIE YET" ...

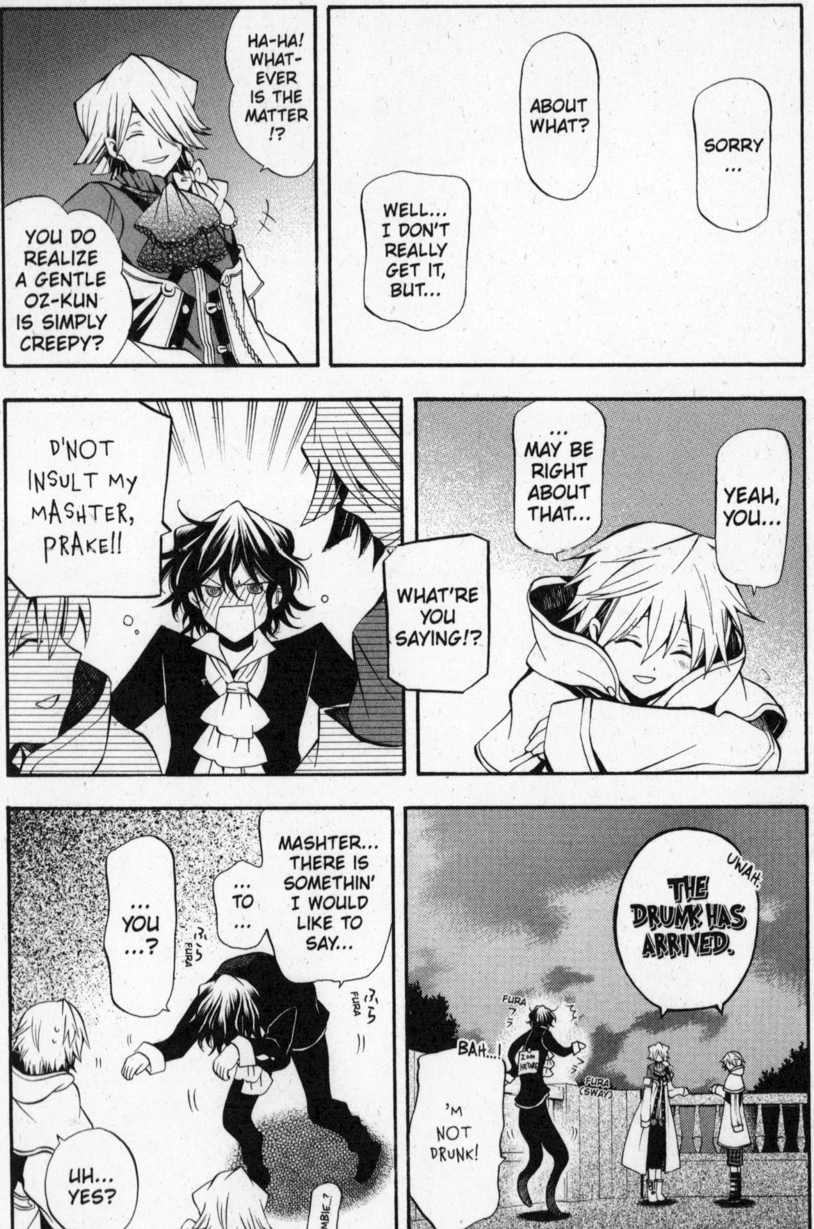
SORRY ...
ABOUT WHAT?
WELL... I DON'T REALLY GET IT, BUT...
HA-HA! WHAT-EVER IS THE MATTER !?
YOU DO REALIZE A GENTLE OZ-KUN IS SIMPLY CREEPY?
YEAH, YOU...
... MAY BE RIGHT ABOUT THAT...
WHAT'RE YOU SAYING!?
D'NOT INSULT MY MASHTER, PRAKE!!
UWAH.
THE DRUNK HAS ARRIVED.
FURA
BAH...!
FURA (SWAY)
'M NOT DRUNK!
MASHTER... THERE IS SOMETHIN' I WOULD LIKE TO SAY...
FURA
... TO ...
... YOU ...?
FURA
UH... YES?
A ZOMBIE...?

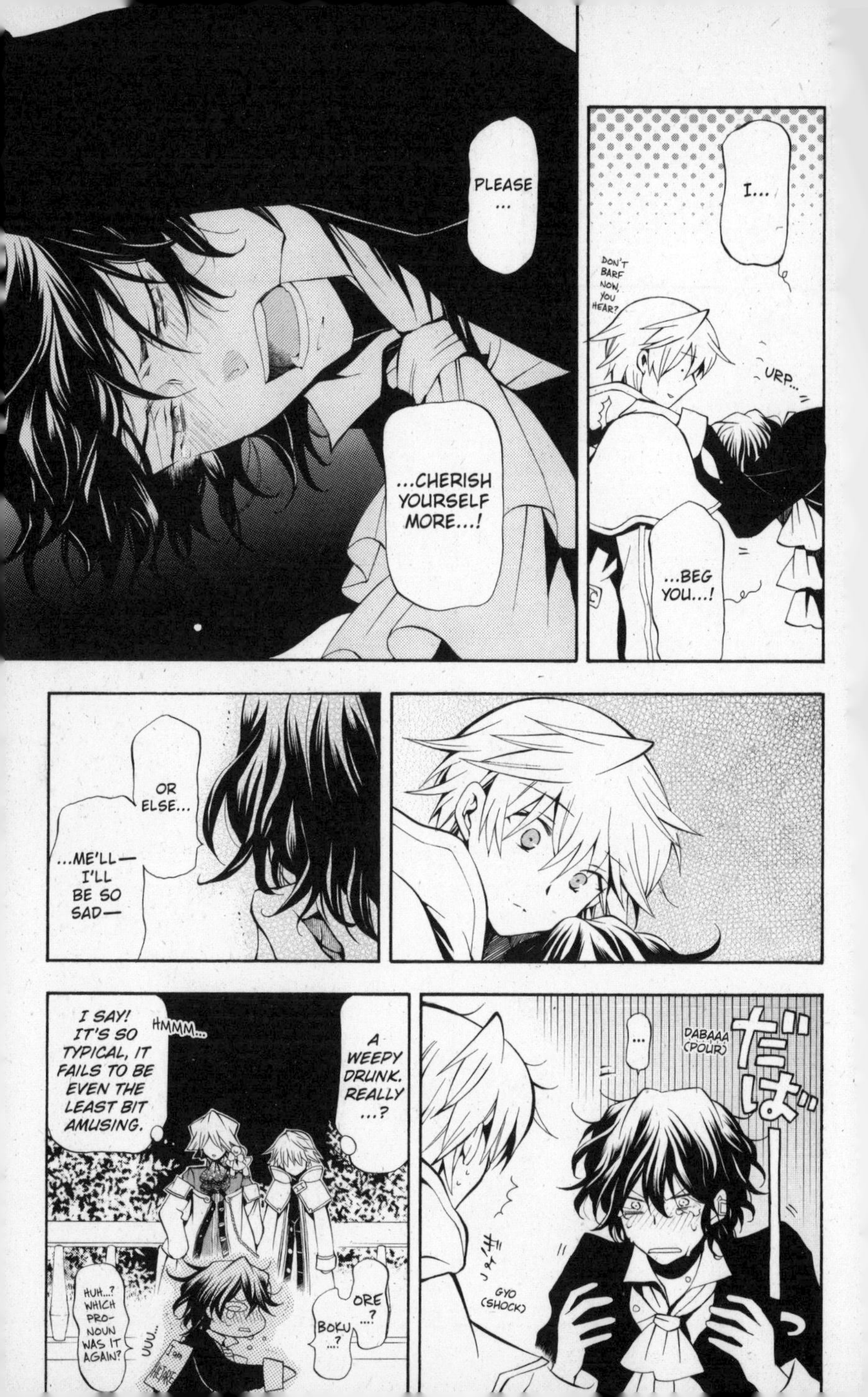
I...
DON'T BARF NOW, YOU HEAR?
URP...
...BEG YOU...!
PLEASE...
...CHERISH YOURSELF MORE...!
OR ELSE...
...ME'LL— I'LL BE SO SAD—
...
DABAAA (POUR)
GYO (SHOCK)
A WEEPY DRUNK. REALLY...?
HMMM...
I SAY! IT'S SO TYPICAL, IT FAILS TO BE EVEN THE LEAST BIT AMUSING.
ORE...?
BOKU...?
HUH...? WHICH PRONOUN WAS IT AGAIN?
UUU...

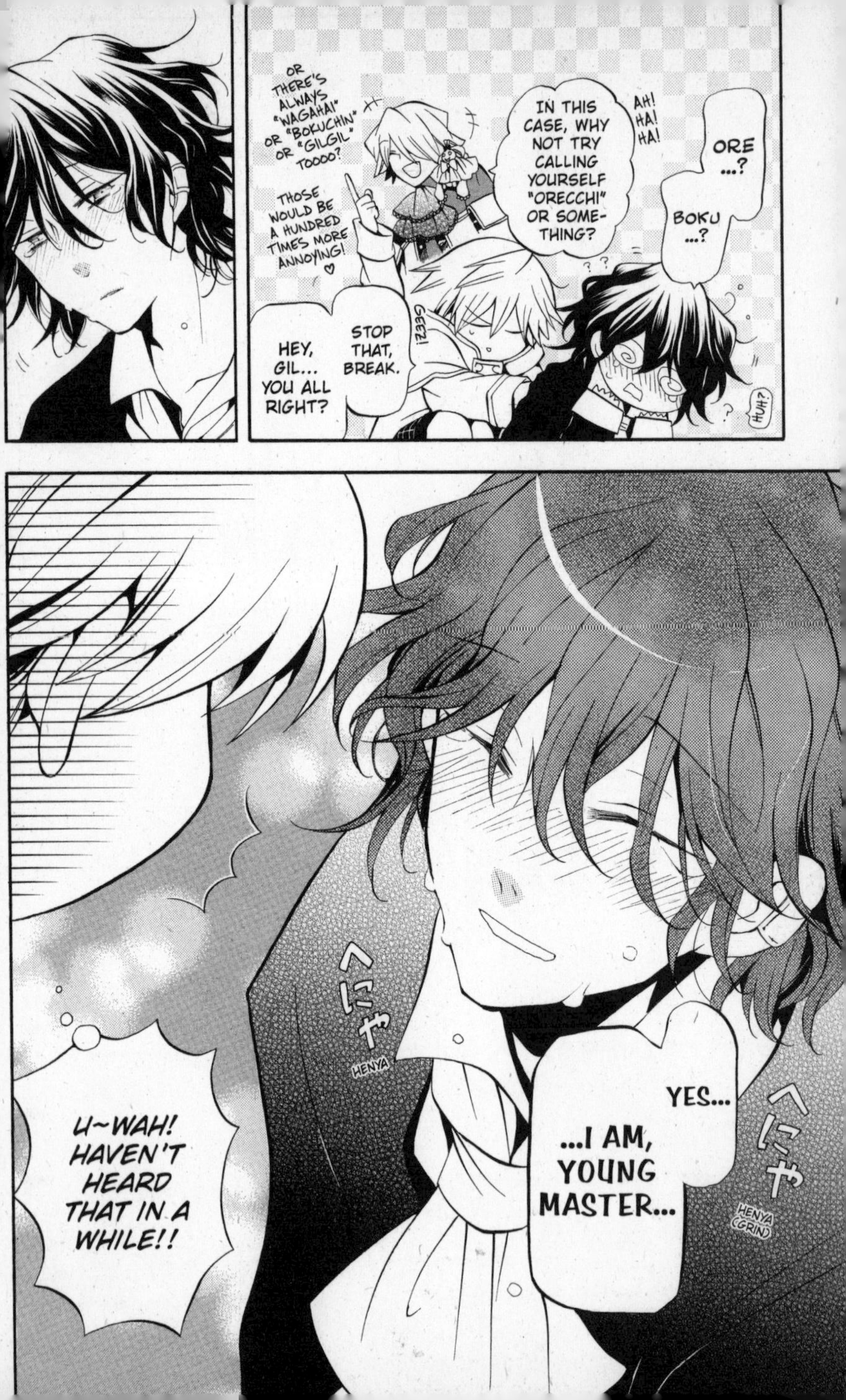
ORE ...?
BOKU ...?
AH! HA! HA!
IN THIS CASE, WHY NOT TRY CALLING YOURSELF "ORECCHI" OR SOME-THING?
OR THERE'S ALWAYS "WAGAHAI" OR "BOKUCHIN" OR "GILGIL" TOOOO?
THOSE WOULD BE A HUNDRED TIMES MORE ANNOYING! ♡
HUH?
GEEZ!
STOP THAT, BREAK.
HEY, GIL... YOU ALL RIGHT?
へにゃ
HENYA (GRIN)
YES...
...I AM, YOUNG MASTER...
へにゃ
HENYA
U~WAH! HAVEN'T HEARD THAT IN A WHILE!!

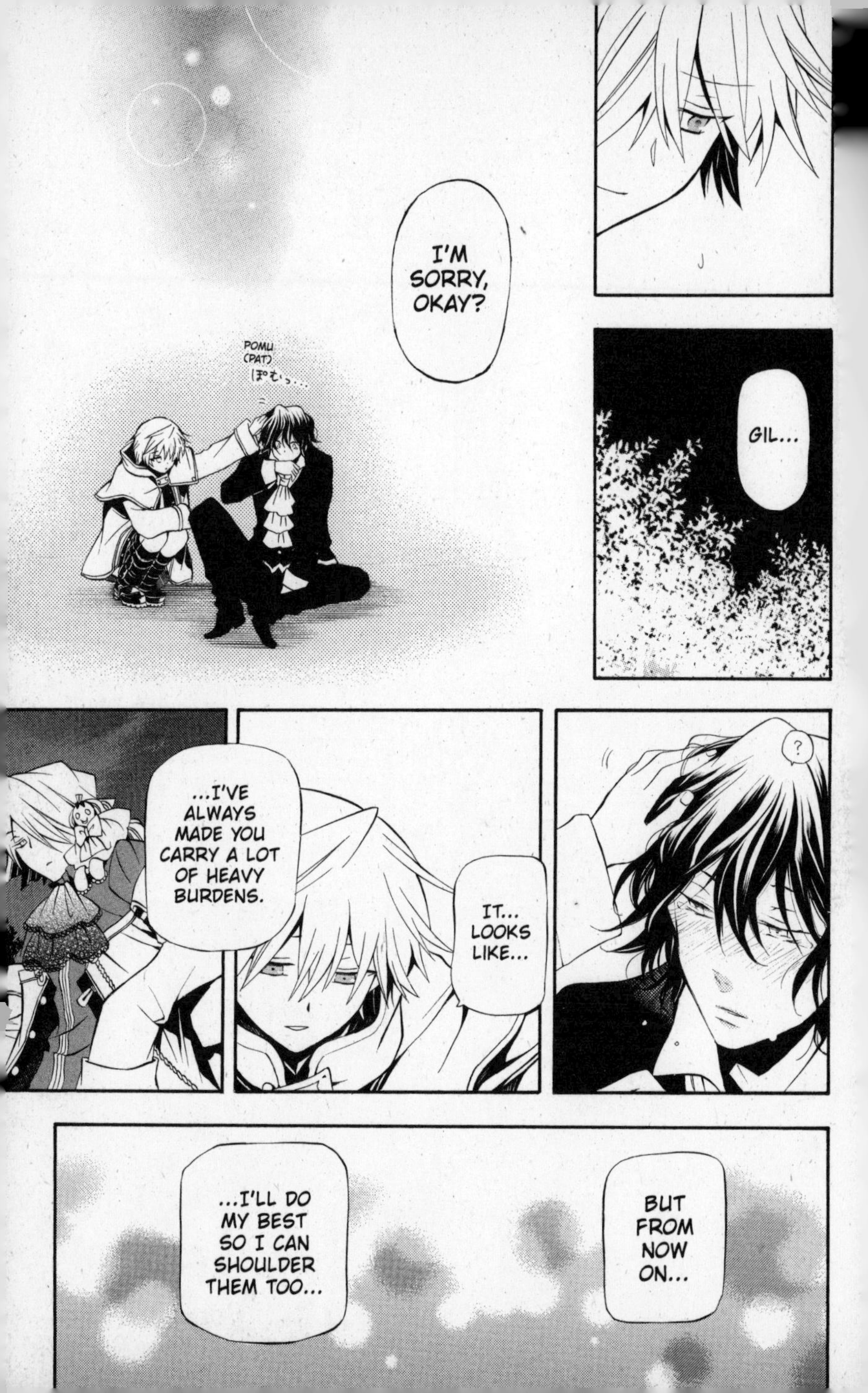
GIL...
I'M SORRY, OKAY?
POMU (PAT)
ぽむっ…
?
IT... LOOKS LIKE...
...I'VE ALWAYS MADE YOU CARRY A LOT OF HEAVY BURDENS.
BUT FROM NOW ON...
...I'LL DO MY BEST SO I CAN SHOULDER THEM TOO...

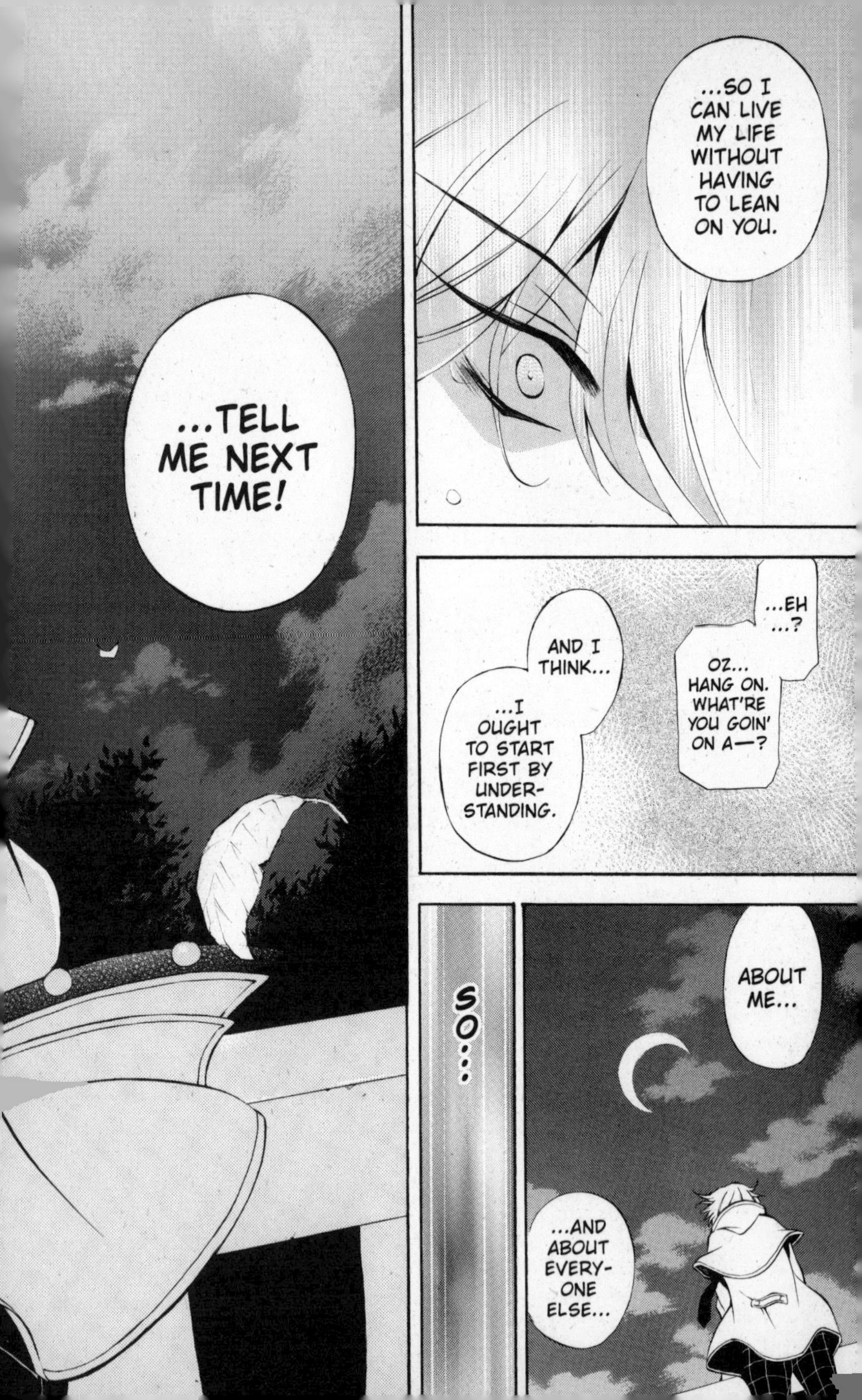
...SO I CAN LIVE MY LIFE WITHOUT HAVING TO LEAN ON YOU.
...EH ...?
OZ... HANG ON. WHAT'RE YOU GOIN' ON A—?
AND I THINK...
...I OUGHT TO START FIRST BY UNDER-STANDING.
ABOUT ME...
SO...
...AND ABOUT EVERY-ONE ELSE...
...TELL ME NEXT TIME!

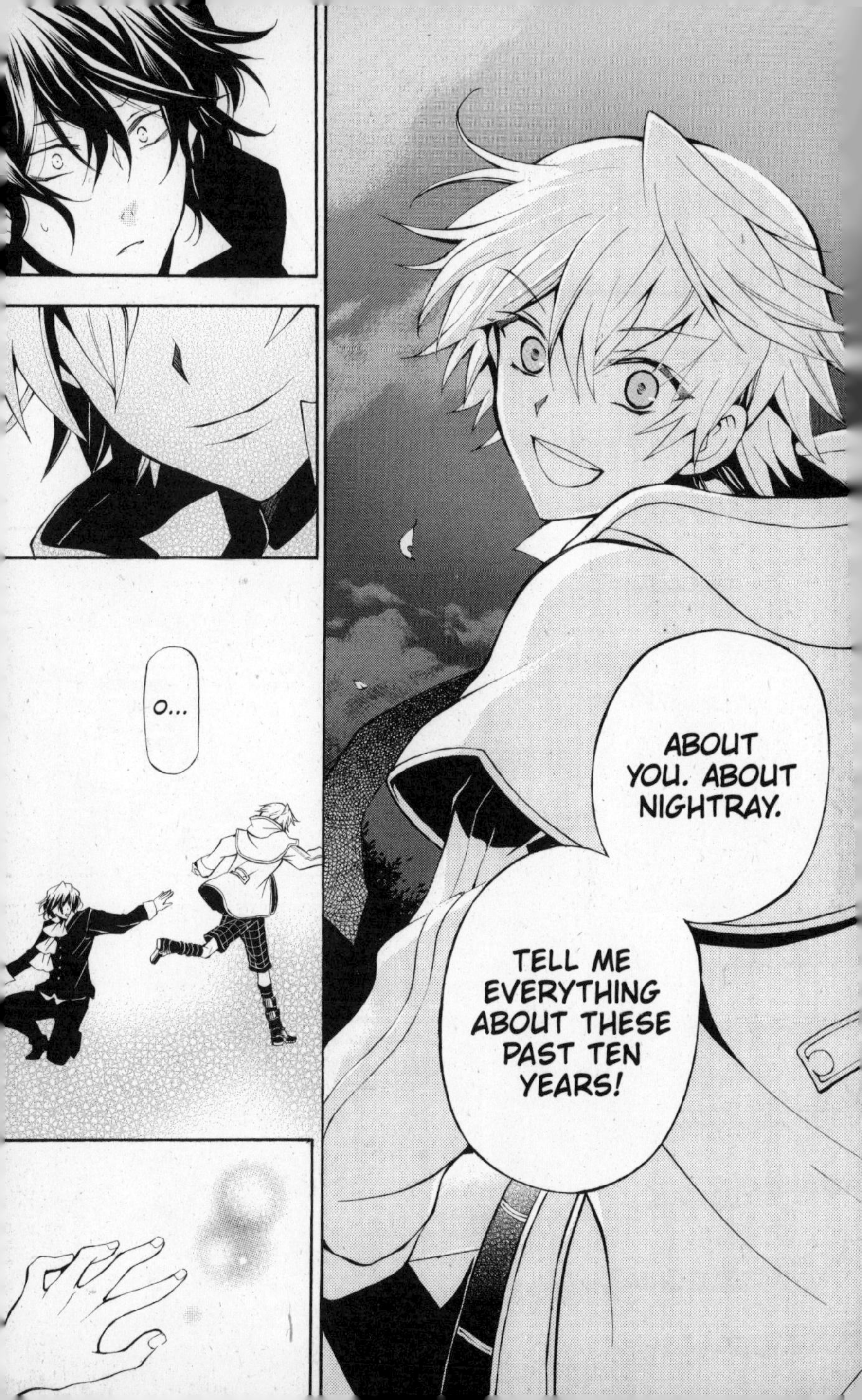
ABOUT YOU. ABOUT NIGHTRAY.
TELL ME EVERYTHING ABOUT THESE PAST TEN YEARS!
O...

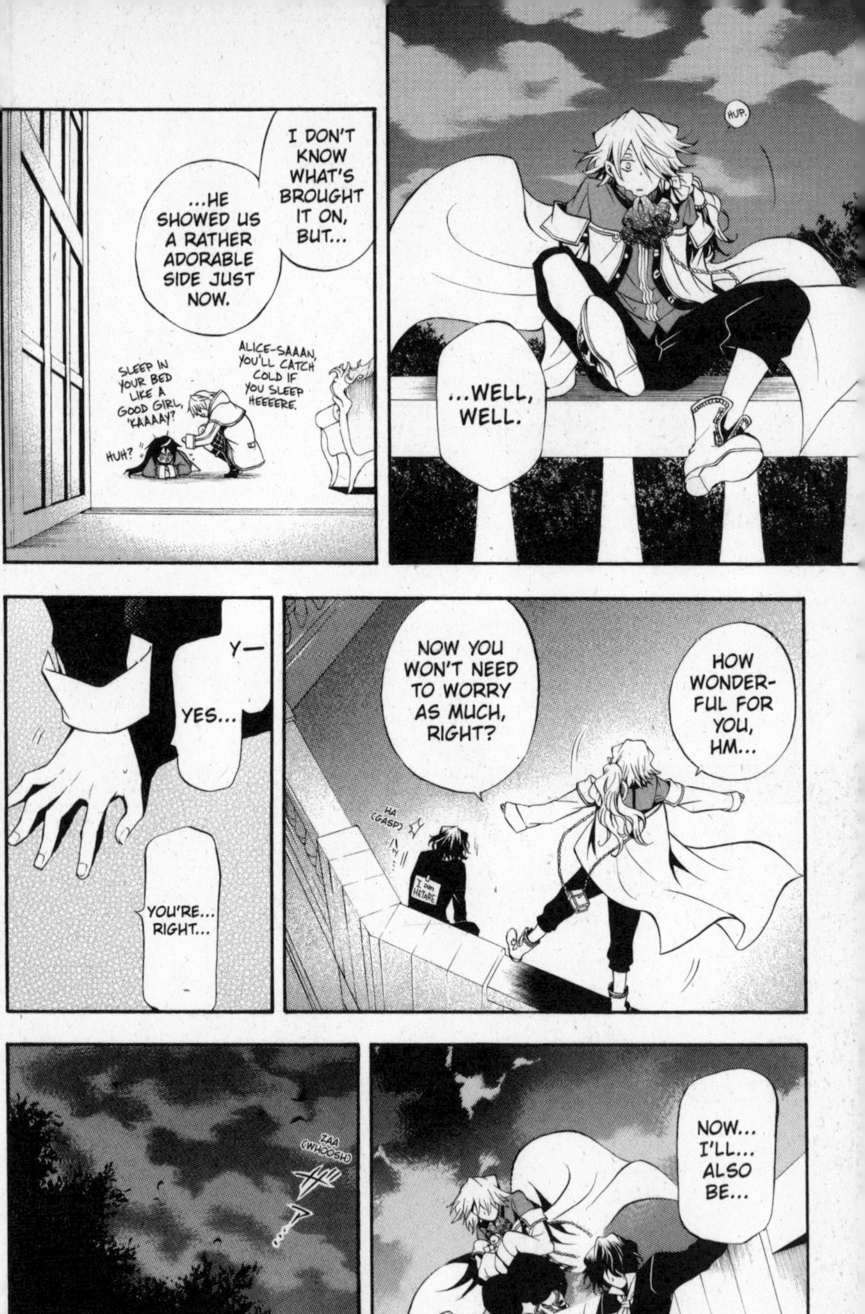
HUP.
...WELL, WELL.
I DON'T KNOW WHAT'S BROUGHT IT ON, BUT...
...HE SHOWED US A RATHER ADORABLE SIDE JUST NOW.
ALICE-SAAAN, YOU'LL CATCH COLD IF YOU SLEEP HEEEERE.
SLEEP IN YOUR BED LIKE A GOOD GIRL, 'KAAAAY?
HUH?
HOW WONDER-FUL FOR YOU, HM...
NOW YOU WON'T NEED TO WORRY AS MUCH, RIGHT?
HA (GASP)
I am HETARE
Y—
YES...
YOU'RE... RIGHT...
NOW... I'LL... ALSO BE...
ZAA (WHOOSH)

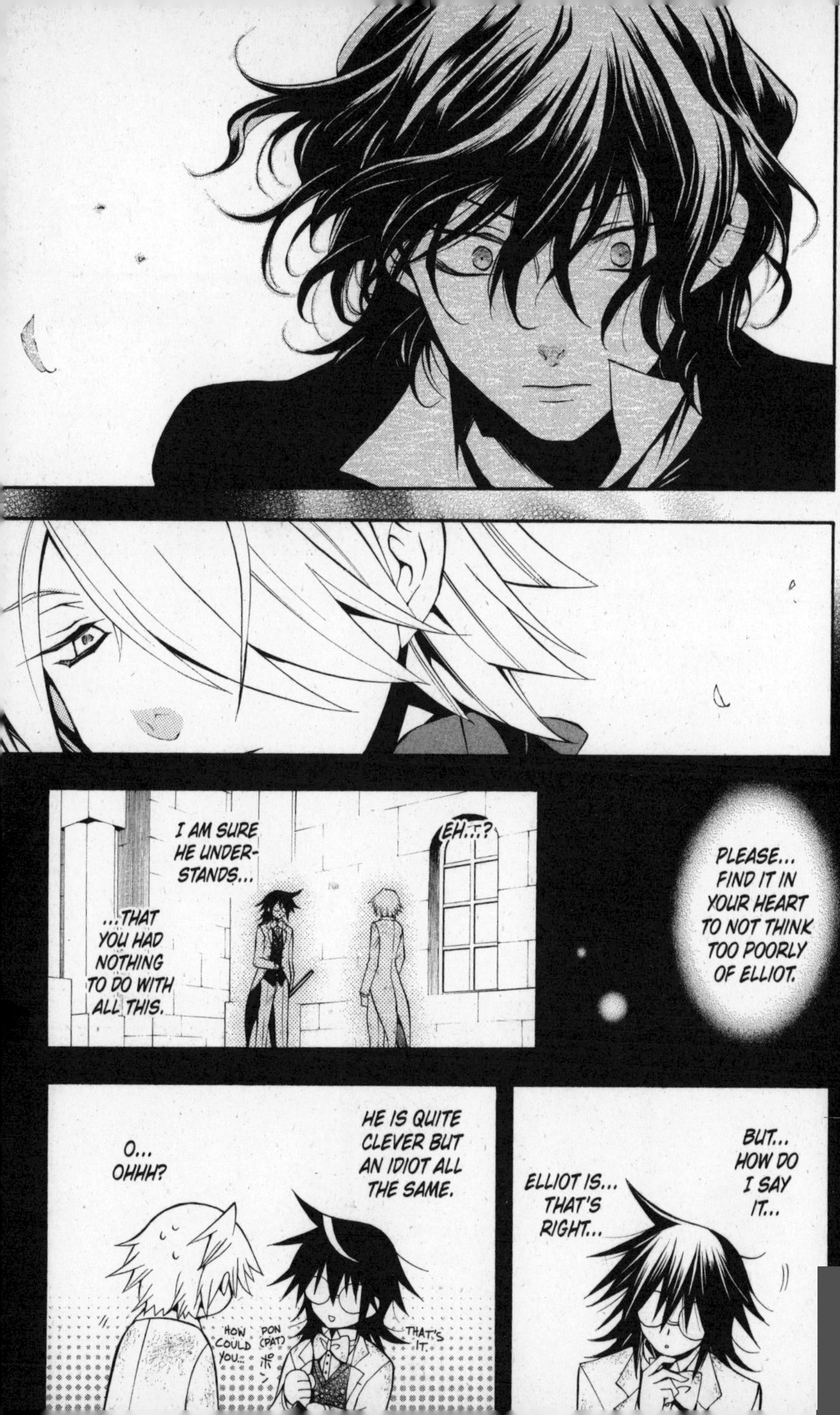
PLEASE... FIND IT IN YOUR HEART TO NOT THINK TOO POORLY OF ELLIOT.
EH...?
I AM SURE HE UNDER-STANDS...
...THAT YOU HAD NOTHING TO DO WITH ALL THIS.
BUT... HOW DO I SAY IT...
ELLIOT IS... THAT'S RIGHT...
HE IS QUITE CLEVER BUT AN IDIOT ALL THE SAME.
THAT'S IT.
PON (PAT)
O... OHHH?
HOW COULD YOU...

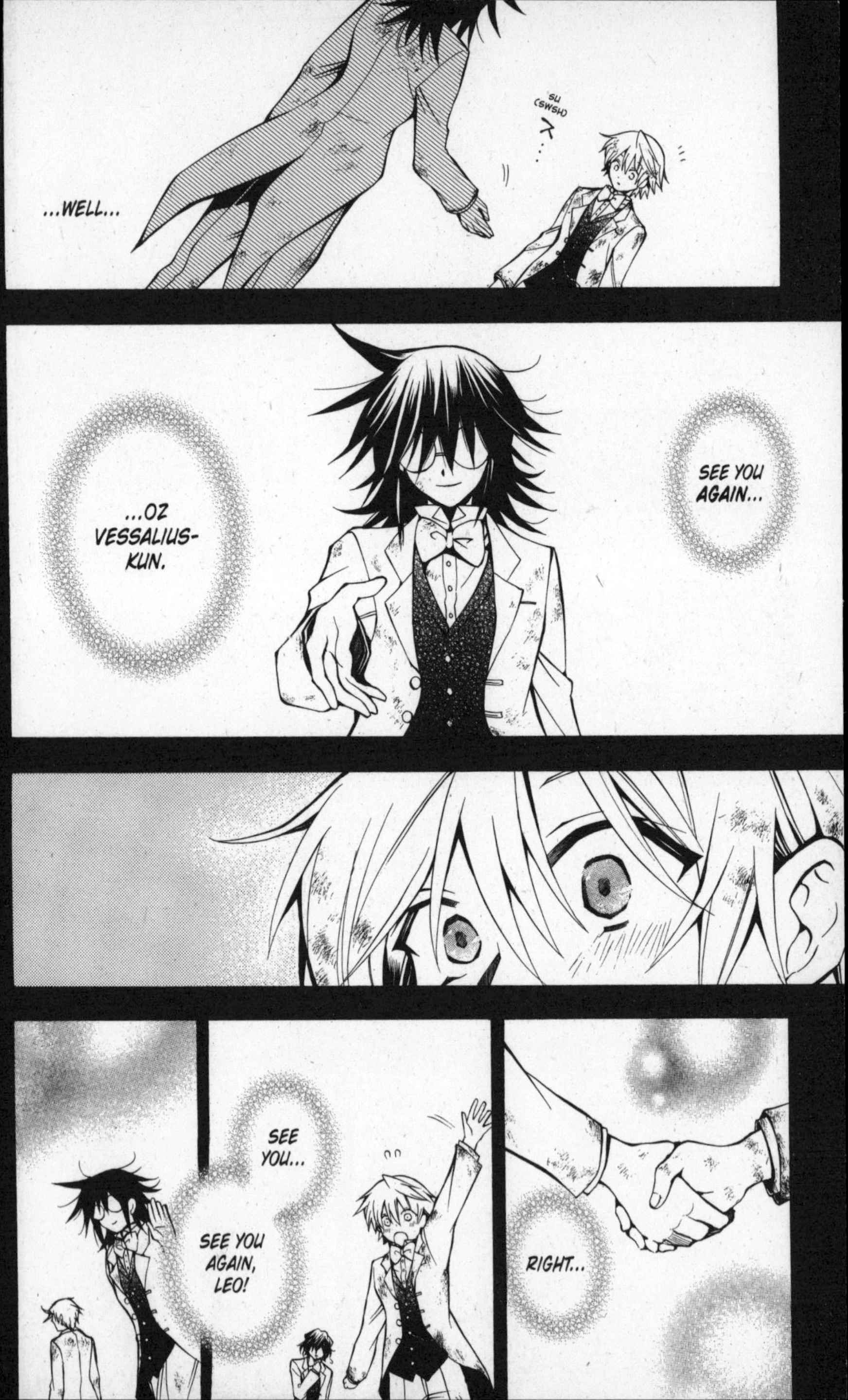
SU (SWSH)
...WELL...
SEE YOU AGAIN...
...OZ VESSALIUS-KUN.
RIGHT...
SEE YOU...
SEE YOU AGAIN, LEO!

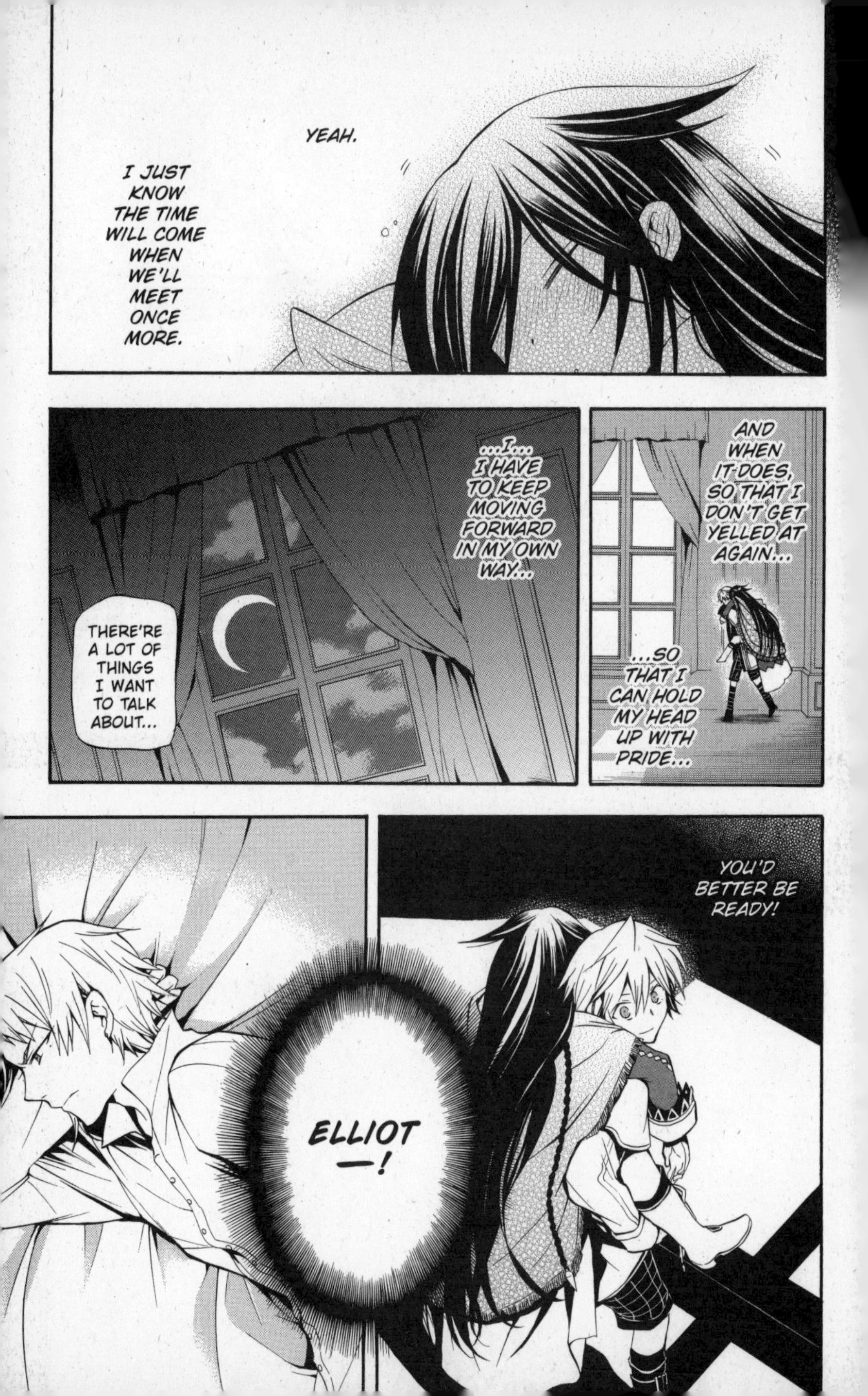
YEAH.
I JUST KNOW THE TIME WILL COME WHEN WE'LL MEET ONCE MORE.
AND WHEN IT DOES, SO THAT I DON'T GET YELLED AT AGAIN...
...SO THAT I CAN HOLD MY HEAD UP WITH PRIDE...
...I... I HAVE TO KEEP MOVING FORWARD IN MY OWN WAY...
THERE'RE A LOT OF THINGS I WANT TO TALK ABOUT...
YOU'D BETTER BE READY!
ELLIOT—!

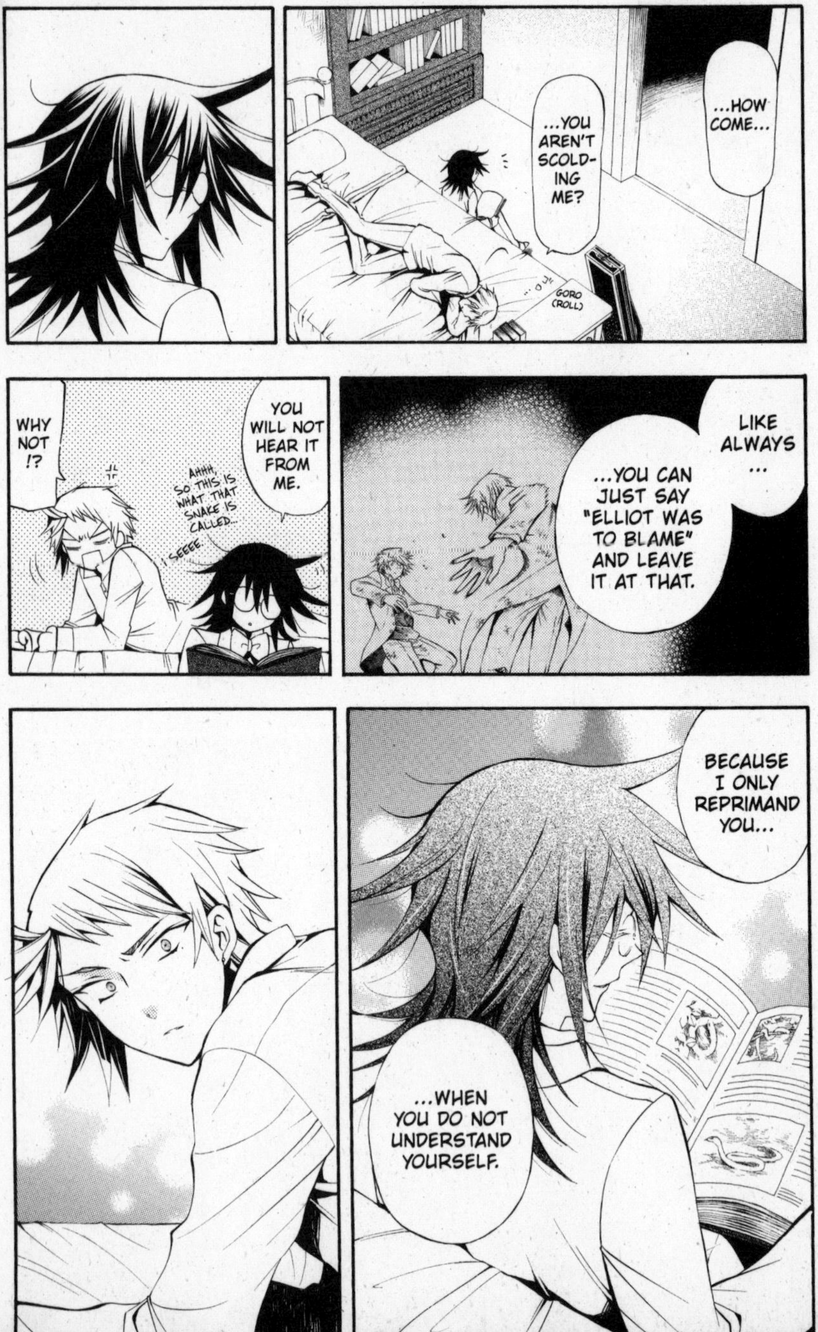

...HOW COME...
...YOU AREN'T SCOLD-ING ME?
GORO (ROLL)
LIKE ALWAYS ...
...YOU CAN JUST SAY "ELLIOT WAS TO BLAME" AND LEAVE IT AT THAT.
YOU WILL NOT HEAR IT FROM ME.
WHY NOT !?
AHHH, SO THIS IS WHAT THAT SNAKE IS CALLED...
SEEEE.
BECAUSE I ONLY REPRIMAND YOU...
...WHEN YOU DO NOT UNDERSTAND YOURSELF.

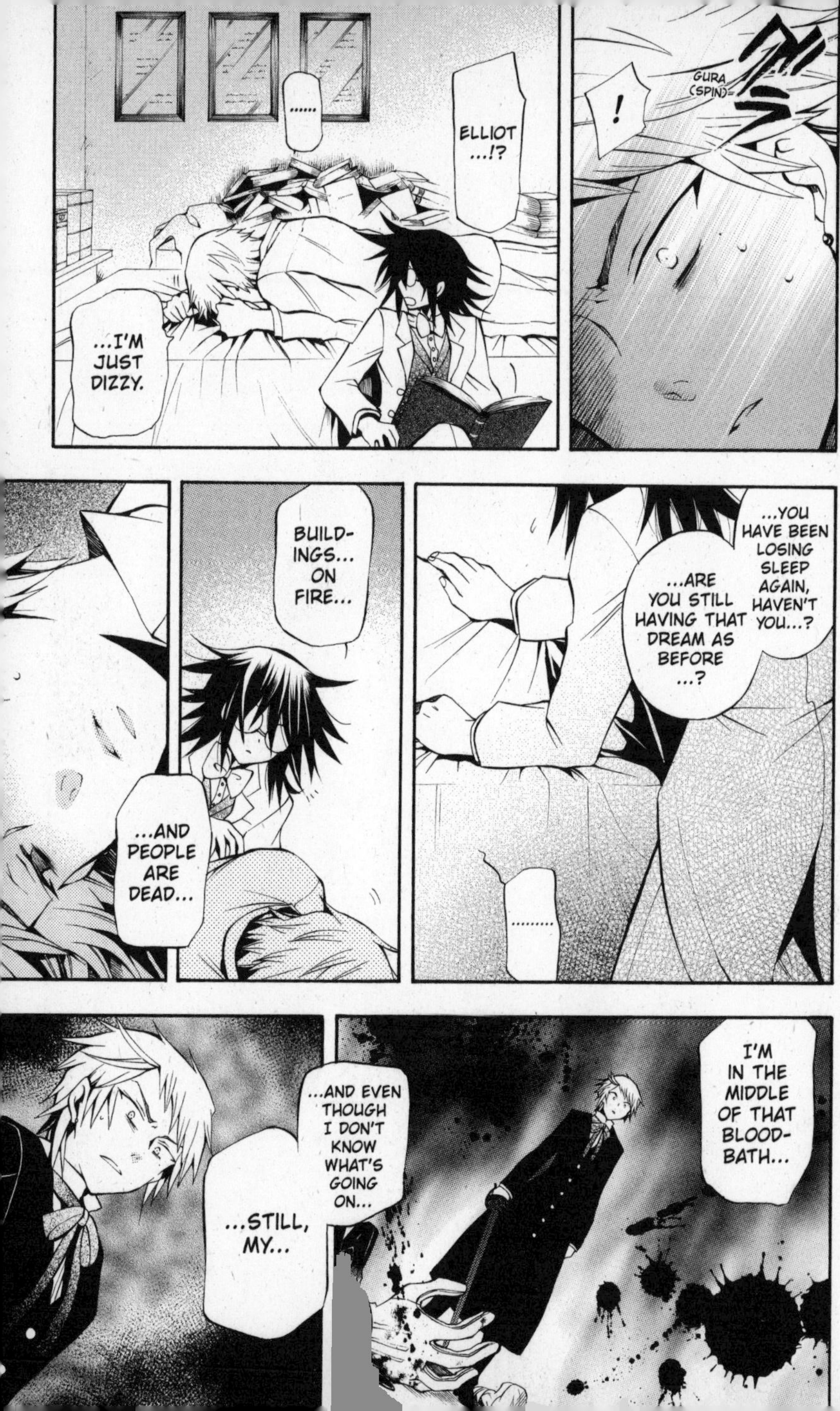
GURA (SPIN)
!
ELLIOT ...!?
......
...I'M JUST DIZZY.
...YOU HAVE BEEN LOSING SLEEP AGAIN, HAVEN'T YOU...?
...ARE YOU STILL HAVING THAT DREAM AS BEFORE ...?
....
BUILD-INGS... ON FIRE...
...AND PEOPLE ARE DEAD...
I'M IN THE MIDDLE OF THAT BLOOD-BATH...
...AND EVEN THOUGH I DON'T KNOW WHAT'S GOING ON...
...STILL, MY...

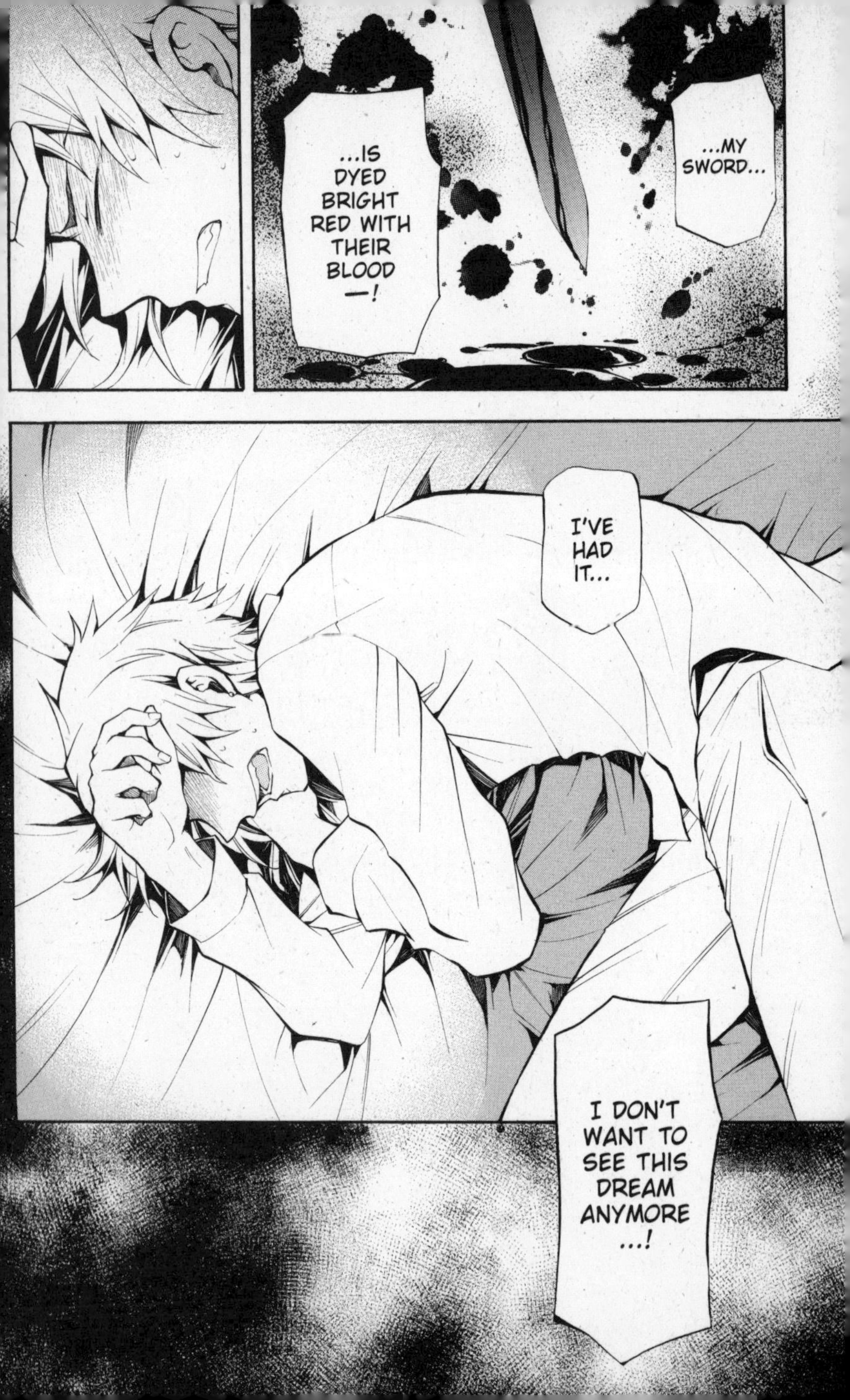
...MY SWORD...
...IS DYED BRIGHT RED WITH THEIR BLOOD—!
I'VE HAD IT...
I DON'T WANT TO SEE THIS DREAM ANYMORE...!

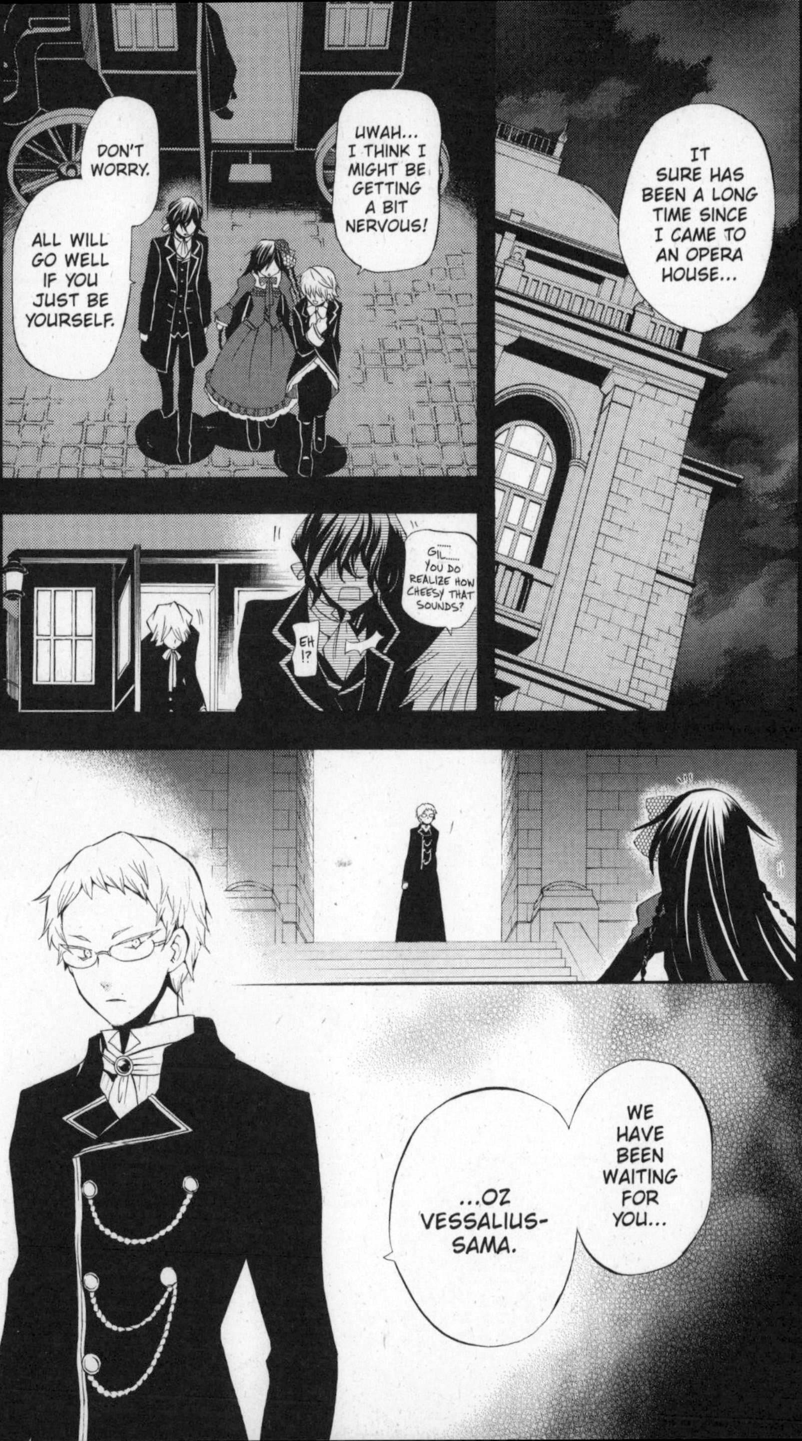
IT SURE HAS BEEN A LONG TIME SINCE I CAME TO AN OPERA HOUSE...
UWAH... I THINK I MIGHT BE GETTING A BIT NERVOUS!
DON'T WORRY.
ALL WILL GO WELL IF YOU JUST BE YOURSELF.
GIL...... YOU DO REALIZE HOW CHEESY THAT SOUNDS?
EH!?
WE HAVE BEEN WAITING FOR YOU...
...OZ VESSALIUS-SAMA.

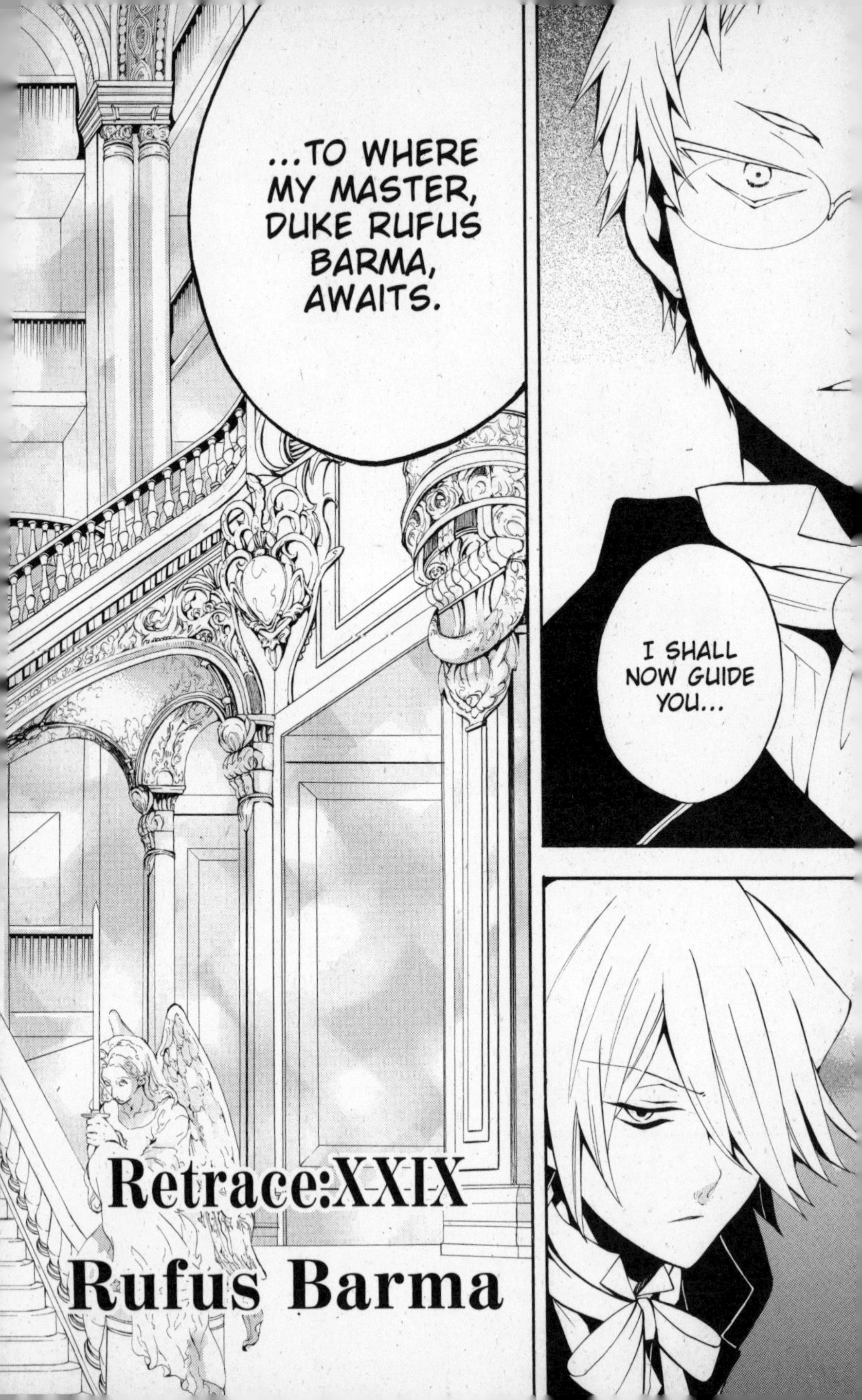
I SHALL NOW GUIDE YOU...
...TO WHERE MY MASTER, DUKE RUFUS BARMA, AWAITS.
Retrace:XXIX
Rufus Barma

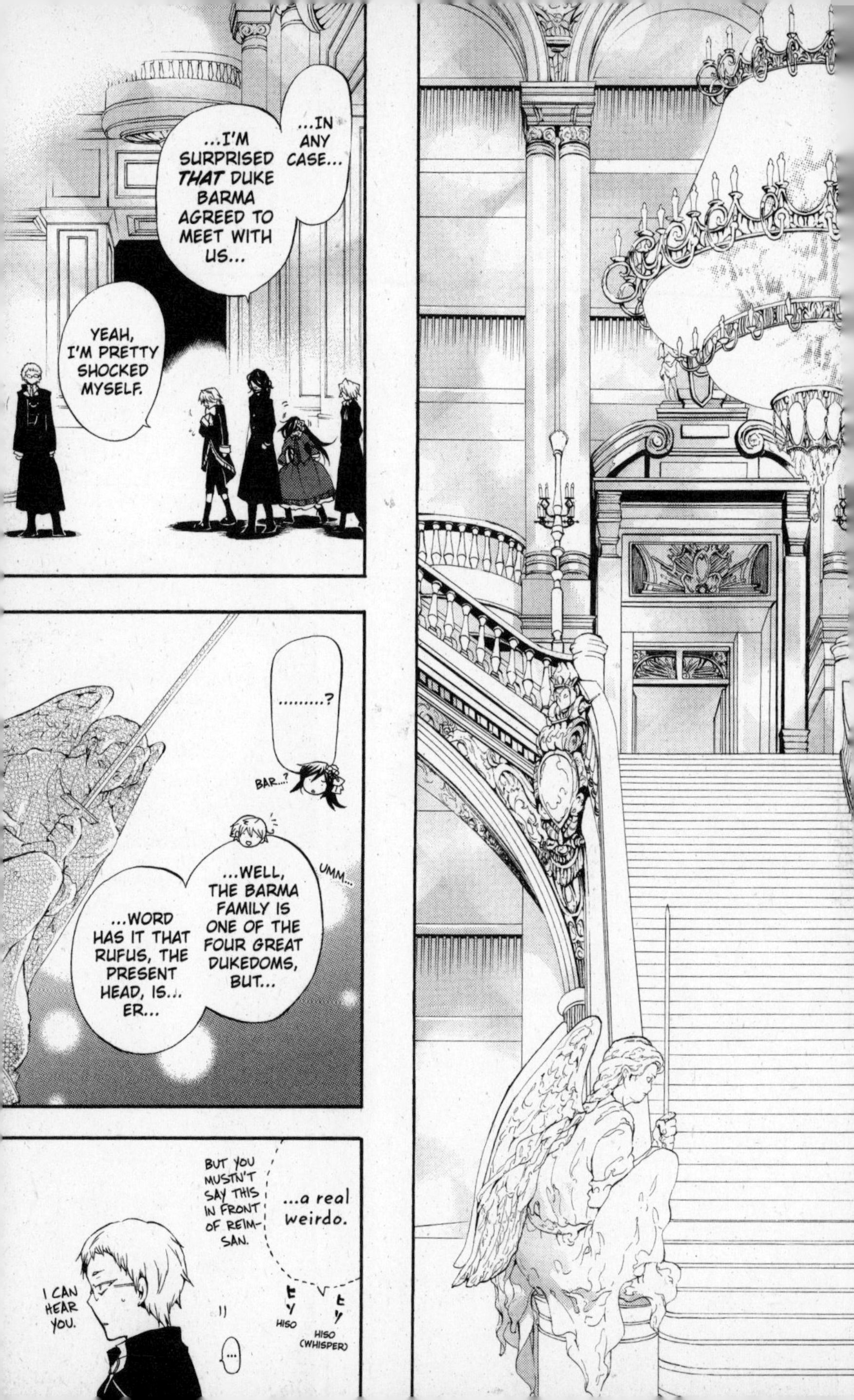

...IN ANY CASE...
...I'M SURPRISED THAT DUKE BARMA AGREED TO MEET WITH US...
YEAH, I'M PRETTY SHOCKED MYSELF.
.........?
BAR...?
UMM...
...WELL, THE BARMA FAMILY IS ONE OF THE FOUR GREAT DUKEDOMS, BUT...
...WORD HAS IT THAT RUFUS, THE PRESENT HEAD, IS... ER...
...a real weirdo.
BUT YOU MUSTN'T SAY THIS IN FRONT OF REIM-SAN.
ヒソ
HISO (WHISPER)
ヒソ
HISO
I CAN HEAR YOU.
...

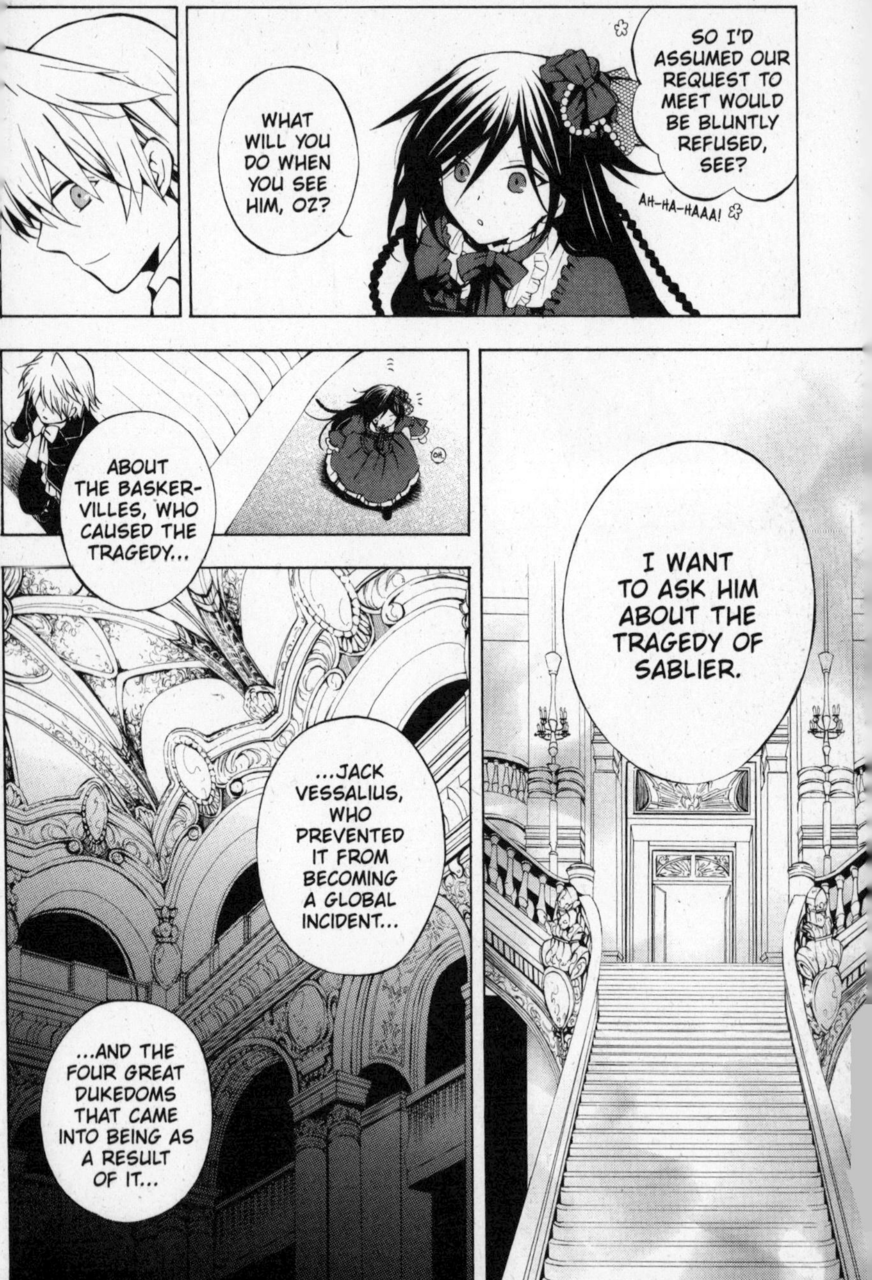
SO I'D ASSUMED OUR REQUEST TO MEET WOULD BE BLUNTLY REFUSED, SEE?
AH-HA-HAAA!
WHAT WILL YOU DO WHEN YOU SEE HIM, OZ?
I WANT TO ASK HIM ABOUT THE TRAGEDY OF SABLIER.
OH.
ABOUT THE BASKER-VILLES, WHO CAUSED THE TRAGEDY...
...JACK VESSALIUS, WHO PREVENTED IT FROM BECOMING A GLOBAL INCIDENT...
...AND THE FOUR GREAT DUKEDOMS THAT CAME INTO BEING AS A RESULT OF IT...

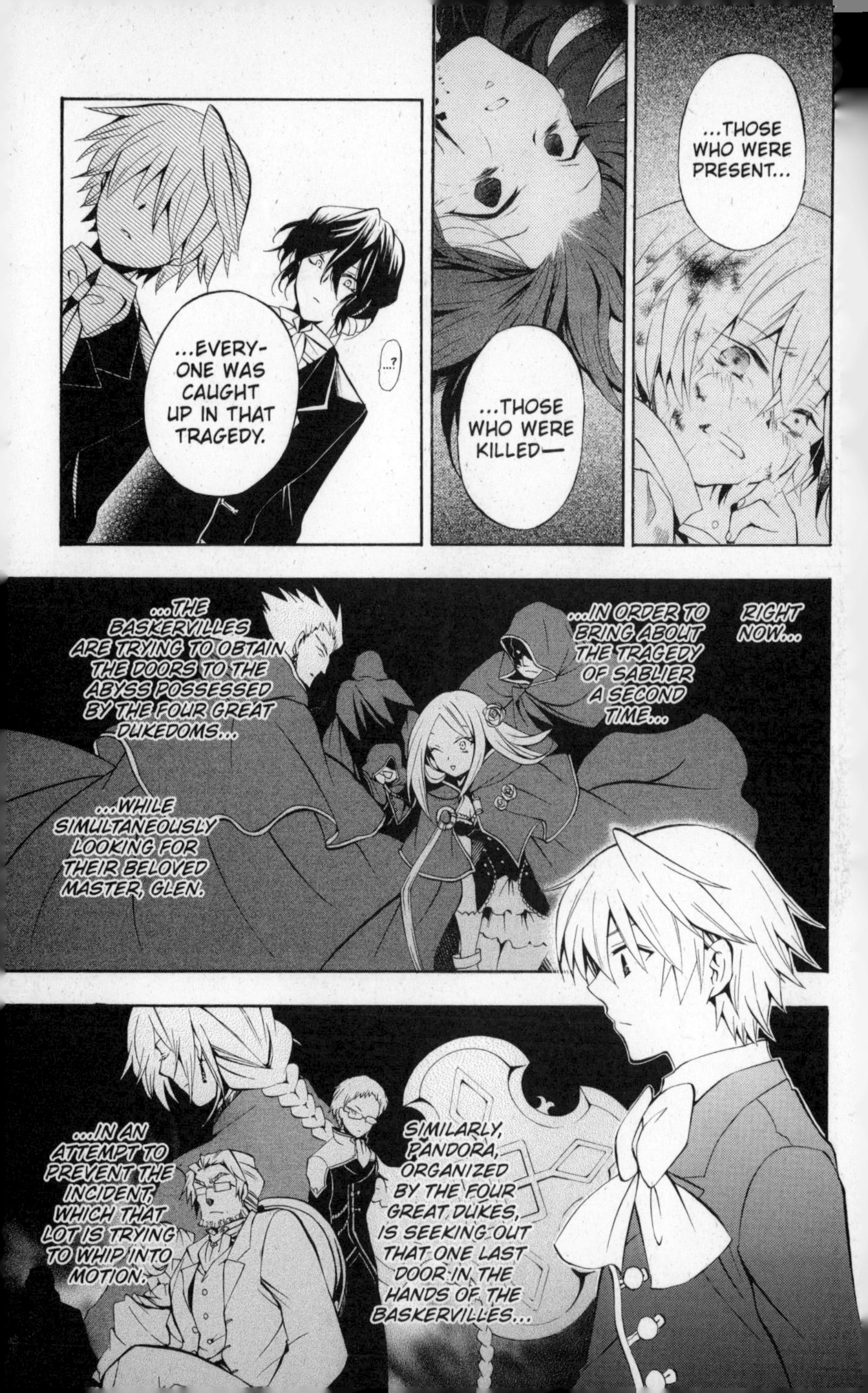
...THOSE WHO WERE PRESENT...
...THOSE WHO WERE KILLED—
...?
...EVERY-ONE WAS CAUGHT UP IN THAT TRAGEDY.
RIGHT NOW...
...IN ORDER TO BRING ABOUT THE TRAGEDY OF SABLIER A SECOND TIME...
...THE BASKERVILLES ARE TRYING TO OBTAIN THE DOORS TO THE ABYSS POSSESSED BY THE FOUR GREAT DUKEDOMS...
...WHILE SIMULTANEOUSLY LOOKING FOR THEIR BELOVED MASTER, GLEN.
SIMILARLY, PANDORA, ORGANIZED BY THE FOUR GREAT DUKES, IS SEEKING OUT THAT ONE LAST DOOR IN THE HANDS OF THE BASKERVILLES...
...IN AN ATTEMPT TO PREVENT THE INCIDENT, WHICH THAT LOT IS TRYING TO WHIP INTO MOTION.

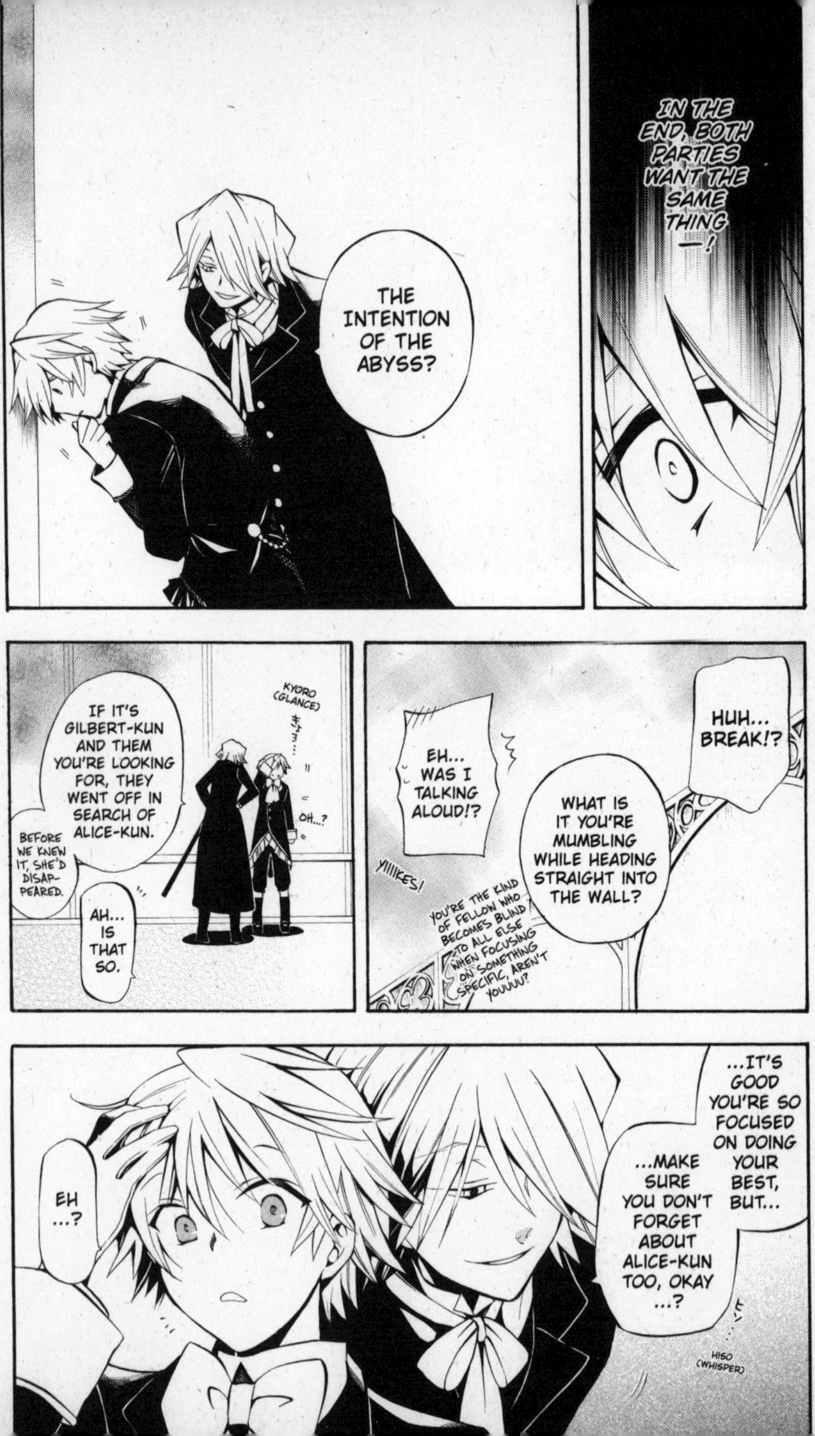
IN THE END, BOTH PARTIES WANT THE SAME THING—!
THE INTENTION OF THE ABYSS?
HUH... BREAK!?
WHAT IS IT YOU'RE MUMBLING WHILE HEADING STRAIGHT INTO THE WALL?
EH... WAS I TALKING ALOUD!?
YOU'RE THE KIND OF FELLOW WHO BECOMES BLIND TO ALL ELSE WHEN FOCUSING ON SOMETHING SPECIFIC, AREN'T YOUUUU?
YIIIIKES!
KYORO (GLANCE)
OH...?
IF IT'S GILBERT-KUN AND THEM YOU'RE LOOKING FOR, THEY WENT OFF IN SEARCH OF ALICE-KUN.
BEFORE WE KNEW IT, SHE'D DISAPPEARED.
AH... IS THAT SO.
...IT'S GOOD YOU'RE SO FOCUSED ON DOING YOUR BEST, BUT...
...MAKE SURE YOU DON'T FORGET ABOUT ALICE-KUN TOO, OKAY ...?
HISO (WHISPER)
EH ...?

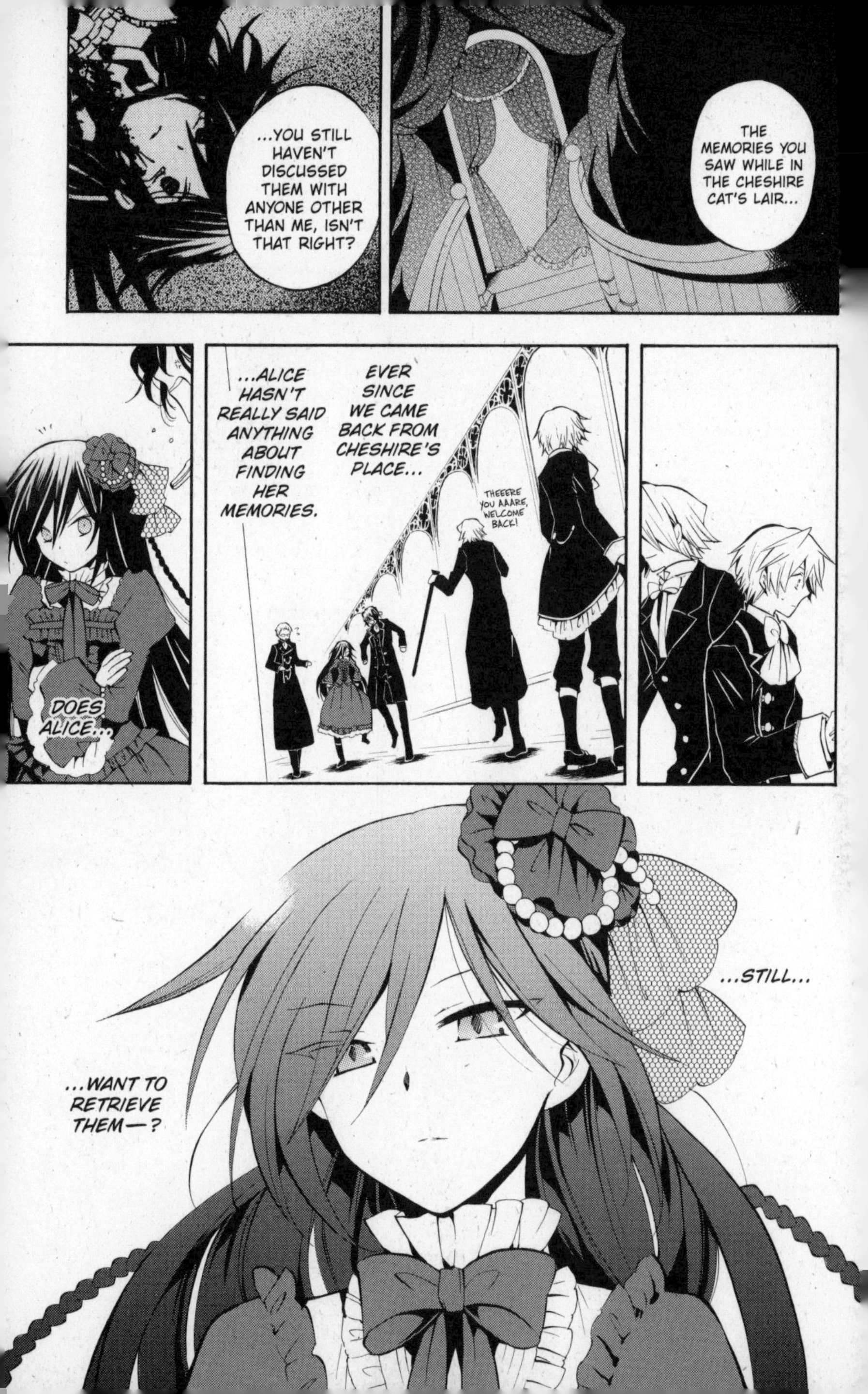
THE MEMORIES YOU SAW WHILE IN THE CHESHIRE CAT'S LAIR...
...YOU STILL HAVEN'T DISCUSSED THEM WITH ANYONE OTHER THAN ME, ISN'T THAT RIGHT?
THEEERE YOU AAARE, WELCOME BACK!
EVER SINCE WE CAME BACK FROM CHESHIRE'S PLACE...
...ALICE HASN'T REALLY SAID ANYTHING ABOUT FINDING HER MEMORIES.
DOES ALICE...
...STILL...
...WANT TO RETRIEVE THEM—?

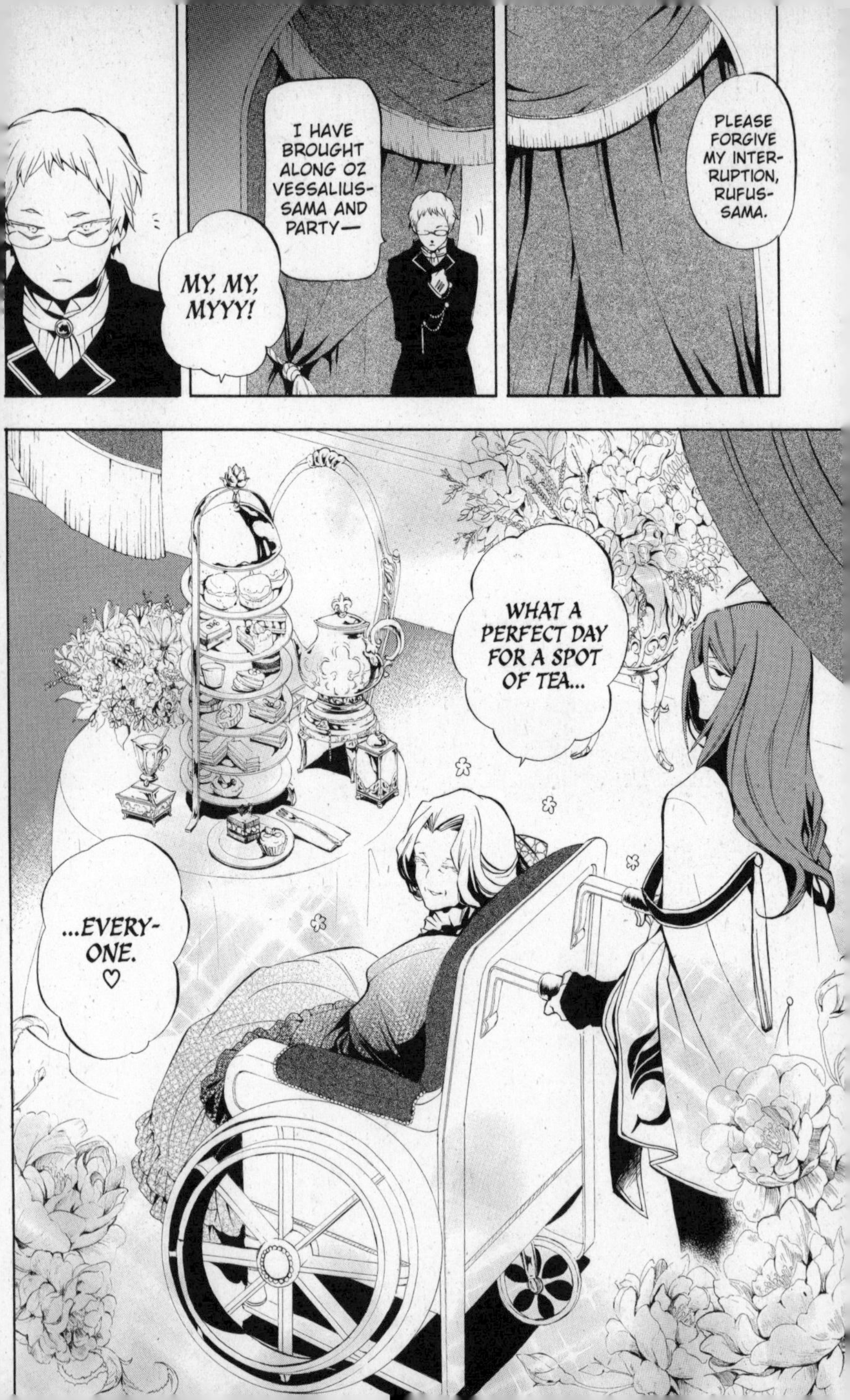
PLEASE FORGIVE MY INTER-RUPTION, RUFUS-SAMA.
I HAVE BROUGHT ALONG OZ VESSALIUS-SAMA AND PARTY—
MY, MY, MYYY!
WHAT A PERFECT DAY FOR A SPOT OF TEA...
...EVERY-ONE. ♡

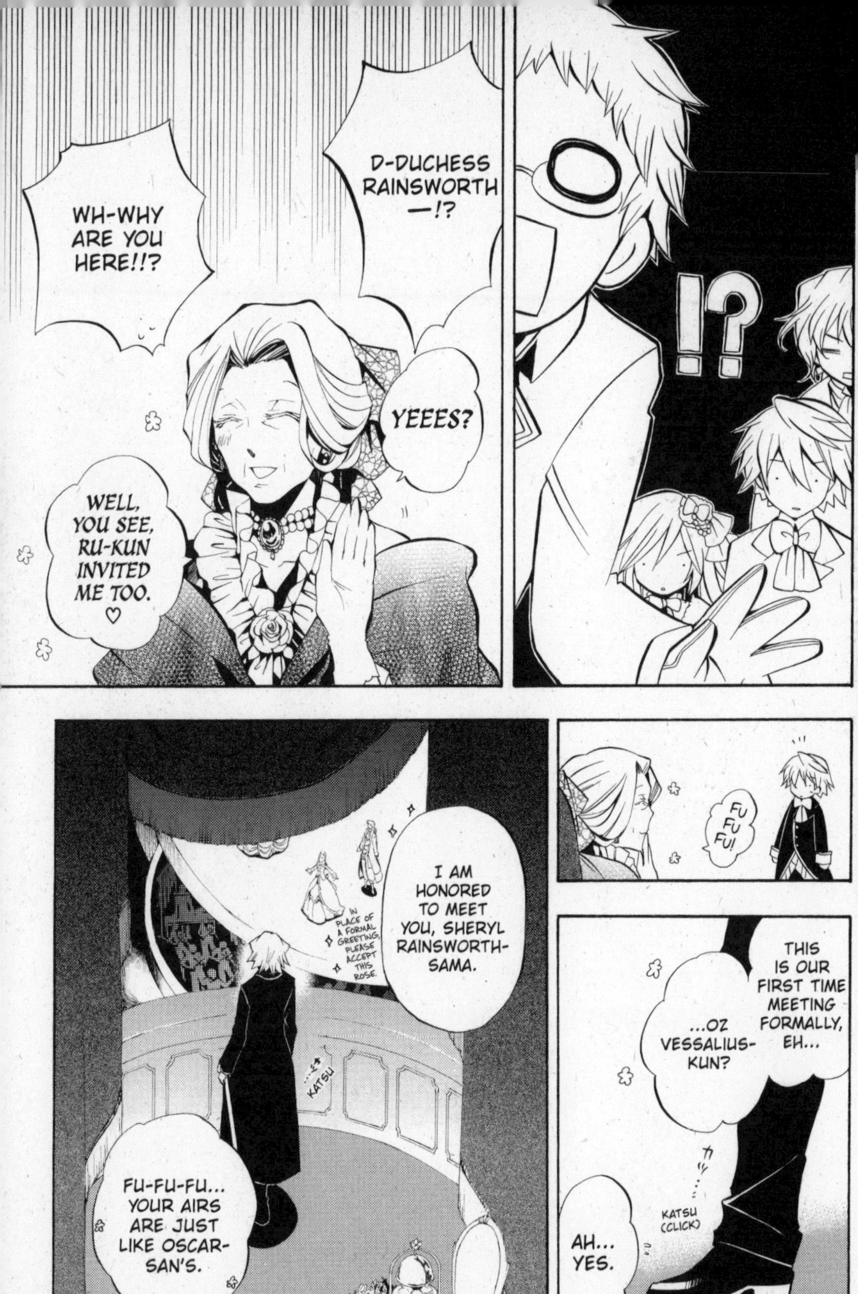
!?
D-DUCHESS RAINSWORTH—!?
WH-WHY ARE YOU HERE!!?
YEEES?
WELL, YOU SEE, RU-KUN INVITED ME TOO. ♡
FU FU FU!
THIS IS OUR FIRST TIME MEETING FORMALLY, EH...
...OZ VESSALIUS-KUN?
KATSU (CLICK)
AH... YES.
I AM HONORED TO MEET YOU, SHERYL RAINSWORTH-SAMA.
IN PLACE OF A FORMAL GREETING, PLEASE ACCEPT THIS ROSE.
KATSU
FU-FU-FU... YOUR AIRS ARE JUST LIKE OSCAR-SAN'S.

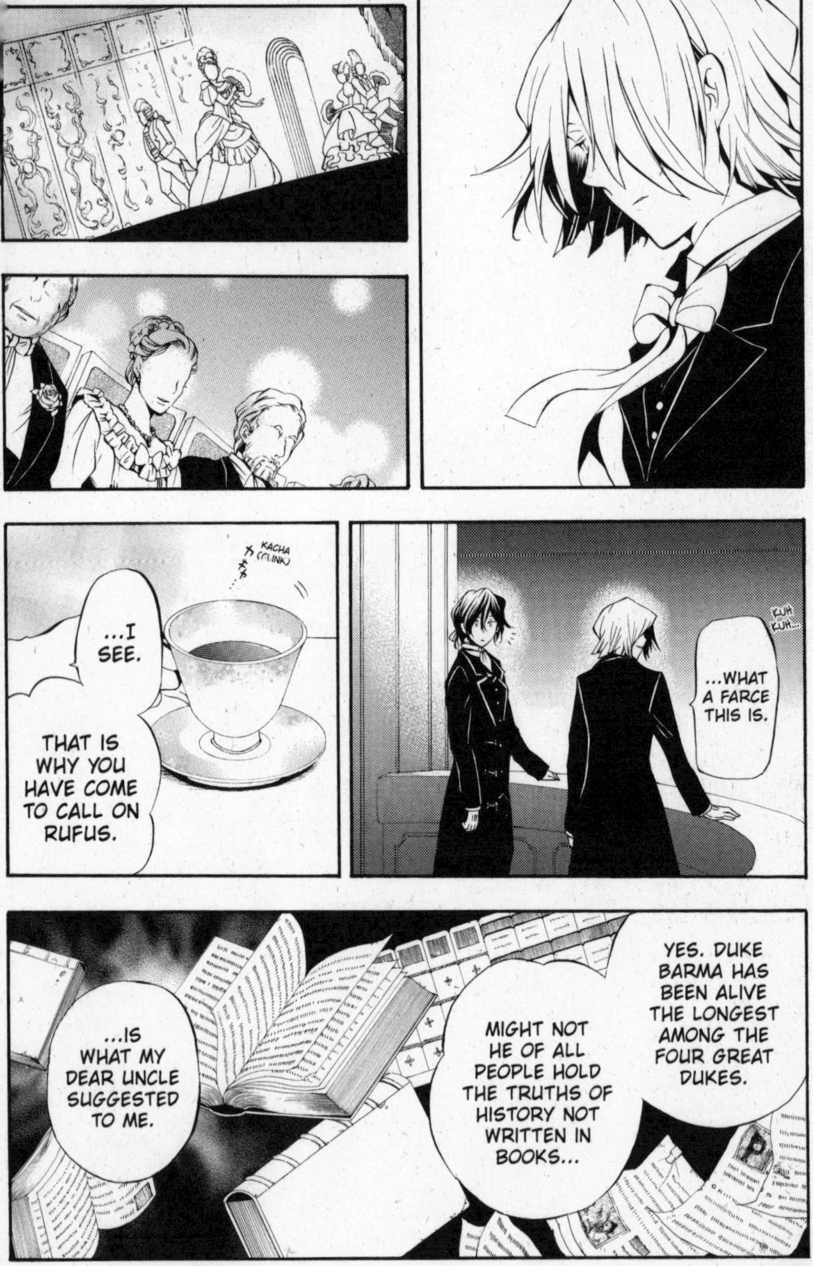
KUH KUH...
...WHAT A FARCE THIS IS.
KACHA (CLINK)
...I SEE.
THAT IS WHY YOU HAVE COME TO CALL ON RUFUS.
YES. DUKE BARMA HAS BEEN ALIVE THE LONGEST AMONG THE FOUR GREAT DUKES.
MIGHT NOT HE OF ALL PEOPLE HOLD THE TRUTHS OF HISTORY NOT WRITTEN IN BOOKS...
...IS WHAT MY DEAR UNCLE SUGGESTED TO ME.

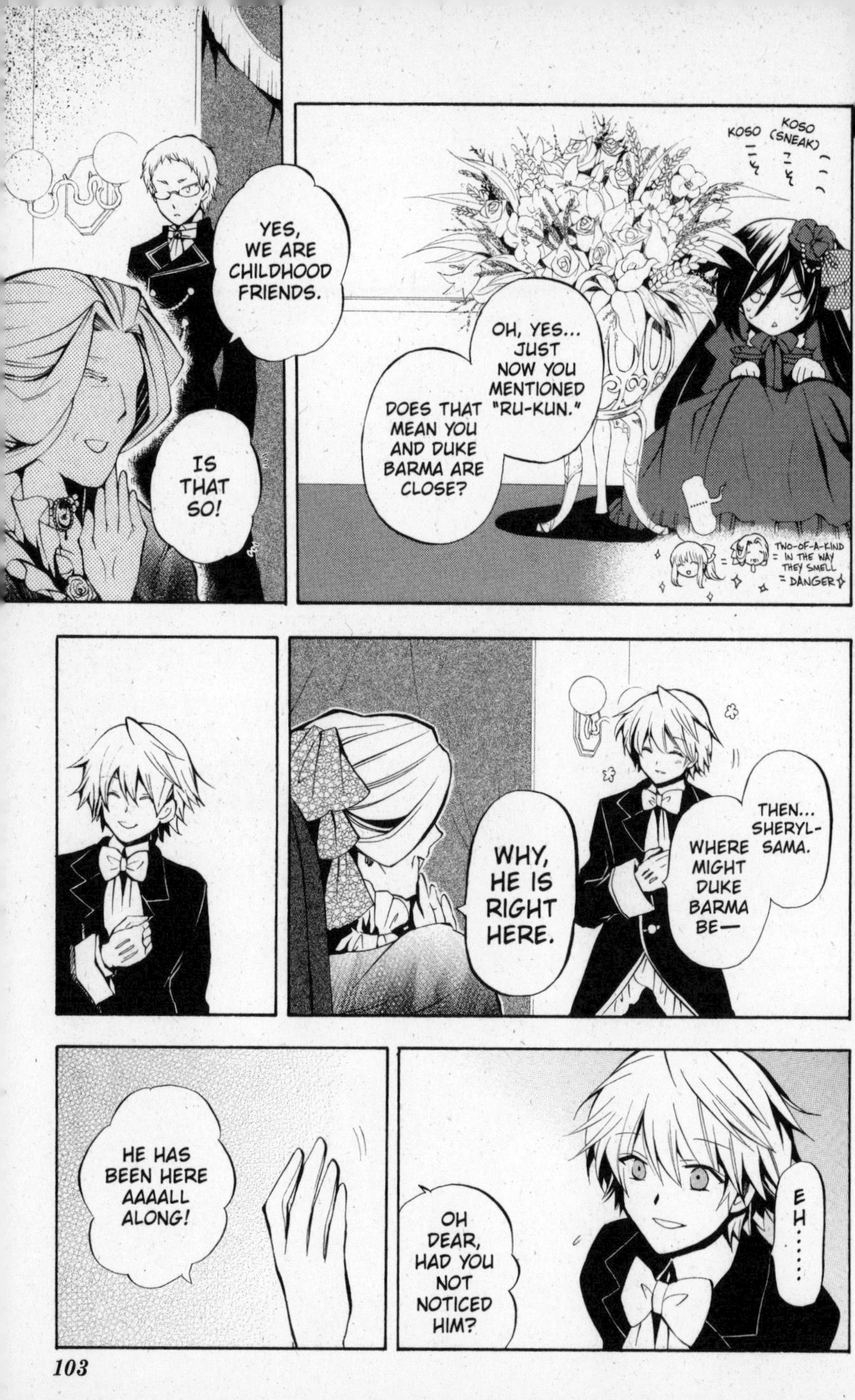
KOSO
KOSO (SNEAK)
OH, YES... JUST NOW YOU MENTIONED "RU-KUN."
DOES THAT MEAN YOU AND DUKE BARMA ARE CLOSE?
TWO-OF-A-KIND = IN THE WAY THEY SMELL = DANGER
YES, WE ARE CHILDHOOD FRIENDS.
IS THAT SO!
THEN... SHERYL-SAMA.
WHERE MIGHT DUKE BARMA BE—
WHY, HE IS RIGHT HERE.
EH......
OH DEAR, HAD YOU NOT NOTICED HIM?
HE HAS BEEN HERE AAAALL ALONG!

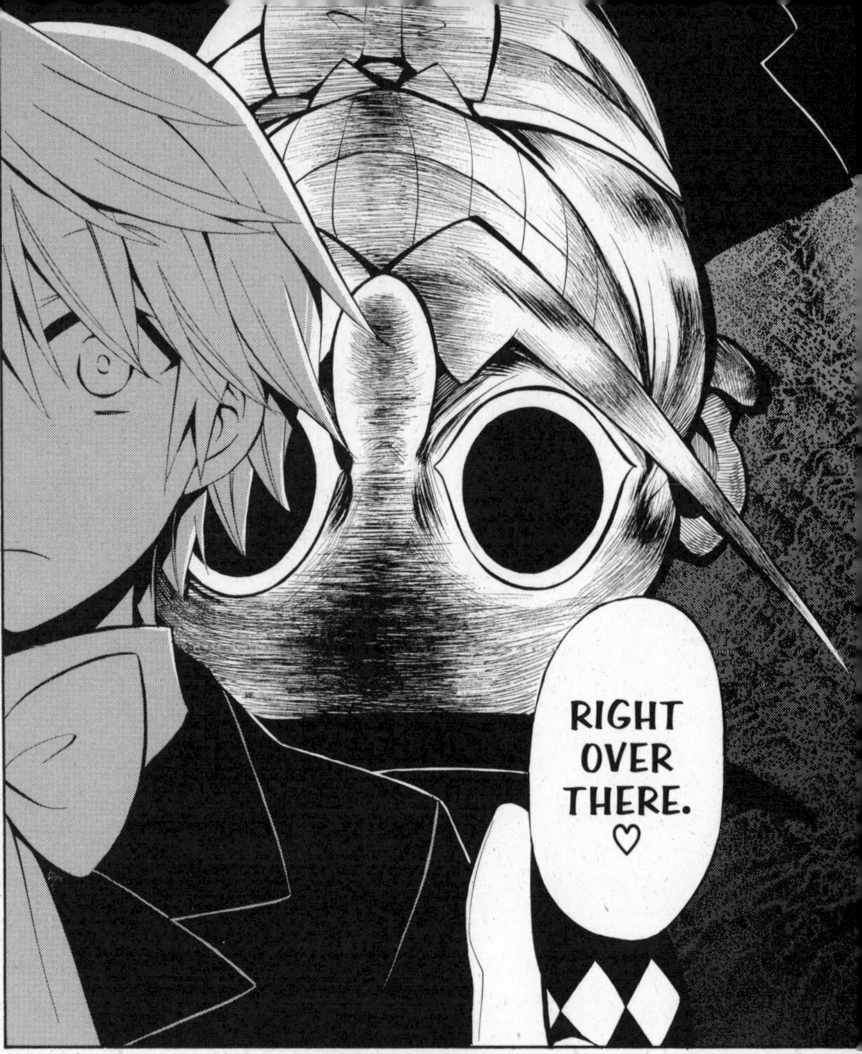
RIGHT OVER THERE. ♡

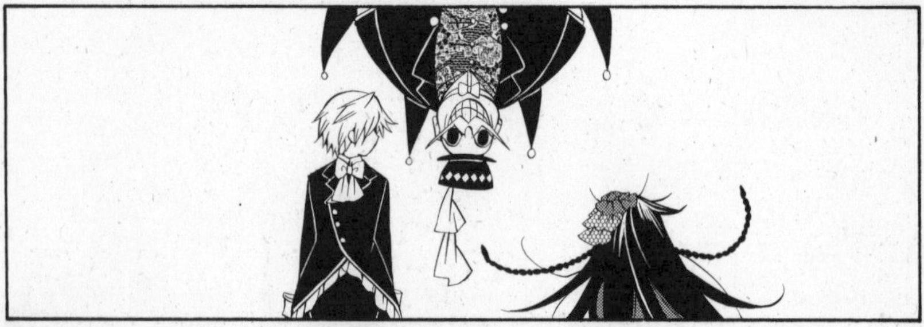

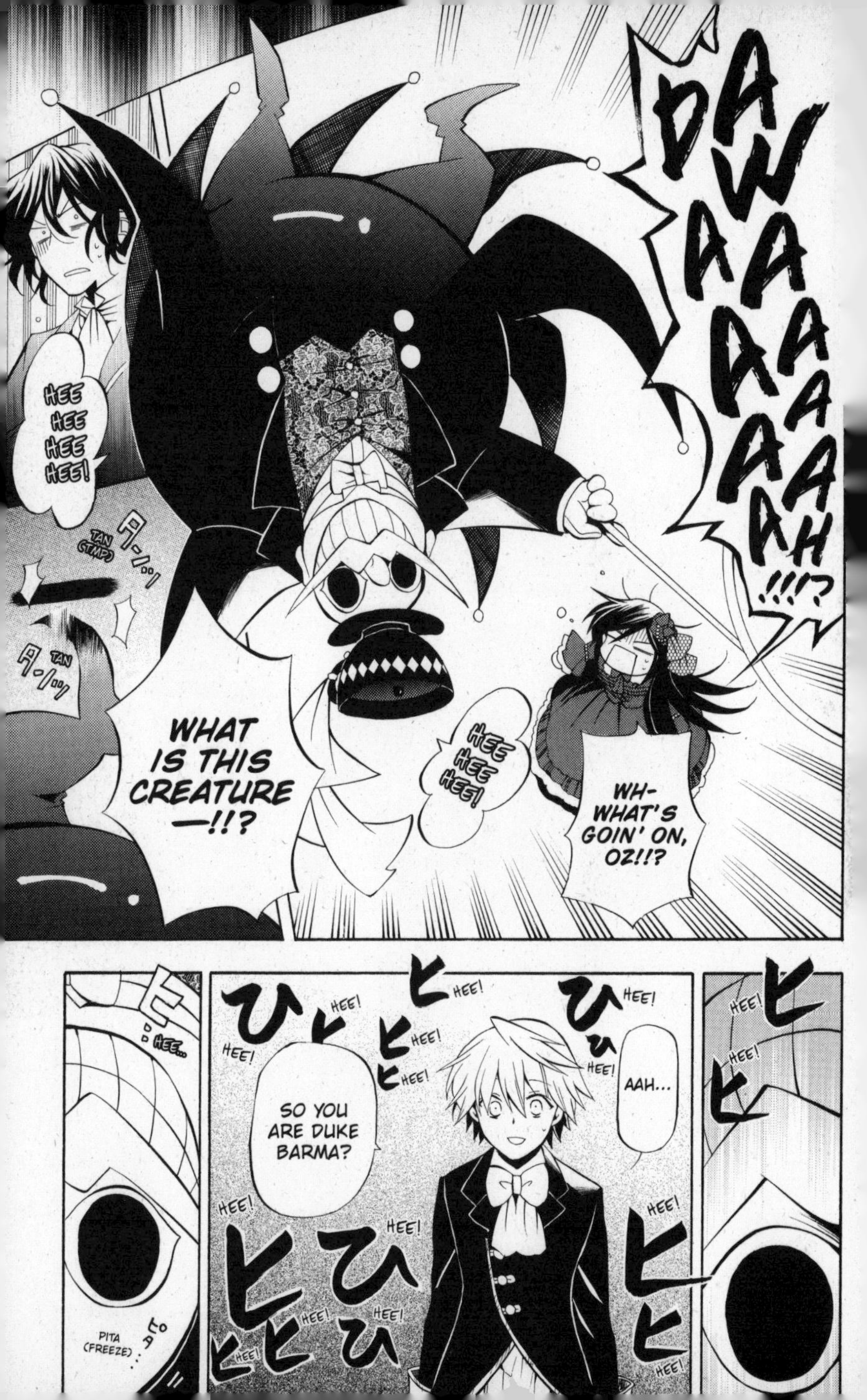
DAWAAAAAAAAAAH!!!?
WH-WHAT'S GOIN' ON, OZ!!?
HEE HEE HEE!
WHAT IS THIS CREATURE—!!?
HEE HEE HEE HEE!
TAN (TMP)
TAN
HEE!
HEE!
HEE!
HEE!
AAH...
HEE!
HEE!
HEE!
SO YOU ARE DUKE BARMA?
HEE!
HEE!
HEE!
HEE!
HEE!
HEE!
HEE!
HEE!
HEE...
PITA (FREEZE)

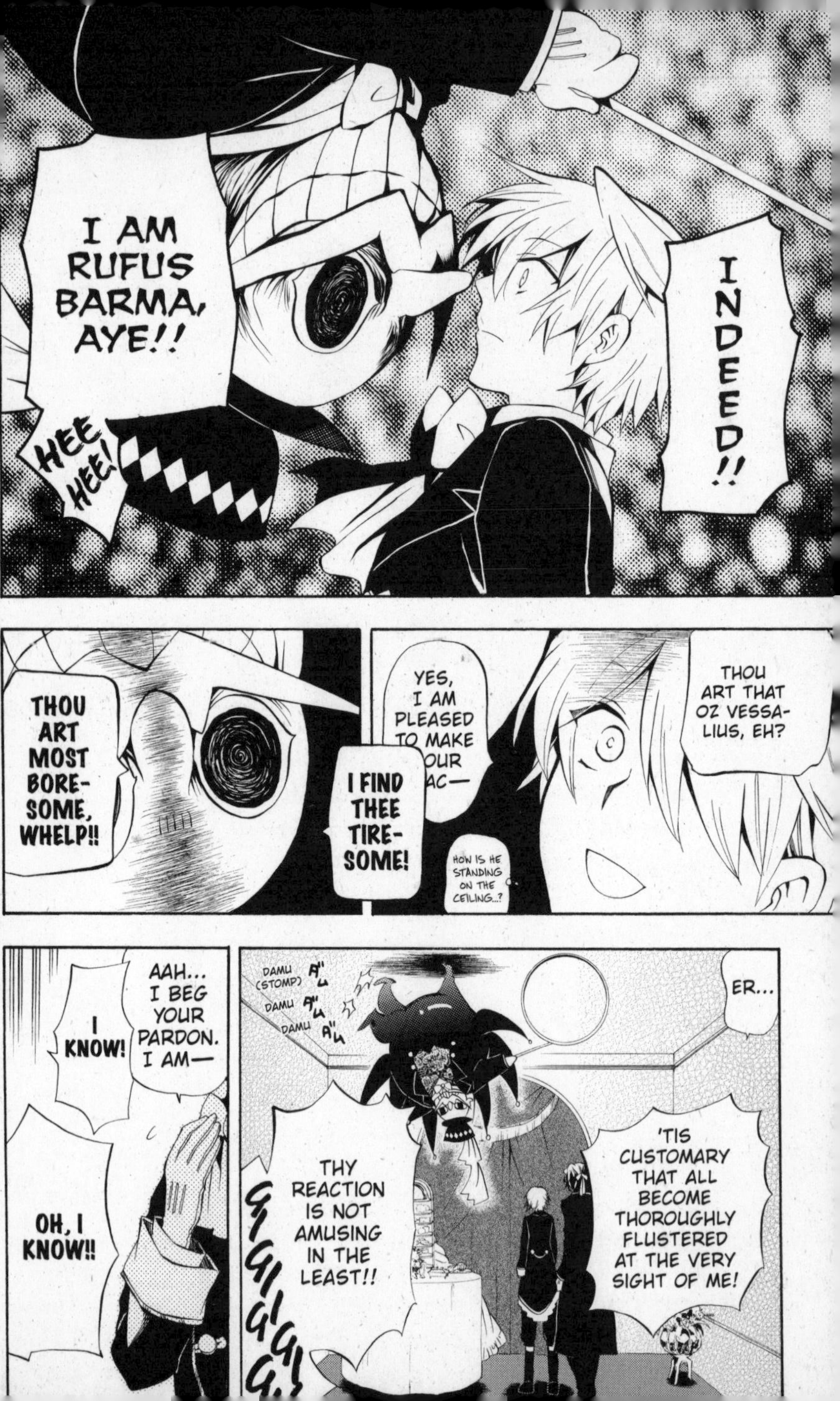
INDEED!!
I AM RUFUS BARMA, AYE!!
HEE HEE!
THOU ART THAT OZ VESSA-LIUS, EH?
YES, I AM PLEASED TO MAKE YOUR AC—
HOW IS HE STANDING ON THE CEILING...?
I FIND THEE TIRE-SOME!
THOU ART MOST BORE-SOME, WHELP!!
ER...
DAMU (STOMP)
DAMU
DAMU
'TIS CUSTOMARY THAT ALL BECOME THOROUGHLY FLUSTERED AT THE VERY SIGHT OF ME!
THY REACTION IS NOT AMUSING IN THE LEAST!!
AAH... I BEG YOUR PARDON. I AM—
I KNOW!
OH, I KNOW!!

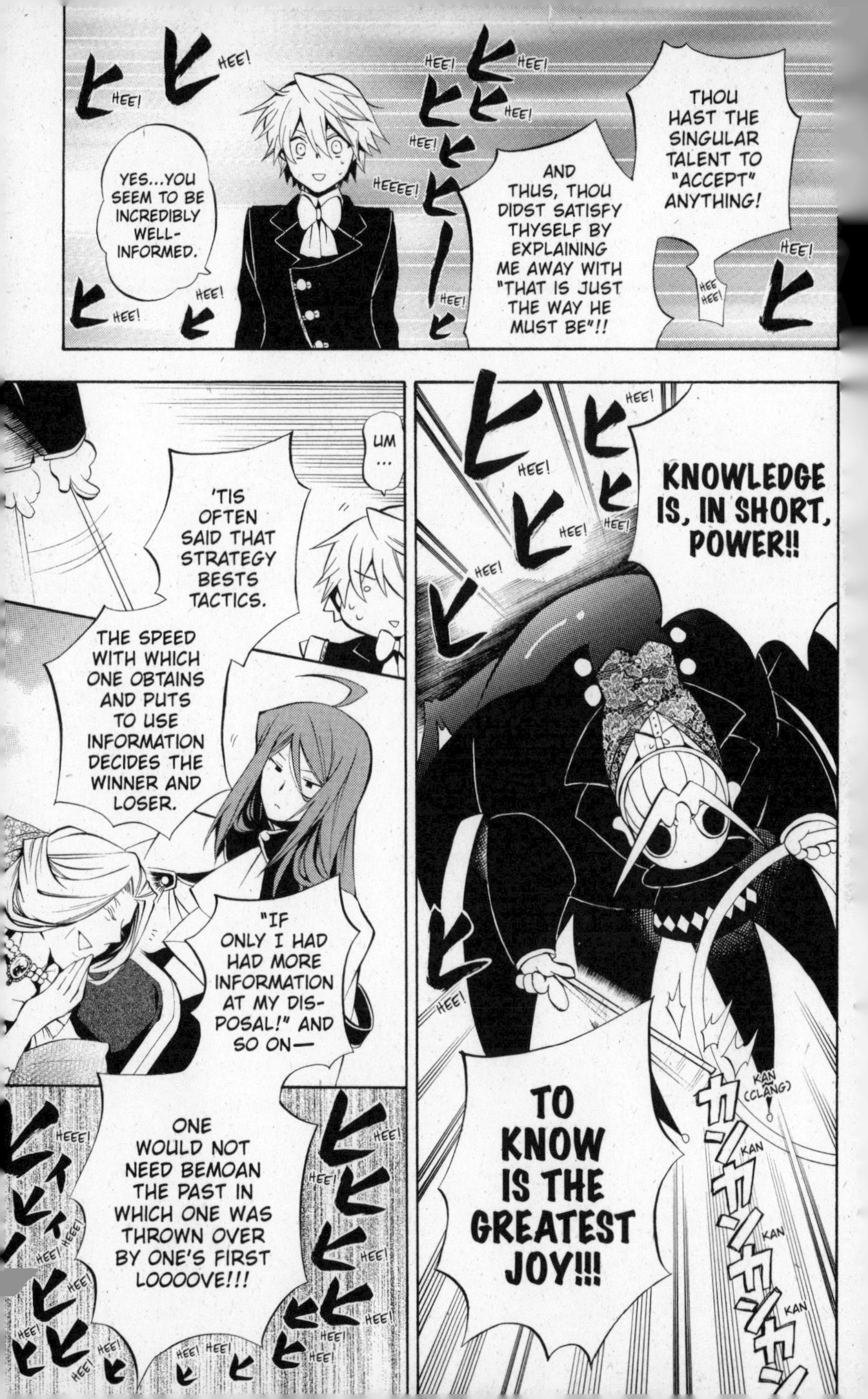
HEE!
THOU HAST THE SINGULAR TALENT TO "ACCEPT" ANYTHING!
HEE HEE!
HEE!
HEE!
HEEEE!
AND THUS, THOU DIDST SATISFY THYSELF BY EXPLAINING ME AWAY WITH "THAT IS JUST THE WAY HE MUST BE"!!
HEE!
HEE!
HEE!
YES...YOU SEEM TO BE INCREDIBLY WELL-INFORMED.
HEE!
HEE!
HEE!
KNOWLEDGE IS, IN SHORT, POWER!!
HEE!
HEE!
HEE!
HEE!
HEE!
HEE!
TO KNOW IS THE GREATEST JOY!!!
KAN (CLANG)
KAN
KAN
KAN
UM ...
'TIS OFTEN SAID THAT STRATEGY BESTS TACTICS.
THE SPEED WITH WHICH ONE OBTAINS AND PUTS TO USE INFORMATION DECIDES THE WINNER AND LOSER.
"IF ONLY I HAD HAD MORE INFORMATION AT MY DISPOSAL!" AND SO ON—
HEEE!
HEE!
HEE!
HEE!
HEE!
HEE!
ONE WOULD NOT NEED BEMOAN THE PAST IN WHICH ONE WAS THROWN OVER BY ONE'S FIRST LOOOOVE!!!
HEEE!
HEEE!
HEE!
HEE!
HEE!
HEE!
HEE!
HEE!

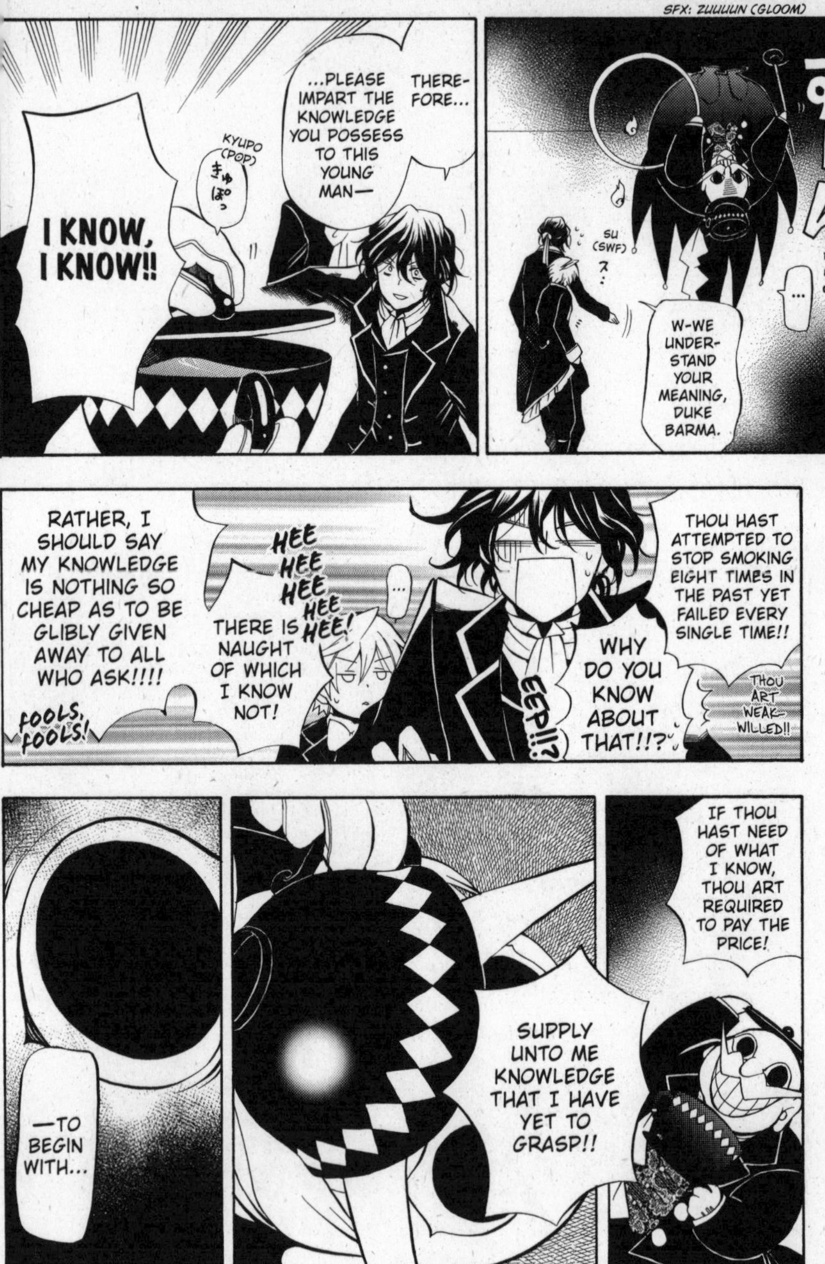
SFX: ZUUUUN (GLOOM)
ずーん…
…
W-WE UNDERSTAND YOUR MEANING, DUKE BARMA.
SU (SWF)
ス…
THEREFORE…
…PLEASE IMPART THE KNOWLEDGE YOU POSSESS TO THIS YOUNG MAN—
KYUPO (POP)
きゅぽっ
I KNOW, I KNOW!!
THOU HAST ATTEMPTED TO STOP SMOKING EIGHT TIMES IN THE PAST YET FAILED EVERY SINGLE TIME!!
THOU ART WEAK-WILLED!!
WHY DO YOU KNOW ABOUT THAT!!?
EEP!!?
…
HEE HEE HEE HEE HEE!
THERE IS NAUGHT OF WHICH I KNOW NOT!
RATHER, I SHOULD SAY MY KNOWLEDGE IS NOTHING SO CHEAP AS TO BE GLIBLY GIVEN AWAY TO ALL WHO ASK!!!!
FOOLS, FOOLS!
IF THOU HAST NEED OF WHAT I KNOW, THOU ART REQUIRED TO PAY THE PRICE!
SUPPLY UNTO ME KNOWLEDGE THAT I HAVE YET TO GRASP!!
—TO BEGIN WITH…

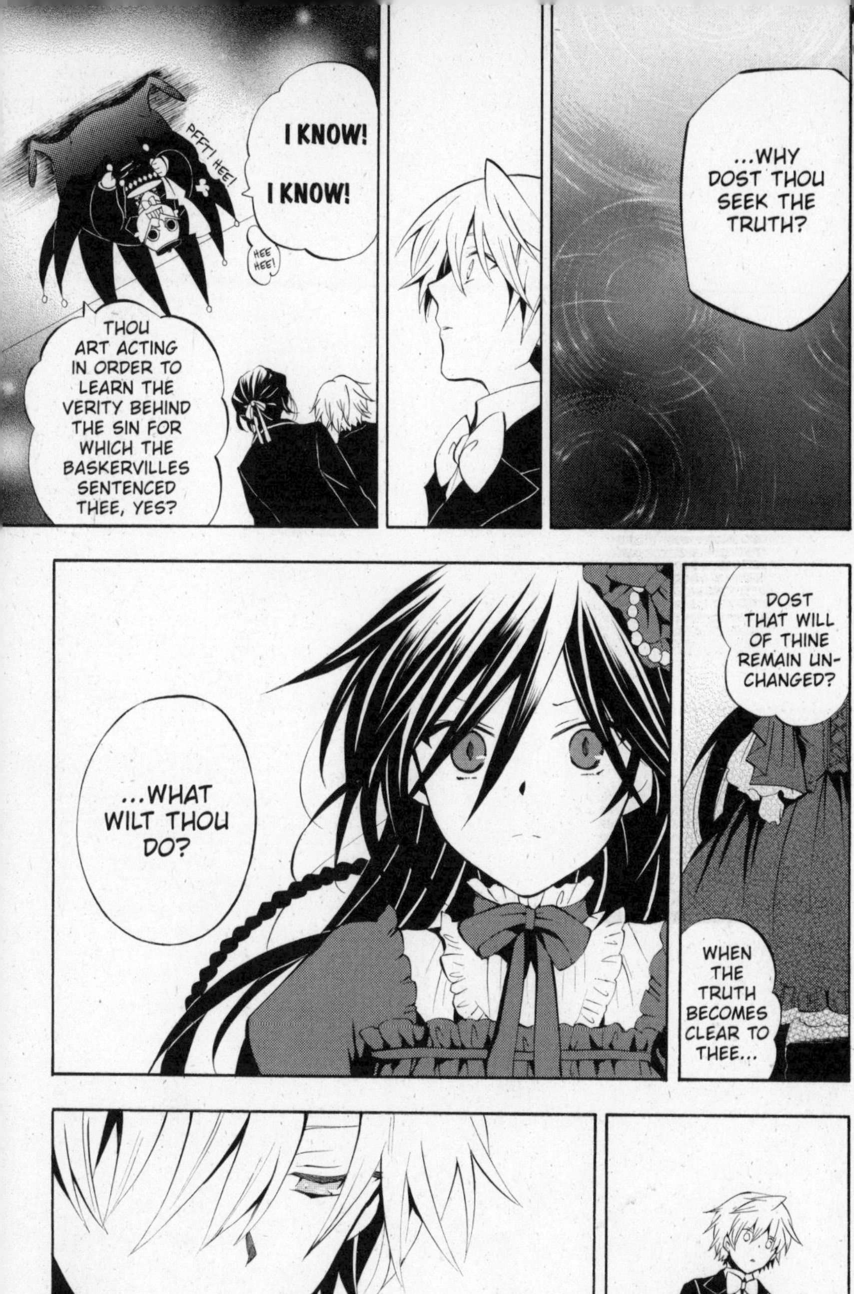
...WHY DOST THOU SEEK THE TRUTH?
I KNOW!
I KNOW!
PFFT! HEE!
HEE HEE!
THOU ART ACTING IN ORDER TO LEARN THE VERITY BEHIND THE SIN FOR WHICH THE BASKERVILLES SENTENCED THEE, YES?
DOST THAT WILL OF THINE REMAIN UN-CHANGED?
WHEN THE TRUTH BECOMES CLEAR TO THEE...
...WHAT WILT THOU DO?

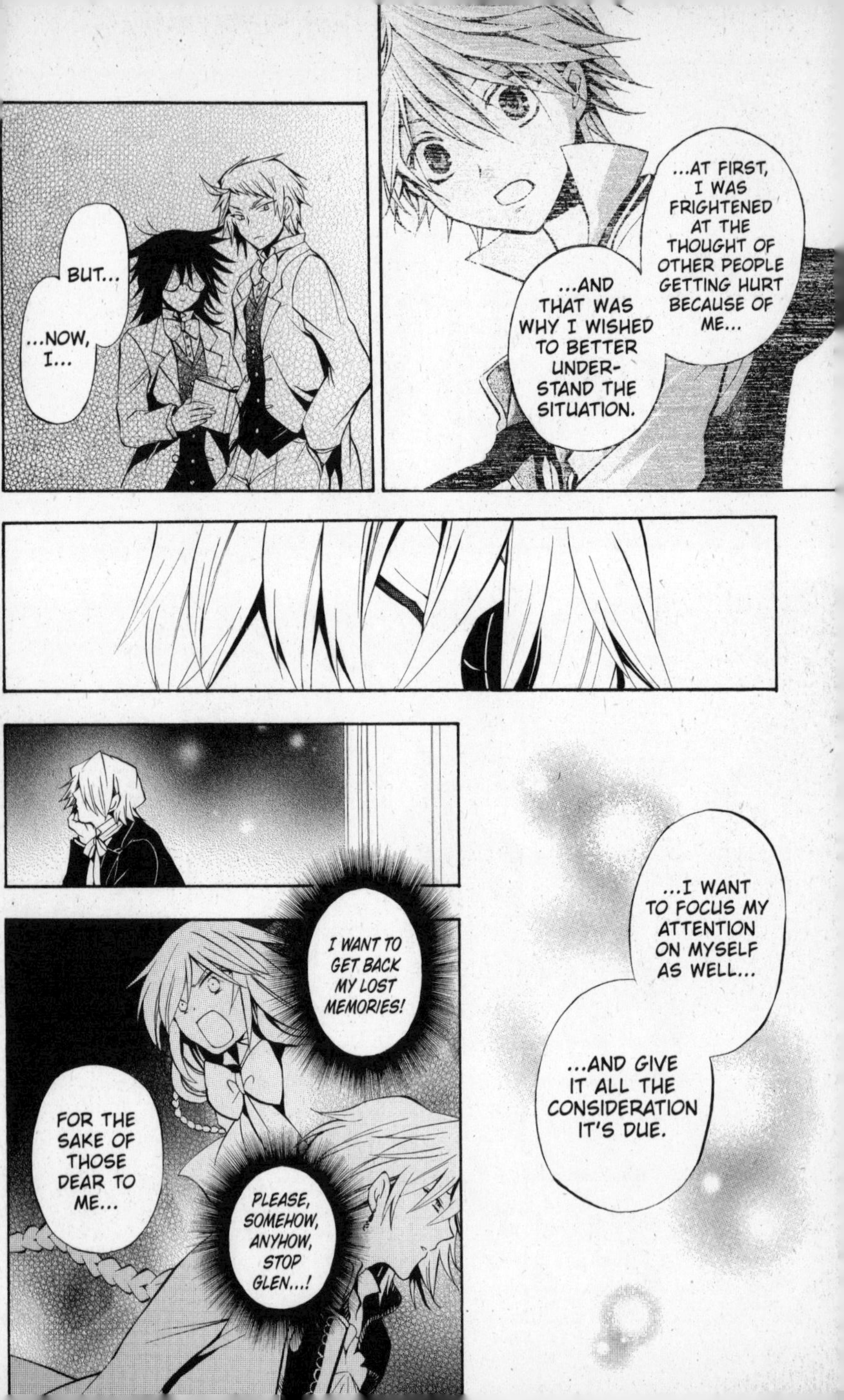
...AT FIRST, I WAS FRIGHTENED AT THE THOUGHT OF OTHER PEOPLE GETTING HURT BECAUSE OF ME...
...AND THAT WAS WHY I WISHED TO BETTER UNDER-STAND THE SITUATION.
BUT...
...NOW, I...
...I WANT TO FOCUS MY ATTENTION ON MYSELF AS WELL...
...AND GIVE IT ALL THE CONSIDERATION IT'S DUE.
I WANT TO GET BACK MY LOST MEMORIES!
FOR THE SAKE OF THOSE DEAR TO ME...
PLEASE, SOMEHOW, ANYHOW, STOP GLEN...!

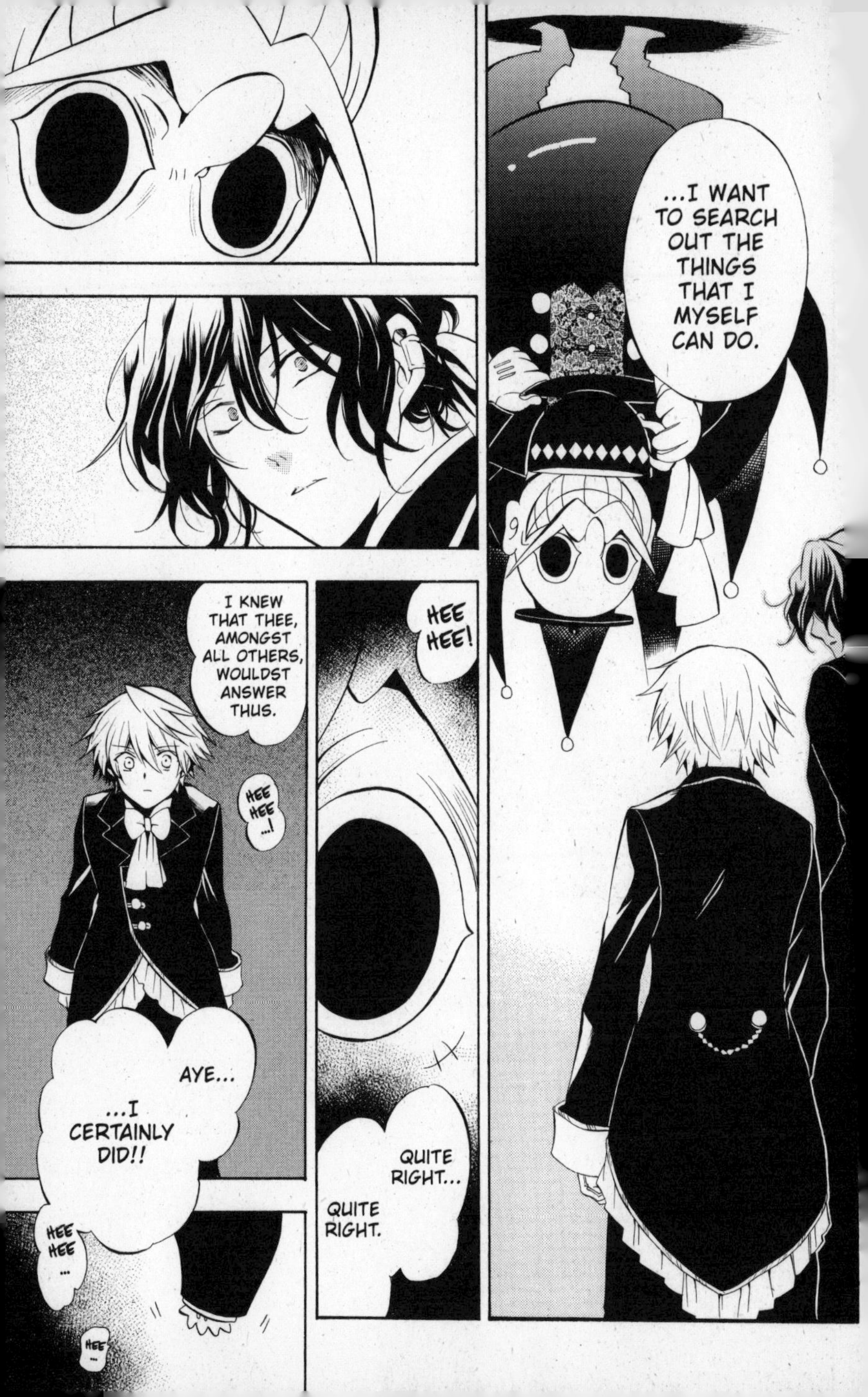
...I WANT TO SEARCH OUT THE THINGS THAT I MYSELF CAN DO.
HEE HEE!
I KNEW THAT THEE, AMONGST ALL OTHERS, WOULDST ANSWER THUS.
HEE HEE ...!
QUITE RIGHT...
QUITE RIGHT.
AYE...
...I CERTAINLY DID!!
HEE HEE ...
HEE ...

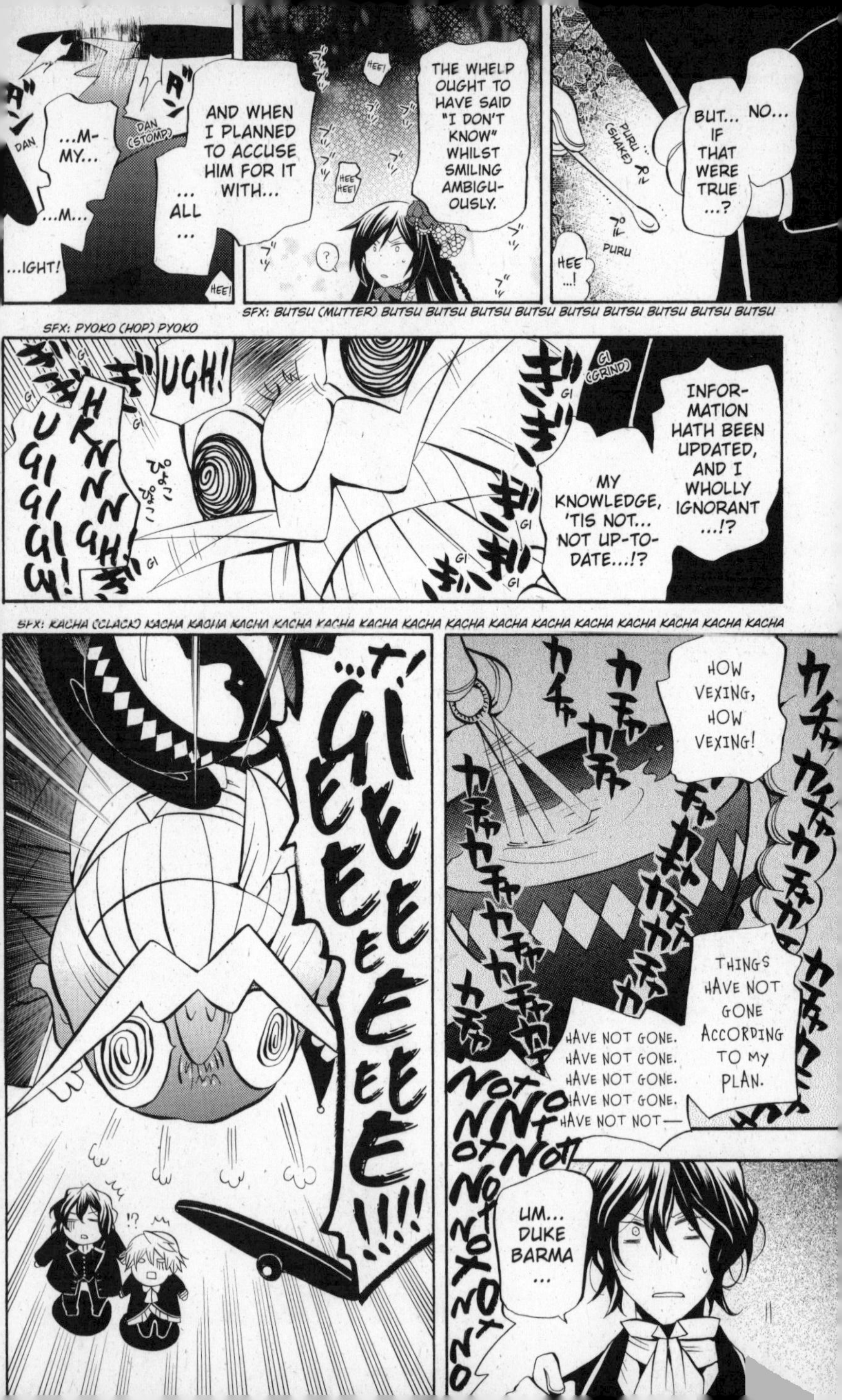
NO...
BUT... IF THAT WERE TRUE ...?
PURU (SHAKE)
PURU
HEE ...!
THE WHELP OUGHT TO HAVE SAID "I DON'T KNOW" WHILST SMILING AMBIGUOUSLY.
HEE!
HEE HEE!
?
AND WHEN I PLANNED TO ACCUSE HIM FOR IT WITH...
... ALL ...
DAN (STOMP)
...M-MY...
DAN
...M...
...IGHT!
HEE!
SFX: BUTSU (MUTTER) BUTSU BUTSU BUTSU BUTSU BUTSU BUTSU BUTSU BUTSU BUTSU
SFX: PYOKO (HOP) PYOKO
INFORMATION HATH BEEN UPDATED, AND I WHOLLY IGNORANT ...!?
MY KNOWLEDGE, 'TIS NOT... NOT UP-TO-DATE...!?
GI (GRIND)
GI
GI
GI
GI
UGH!
HRNNNNGH!
UGIGIGIGI!
SFX: KACHA (CLACK) KACHA KACHA KACHA KACHA KACHA KACHA KACHA KACHA KACHA KACHA KACHA KACHA KACHA KACHA KACHA
HOW VEXING, HOW VEXING!
THINGS HAVE NOT GONE ACCORDING TO MY PLAN.
HAVE NOT GONE. HAVE NOT GONE. HAVE NOT GONE. HAVE NOT GONE. HAVE NOT NOT—
NOT NOT NOT NOT NOT NOT NOT NOT NOT NO
UM... DUKE BARMA ...
...T! GIEEEEEEEEEEE!!!
!?

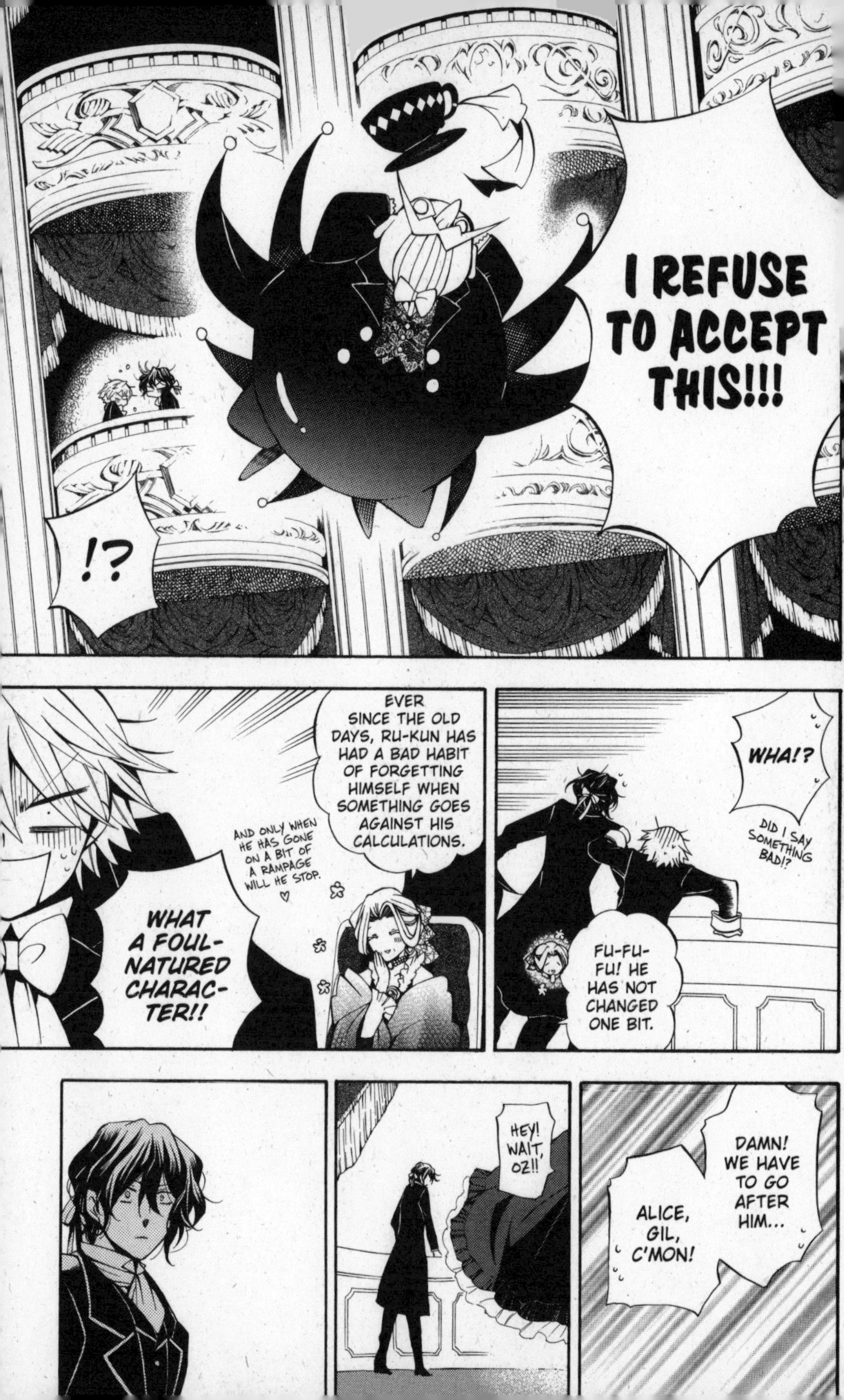
I REFUSE TO ACCEPT THIS!!!
!?
WHA!?
DID I SAY SOMETHING BAD!?
FU-FU-FU! HE HAS NOT CHANGED ONE BIT.
EVER SINCE THE OLD DAYS, RU-KUN HAS HAD A BAD HABIT OF FORGETTING HIMSELF WHEN SOMETHING GOES AGAINST HIS CALCULATIONS.
AND ONLY WHEN HE HAS GONE ON A BIT OF A RAMPAGE WILL HE STOP. ♥
WHAT A FOUL-NATURED CHARACTER!!
DAMN! WE HAVE TO GO AFTER HIM...
ALICE, GIL, C'MON!
HEY! WAIT, OZ!!

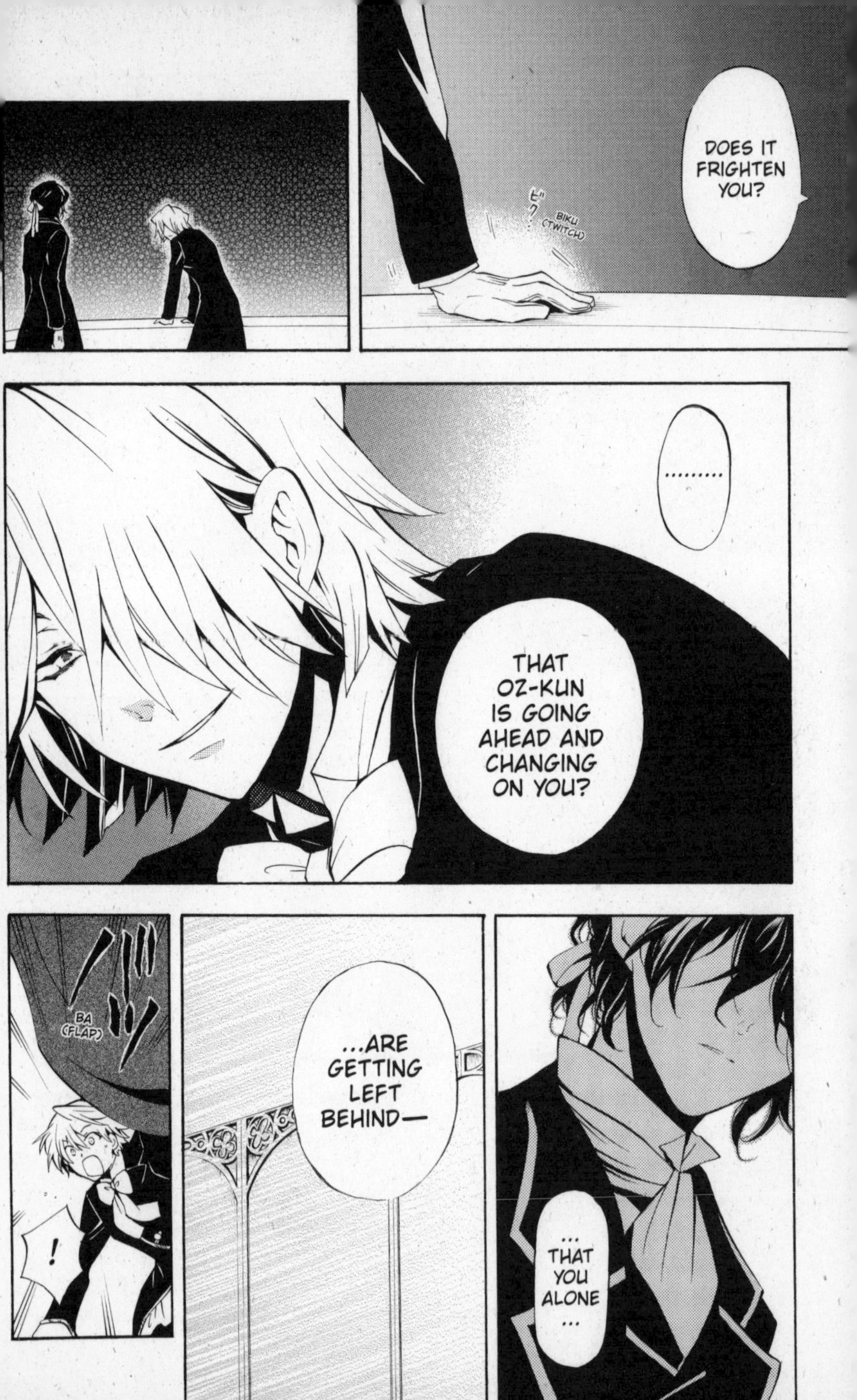
DOES IT FRIGHTEN YOU?
BIKU (TWITCH)
....
THAT OZ-KUN IS GOING AHEAD AND CHANGING ON YOU?
... THAT YOU ALONE ...
...ARE GETTING LEFT BEHIND—
BA (FLAP)
!

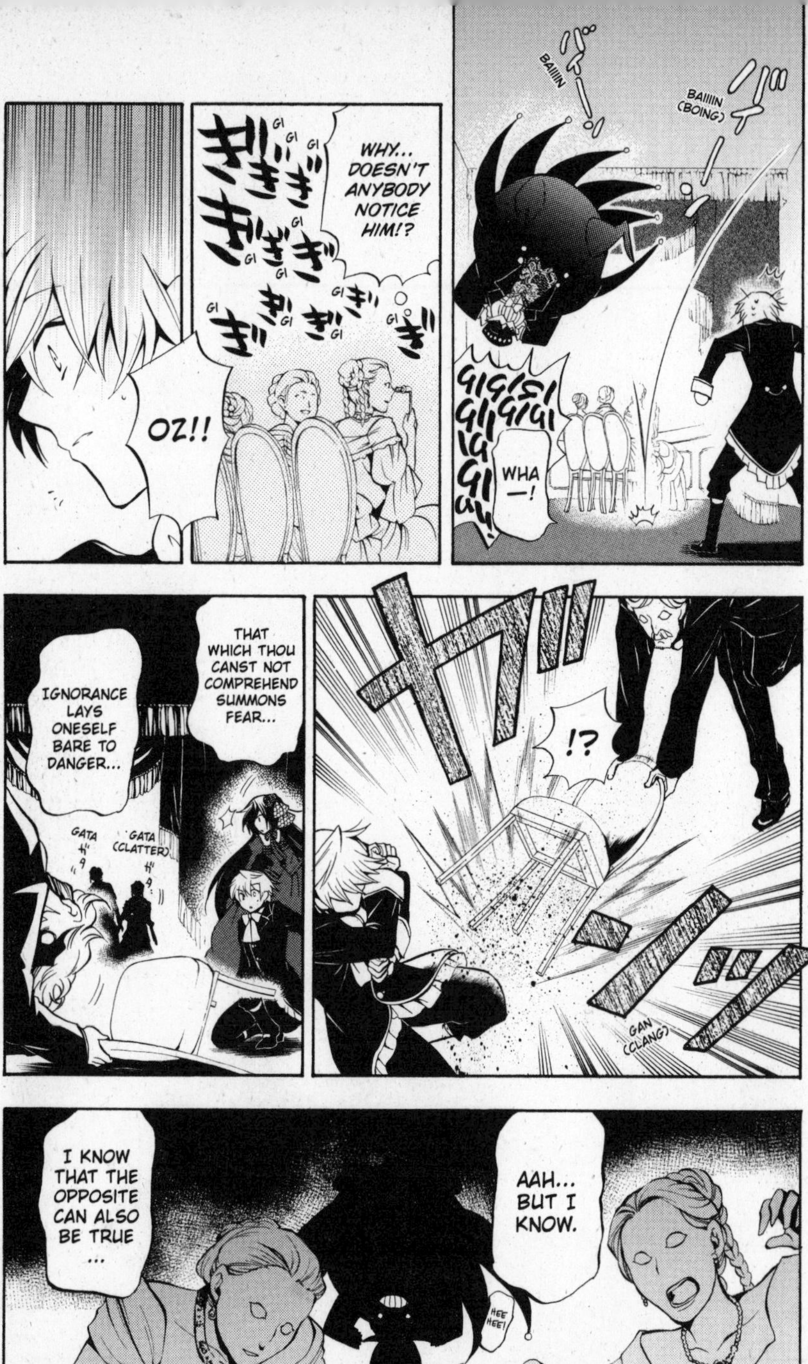
BAIIIN
BAIIIN (BOING)
GIGIGIGIGIGIGIGIGIGIGIGIGIGI!
WHA—!
GI GI GI GI GI GI GI GI GI GI GI GI GI
WHY... DOESN'T ANYBODY NOTICE HIM!?
OZ!!
!?
GAN (CLANG)
THAT WHICH THOU CANST NOT COMPREHEND SUMMONS FEAR...
IGNORANCE LAYS ONESELF BARE TO DANGER...
GATA
GATA (CLATTER)
AAH... BUT I KNOW.
HEE HEE!
I KNOW THAT THE OPPOSITE CAN ALSO BE TRUE...

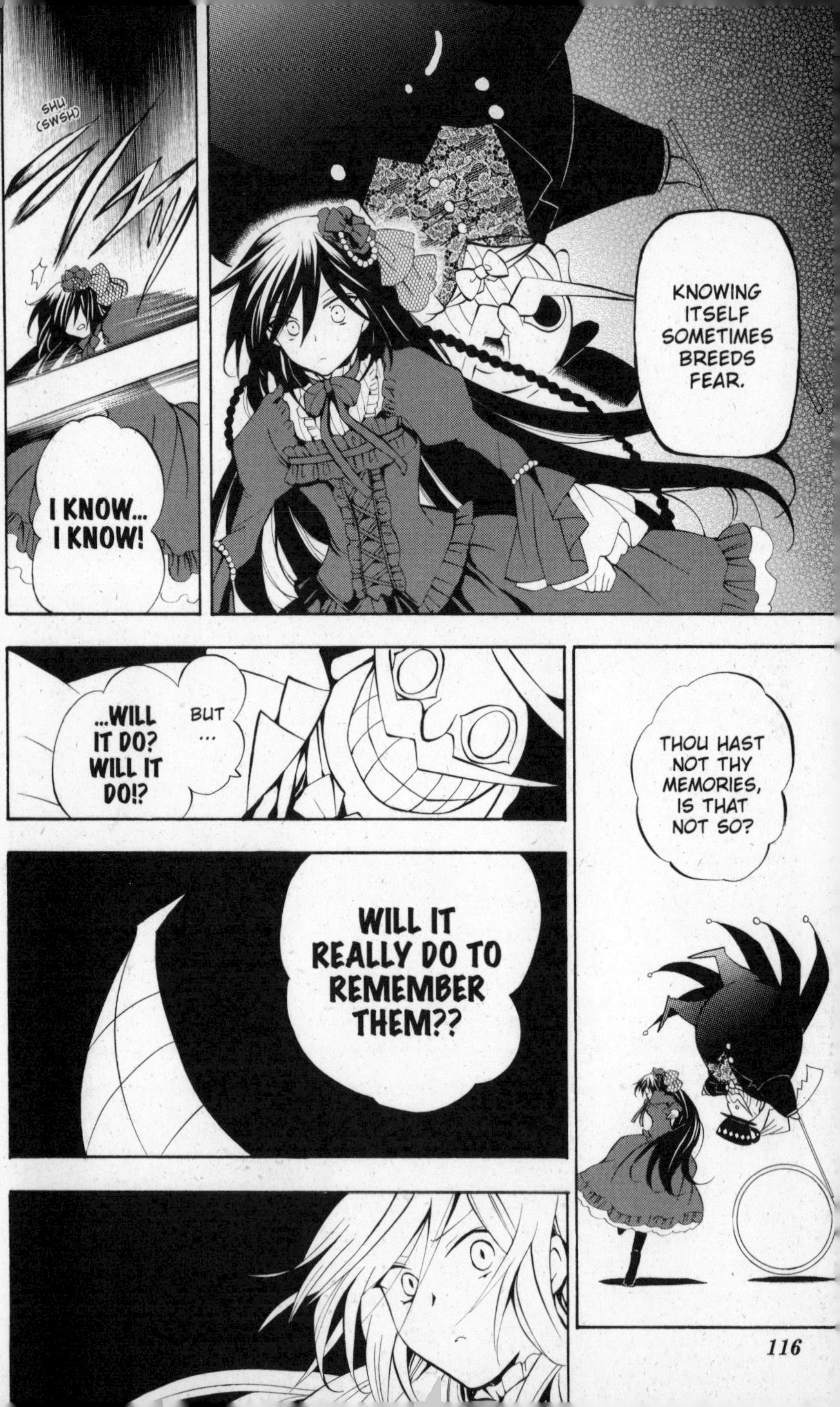
KNOWING ITSELF SOMETIMES BREEDS FEAR.
SHU (SWSH)
I KNOW... I KNOW!
THOU HAST NOT THY MEMORIES, IS THAT NOT SO?
BUT ...
...WILL IT DO? WILL IT DO!?
WILL IT REALLY DO TO REMEMBER THEM??

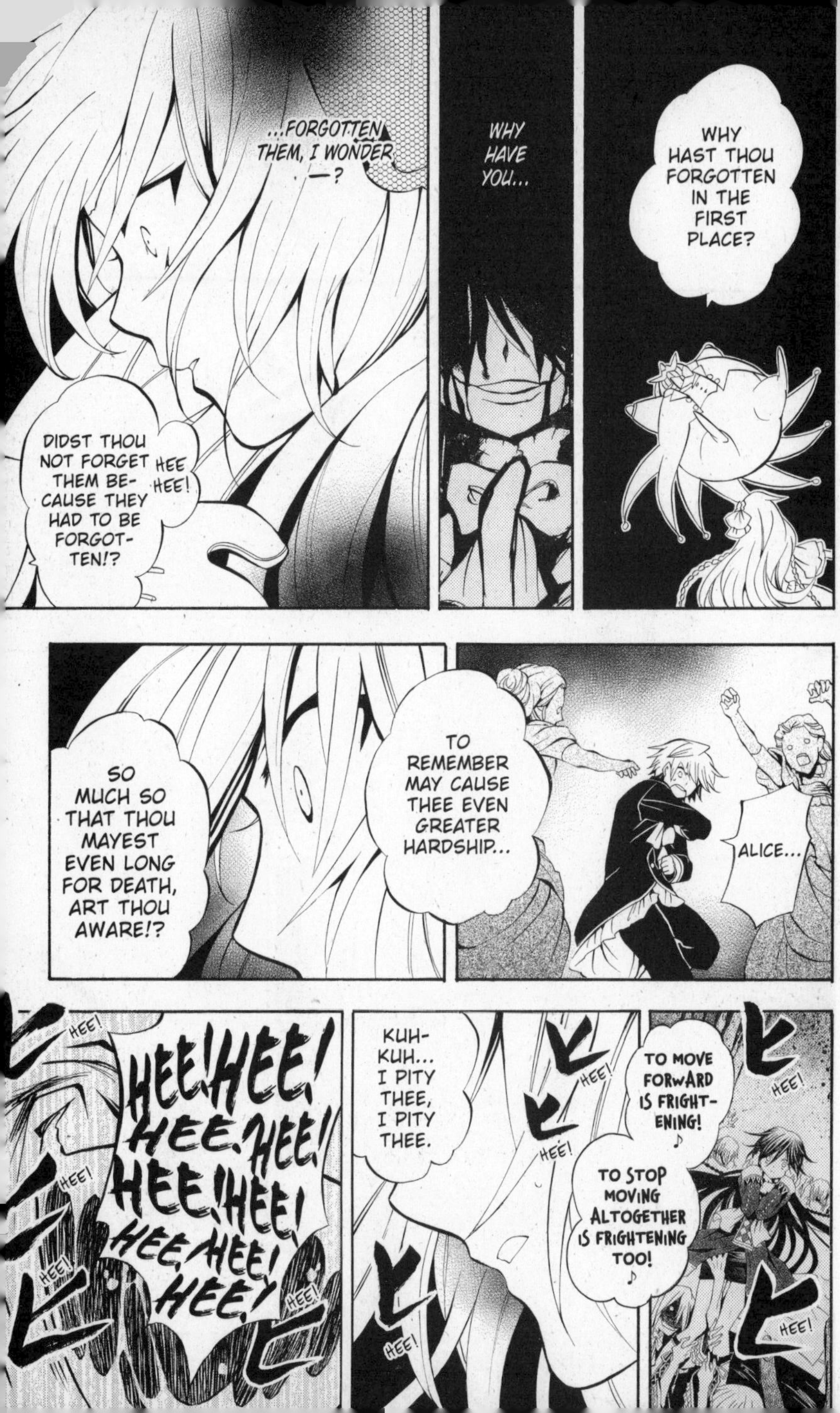
WHY HAST THOU FORGOTTEN IN THE FIRST PLACE?
WHY HAVE YOU...
...FORGOTTEN THEM, I WONDER —?
DIDST THOU NOT FORGET THEM BECAUSE THEY HAD TO BE FORGOTTEN!?
HEE HEE!
ALICE...
TO REMEMBER MAY CAUSE THEE EVEN GREATER HARDSHIP...
SO MUCH SO THAT THOU MAYEST EVEN LONG FOR DEATH, ART THOU AWARE!?
HEE!
TO MOVE FORWARD IS FRIGHTENING! ♪
TO STOP MOVING ALTOGETHER IS FRIGHTENING TOO! ♪
HEE!
KUH-KUH... I PITY THEE, I PITY THEE.
HEE!
HEE!
HEE!
HEE!
HEE! HEE! HEE! HEE! HEE! HEE! HEE! HEE! HEE!
HEE!
HEE!
HEE!

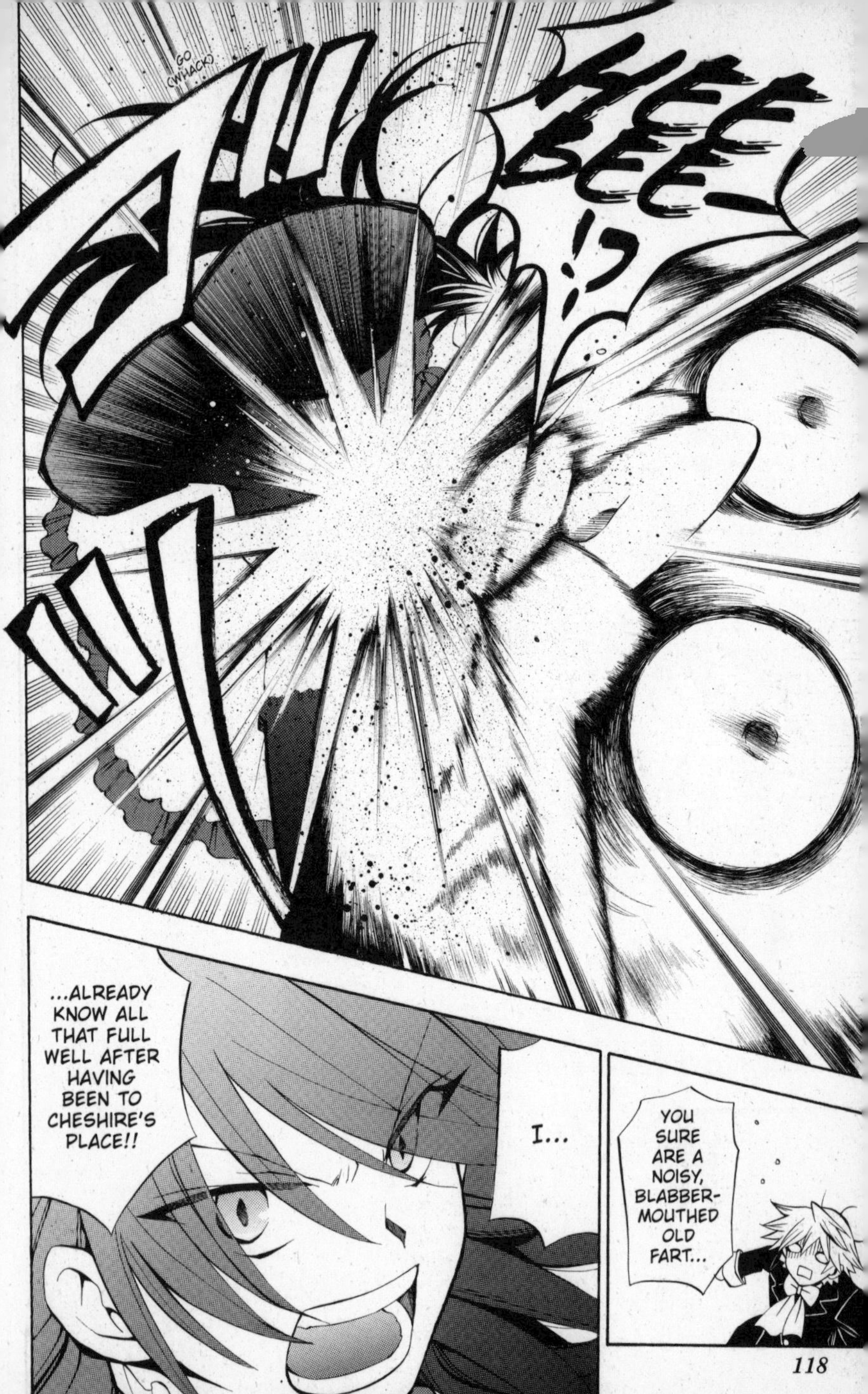
GO (WHACK)
HEE BEE-!?
YOU SURE ARE A NOISY, BLABBER-MOUTHED OLD FART...
I...
...ALREADY KNOW ALL THAT FULL WELL AFTER HAVING BEEN TO CHESHIRE'S PLACE!!

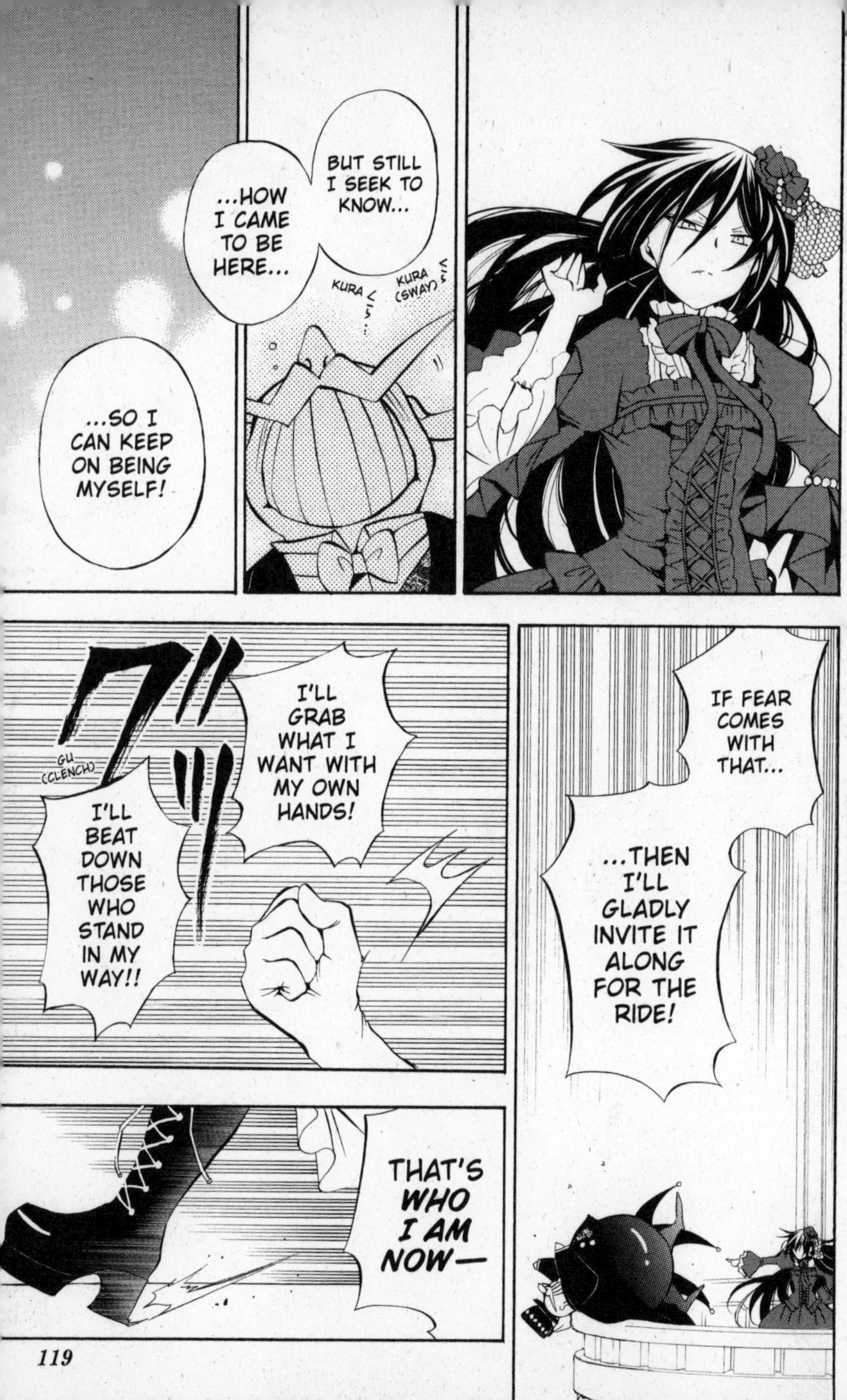
BUT STILL I SEEK TO KNOW...
...HOW I CAME TO BE HERE...
KURA
KURA (SWAY)
...SO I CAN KEEP ON BEING MYSELF!
IF FEAR COMES WITH THAT...
...THEN I'LL GLADLY INVITE IT ALONG FOR THE RIDE!
I'LL GRAB WHAT I WANT WITH MY OWN HANDS!
GU (CLENCH)
I'LL BEAT DOWN THOSE WHO STAND IN MY WAY!!
THAT'S *WHO I AM NOW*—

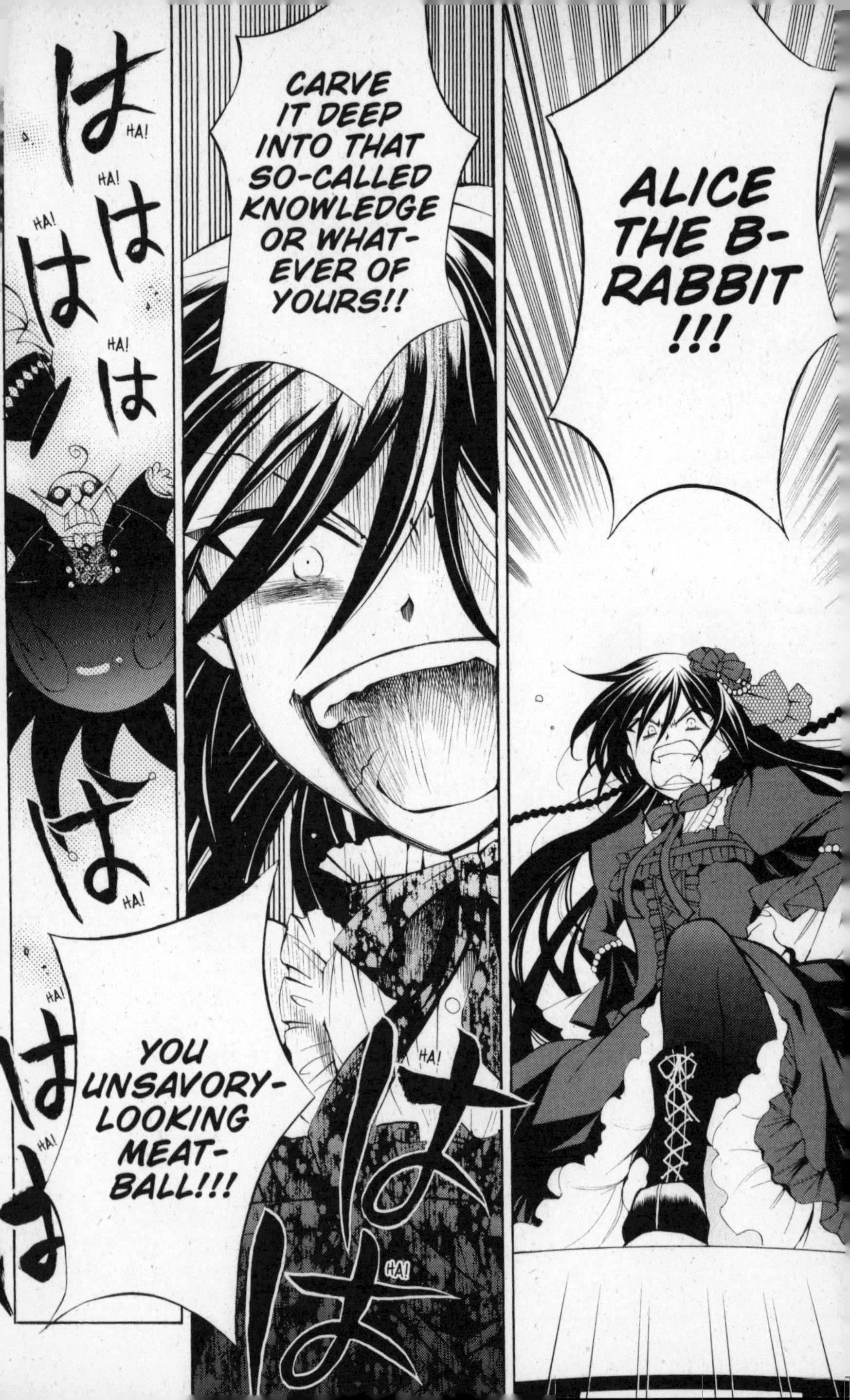
ALICE THE B-RABBIT!!!
CARVE IT DEEP INTO THAT SO-CALLED KNOWLEDGE OR WHATEVER OF YOURS!!
HA! HA! HA! HA! HA!
YOU UNSAVORY-LOOKING MEATBALL!!!
HA! HA!
HA! HA!

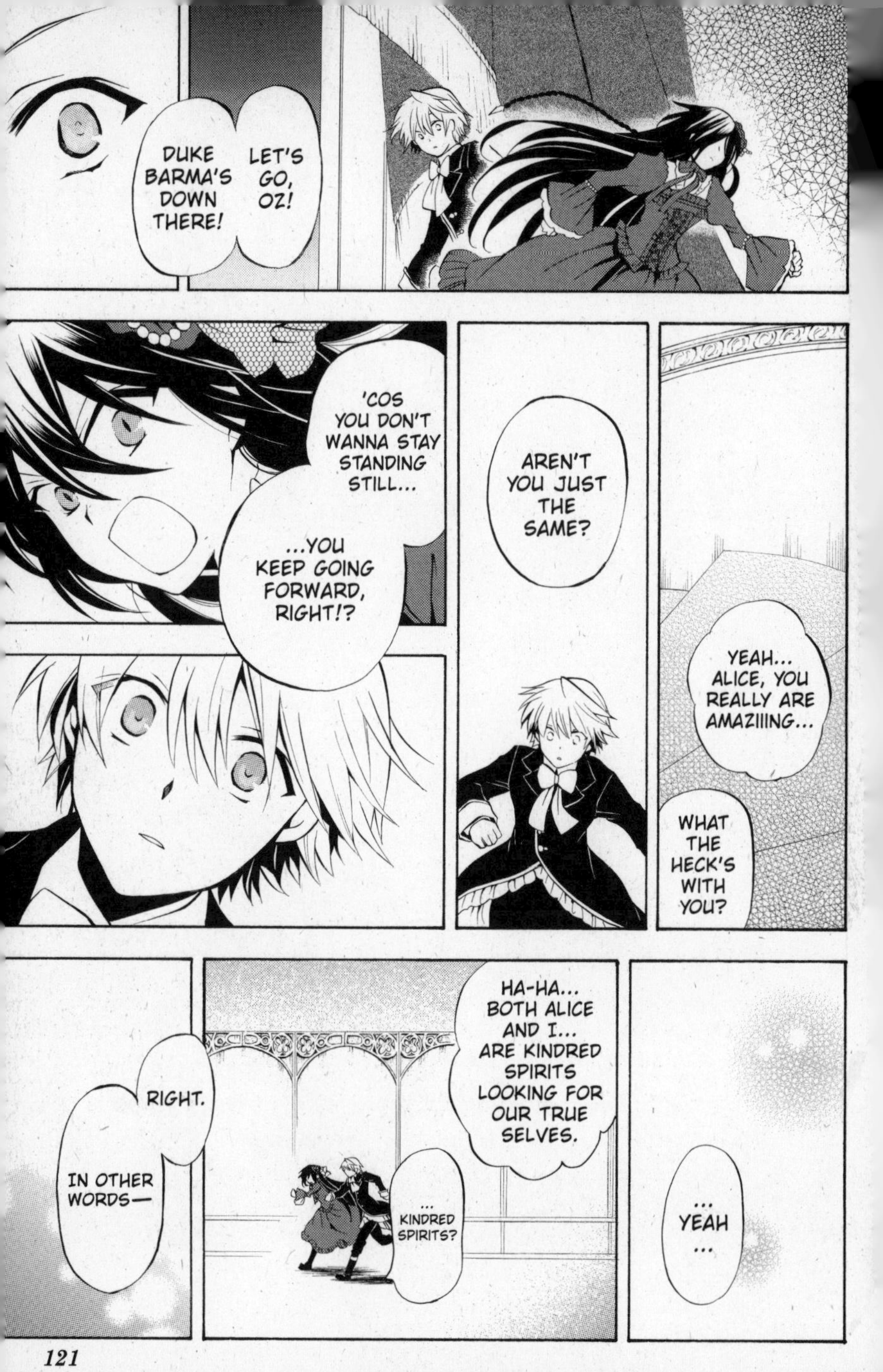
LET'S GO, OZ!
DUKE BARMA'S DOWN THERE!
YEAH... ALICE, YOU REALLY ARE AMAZIIING...
WHAT THE HECK'S WITH YOU?
AREN'T YOU JUST THE SAME?
'COS YOU DON'T WANNA STAY STANDING STILL...
...YOU KEEP GOING FORWARD, RIGHT!?
... YEAH ...
HA-HA... BOTH ALICE AND I... ARE KINDRED SPIRITS LOOKING FOR OUR TRUE SELVES.
... KINDRED SPIRITS?
RIGHT.
IN OTHER WORDS—

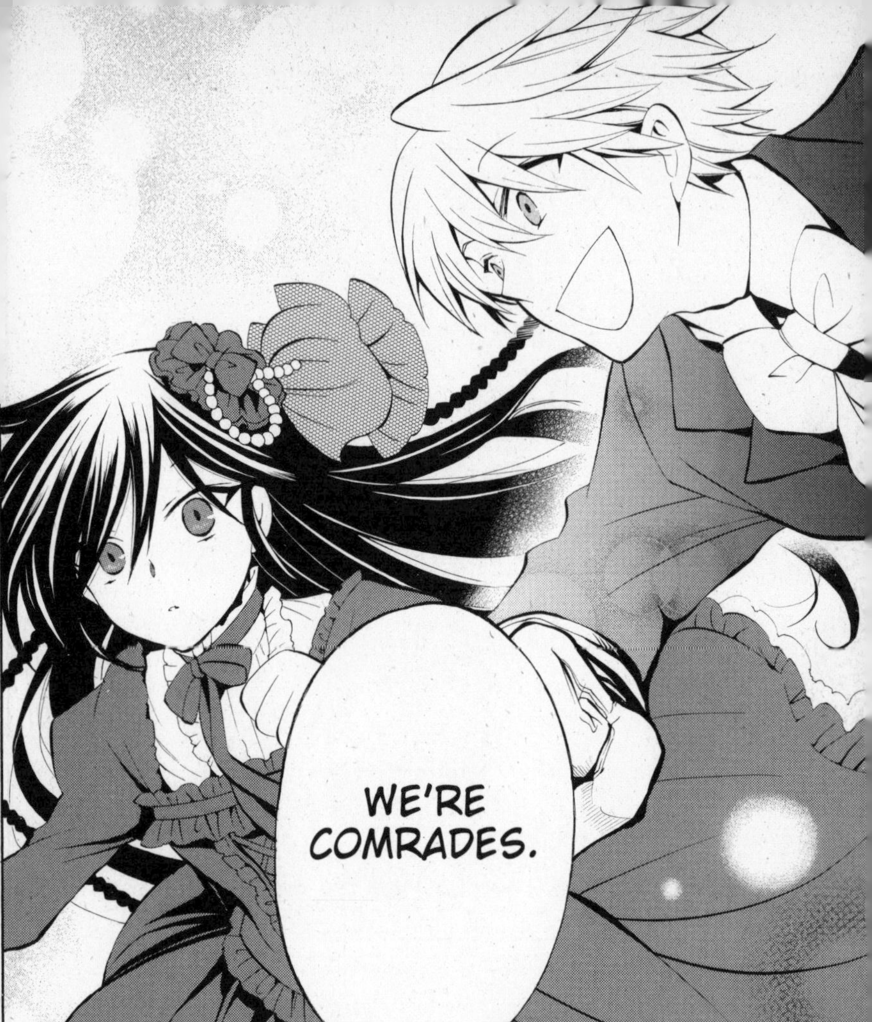
WE'RE COMRADES.
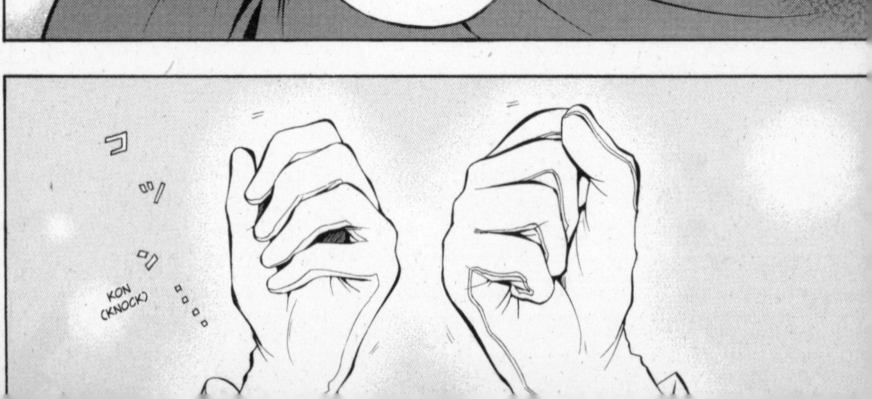
KON (KNOCK)

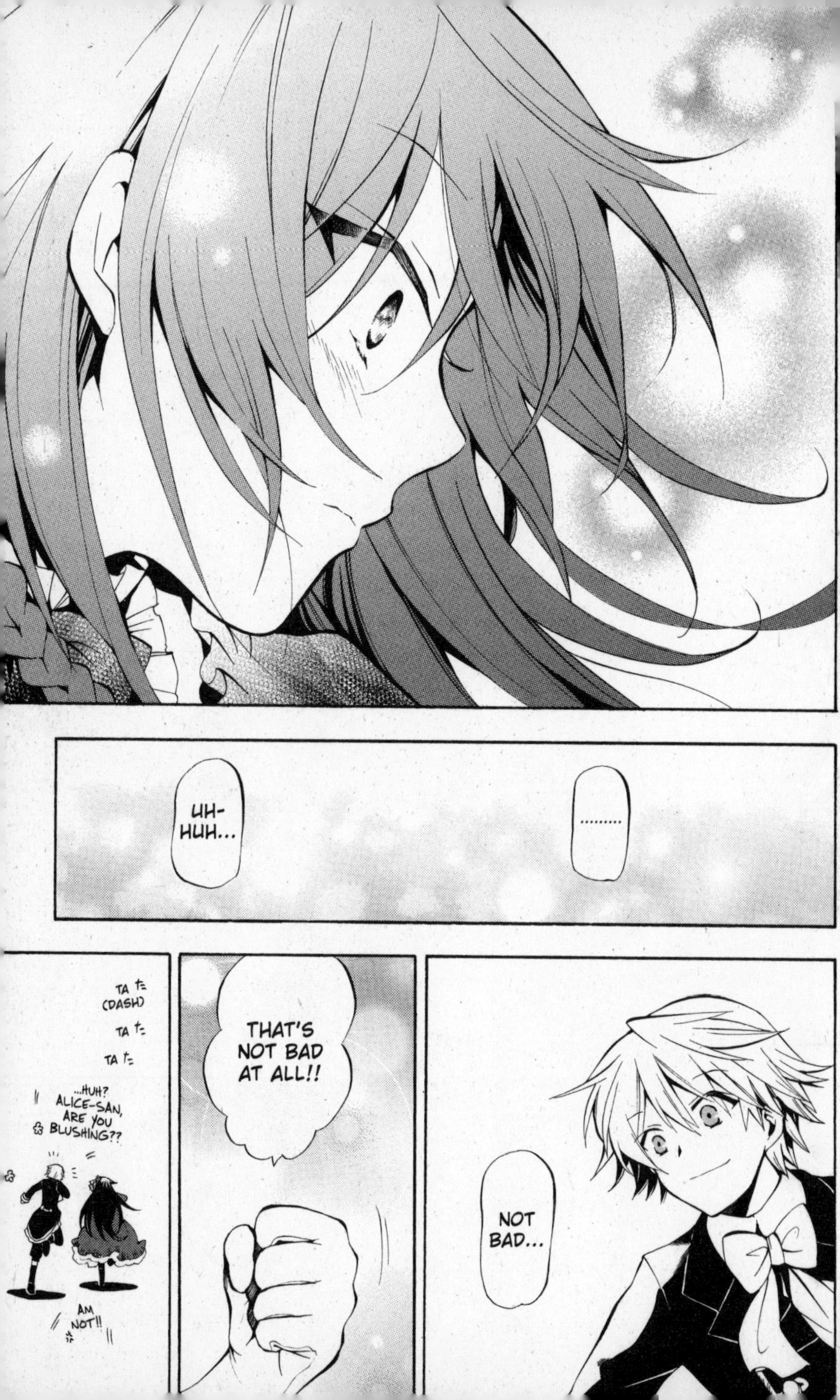
....
UH-HUH...
NOT BAD...
THAT'S NOT BAD AT ALL!!
TA た (DASH)
TA た
TA た
...HUH? ALICE-SAN, ARE YOU BLUSHING??
AM NOT!!

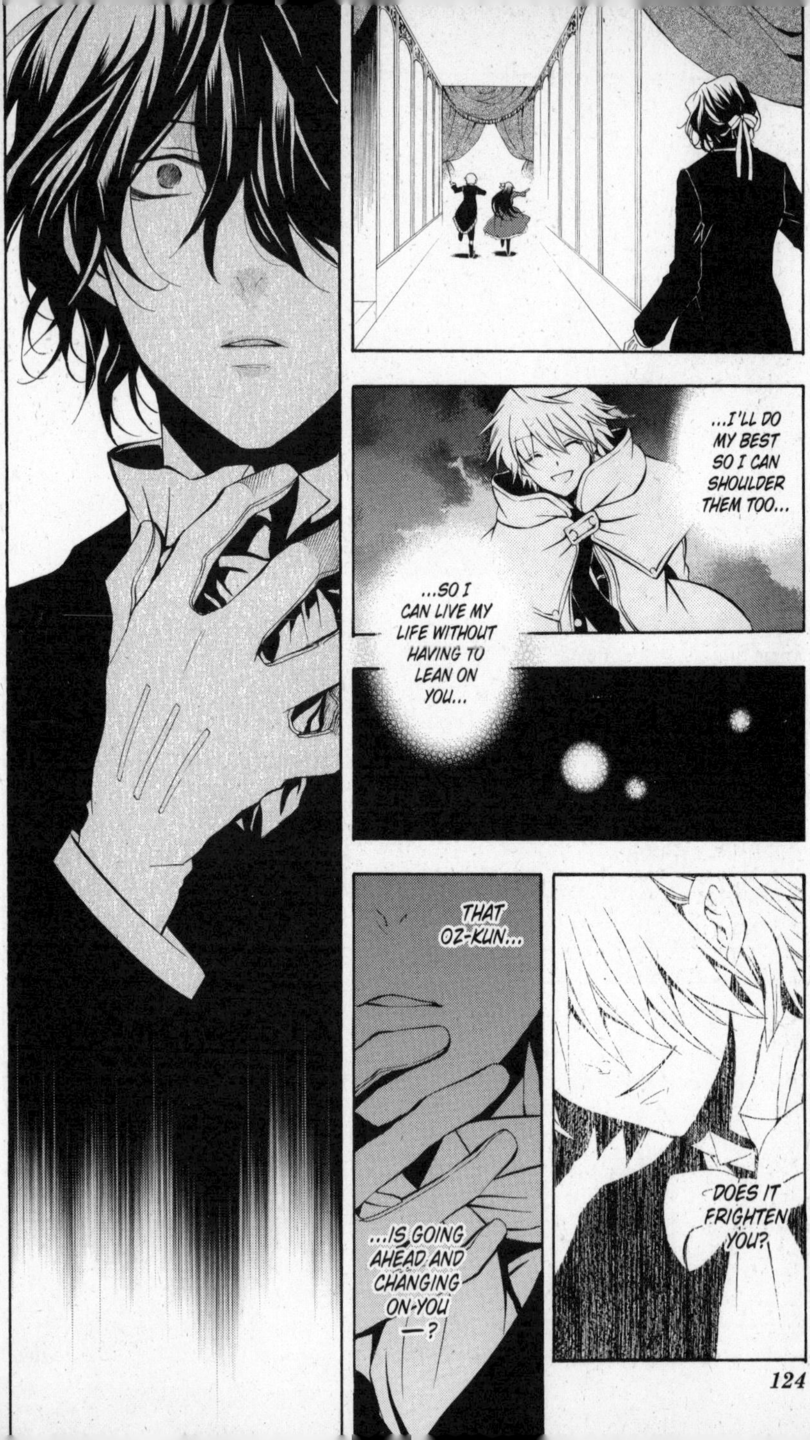

...I'LL DO MY BEST SO I CAN SHOULDER THEM TOO...
...SO I CAN LIVE MY LIFE WITHOUT HAVING TO LEAN ON YOU...
DOES IT FRIGHTEN YOU?
THAT OZ-KUN...
...IS GOING AHEAD AND CHANGING ON YOU —?

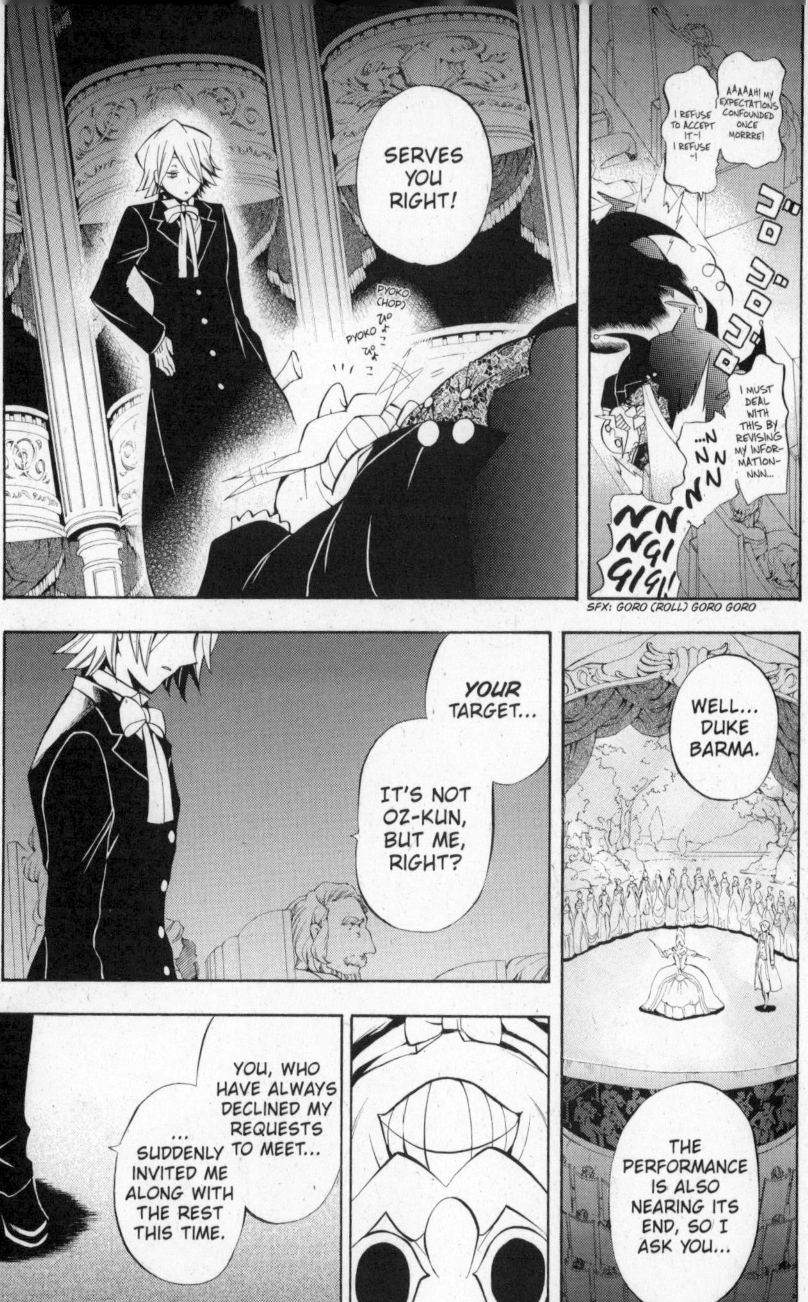
AAAAAH! MY EXPECTATIONS CONFOUNDED ONCE MORRRE!
I REFUSE TO ACCEPT IT~! I REFUSE~!
ゴロ ゴロ ゴロ
I MUST DEAL WITH THIS BY REVISING MY INFOR-MATION-NNN...
...NNNNNNNNNGIGIGI!!
SFX: GORO (ROLL) GORO GORO
SERVES YOU RIGHT!
PYOKO (HOP)
PYOKO
WELL... DUKE BARMA.
THE PERFORMANCE IS ALSO NEARING ITS END, SO I ASK YOU...
YOUR TARGET...
IT'S NOT OZ-KUN, BUT ME, RIGHT?
YOU, WHO HAVE ALWAYS DECLINED MY REQUESTS TO MEET...
...SUDDENLY INVITED ME ALONG WITH THE REST THIS TIME.

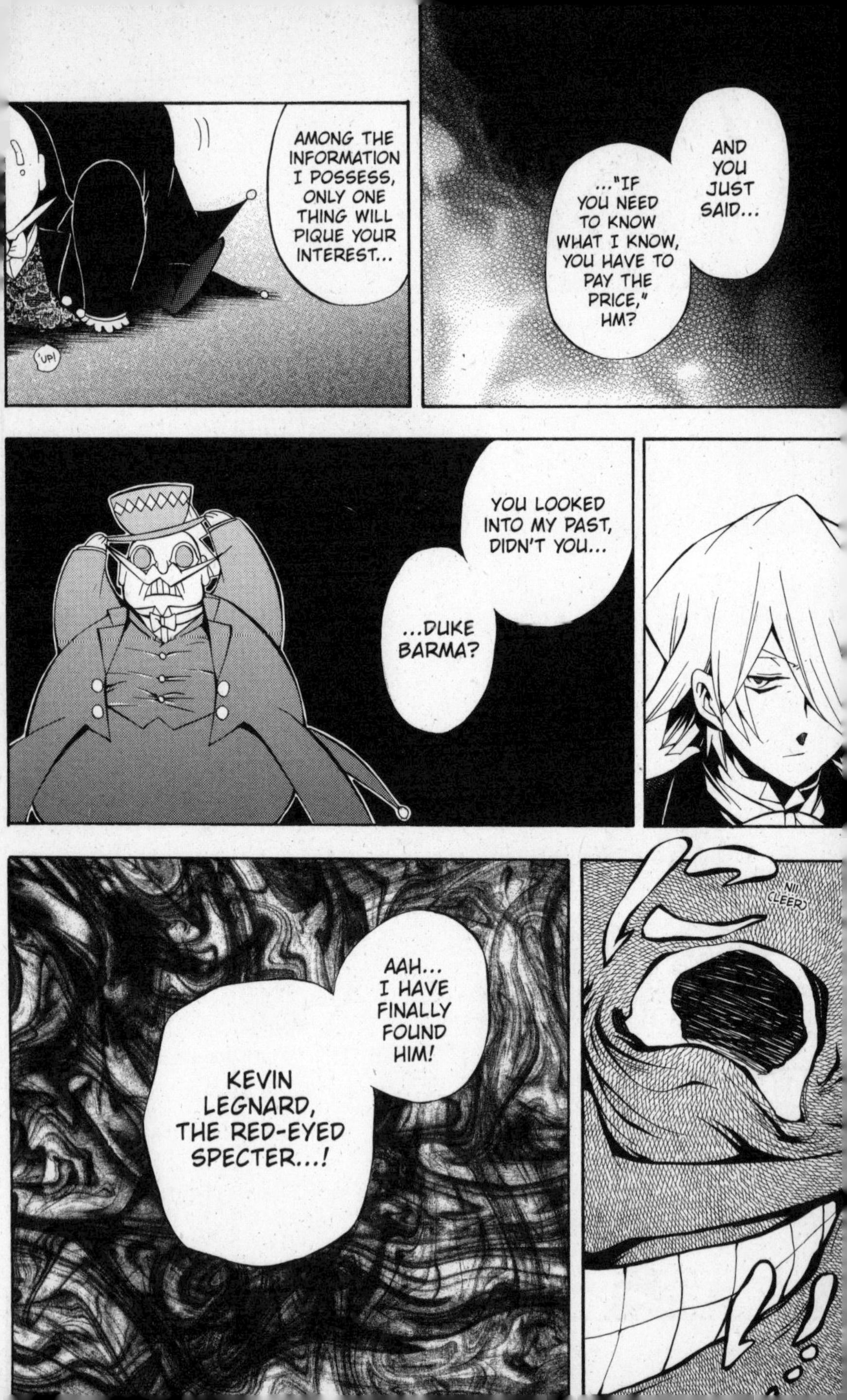
AND YOU JUST SAID...
..."IF YOU NEED TO KNOW WHAT I KNOW, YOU HAVE TO PAY THE PRICE," HM?
AMONG THE INFORMATION I POSSESS, ONLY ONE THING WILL PIQUE YOUR INTEREST...
'UP!
YOU LOOKED INTO MY PAST, DIDN'T YOU...
...DUKE BARMA?
AAH... I HAVE FINALLY FOUND HIM!
KEVIN LEGNARD, THE RED-EYED SPECTER...!

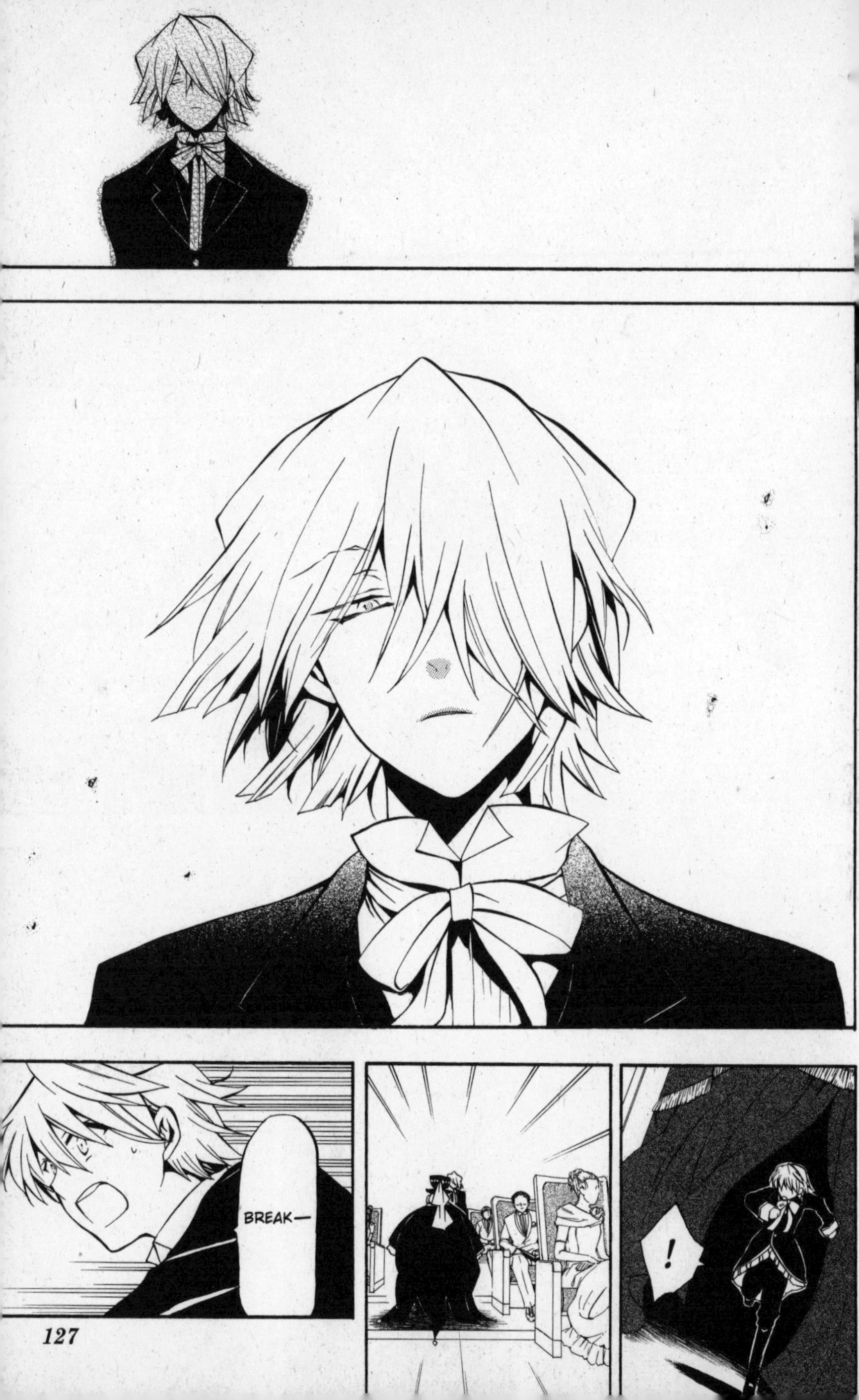
!
BREAK—

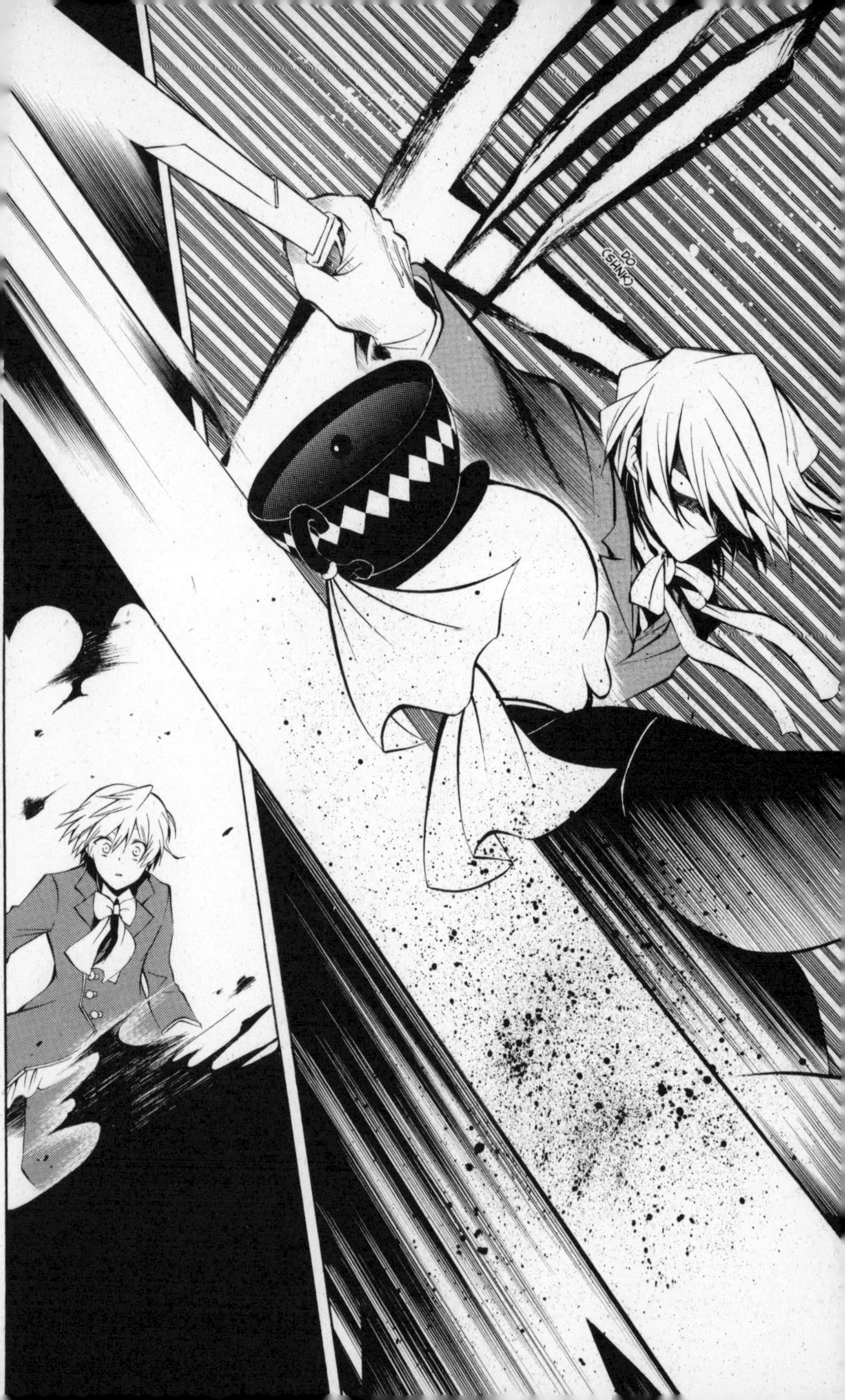

DO
(SHNK)

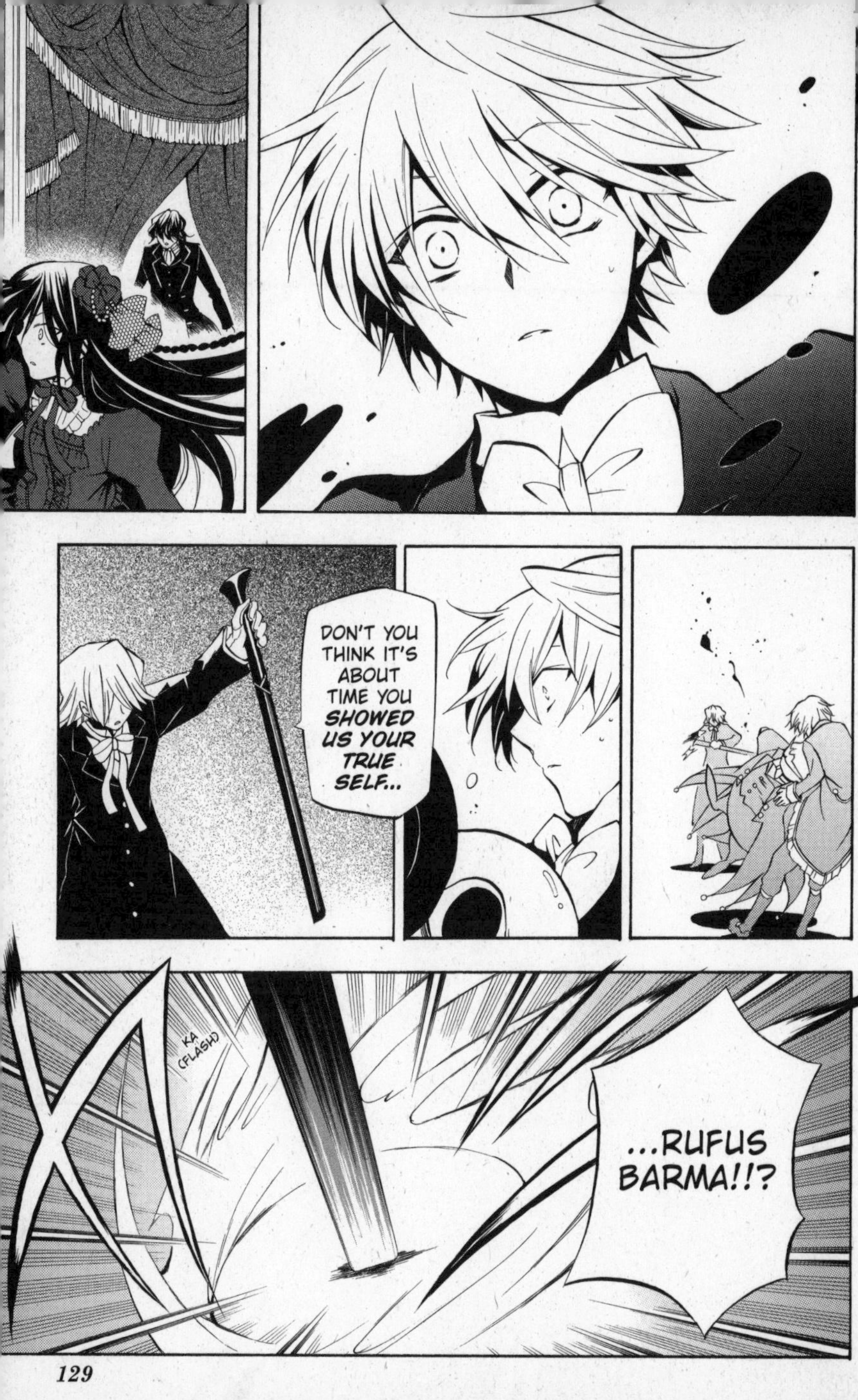
DON'T YOU THINK IT'S ABOUT TIME YOU SHOWED US YOUR TRUE SELF...
KA (FLASH)
...RUFUS BARMA!!?

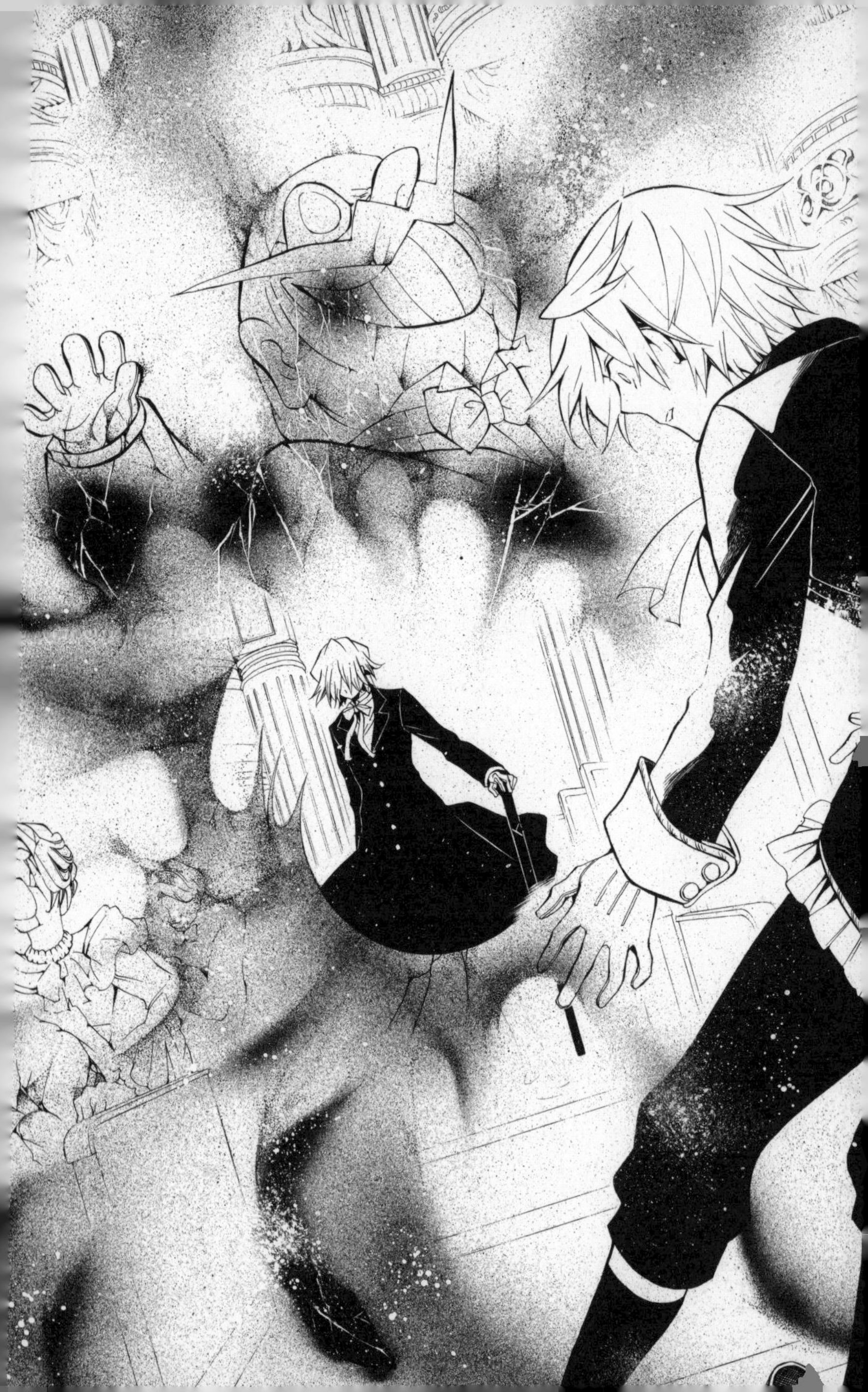

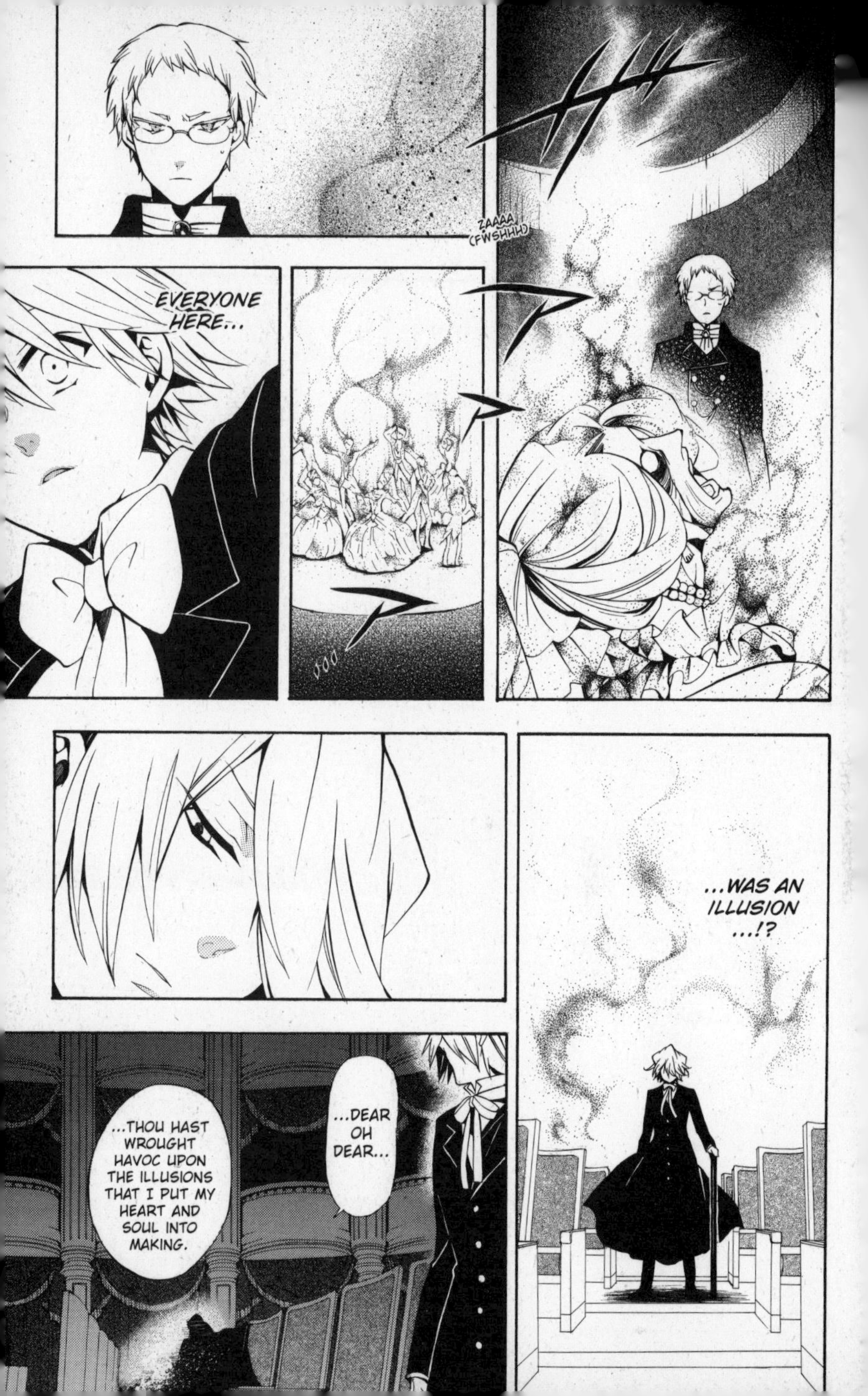
ZAAAA (FWSHHH)
EVERYONE HERE...
...WAS AN ILLUSION ...!?
...DEAR OH DEAR...
...THOU HAST WROUGHT HAVOC UPON THE ILLUSIONS THAT I PUT MY HEART AND SOUL INTO MAKING.

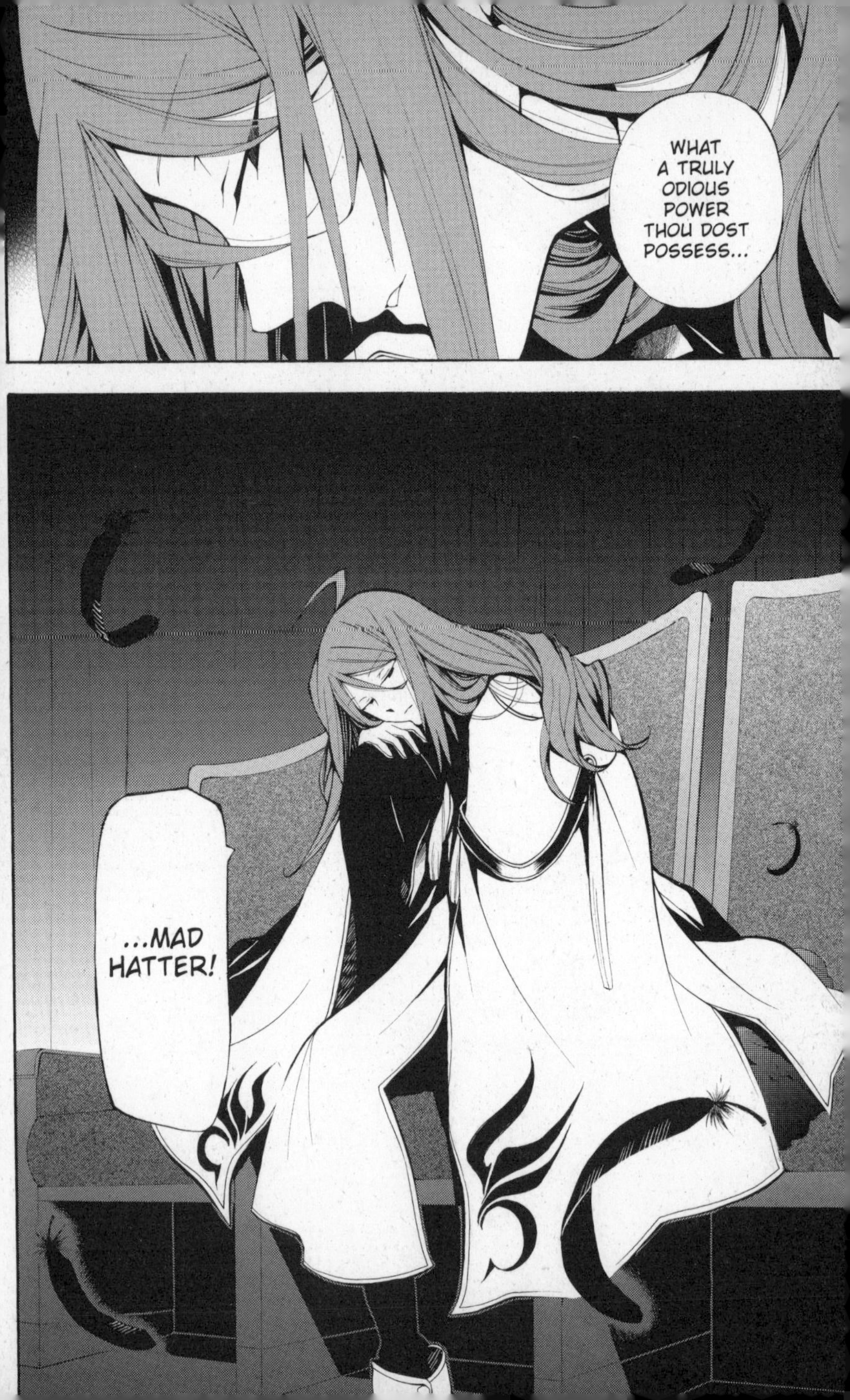
WHAT A TRULY ODIOUS POWER THOU DOST POSSESS...
...MAD HATTER!

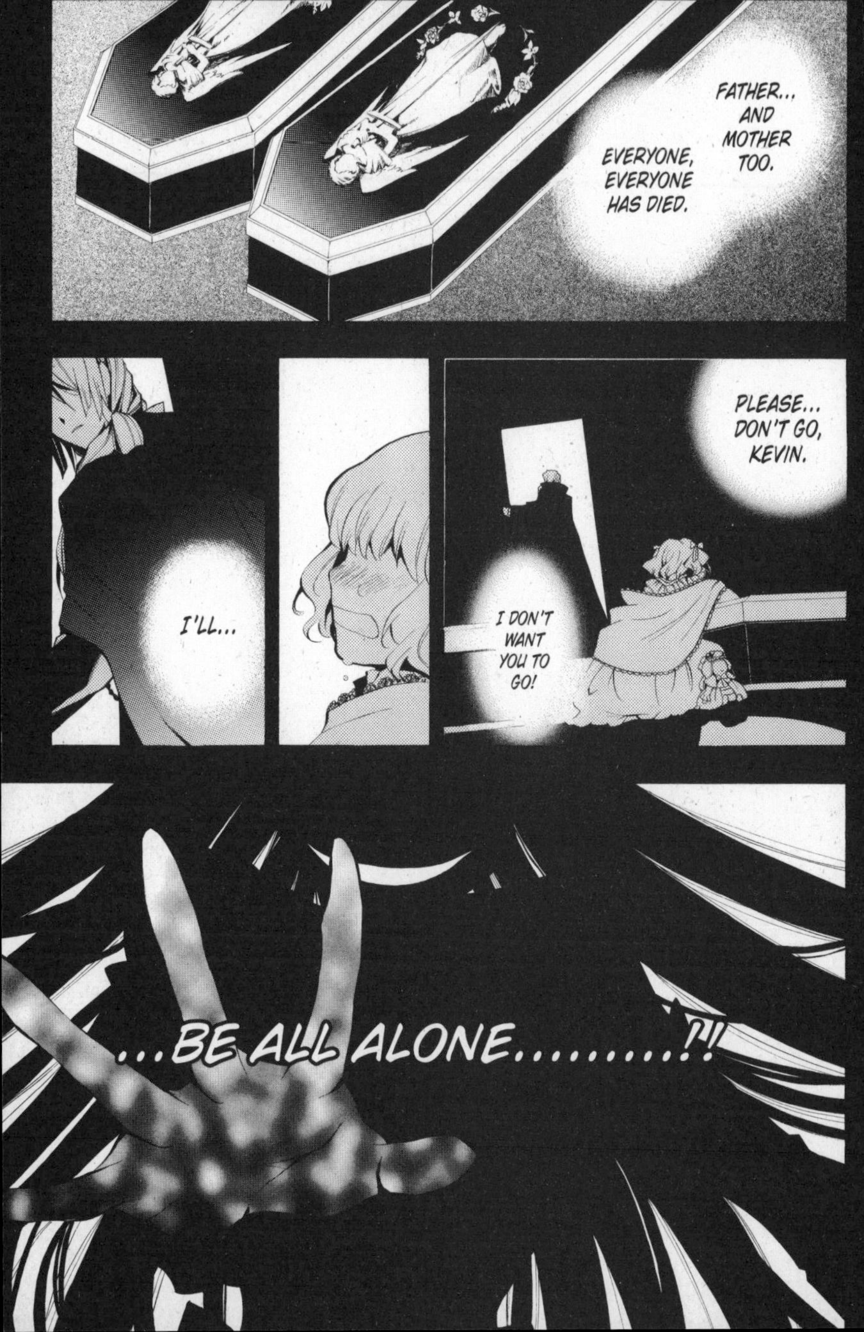
FATHER... AND MOTHER TOO.
EVERYONE, EVERYONE HAS DIED.
PLEASE... DON'T GO, KEVIN.
I DON'T WANT YOU TO GO!
I'LL...
...BE ALL ALONE..........?!

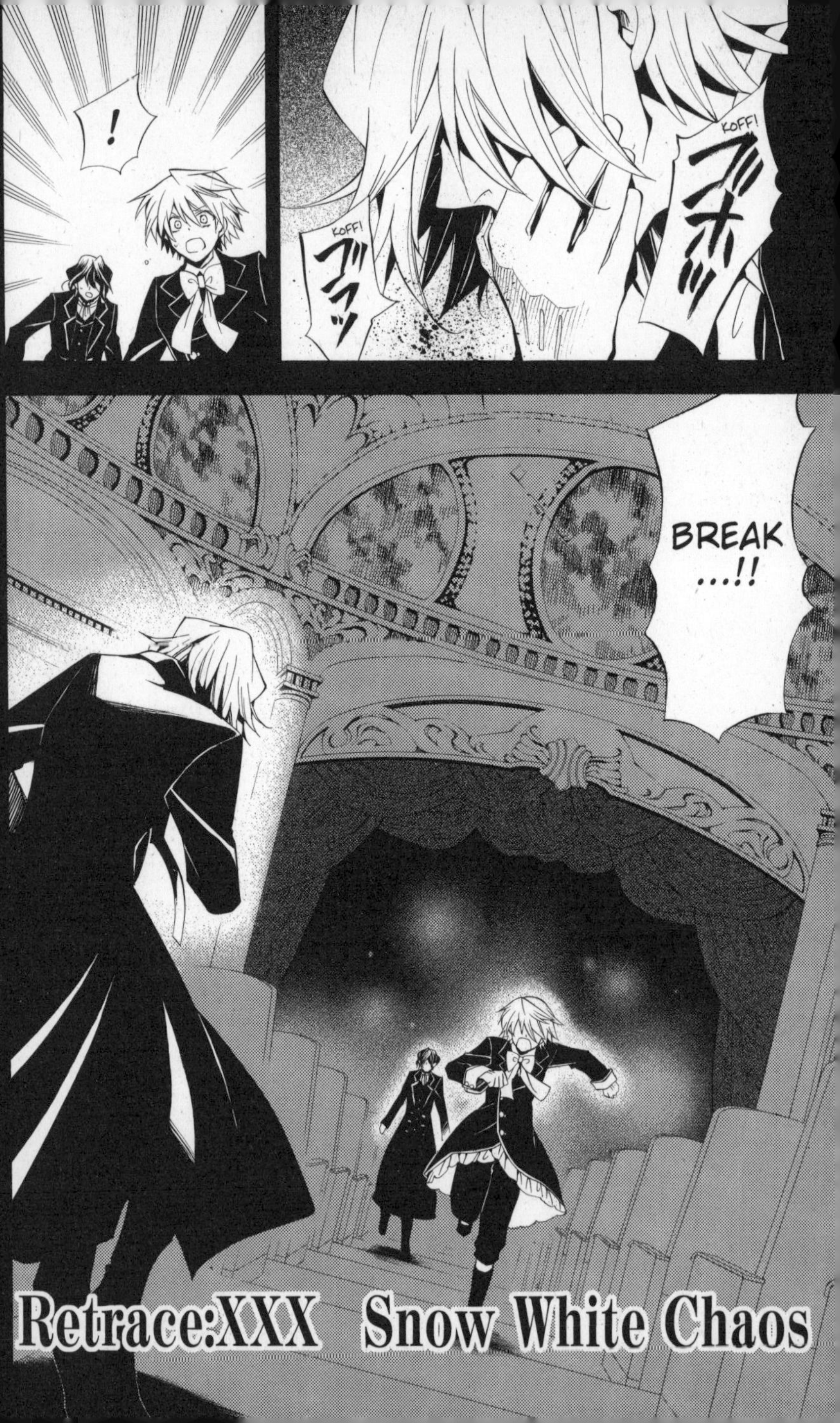
KOFF!
ゴホッ
KOFF!
ゴフッ
!
BREAK ...!!
Retrace:XXX Snow White Chaos

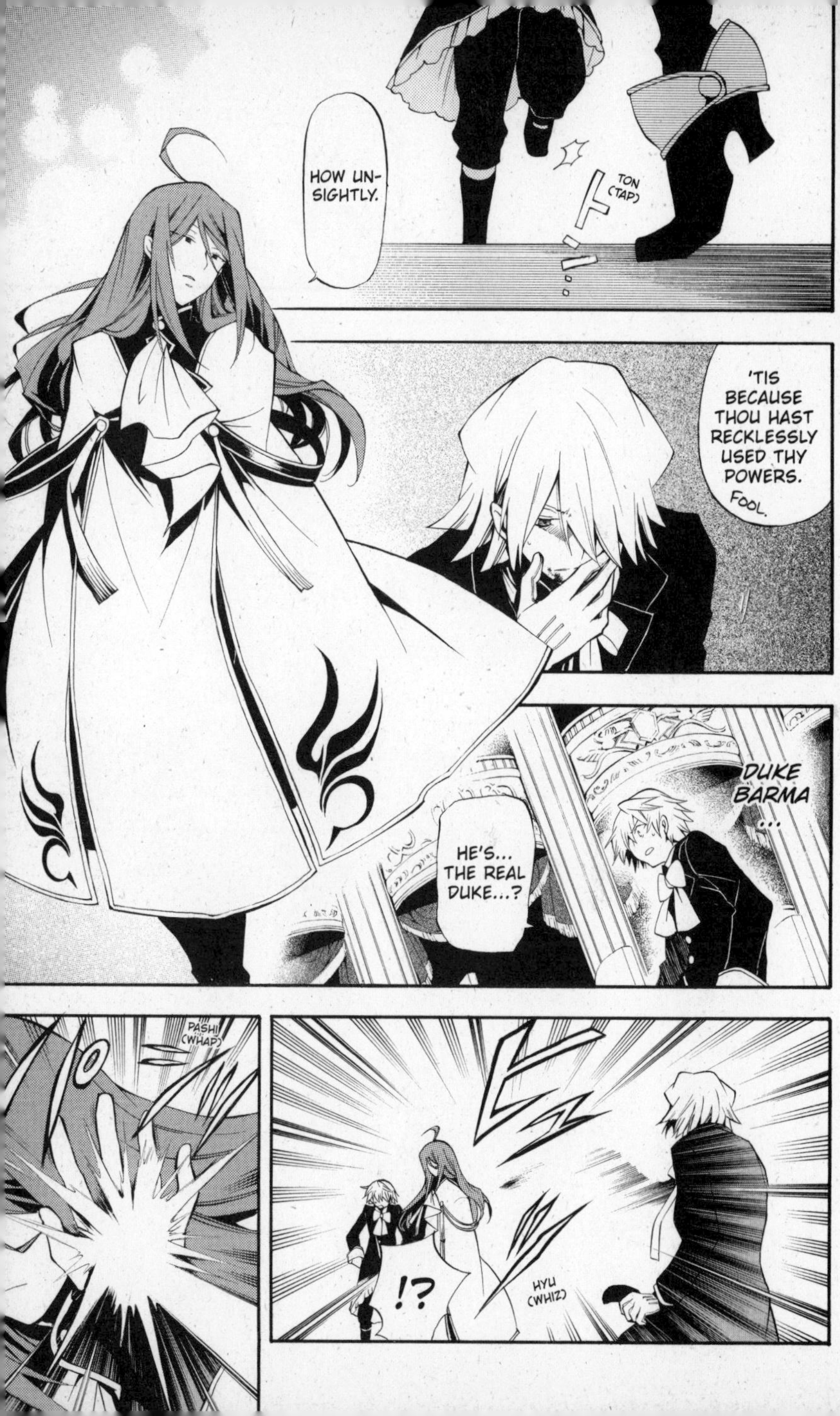

TON (TAP)
HOW UN-SIGHTLY.
'TIS BECAUSE THOU HAST RECKLESSLY USED THY POWERS.
FOOL.
DUKE BARMA...
HE'S... THE REAL DUKE...?
PASHI (WHAP)
HYU (WHIZ)
!?

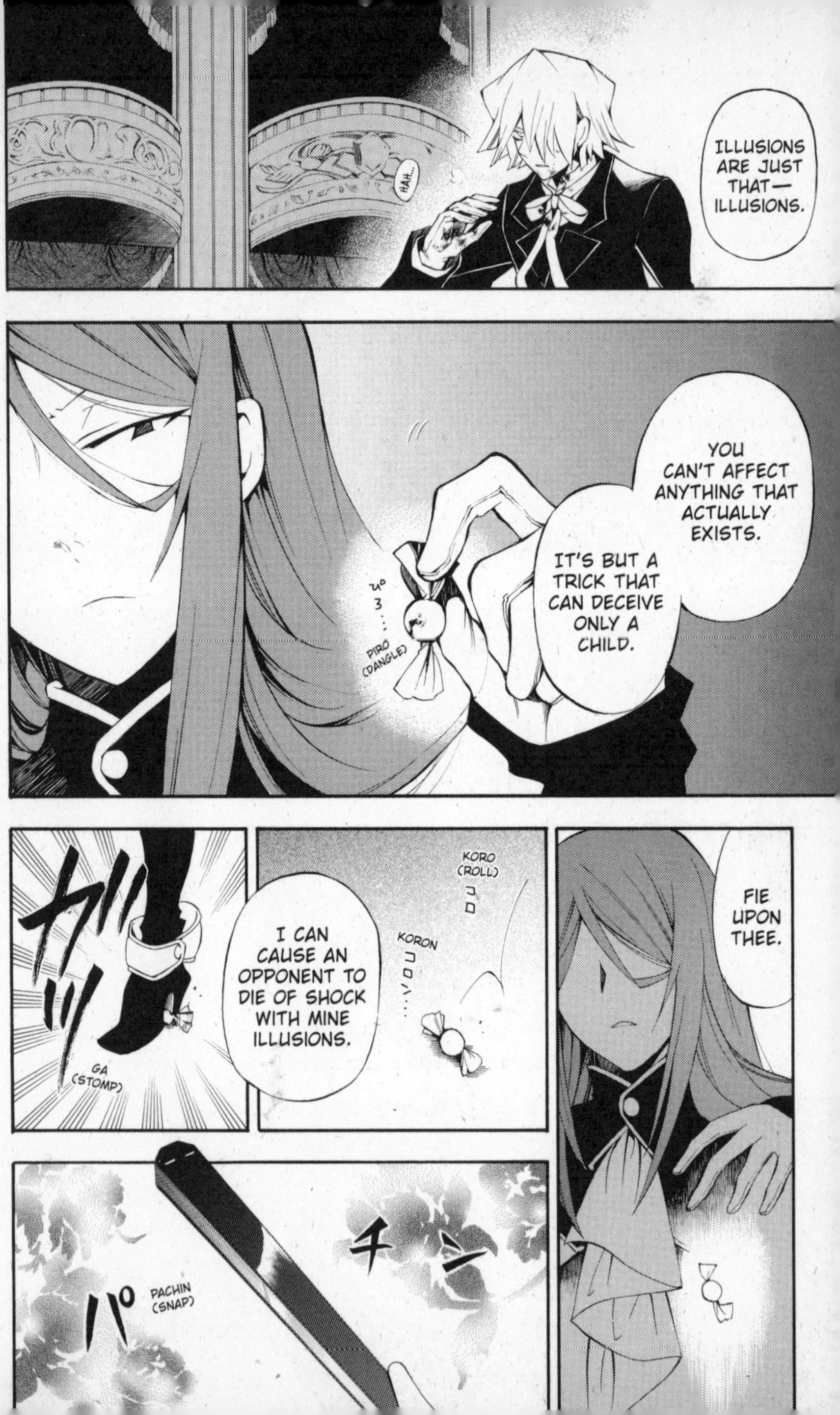
ILLUSIONS ARE JUST THAT— ILLUSIONS.
HAH...
YOU CAN'T AFFECT ANYTHING THAT ACTUALLY EXISTS.
IT'S BUT A TRICK THAT CAN DECEIVE ONLY A CHILD.
PIRO (DANGLE)
FIE UPON THEE.
KORO (ROLL)
I CAN CAUSE AN OPPONENT TO DIE OF SHOCK WITH MINE ILLUSIONS.
KORON
GA (STOMP)
PACHIN (SNAP)

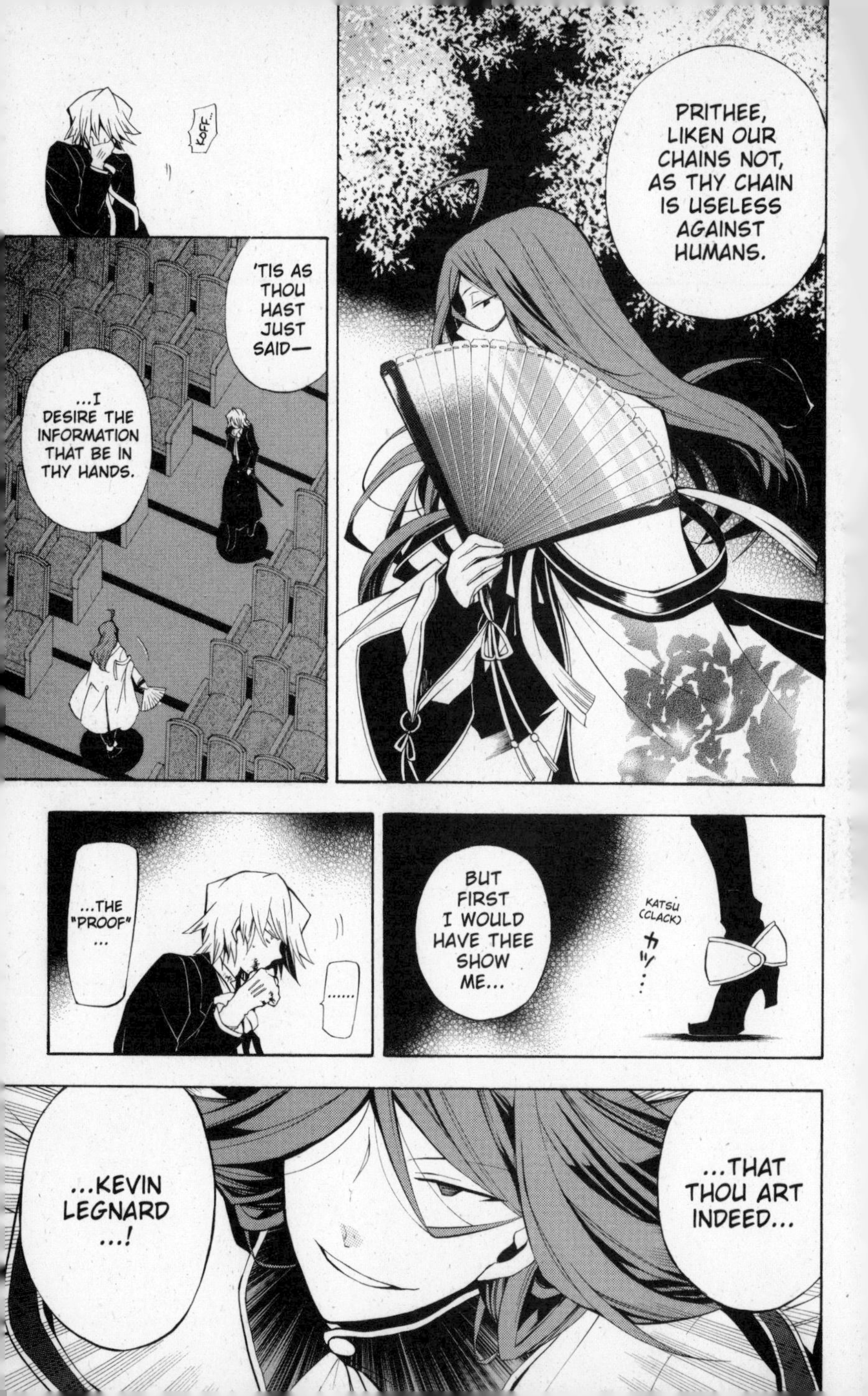
PRITHEE, LIKEN OUR CHAINS NOT, AS THY CHAIN IS USELESS AGAINST HUMANS.
KOFF...
'TIS AS THOU HAST JUST SAID—
...I DESIRE THE INFORMATION THAT BE IN THY HANDS.
BUT FIRST I WOULD HAVE THEE SHOW ME...
KATSU (CLACK)
カッ…
......
...THE "PROOF"...
...THAT THOU ART INDEED...
...KEVIN LEGNARD...!

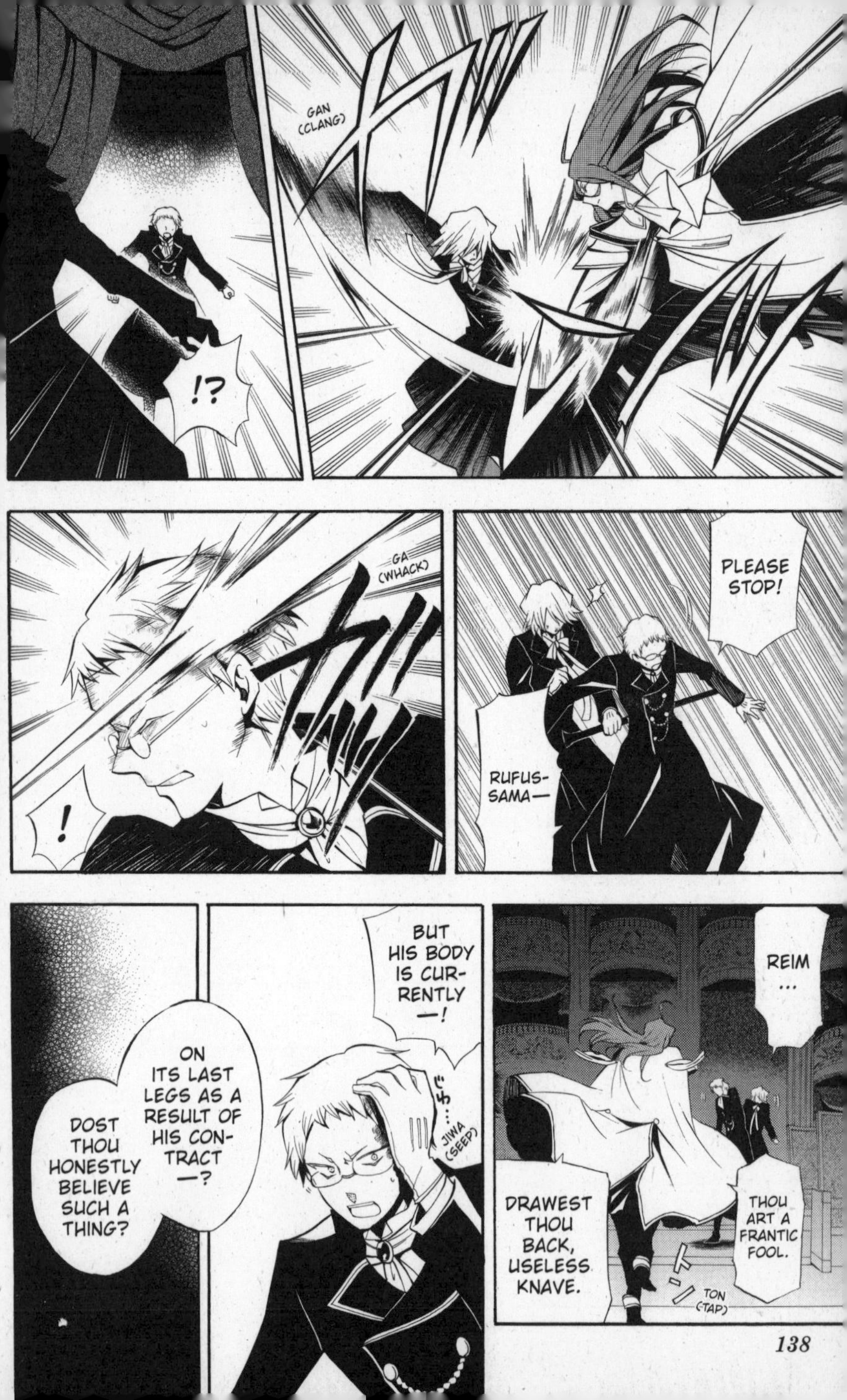
GAN (CLANG)
!?
PLEASE STOP!
RUFUS-SAMA—
GA (WHACK)
!
REIM …
THOU ART A FRANTIC FOOL.
DRAWEST THOU BACK, USELESS KNAVE.
TON (TAP)
BUT HIS BODY IS CUR-RENTLY—!
じわ… JIWA (SEEP)
ON ITS LAST LEGS AS A RESULT OF HIS CON-TRACT—?
DOST THOU HONESTLY BELIEVE SUCH A THING?

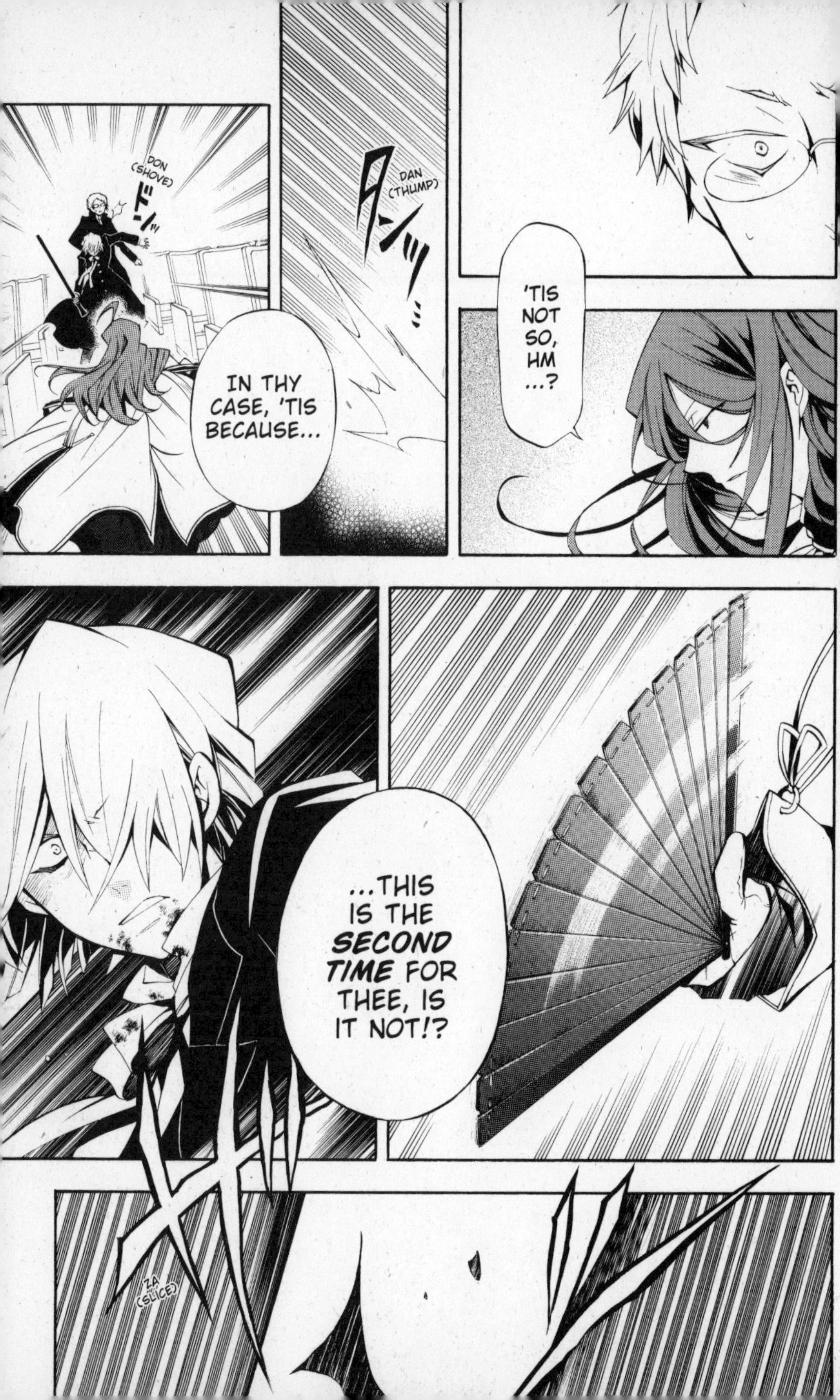
'TIS NOT SO, HM ...?
DAN (THUMP)
IN THY CASE, 'TIS BECAUSE...
DON (SHOVE)
...THIS IS THE **SECOND TIME** FOR THEE, IS IT NOT!?
ZA (SLICE)

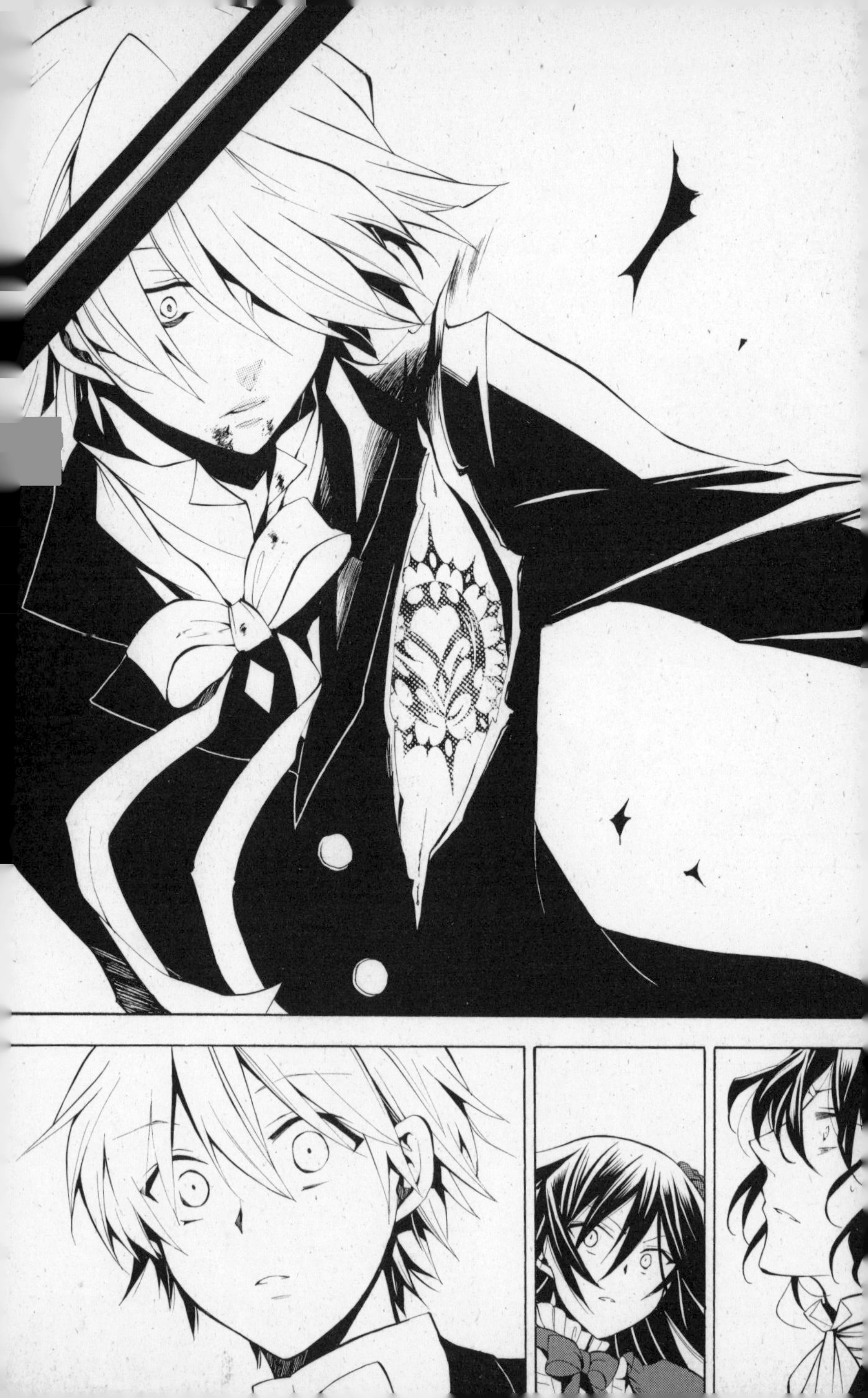

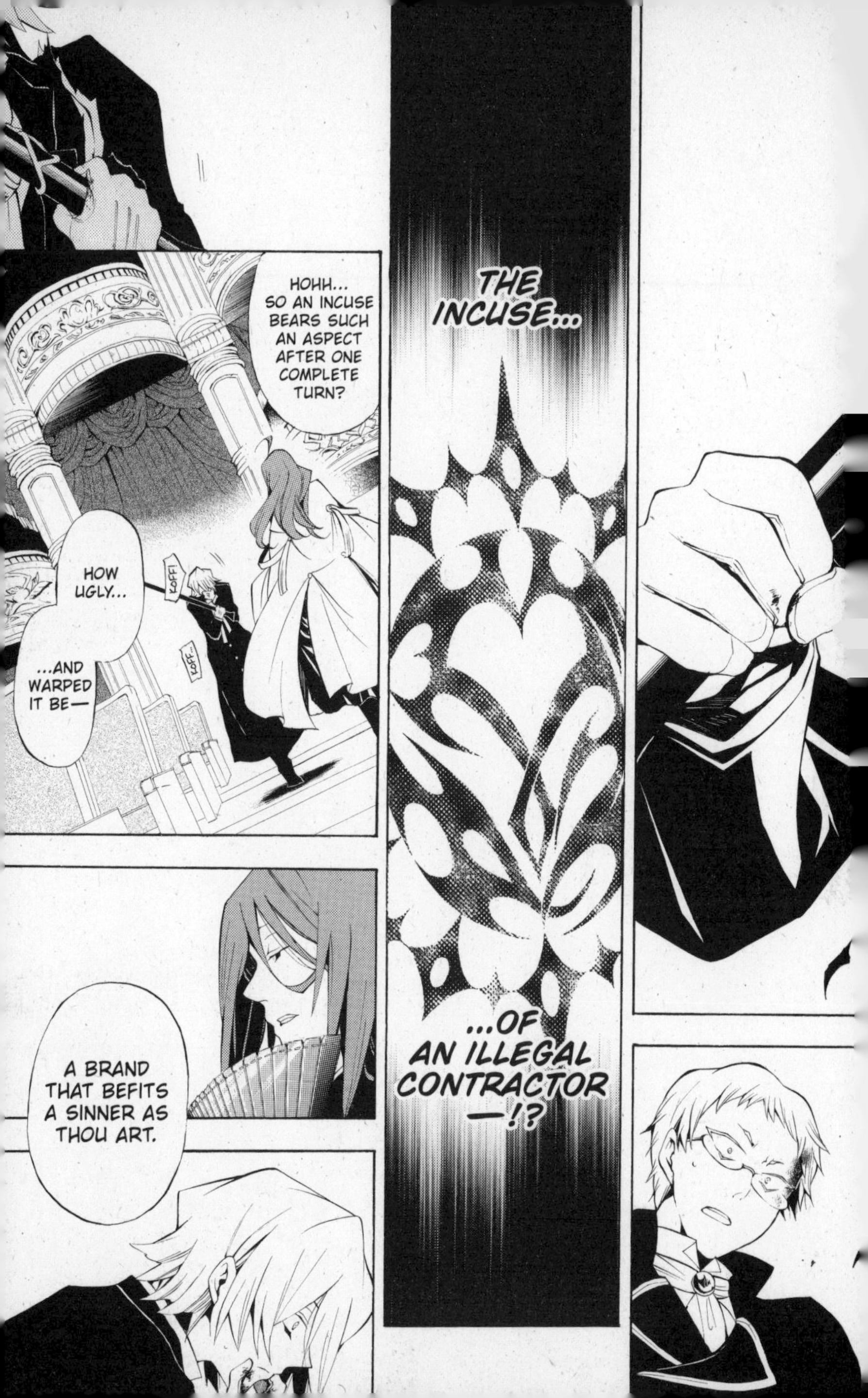
THE INCUSE...
...OF AN ILLEGAL CONTRACTOR—!?
HOHH... SO AN INCUSE BEARS SUCH AN ASPECT AFTER ONE COMPLETE TURN?
KOFF!
KOFF...
HOW UGLY...
...AND WARPED IT BE—
A BRAND THAT BEFITS A SINNER AS THOU ART.

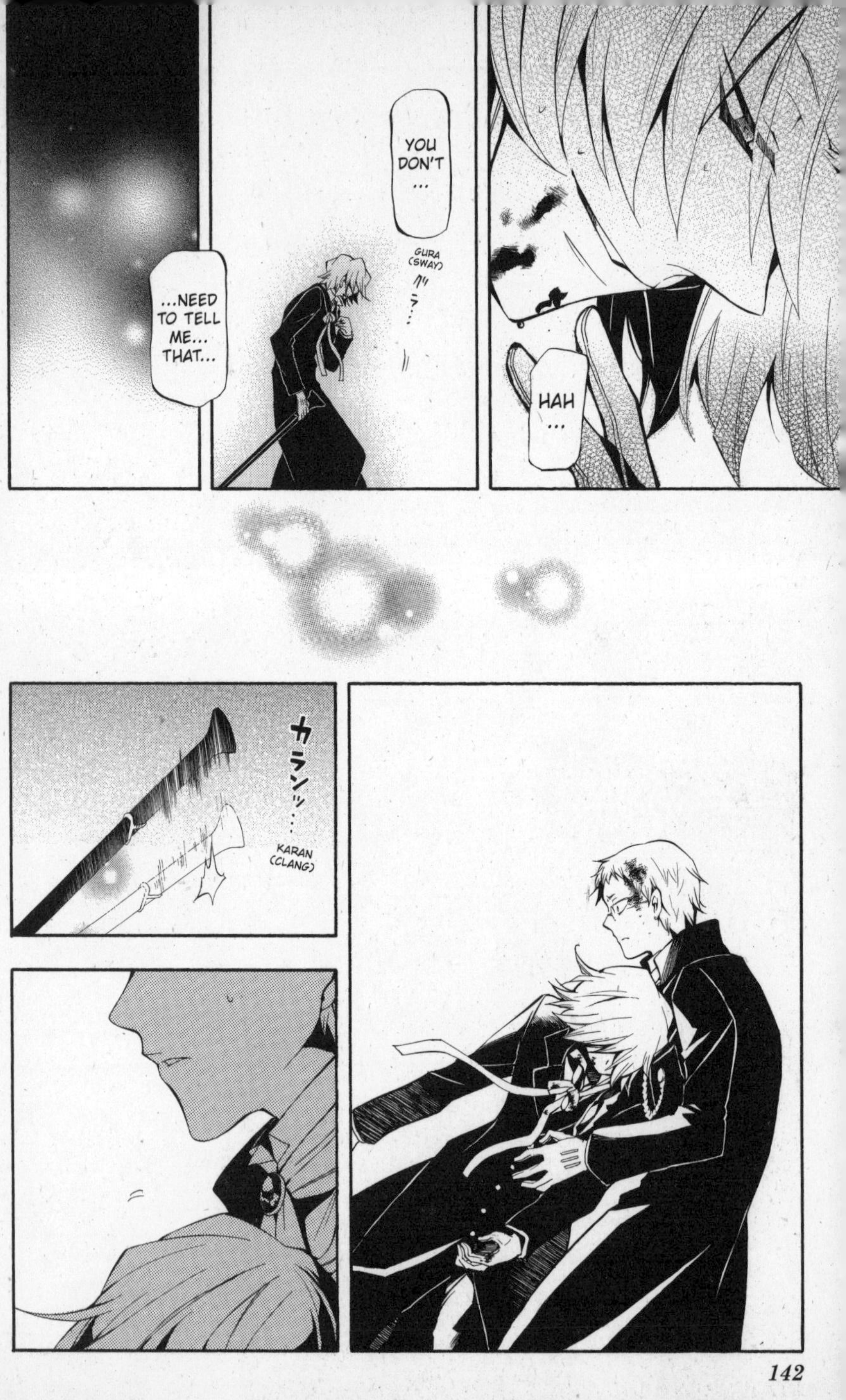
HAH ...
YOU DON'T ...
GURA (SWAY)
グラ…
...NEED TO TELL ME... THAT...
カランッ…
KARAN (CLANG)

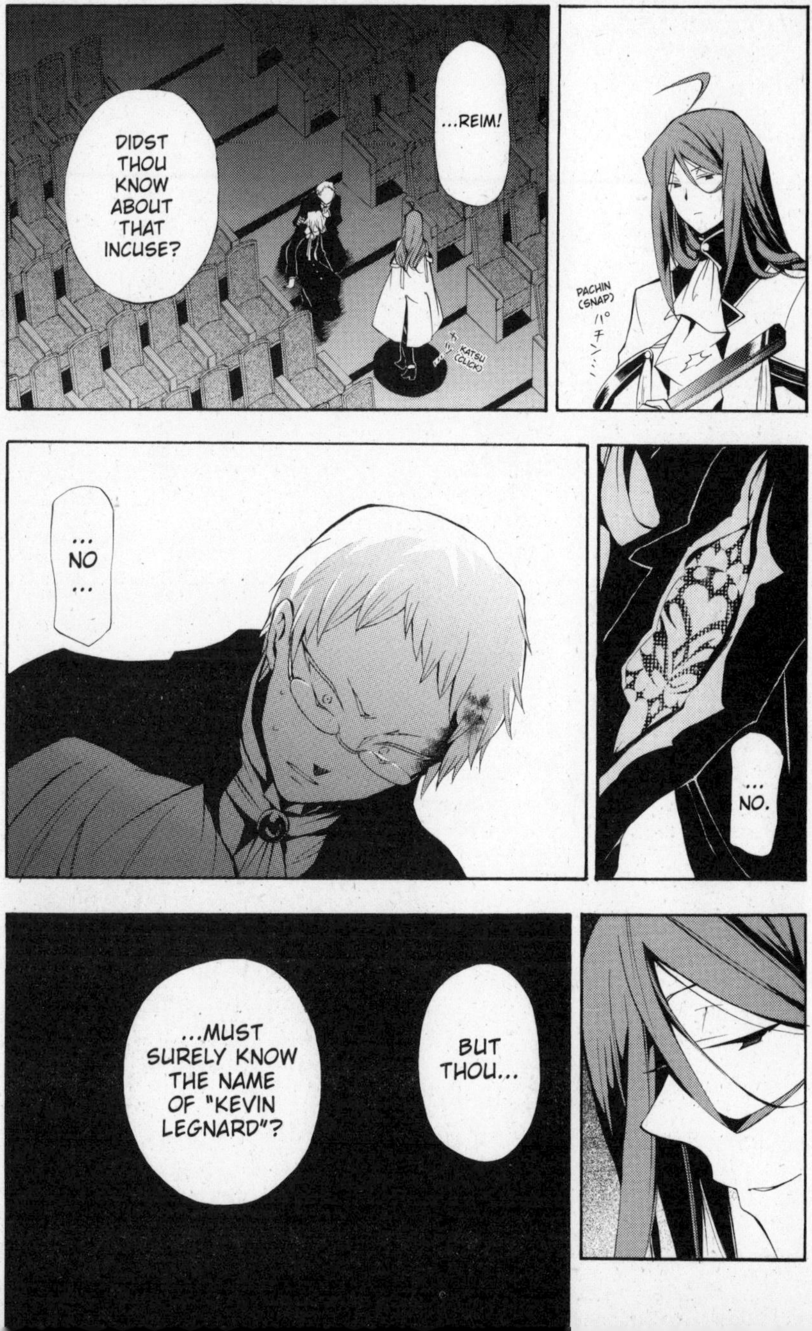
PACHIN (SNAP)
パチン
...REIM!
DIDST THOU KNOW ABOUT THAT INCUSE?
KATSU (CLICK)
... NO.
... NO ...
BUT THOU...
...MUST SURELY KNOW THE NAME OF "KEVIN LEGNARD"?

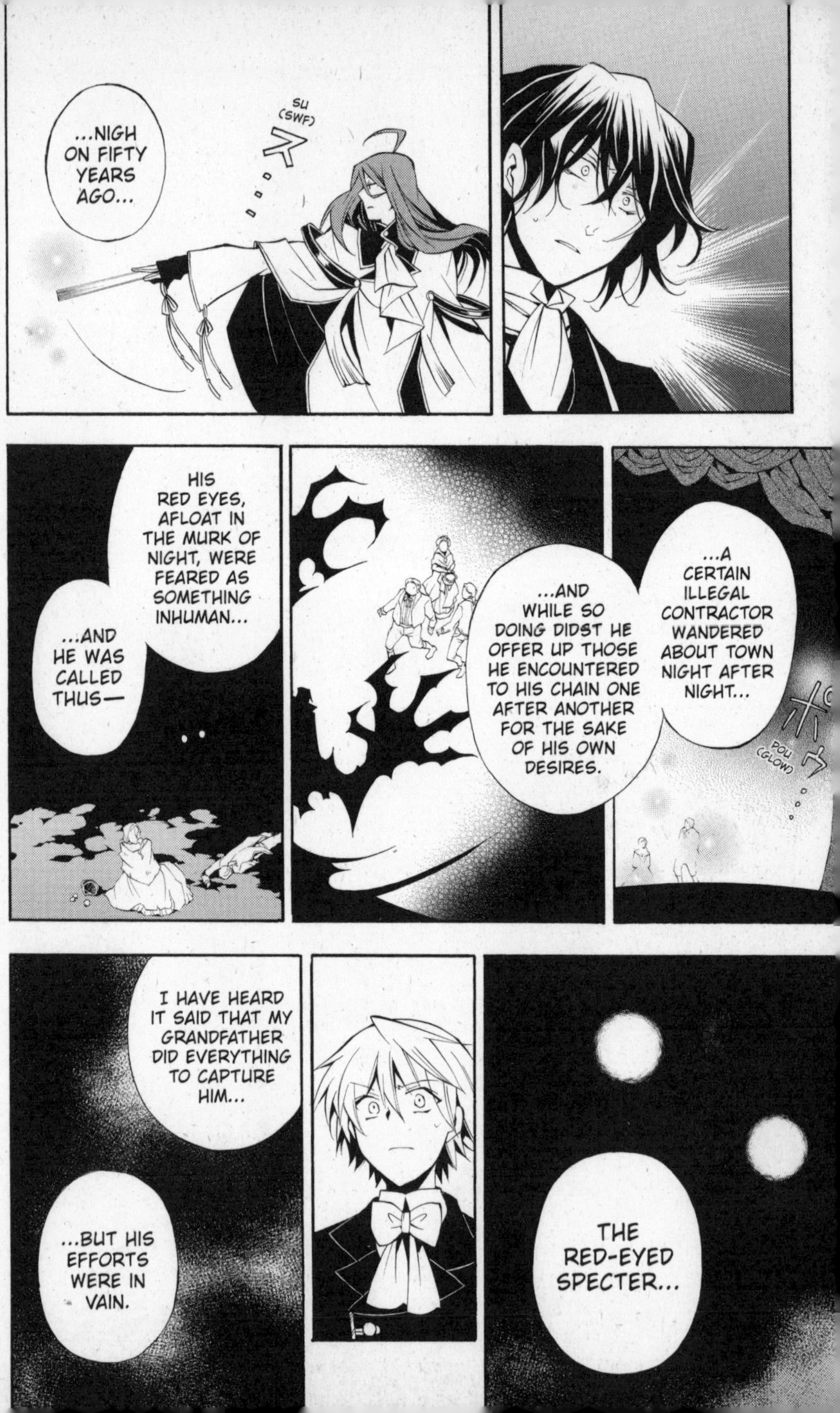
ス
SU (SWF)
...NIGH ON FIFTY YEARS AGO...
...A CERTAIN ILLEGAL CONTRACTOR WANDERED ABOUT TOWN NIGHT AFTER NIGHT...
ポウ
POU (GLOW)
...AND WHILE SO DOING DIDST HE OFFER UP THOSE HE ENCOUNTERED TO HIS CHAIN ONE AFTER ANOTHER FOR THE SAKE OF HIS OWN DESIRES.
HIS RED EYES, AFLOAT IN THE MURK OF NIGHT, WERE FEARED AS SOMETHING INHUMAN...
...AND HE WAS CALLED THUS—
THE RED-EYED SPECTER...
I HAVE HEARD IT SAID THAT MY GRANDFATHER DID EVERYTHING TO CAPTURE HIM...
...BUT HIS EFFORTS WERE IN VAIN.

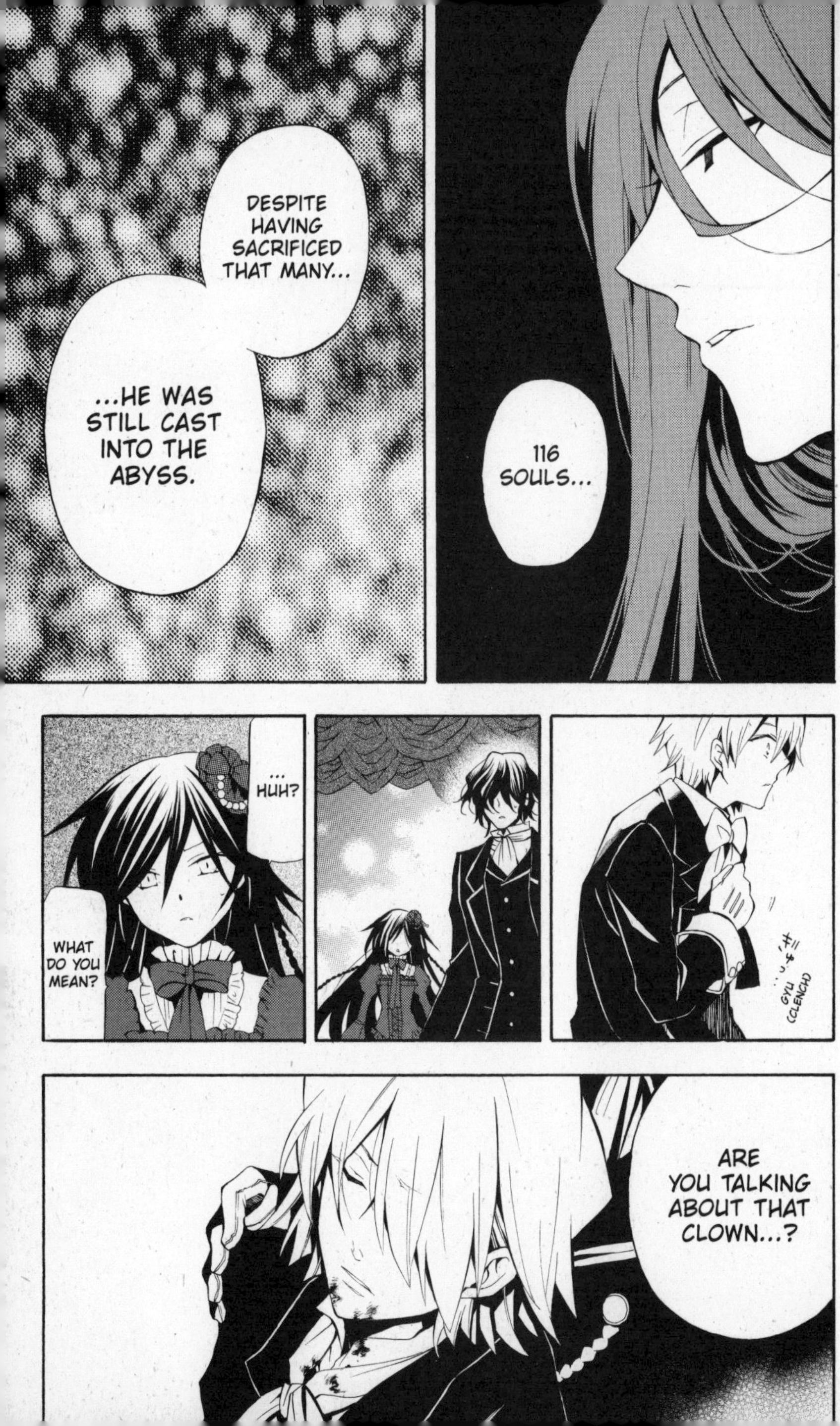
116 SOULS...
DESPITE HAVING SACRIFICED THAT MANY...
...HE WAS STILL CAST INTO THE ABYSS.
GYU (CLENCH)
...HUH?
WHAT DO YOU MEAN?
ARE YOU TALKING ABOUT THAT CLOWN...?

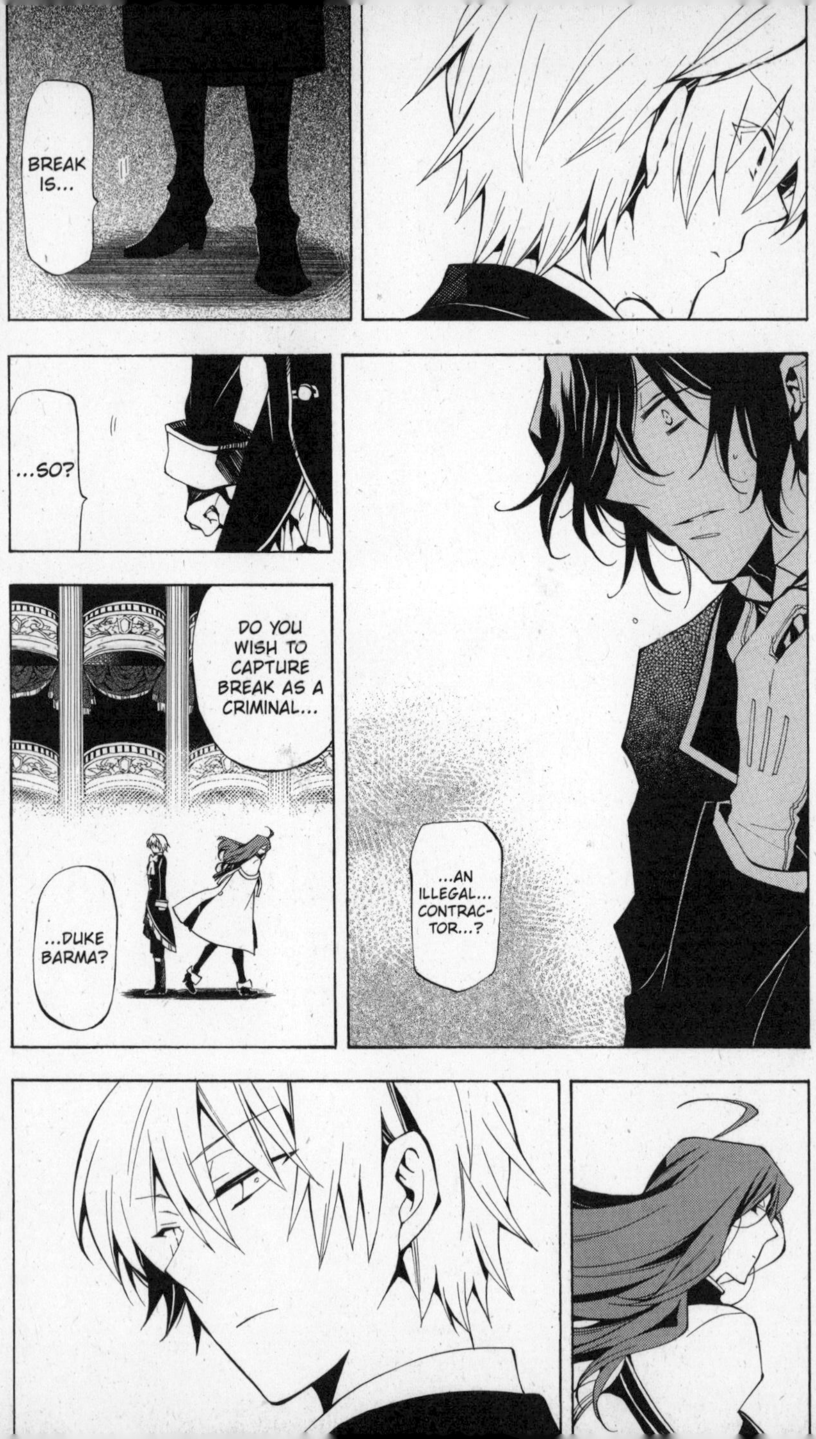
BREAK IS...
...AN ILLEGAL... CONTRAC-TOR...?
...SO?
DO YOU WISH TO CAPTURE BREAK AS A CRIMINAL...
...DUKE BARMA?

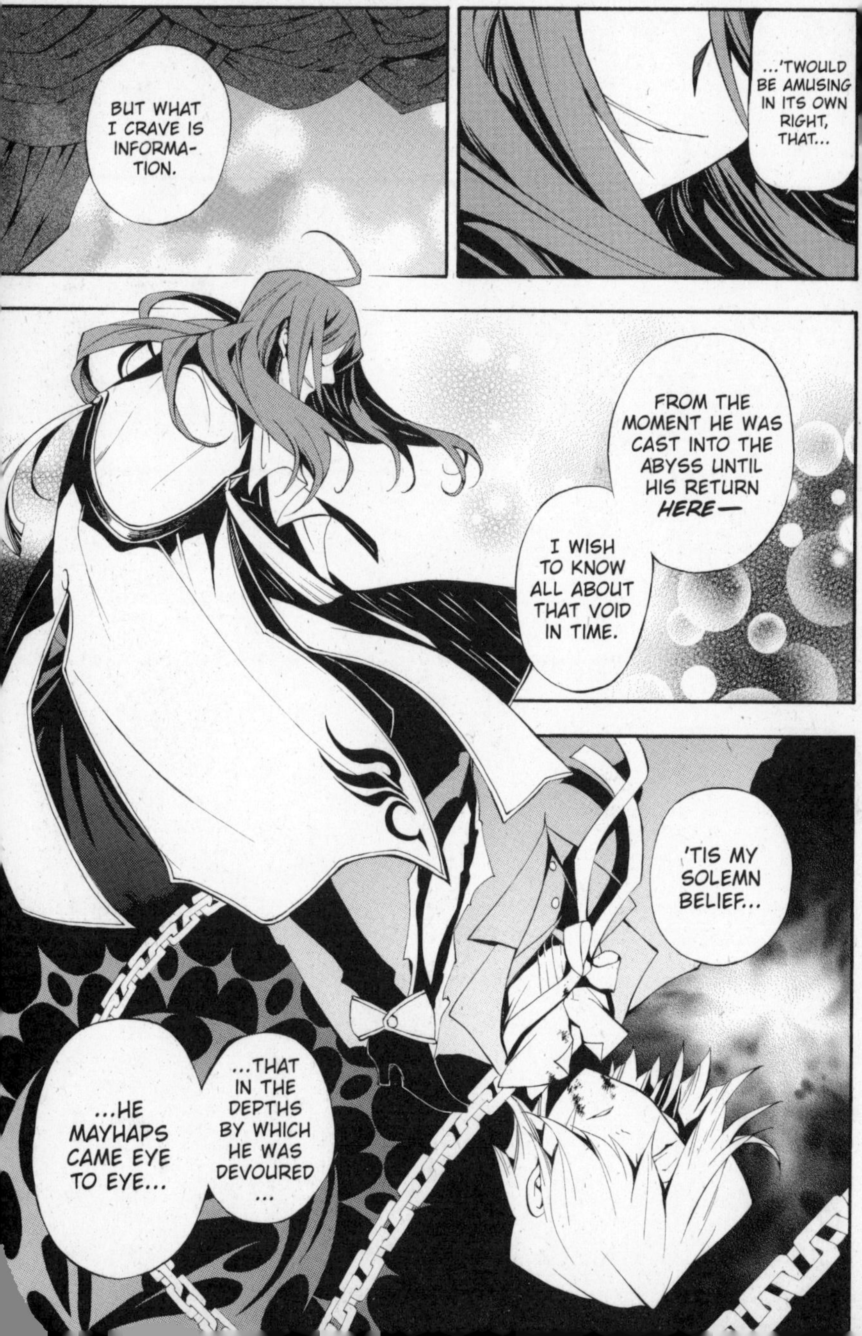
...'TWOULD BE AMUSING IN ITS OWN RIGHT, THAT...
BUT WHAT I CRAVE IS INFORMATION.
FROM THE MOMENT HE WAS CAST INTO THE ABYSS UNTIL HIS RETURN *HERE*—
I WISH TO KNOW ALL ABOUT THAT VOID IN TIME.
'TIS MY SOLEMN BELIEF...
...THAT IN THE DEPTHS BY WHICH HE WAS DEVOURED...
...HE MAYHAPS CAME EYE TO EYE...

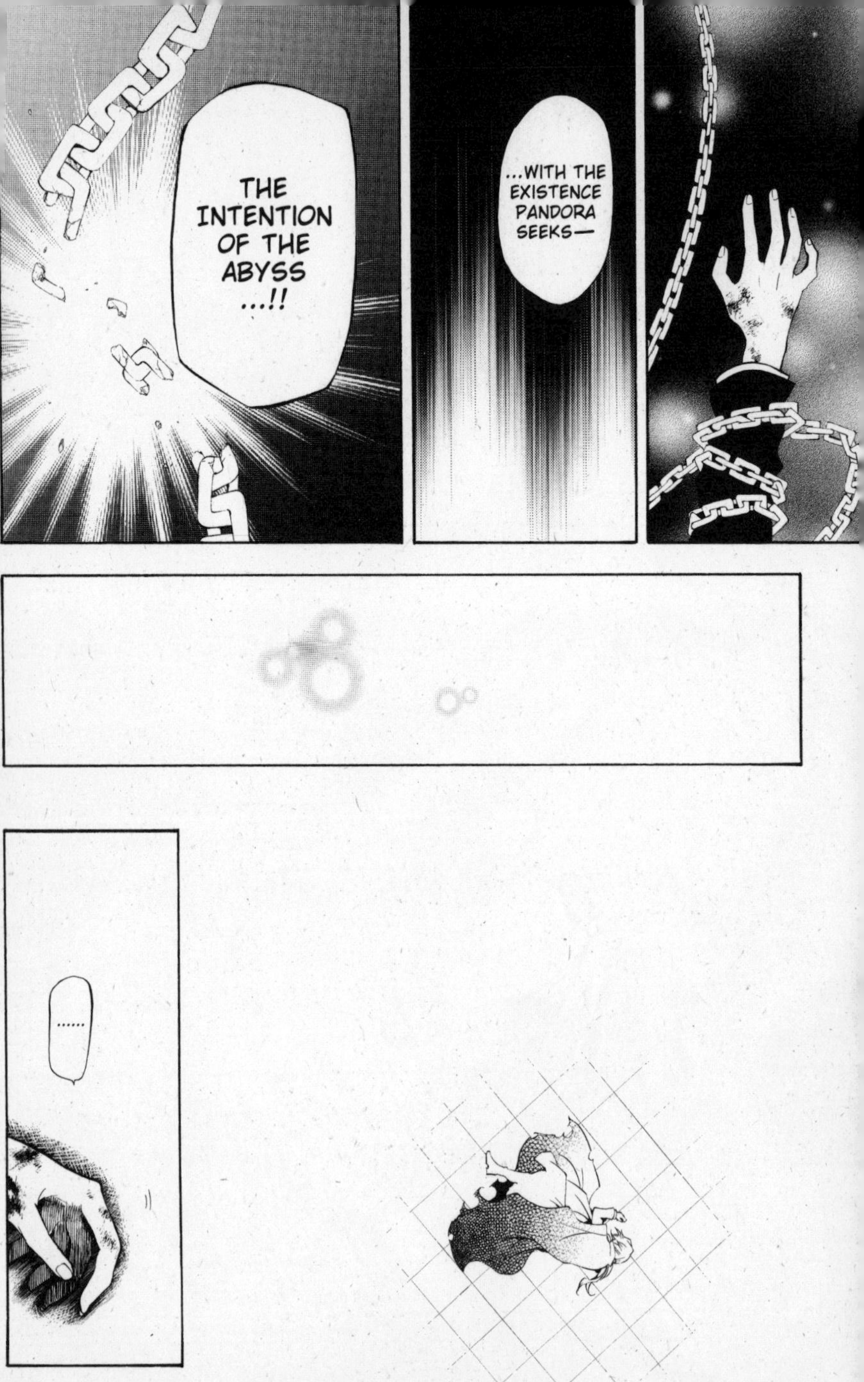
...WITH THE EXISTENCE PANDORA SEEKS—
THE INTENTION OF THE ABYSS ...!!
......

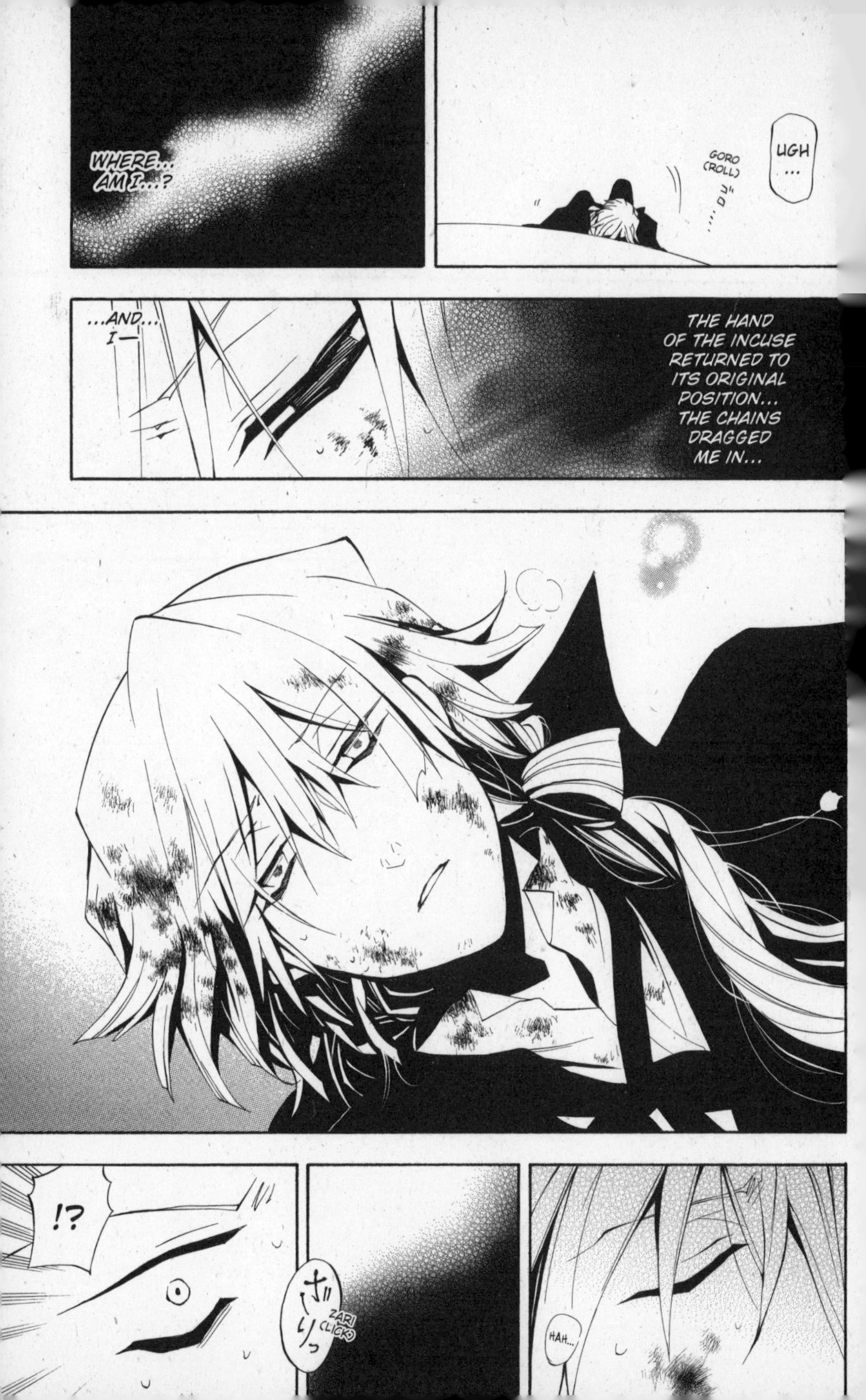
UGH ...
GORO (ROLL)
WHERE... AM I...?
THE HAND OF THE INCUSE RETURNED TO ITS ORIGINAL POSITION... THE CHAINS DRAGGED ME IN...
...AND... I—
HAH...
ZARI (CLICK)
!?

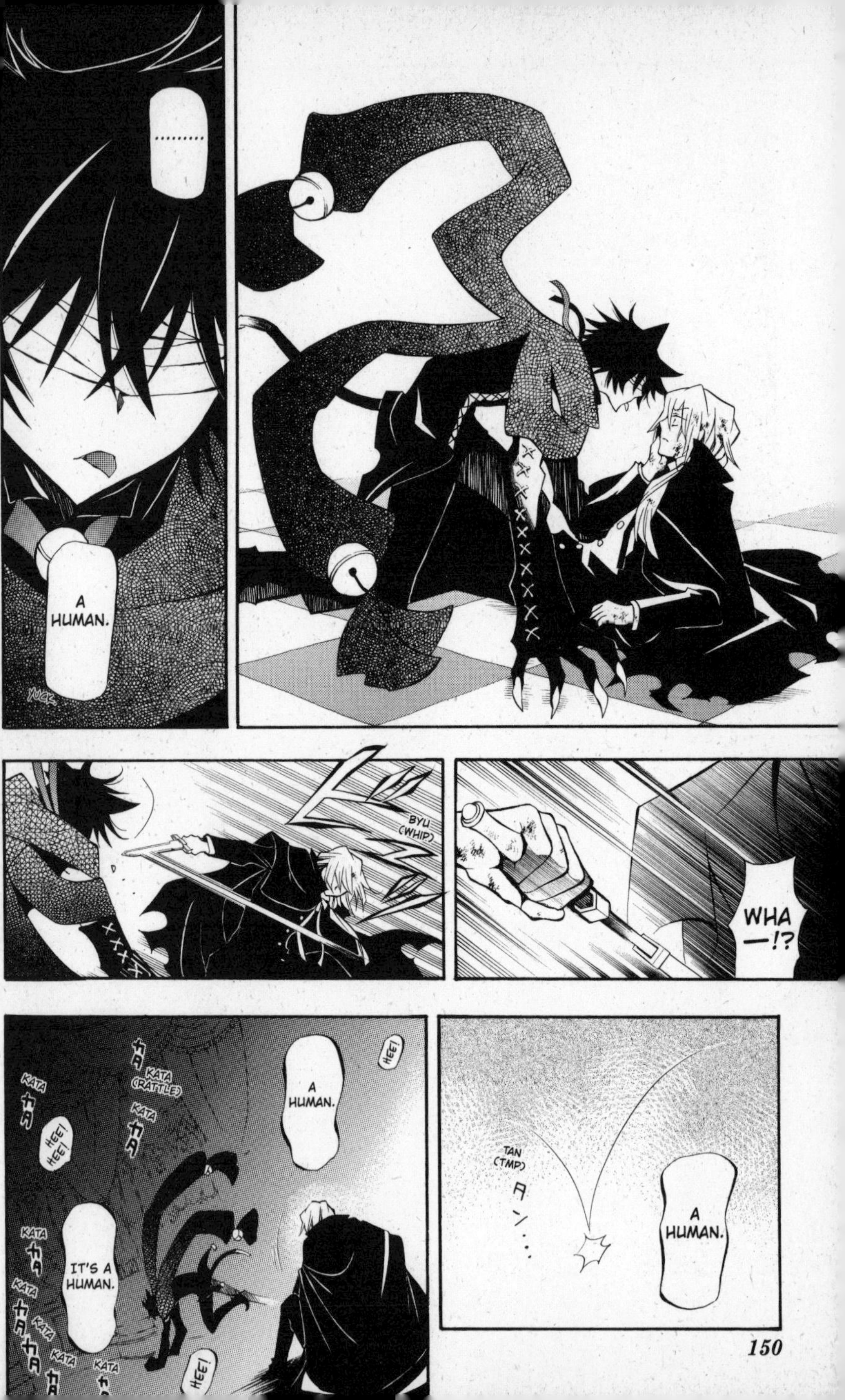
……
A HUMAN.
YUCK
WHA—!?
BYU (WHIP)
TAN (TMP)
A HUMAN.
HEE!
A HUMAN.
KATA (RATTLE)
KATA
KATA
HEE! HEE!
IT'S A HUMAN.
KATA
KATA
KATA
KATA
KATA
HEE!

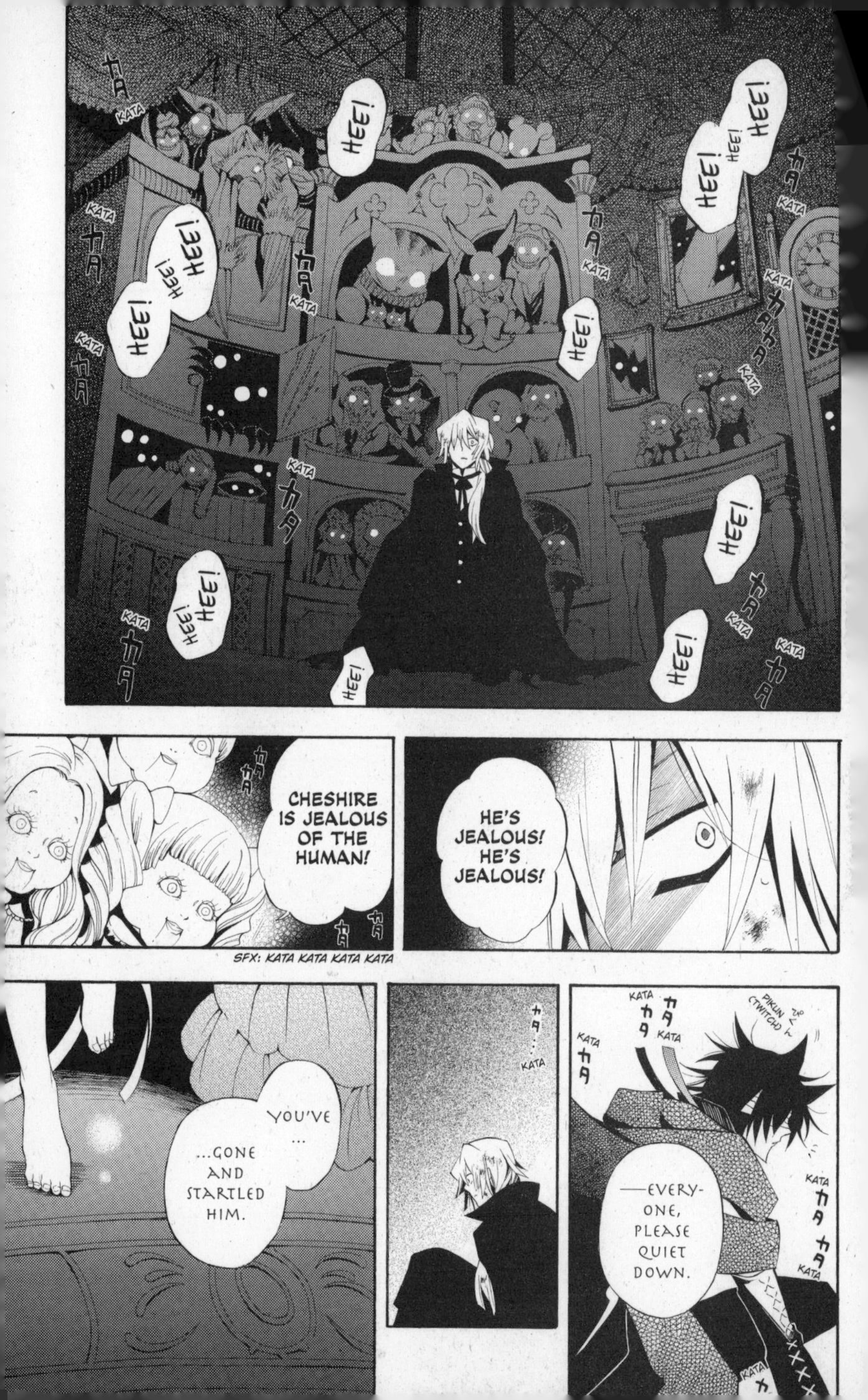

HEE! HEE! HEE!
KATA
KATA
KATA
KATA
HEE!
HEE!
KATA
HEE!
KATA
HEE!
KATA
HEE! HEE! HEE!
KATA
KATA
HEE! HEE!
KATA
HEE!
HE'S JEALOUS! HE'S JEALOUS!
CHESHIRE IS JEALOUS OF THE HUMAN!
SFX: KATA KATA KATA KATA
KATA
KATA
KATA
PIKUN (TWITCH)
KATA
—EVERYONE, PLEASE QUIET DOWN.
KATA
KATA
KATA
KATA
YOU'VE ...
...GONE AND STARTLED HIM.

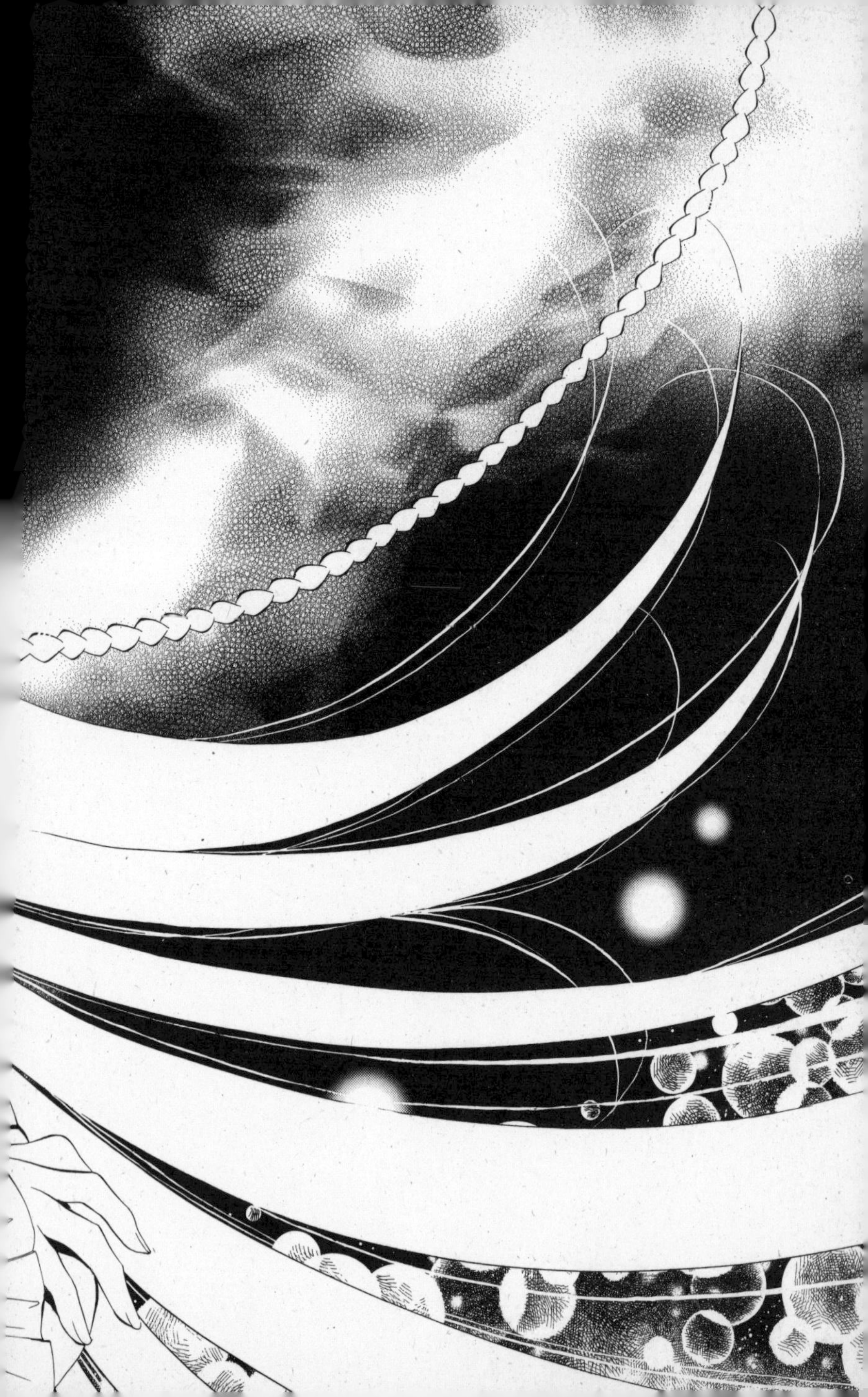

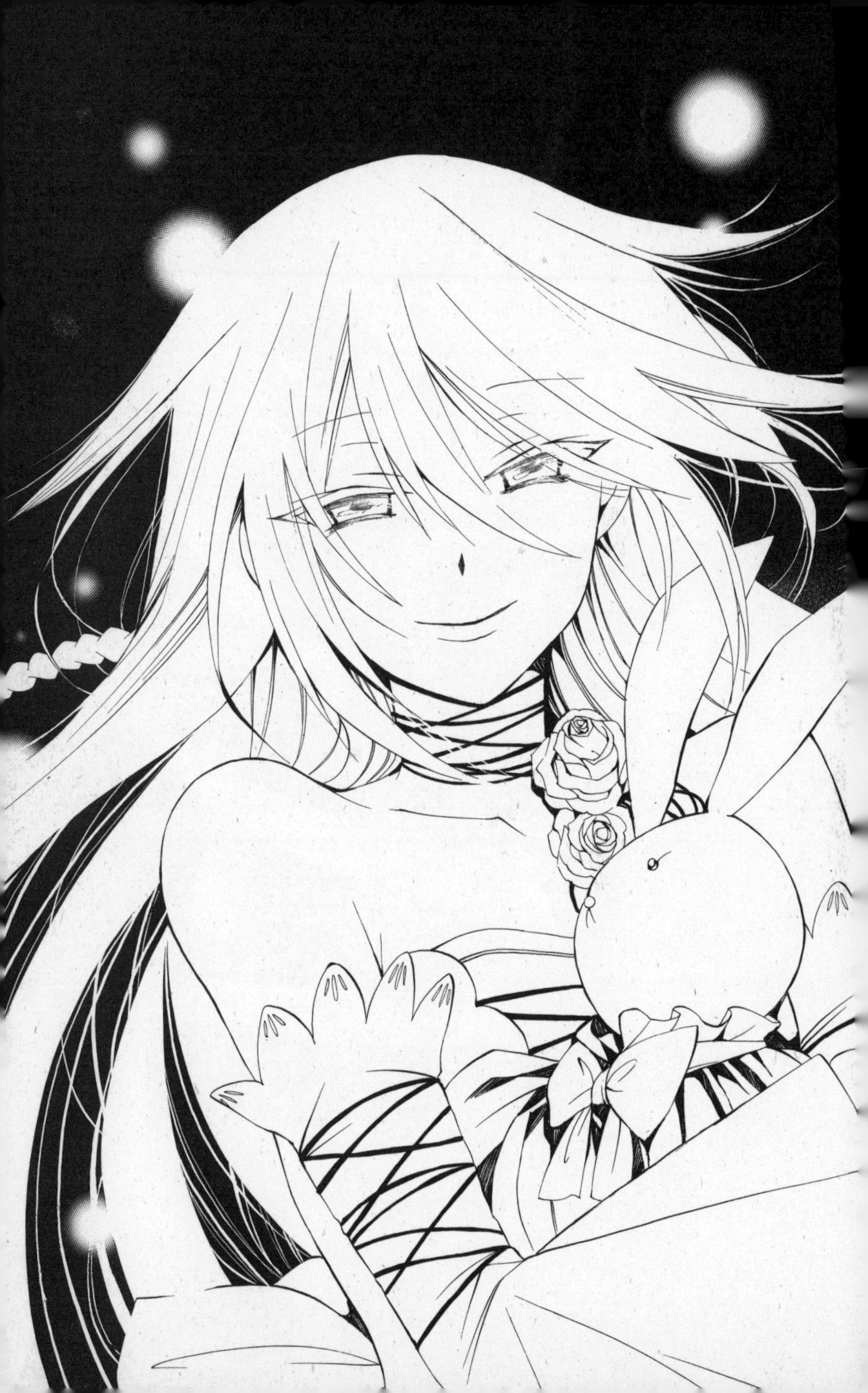

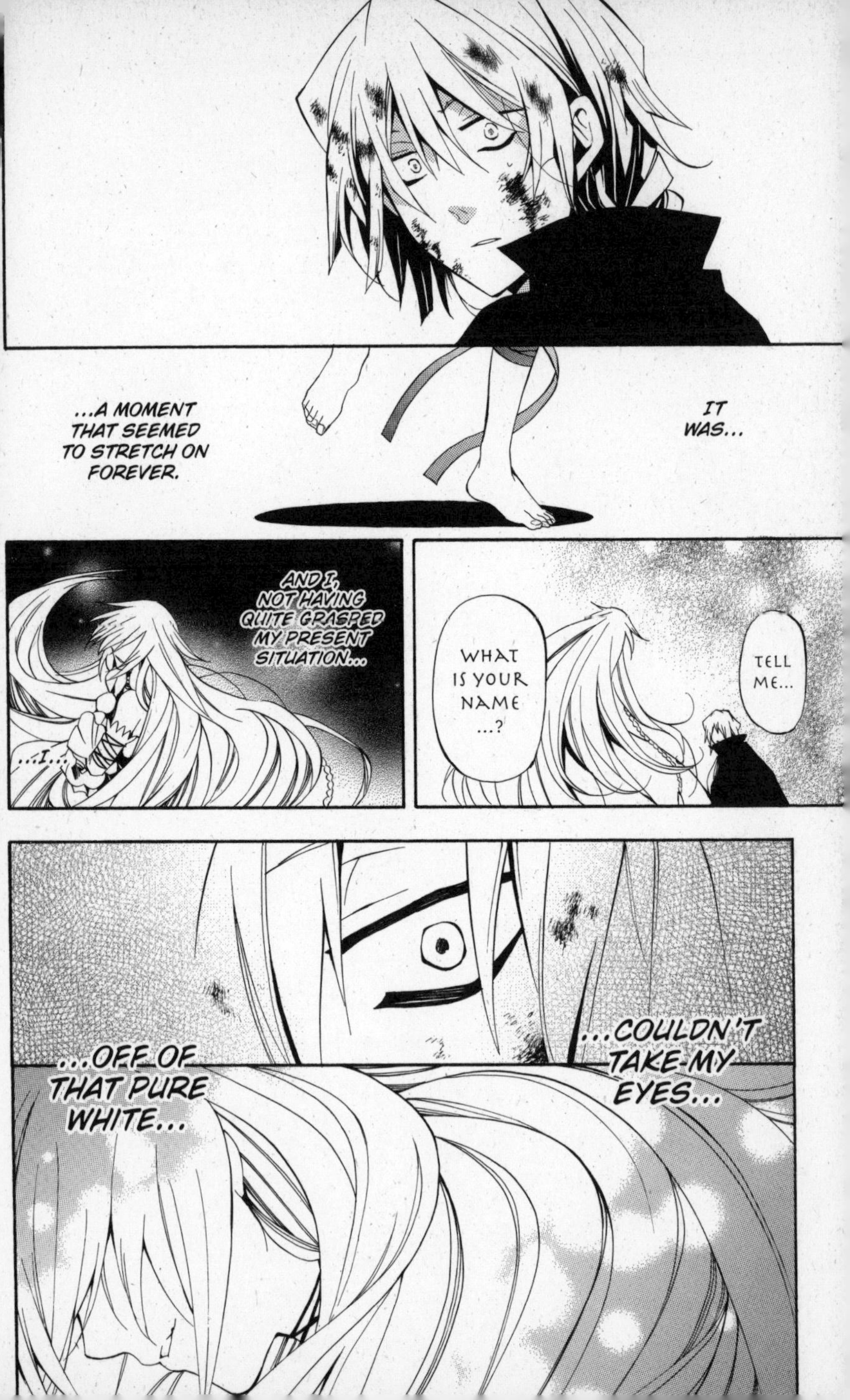
IT WAS...
...A MOMENT THAT SEEMED TO STRETCH ON FOREVER.
TELL ME...
WHAT IS YOUR NAME ...?
AND I, NOT HAVING QUITE GRASPED MY PRESENT SITUATION...
...I...
...COULDN'T TAKE MY EYES...
...OFF OF THAT PURE WHITE...

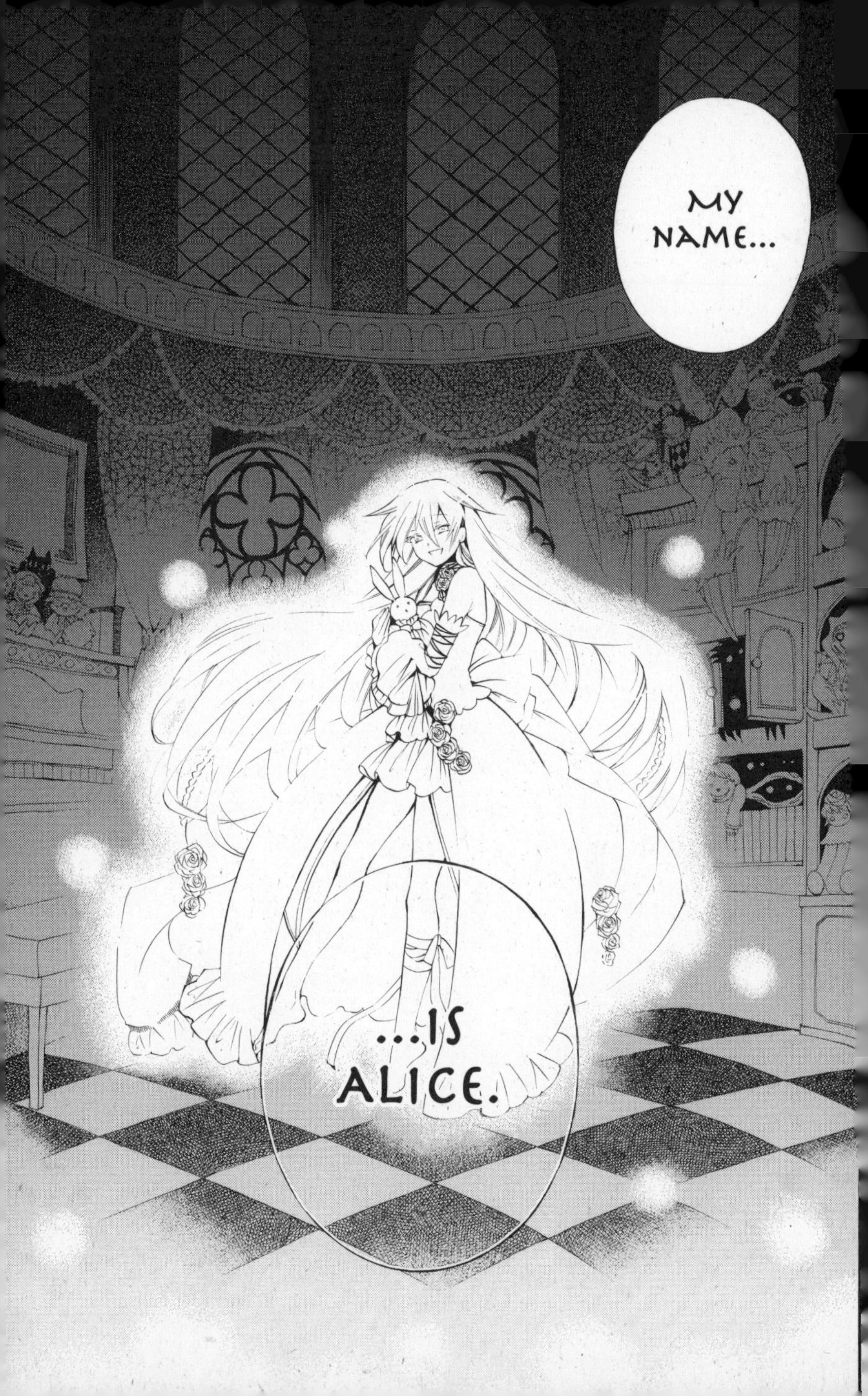
MY NAME...
...IS ALICE.

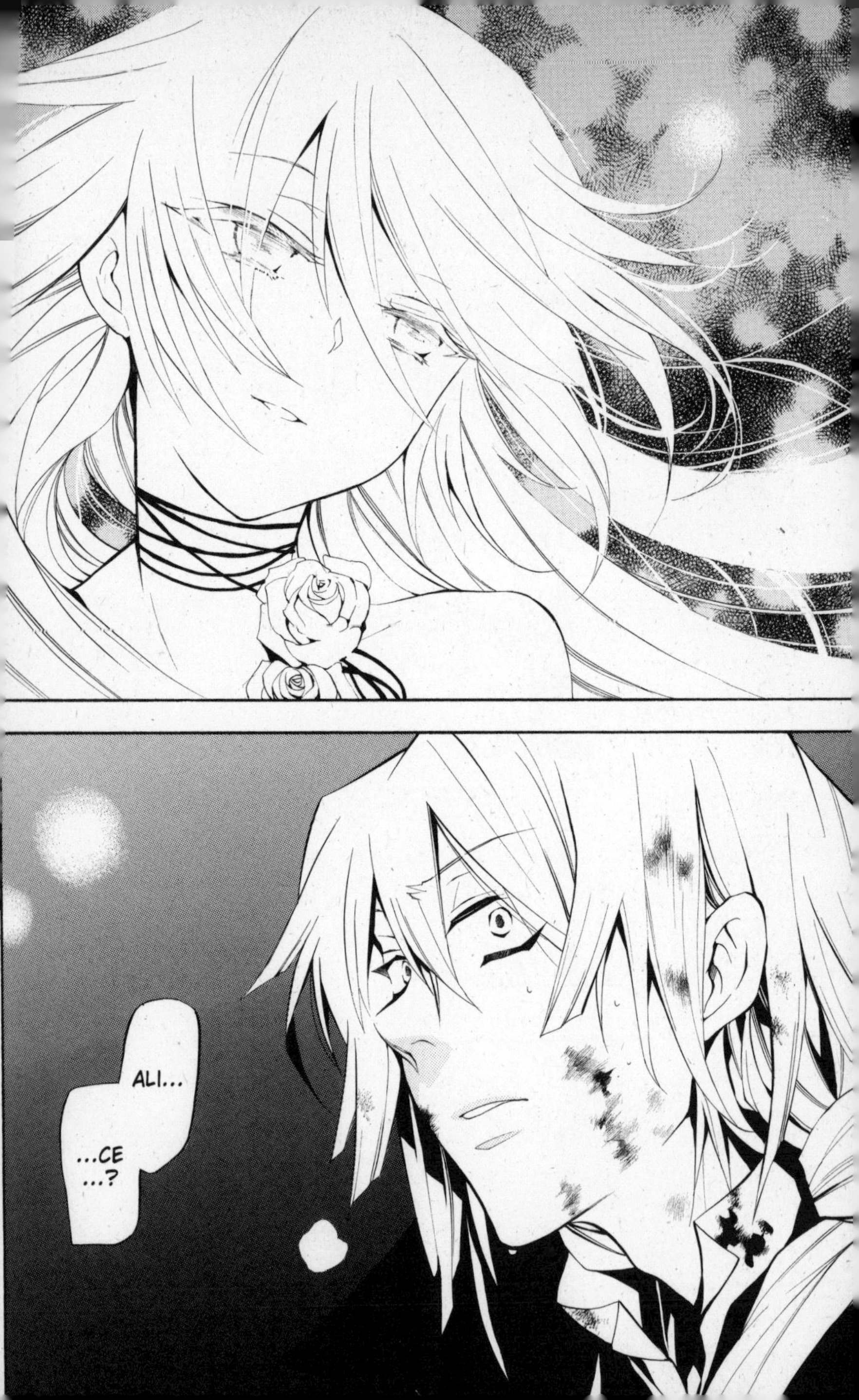
ALI...
...CE
...?

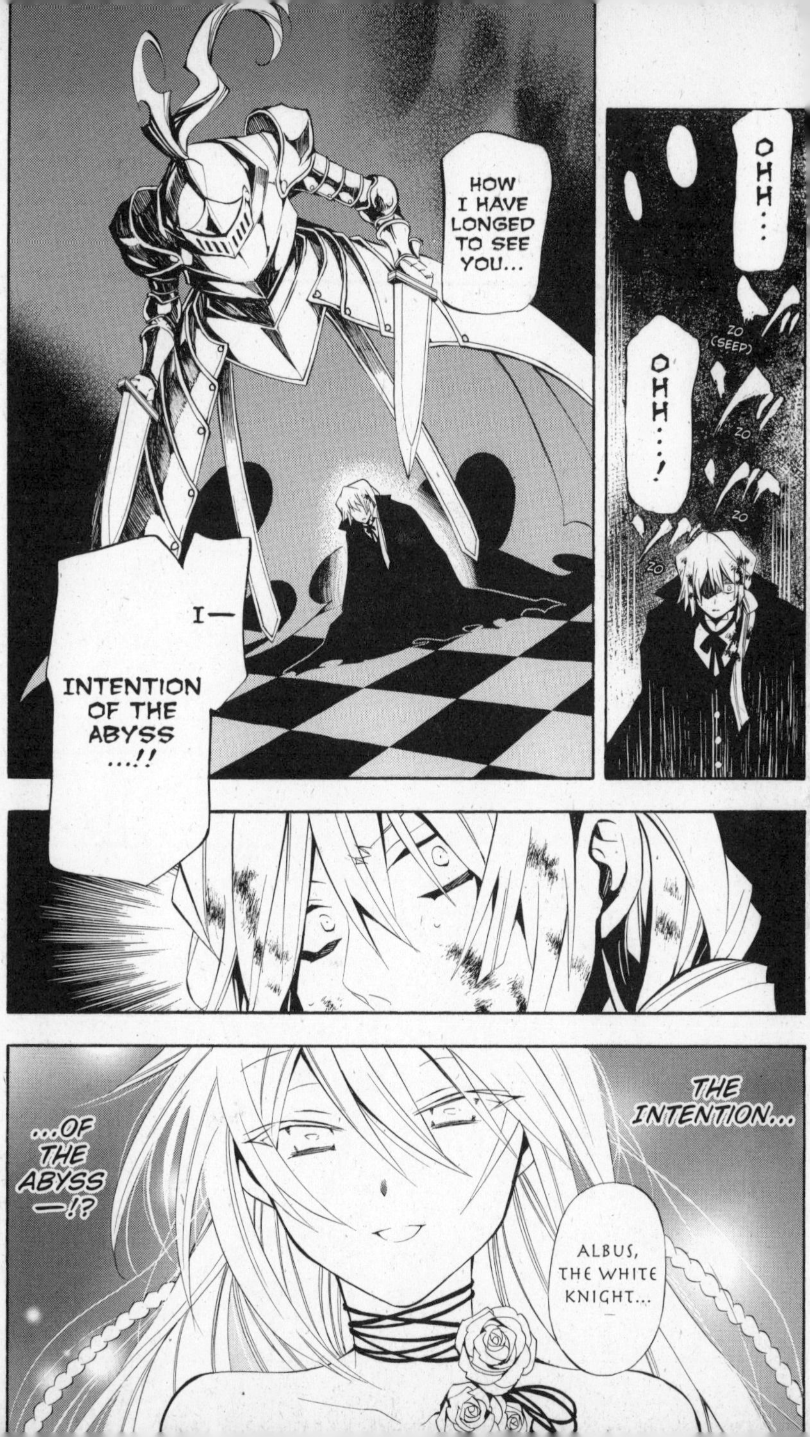
OHH...
ZO (SEEP)
OHH...!
ZO
ZO
ZO
HOW I HAVE LONGED TO SEE YOU...
I—
INTENTION OF THE ABYSS...!!
THE INTENTION...
...OF THE ABYSS—!?
ALBUS, THE WHITE KNIGHT...

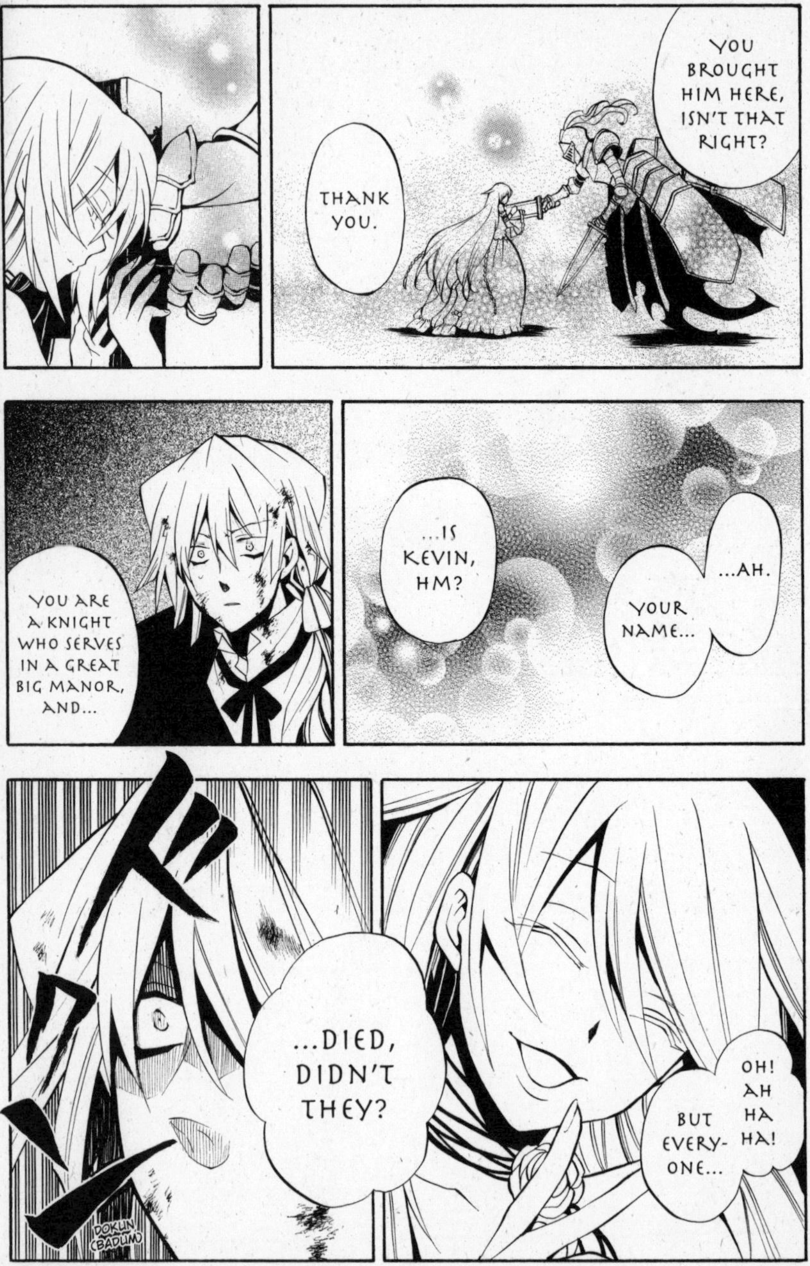
YOU BROUGHT HIM HERE, ISN'T THAT RIGHT?
THANK YOU.
...AH.
YOUR NAME...
...IS KEVIN, HM?
YOU ARE A KNIGHT WHO SERVES IN A GREAT BIG MANOR, AND...
OH! AH HA HA!
BUT EVERY-ONE...
...DIED, DIDN'T THEY?
DOKUN (BADUM)

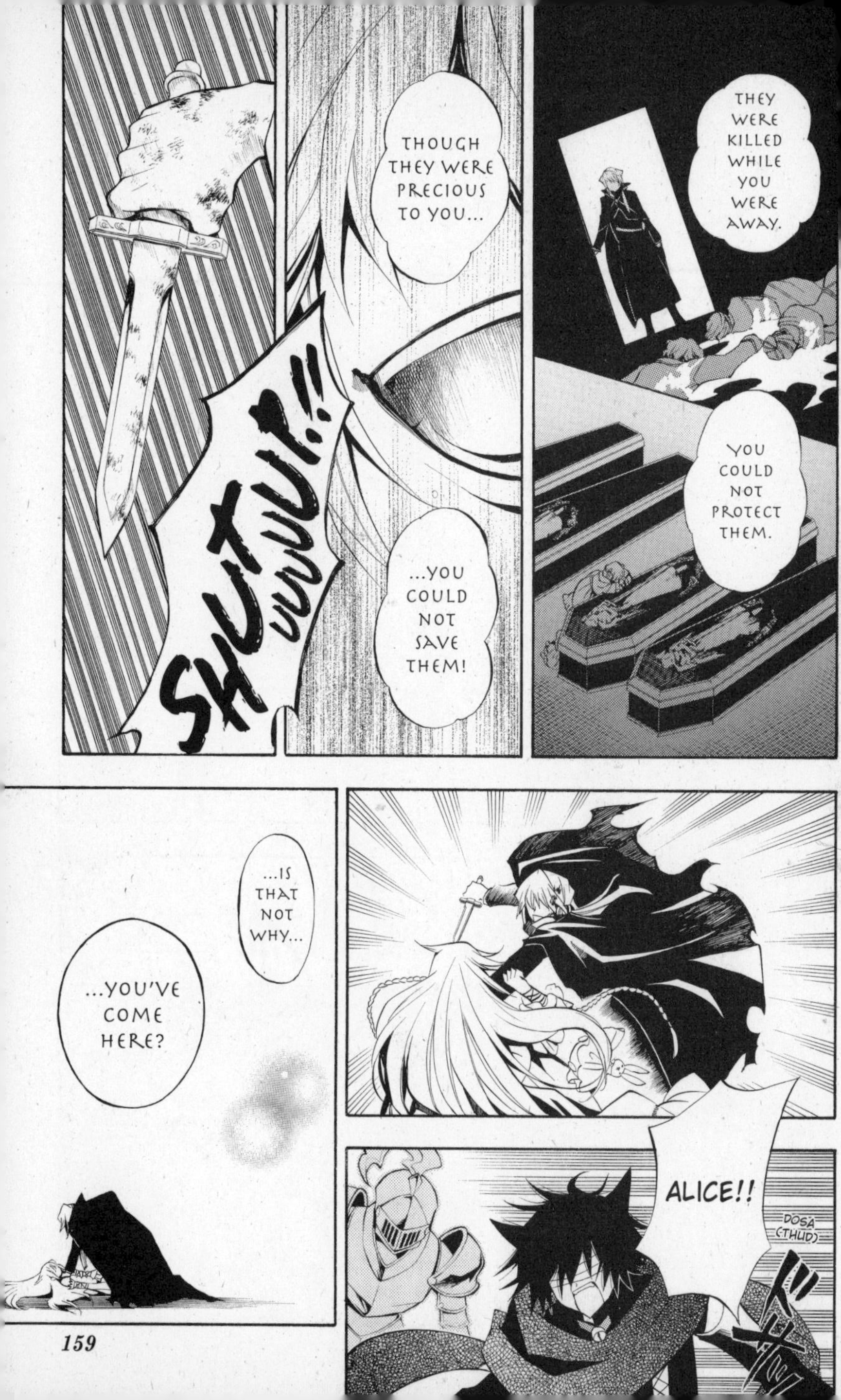
THEY WERE KILLED WHILE YOU WERE AWAY.
YOU COULD NOT PROTECT THEM.
THOUGH THEY WERE PRECIOUS TO YOU...
...YOU COULD NOT SAVE THEM!
SHUTUUUUUP!!
ALICE!!
DOSA (THUD)
ドサ
...IS THAT NOT WHY...
...YOU'VE COME HERE?

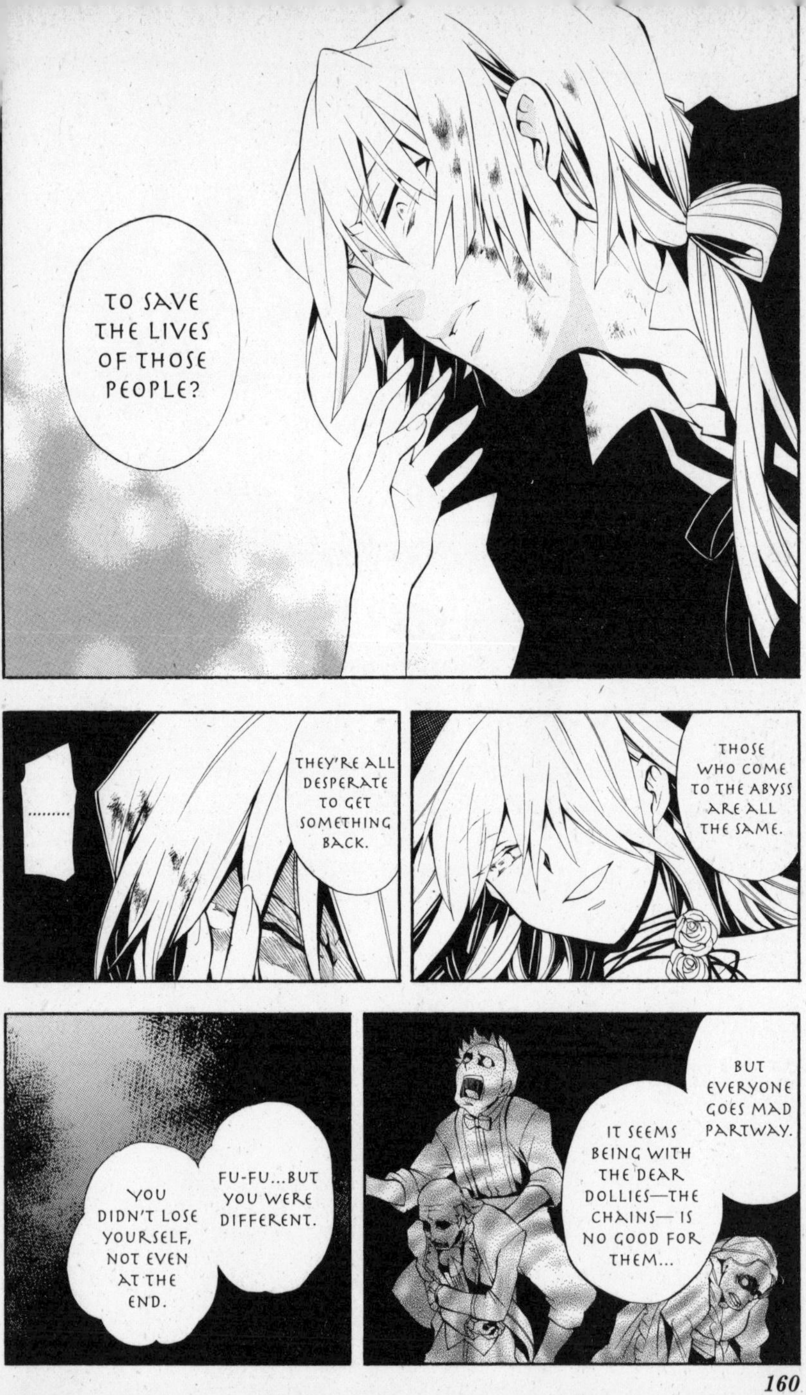
TO SAVE THE LIVES OF THOSE PEOPLE?
THOSE WHO COME TO THE ABYSS ARE ALL THE SAME.
THEY'RE ALL DESPERATE TO GET SOMETHING BACK.
....
BUT EVERYONE GOES MAD PARTWAY.
IT SEEMS BEING WITH THE DEAR DOLLIES—THE CHAINS— IS NO GOOD FOR THEM...
FU-FU...BUT YOU WERE DIFFERENT.
YOU DIDN'T LOSE YOURSELF, NOT EVEN AT THE END.

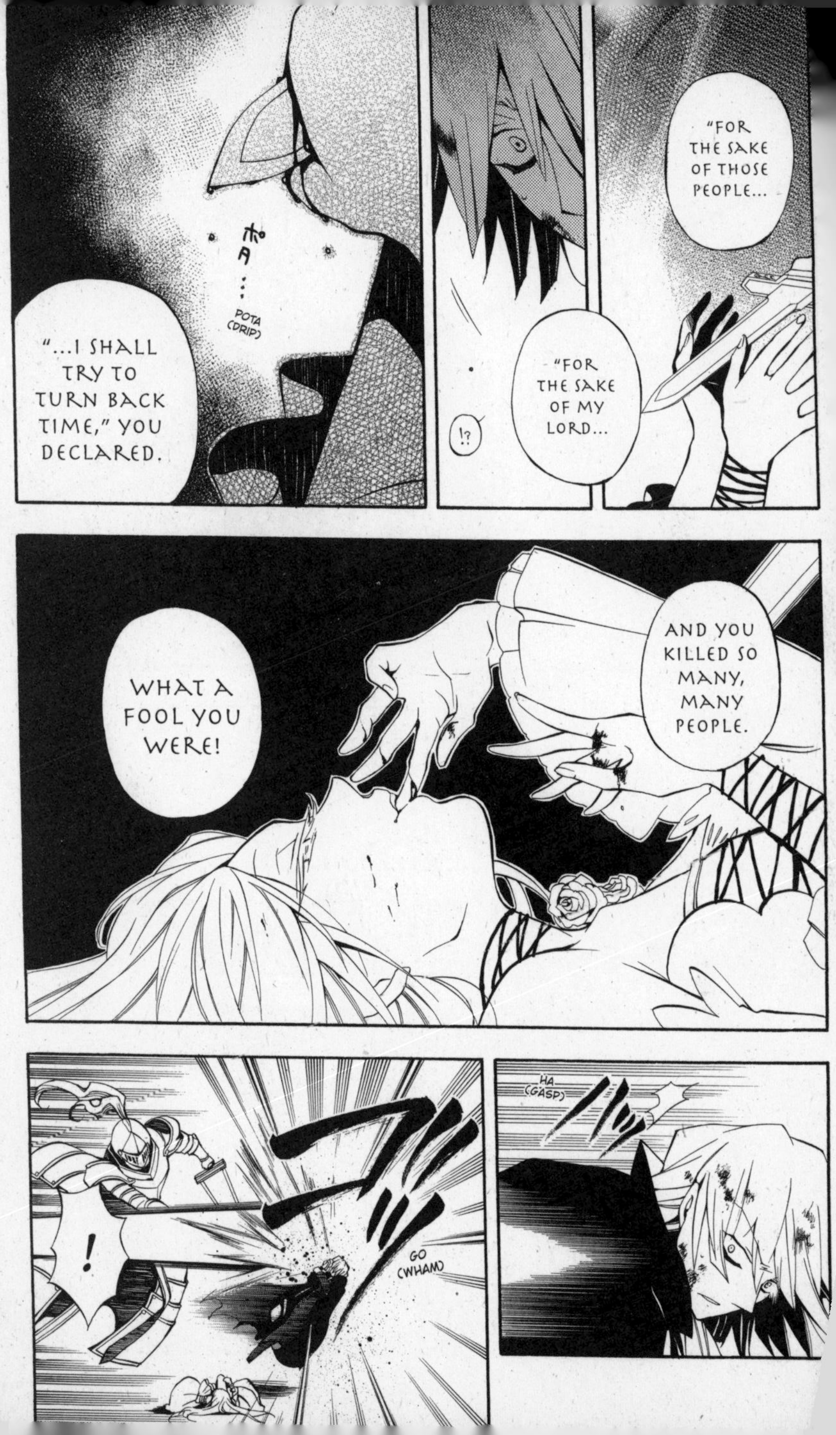

"FOR THE SAKE OF THOSE PEOPLE...
"FOR THE SAKE OF MY LORD...
!?
ポタ…
POTA (DRIP)
"...I SHALL TRY TO TURN BACK TIME," YOU DECLARED.
AND YOU KILLED SO MANY, MANY PEOPLE.
WHAT A FOOL YOU WERE!
HA (GASP)
GO (WHAM)
!

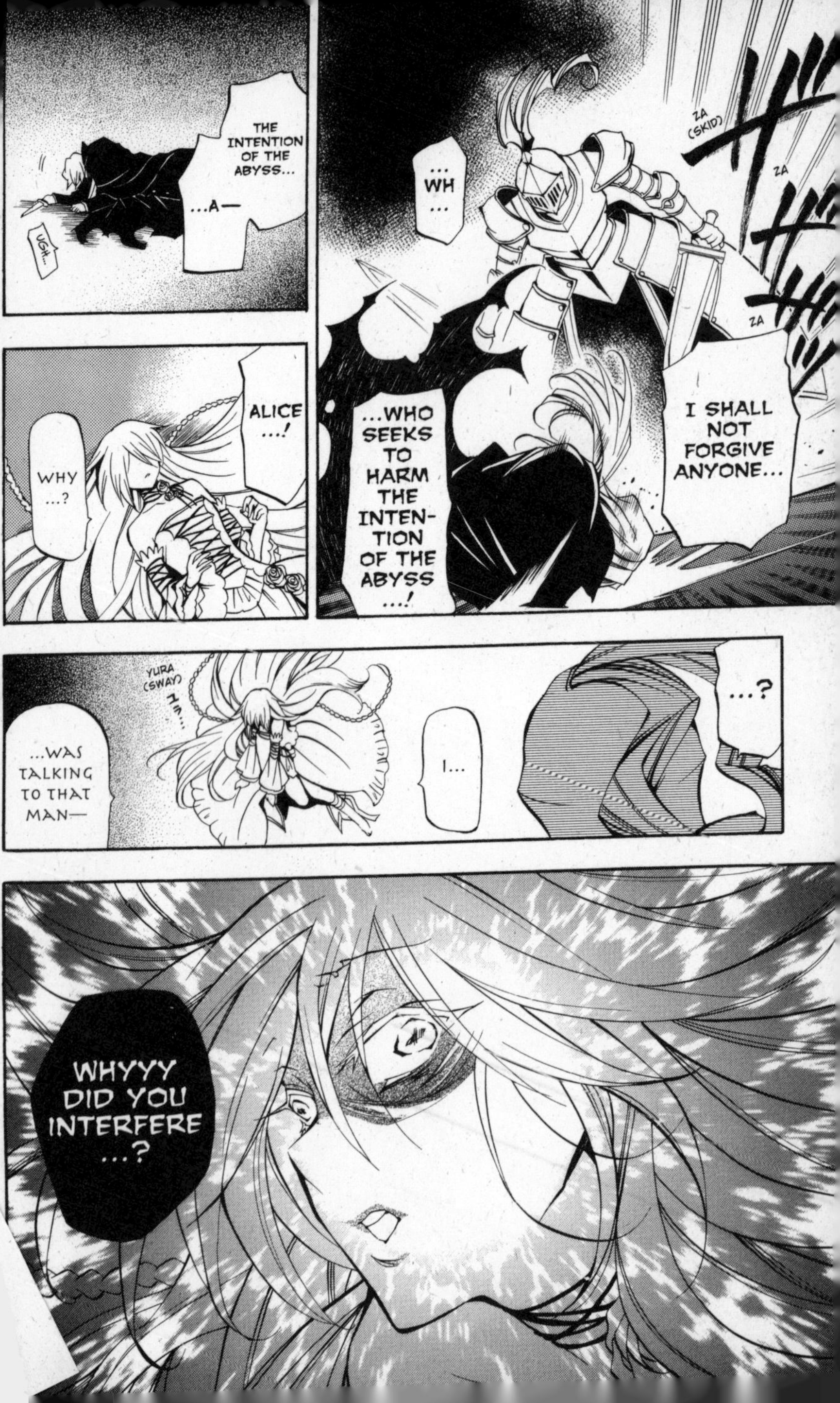
ZA (SKID)
ZA
ZA
...WH...
I SHALL NOT FORGIVE ANYONE...
...WHO SEEKS TO HARM THE INTENTION OF THE ABYSS...!
THE INTENTION OF THE ABYSS...
...A—
UGH...
ALICE...!
WHY...?
...?
I...
YURA (SWAY)
...WAS TALKING TO THAT MAN—
WHYYY DID YOU INTERFERE...?

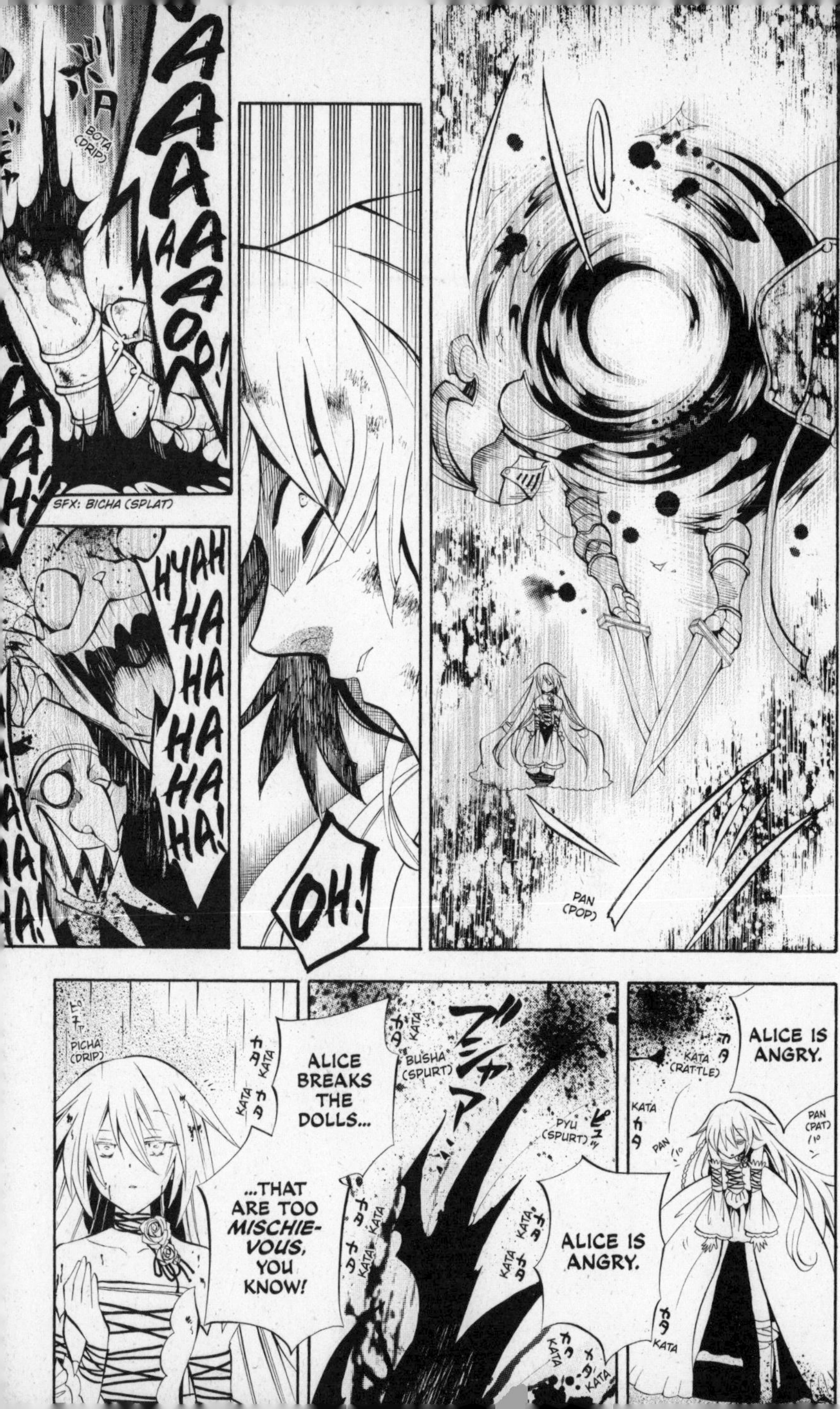

PAN (POP)
OH!
AAAAAAAOOO!
BOTA (DRIP)
AAH AH!
SFX: BICHA (SPLAT)
HYAH HA HA HA HA HA HA!
HAHA HA!
ALICE IS ANGRY.
KATA (RATTLE)
KATA
PAN
PAN (PAT)
KATA
BUSHA (SPURT)
KATA
PYU (SPURT)
ALICE IS ANGRY.
KATA KATA KATA KATA
KATA KATA KATA
PICHA (DRIP)
KATA KATA
KATA
ALICE BREAKS THE DOLLS...
...THAT ARE TOO MISCHIEVOUS, YOU KNOW!

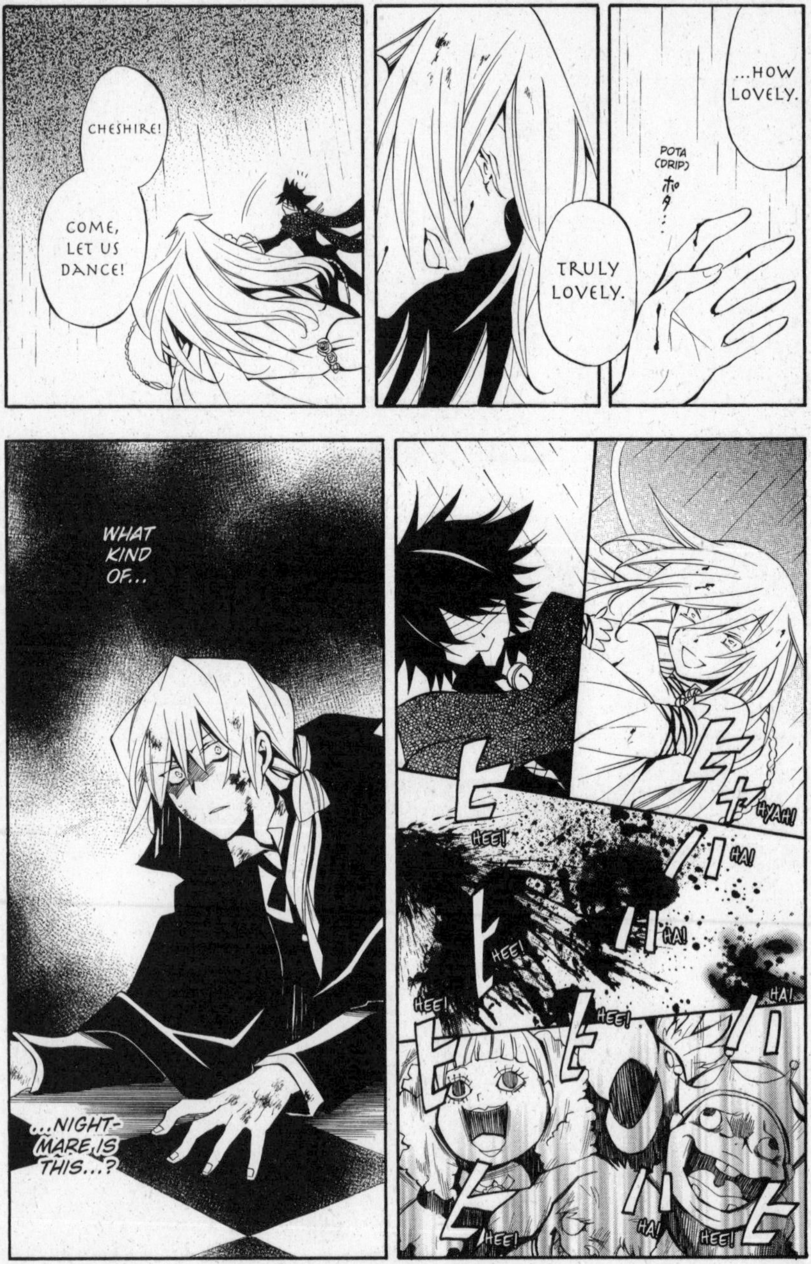
...HOW LOVELY.
POTA (DRIP)
ポタ...
TRULY LOVELY.
CHESHIRE!
COME, LET US DANCE!
HYAH!
HEE!
HA!
HEE!
HA!
HEE!
HEE!
HA!
HEE!
HA!
HEE!
WHAT KIND OF...
...NIGHT-MARE IS THIS...?

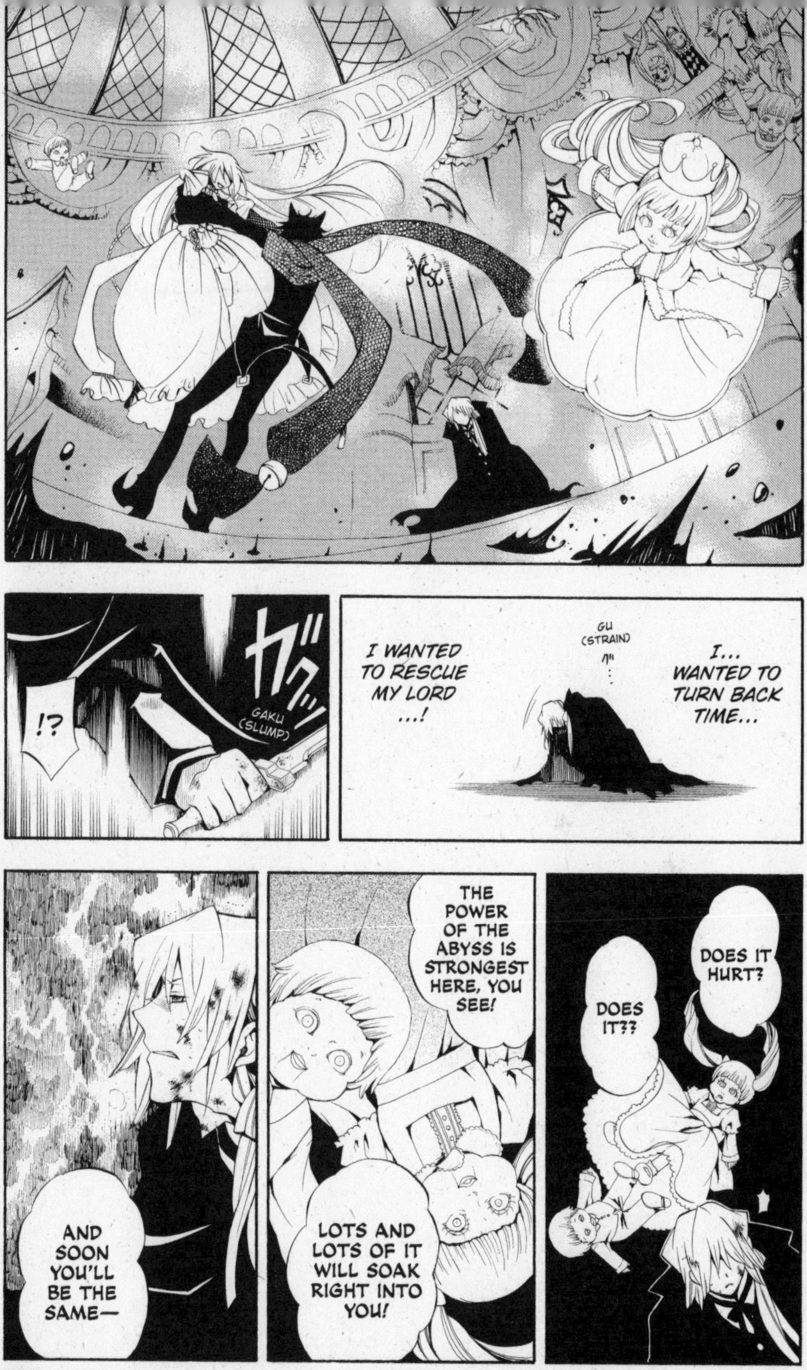
I... WANTED TO TURN BACK TIME...
GU (STRAIN)
I WANTED TO RESCUE MY LORD ...!
GAKU (SLUMP)
!?
DOES IT HURT?
DOES IT??
THE POWER OF THE ABYSS IS STRONGEST HERE, YOU SEE!
LOTS AND LOTS OF IT WILL SOAK RIGHT INTO YOU!
AND SOON YOU'LL BE THE SAME—

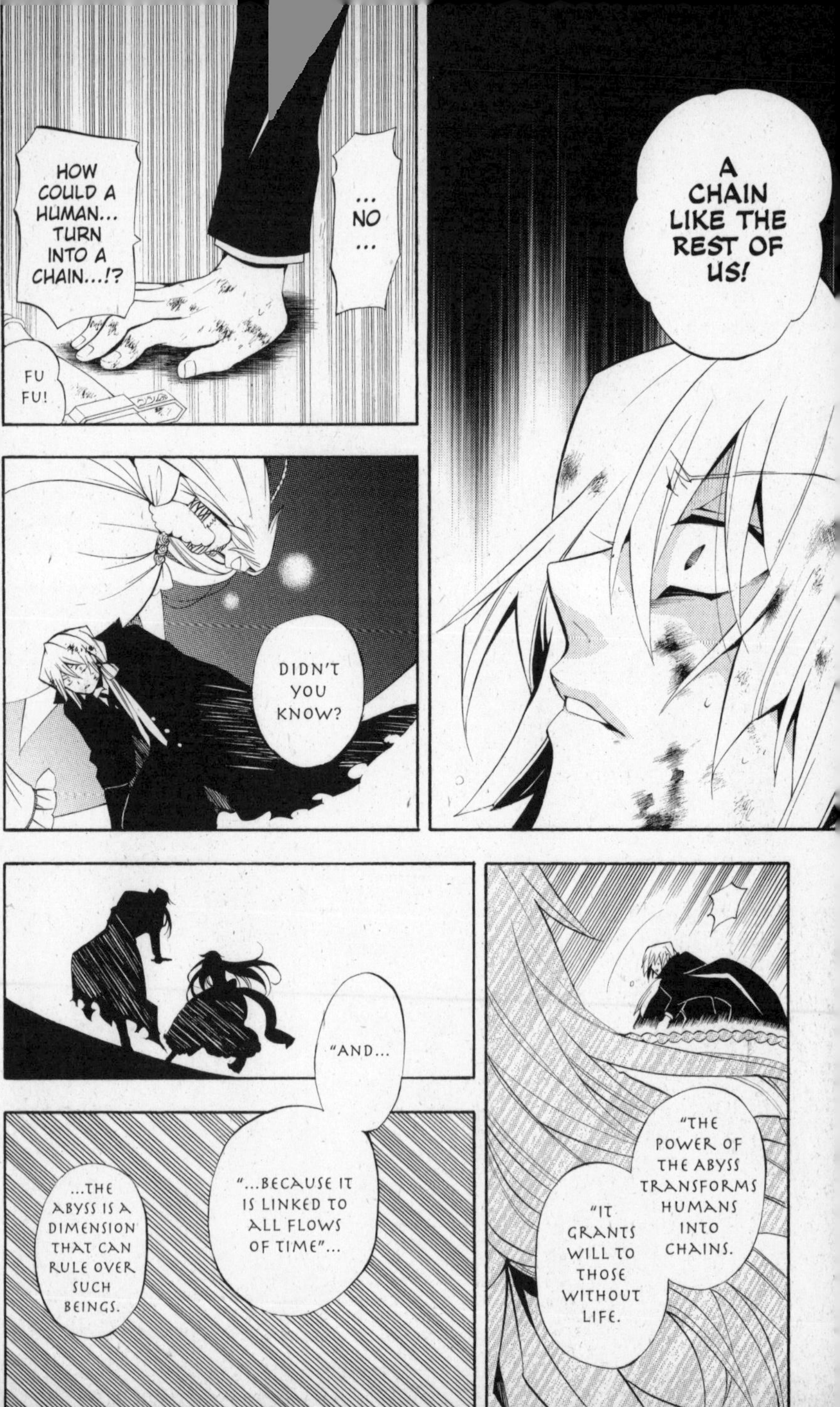
A CHAIN LIKE THE REST OF US!
...NO...
HOW COULD A HUMAN... TURN INTO A CHAIN...!?
FU FU!
DIDN'T YOU KNOW?
"THE POWER OF THE ABYSS TRANSFORMS HUMANS INTO CHAINS.
"IT GRANTS WILL TO THOSE WITHOUT LIFE.
"AND...
"...BECAUSE IT IS LINKED TO ALL FLOWS OF TIME"...
...THE ABYSS IS A DIMENSION THAT CAN RULE OVER SUCH BEINGS.

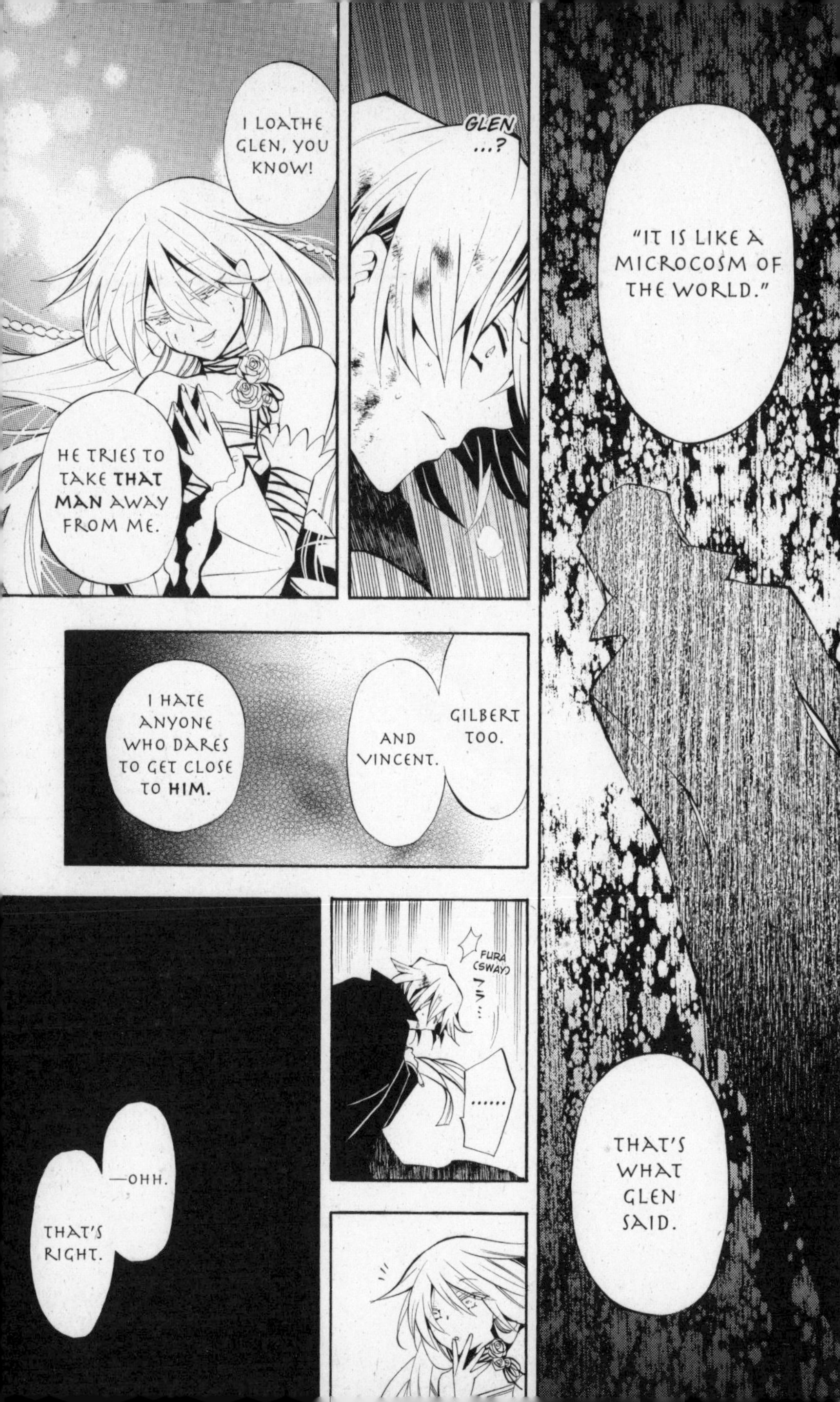
"IT IS LIKE A MICROCOSM OF THE WORLD."
THAT'S WHAT GLEN SAID.
GLEN ...?
I LOATHE GLEN, YOU KNOW!
HE TRIES TO TAKE **THAT MAN** AWAY FROM ME.
GILBERT TOO.
AND VINCENT.
I HATE ANYONE WHO DARES TO GET CLOSE TO **HIM.**
FURA (SWAY)
フラ…
......
—OHH.
THAT'S RIGHT.

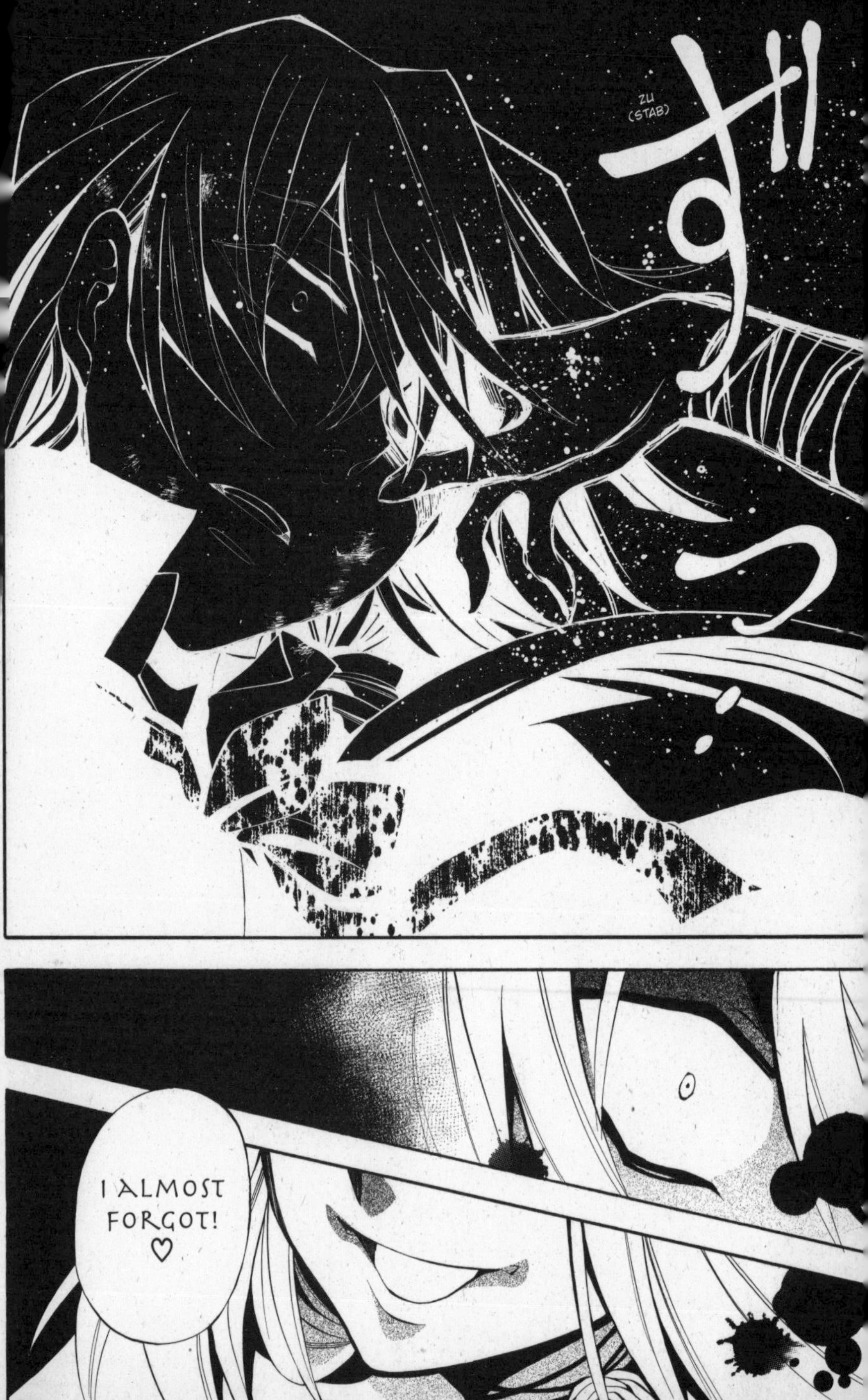
ZU (STAB)
I ALMOST FORGOT! ♡

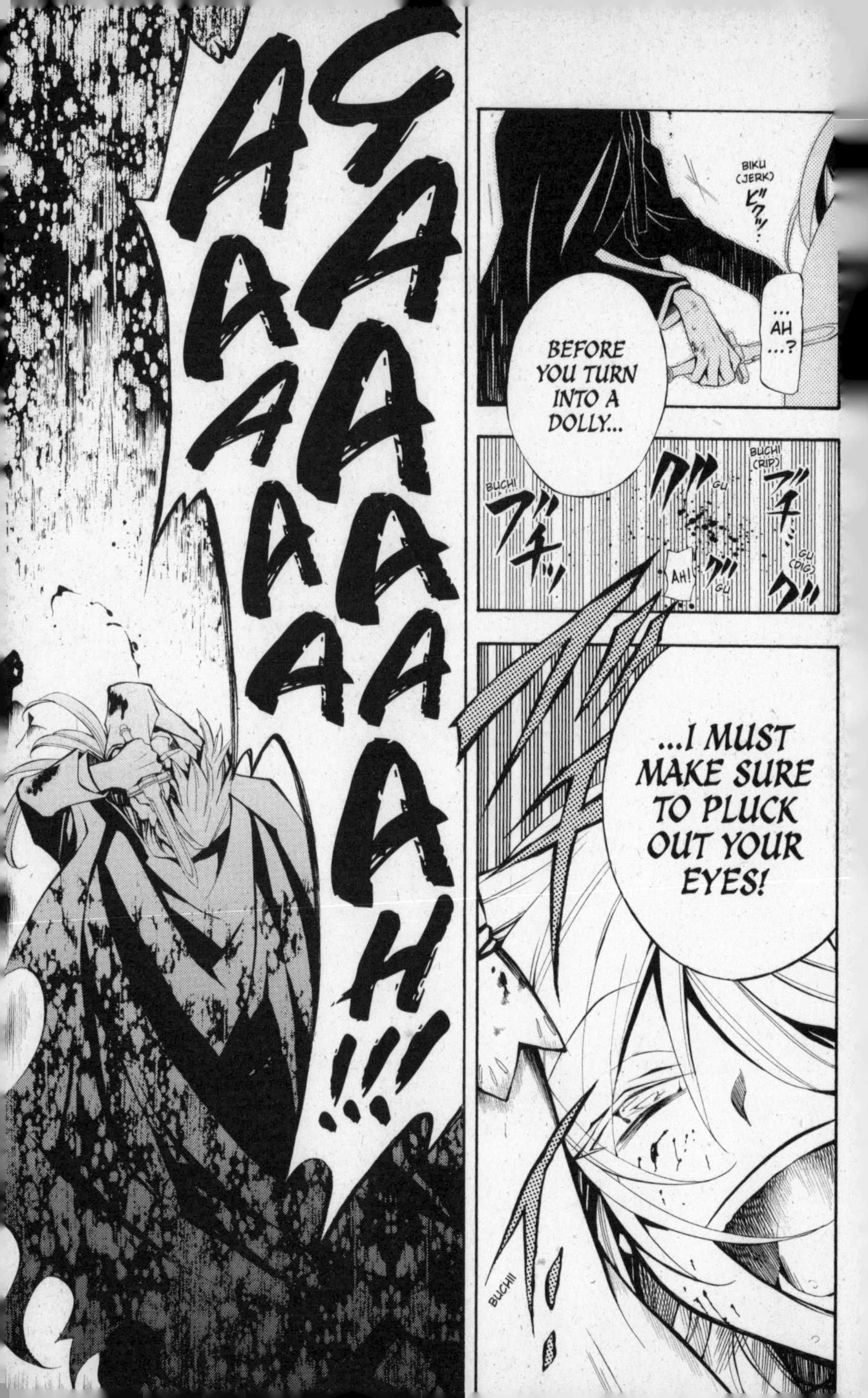
BIKU (JERK)
...AH...?
BEFORE YOU TURN INTO A DOLLY...
BUCHI (RIP)
GU (DIG)
GU
AH!
GU
BUCHI
...I MUST MAKE SURE TO PLUCK OUT YOUR EYES!
BUCHI!
AGAAAAAAAAAAAAAH!!!

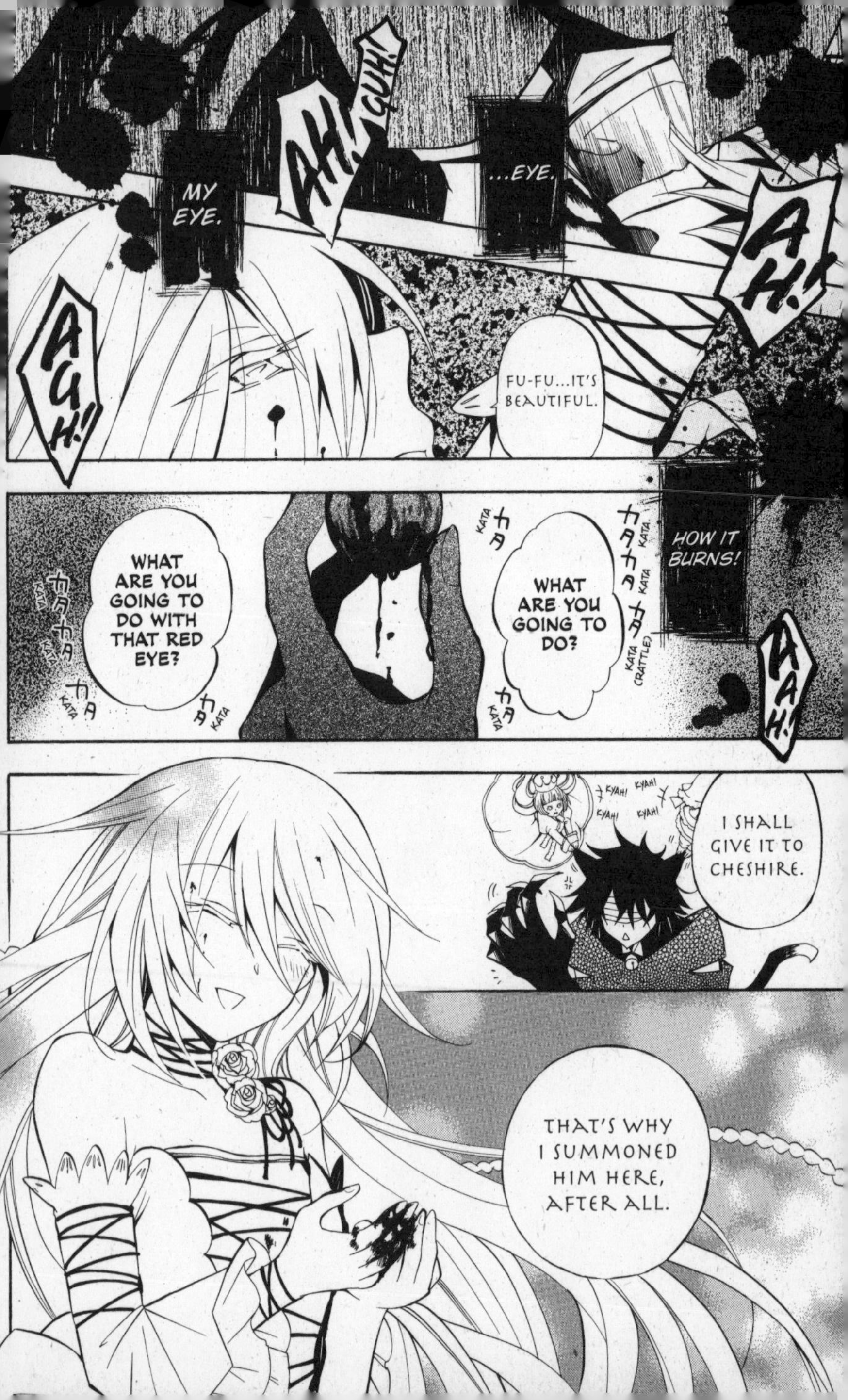

AH!
...EYE.
GUH!
AH!
MY EYE.
FU-FU...IT'S BEAUTIFUL.
AGUH!
HOW IT BURNS!
AAAH!
カタ KATA
カタ KATA
カタ KATA (RATTLE)
WHAT ARE YOU GOING TO DO?
カタ KATA
カタ KATA
WHAT ARE YOU GOING TO DO WITH THAT RED EYE?
カタ KATA
カタ KATA
カタ KATA
I SHALL GIVE IT TO CHESHIRE.
KYAH! KYAH! KYAH! KYAH!
THAT'S WHY I SUMMONED HIM HERE, AFTER ALL.

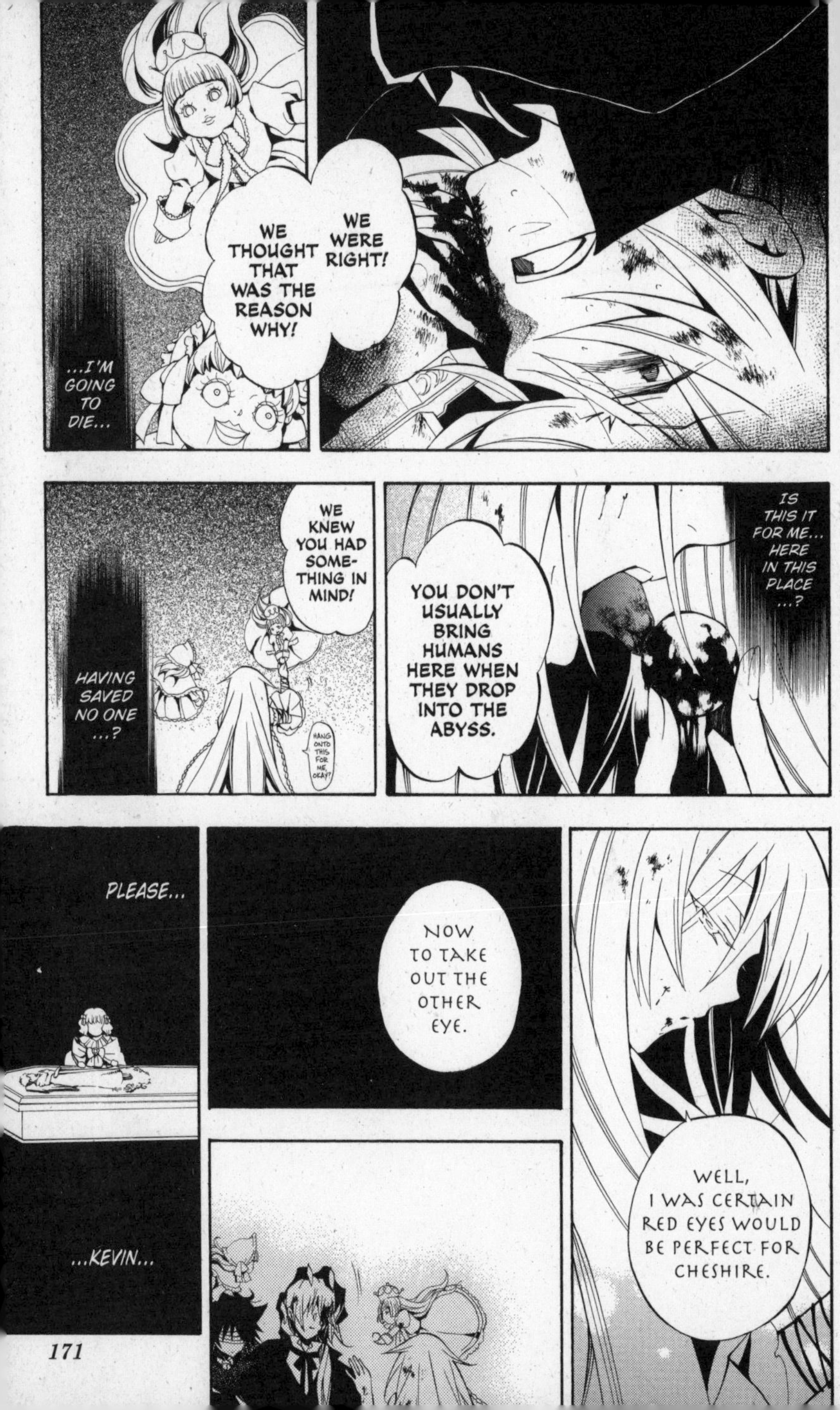
WE WERE RIGHT!
WE THOUGHT THAT WAS THE REASON WHY!
...I'M GOING TO DIE...
IS THIS IT FOR ME... HERE IN THIS PLACE ...?
YOU DON'T USUALLY BRING HUMANS HERE WHEN THEY DROP INTO THE ABYSS.
WE KNEW YOU HAD SOME-THING IN MIND!
HAVING SAVED NO ONE ...?
HANG ONTO THIS FOR ME, OKAY?
WELL, I WAS CERTAIN RED EYES WOULD BE PERFECT FOR CHESHIRE.
NOW TO TAKE OUT THE OTHER EYE.
PLEASE...
...KEVIN...

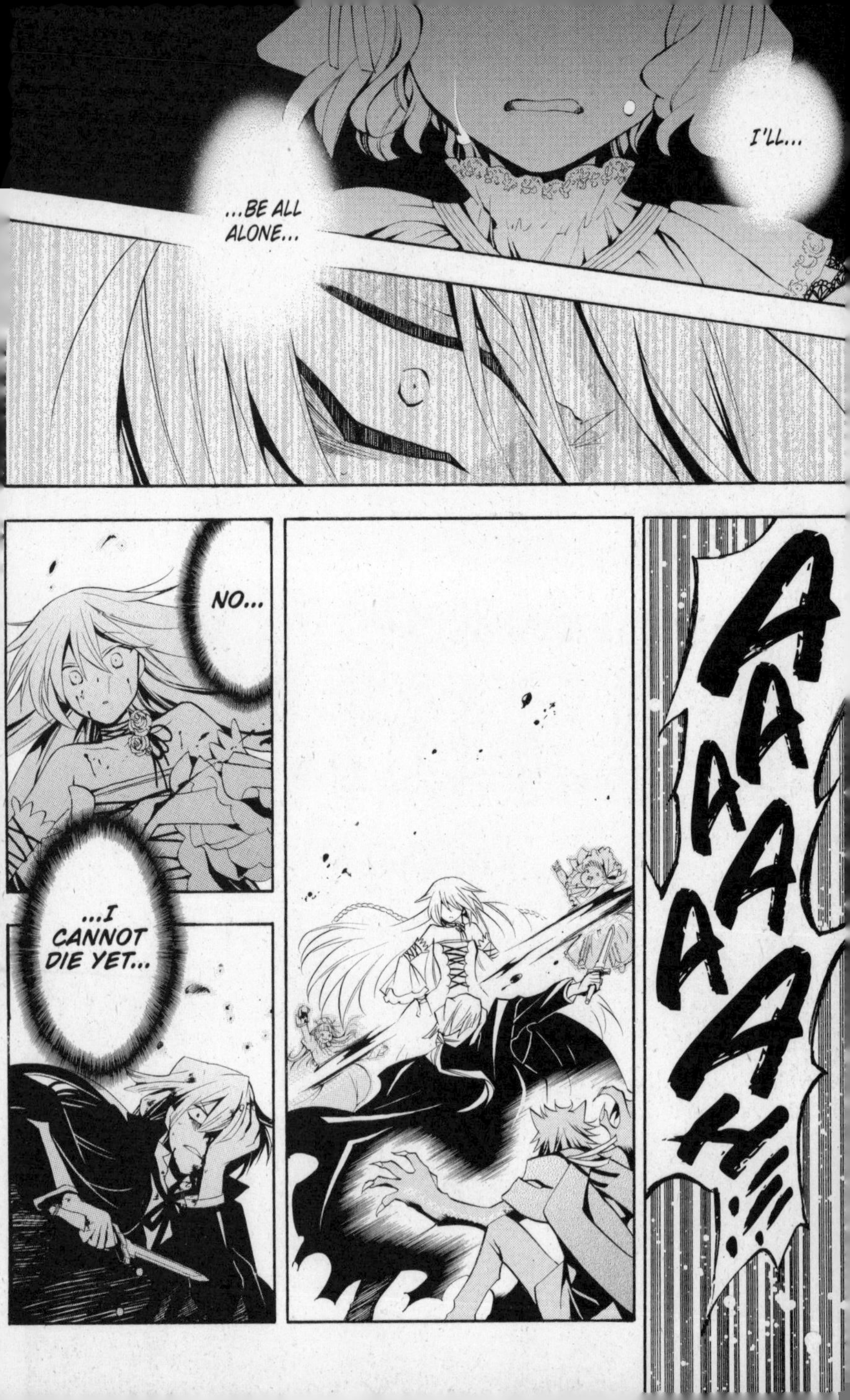
I'LL...
...BE ALL ALONE...
AAAAAAAAH!!!
NO...
...I CANNOT DIE YET...

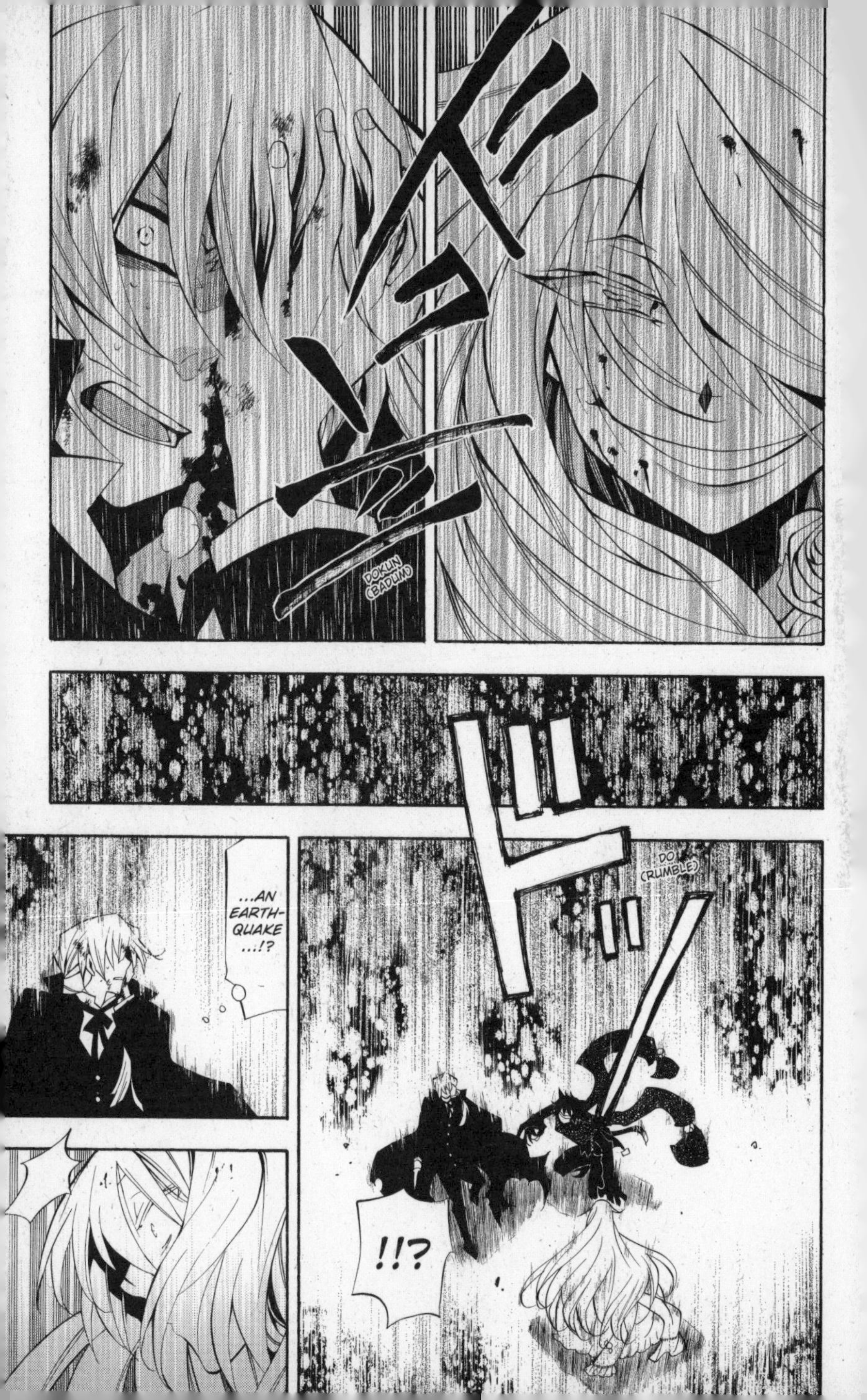
DOKUN (BADUM)
DO (RUMBLE)
!!?
...AN EARTH-QUAKE ...!?

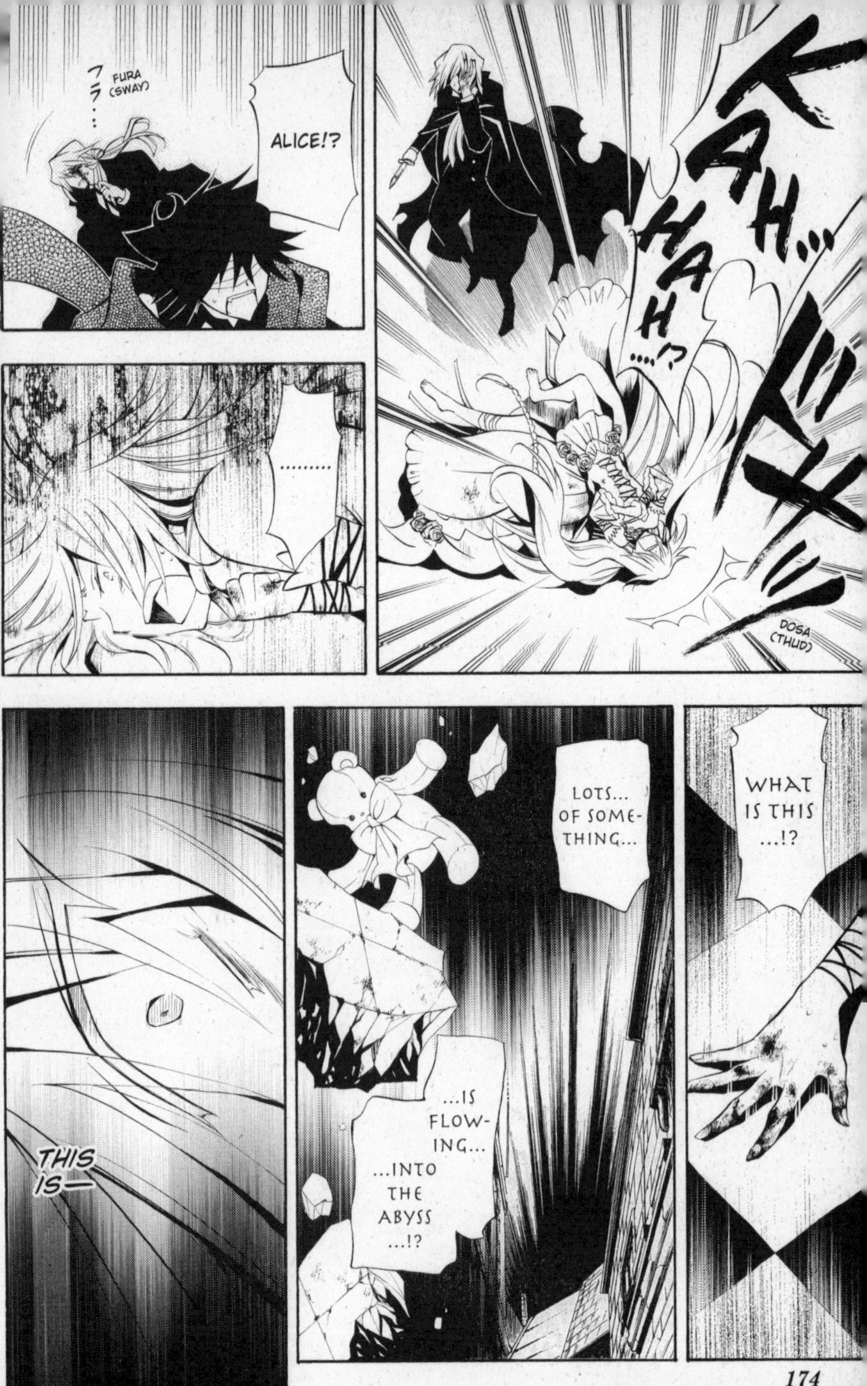
KAH... HAH....!?
DOSA (THUD)
FURA (SWAY)
ALICE!?
....
WHAT IS THIS ...!?
LOTS... OF SOME-THING...
...IS FLOWING...
...INTO THE ABYSS ...!?
THIS IS—

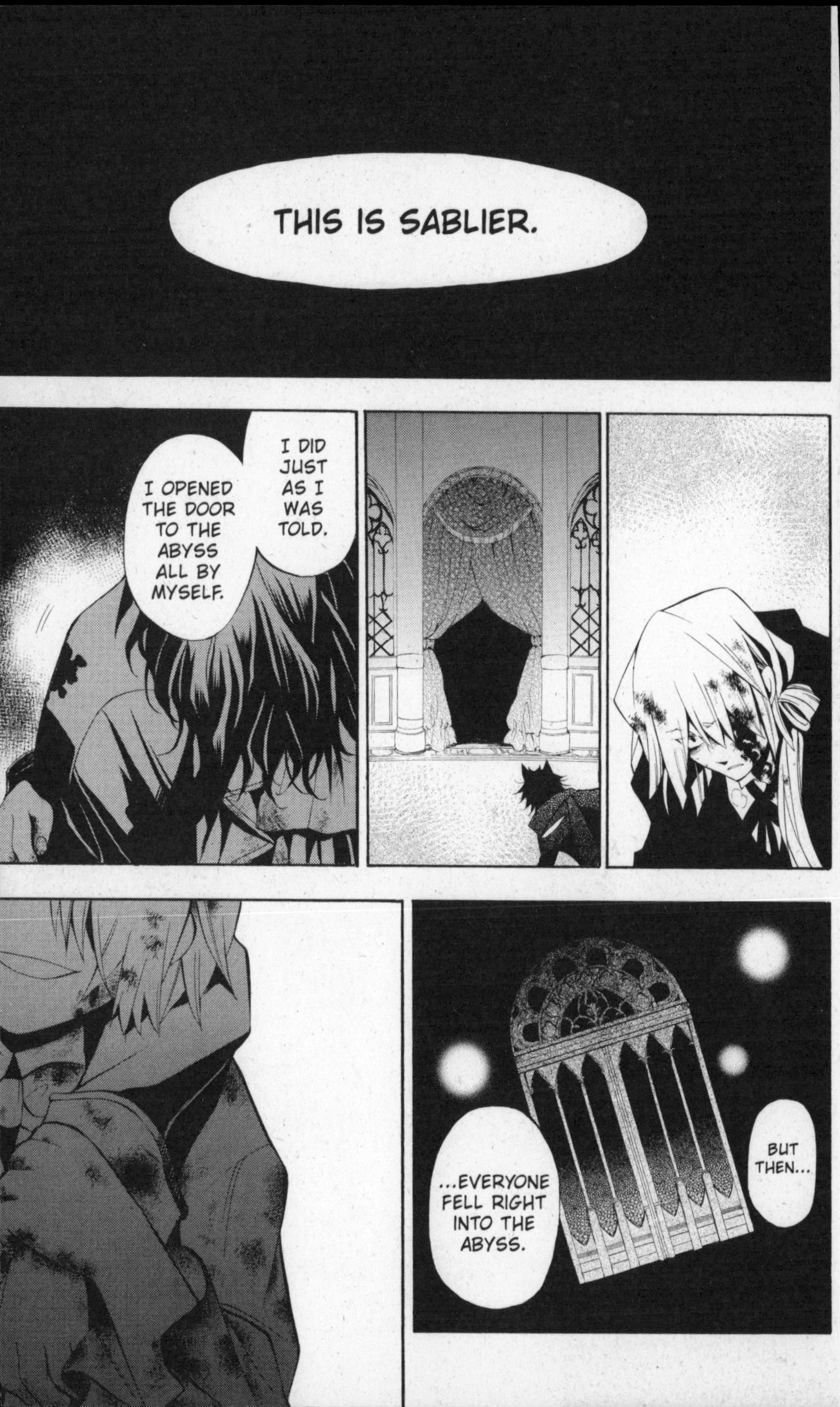
THIS IS SABLIER.
I DID JUST AS I WAS TOLD.
I OPENED THE DOOR TO THE ABYSS ALL BY MYSELF.
BUT THEN...
...EVERYONE FELL RIGHT INTO THE ABYSS.

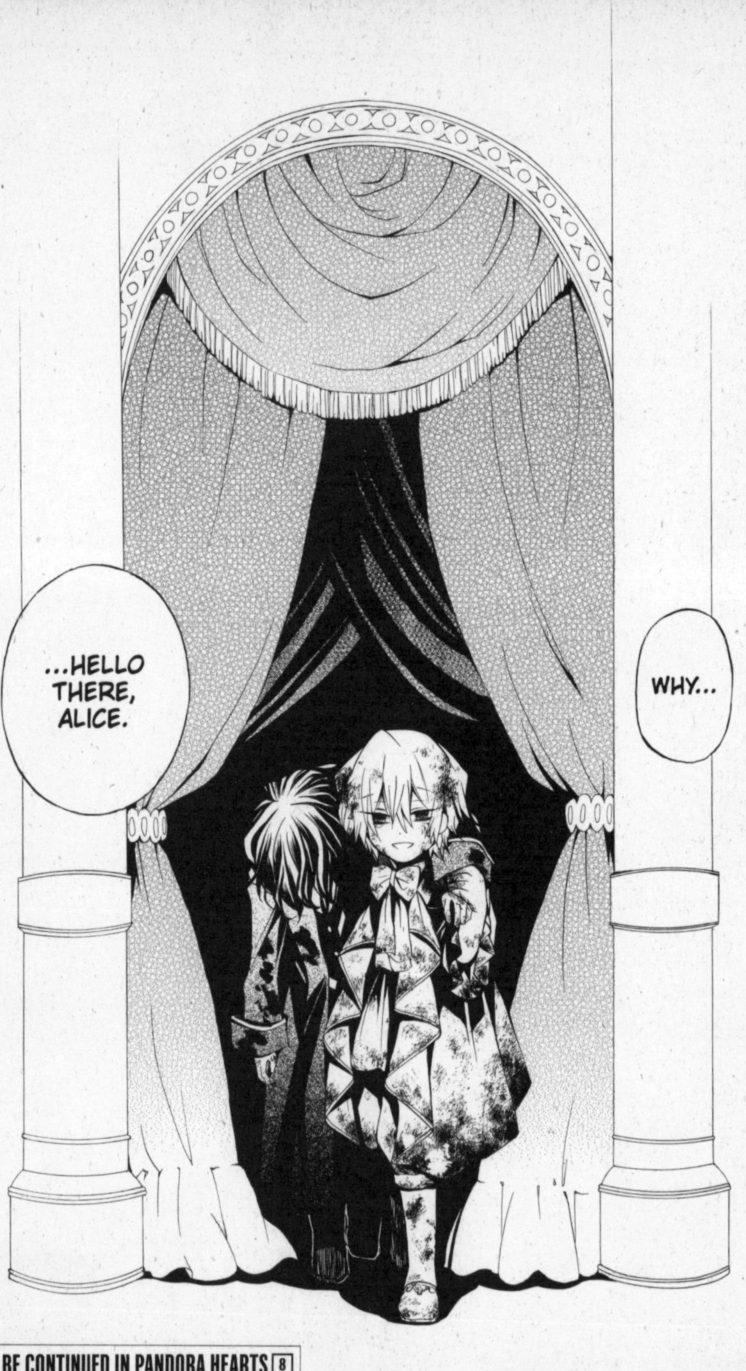
WHY...
...HELLO THERE, ALICE.

TO BE CONTINUED IN PANDORA HEARTS 8

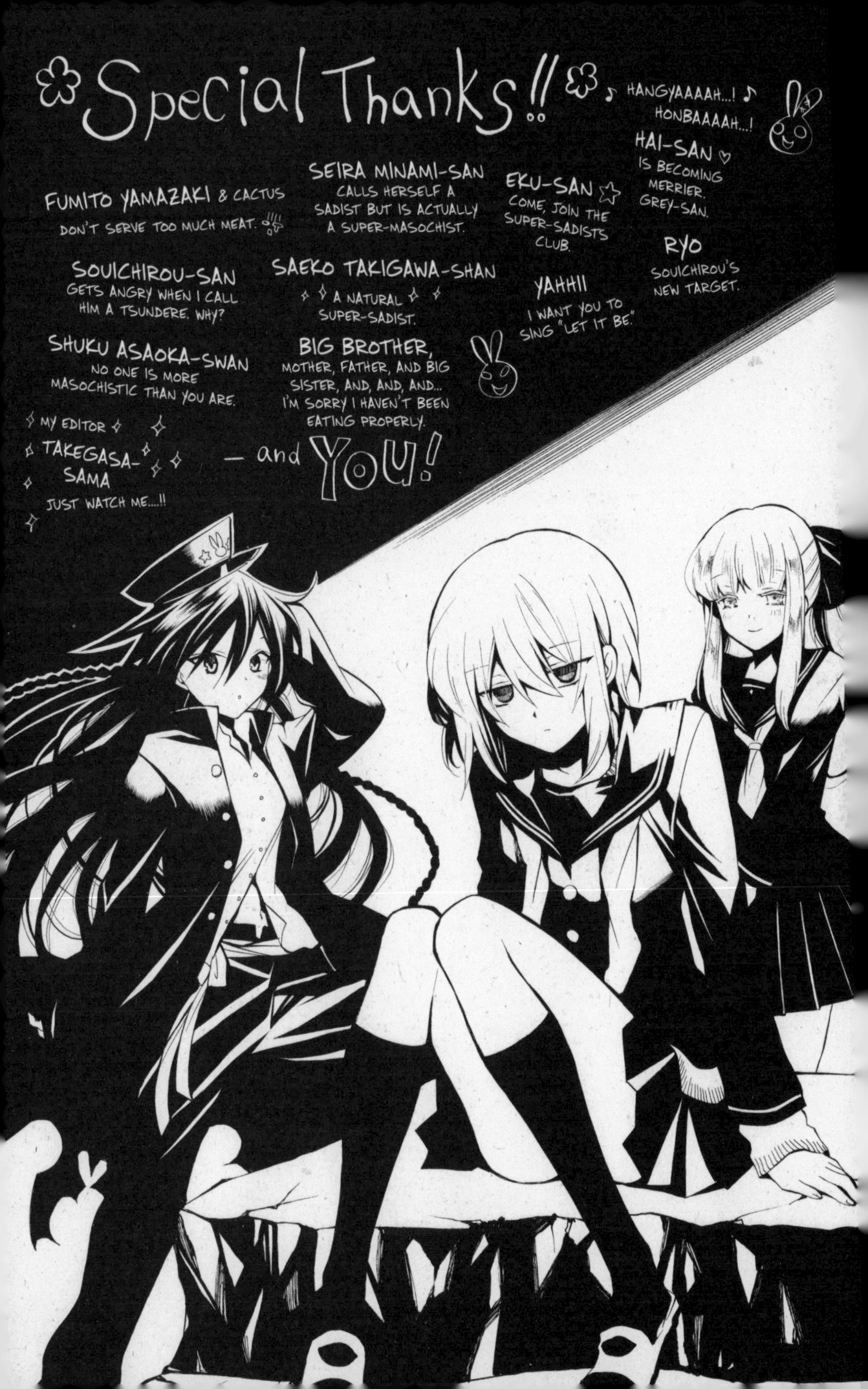
Special Thanks!!
HANGYAAAAH...! ♪ HONBAAAAH...!
FUMITO YAMAZAKI & CACTUS
DON'T SERVE TOO MUCH MEAT.
SEIRA MINAMI-SAN
CALLS HERSELF A SADIST BUT IS ACTUALLY A SUPER-MASOCHIST.
EKU-SAN
COME, JOIN THE SUPER-SADISTS CLUB.
HAI-SAN
IS BECOMING MERRIER. GREY-SAN.
SOUICHIROU-SAN
GETS ANGRY WHEN I CALL HIM A TSUNDERE. WHY?
SAEKO TAKIGAWA-SHAN
A NATURAL SUPER-SADIST.
YAHHI!
I WANT YOU TO SING "LET IT BE."
RYO
SOUICHIROU'S NEW TARGET.
SHUKU ASAOKA-SWAN
NO ONE IS MORE MASOCHISTIC THAN YOU ARE.
BIG BROTHER,
MOTHER, FATHER, AND BIG SISTER, AND, AND, AND... I'M SORRY I HAVEN'T BEEN EATING PROPERLY.
MY EDITOR
TAKEGASA-SAMA
JUST WATCH ME....!!
— and YOU!

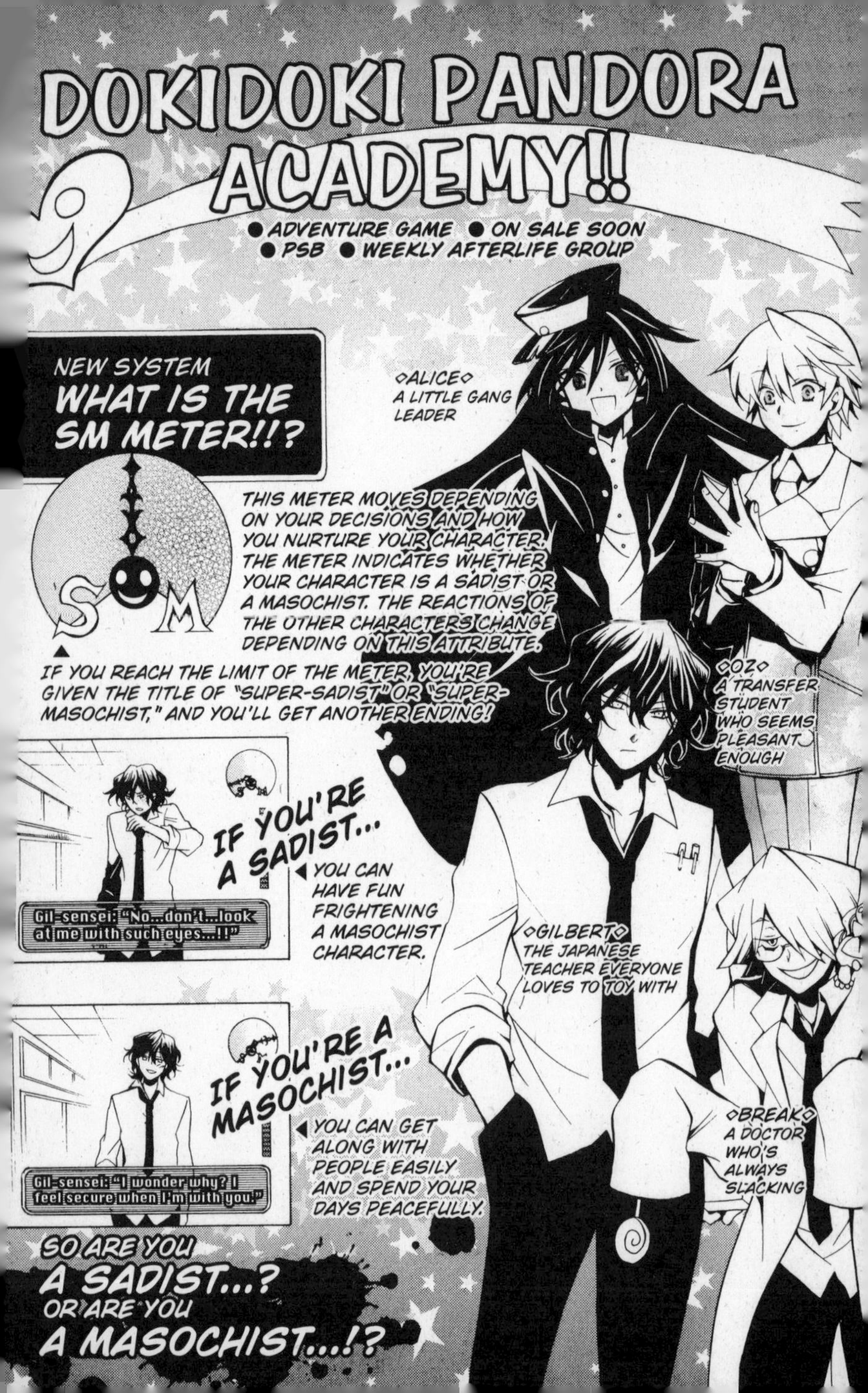
DOKIDOKI PANDORA ACADEMY!!
● ADVENTURE GAME ● ON SALE SOON
● PSB ● WEEKLY AFTERLIFE GROUP
NEW SYSTEM
WHAT IS THE SM METER!!?
◇ALICE◇
A LITTLE GANG LEADER
S M
THIS METER MOVES DEPENDING ON YOUR DECISIONS AND HOW YOU NURTURE YOUR CHARACTER. THE METER INDICATES WHETHER YOUR CHARACTER IS A SADIST OR A MASOCHIST. THE REACTIONS OF THE OTHER CHARACTERS CHANGE DEPENDING ON THIS ATTRIBUTE.
▲ IF YOU REACH THE LIMIT OF THE METER, YOU'RE GIVEN THE TITLE OF "SUPER-SADIST" OR "SUPER-MASOCHIST," AND YOU'LL GET ANOTHER ENDING!
◇OZ◇
A TRANSFER STUDENT WHO SEEMS PLEASANT ENOUGH
IF YOU'RE A SADIST...
◀ YOU CAN HAVE FUN FRIGHTENING A MASOCHIST CHARACTER.
Gil-sensei: "No...don't...look at me with such eyes...!!"
◇GILBERT◇
THE JAPANESE TEACHER EVERYONE LOVES TO TOY WITH
IF YOU'RE A MASOCHIST...
◀ YOU CAN GET ALONG WITH PEOPLE EASILY AND SPEND YOUR DAYS PEACEFULLY.
Gil-sensei: "I wonder why? I feel secure when I'm with you."
◇BREAK◇
A DOCTOR WHO'S ALWAYS SLACKING
SO ARE YOU A SADIST...? OR ARE YOU A MASOCHIST...!?

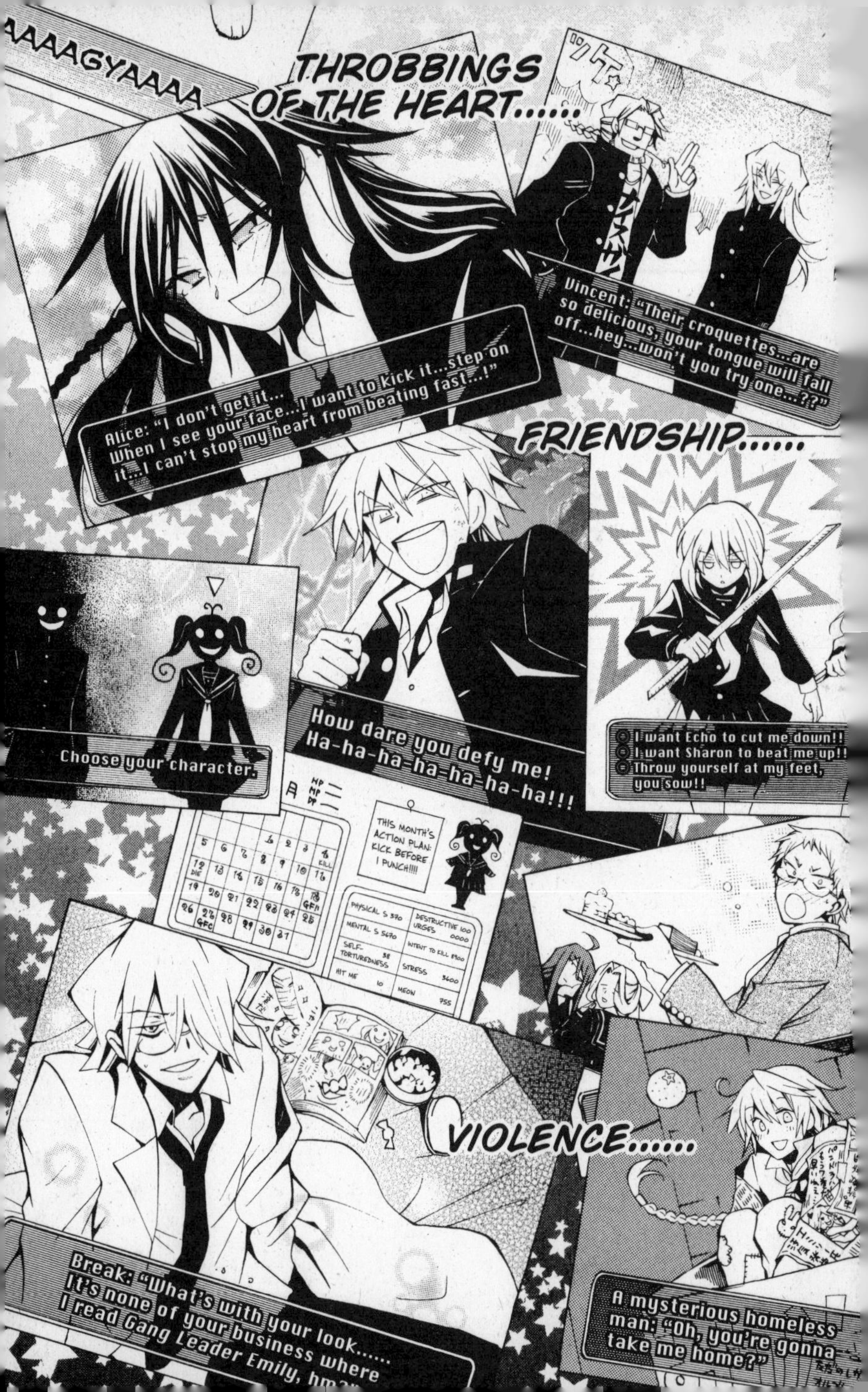
THROBBINGS OF THE HEART......
Vincent: "Their croquettes...are so delicious, your tongue will fall off...hey...won't you try one...??"
AAAAGYAAAA
Alice: "I don't get it... When I see your face...I want to kick it...step on it...I can't stop my heart from beating fast...!"
FRIENDSHIP......
I want Echo to cut me down!!
I want Sharon to beat me up!!
Throw yourself at my feet, you sow!!
How dare you defy me! Ha-ha-ha-ha-ha-ha-ha!!!
Choose your character.
HP
MP
DP
THIS MONTH'S ACTION PLAN: KICK BEFORE I PUNCH!!!!
KILL
DIE
GFC
PHYSICAL S 370
MENTAL S 5670
SELF-TORTUREDNESS 38
HIT ME 10
DESTRUCTIVE URGES 1000000
INTENT TO KILL 8900
STRESS 3600
MEOW 755
VIOLENCE......
A mysterious homeless man: "Oh, you're gonna take me home?"
Break: "What's with your look...... It's none of your business where I read Gang Leader Emily, hm?"

TRANSLATOR'S NOTES

COMMON HONORIFICS

no honorific: Indicates familiarity or closeness; if used without permission or reason, addressing someone in this manner would constitute an insult.

-san: The Japanese equivalent of Mr./Mrs./Miss. If a situation calls for politeness, this is the fail-safe honorific.

-sama: Conveys great respect; may also indicate that the social status of the speaker is lower than that of the addressee.

-kun: Used most often when referring to boys (though it can be applied to girls as well), this indicates affection or familiarity. Occasionally used by older men among their peers, but it may also be used by anyone referring to a person of lower standing.

-chan: An affectionate honorific indicating familiarity used mostly in reference to girls; also used in reference to cute persons or animals of either gender.

-oneesama ***page 68***

A very respectful honorific for a (literal or figurative) big sister.

"I am *Hetare*" ***page 80***

The sign on Gil's back is the equivalent of someone tacking a "kick me" sign to your back; *hetare* is an adjective to describe someone who is incompetent and useless, possibly also a coward.

boku* and *ore ***page 81***

In the original, Gil, who has resolved to use the manlier *ore* to refer to himself, gets confused between it and the more childish *boku*, which he was accustomed to using when he was little. See the bonus comic and translator's notes at the end of ***Pandora Hearts*** vol. 5 for some more background!

orecchi, wagahai, bokuchin,* GilGil** ***page 82

Orecchi is a slangy/silly personal pronoun derived from the informal masculine personal pronoun *ore*. *Wagahai* is an archaic personal pronoun that carries an air of arrogance. *Bokuchin* is a combination of the boyish personal pronoun *boku* and *-chin*, an even more informal version of the honorific *-chan*, which is usually reserved for young children, girls, cute things, or close friends. GilGil is another potential cutesy nickname made from Gil's name.

Cage vs *keiji* ***page 182***

Nicholas Cage in Japanese is homophonic to Nicholas-*keiji*, or "Detective Nicholas," hence the confusion.

PandoraHearts

Nowadays, the neighbor ladies on either side of my place bring me meals. My heart gets all warm and fuzzy then because in modern Japan, you don't associate much with your neighbors. The tofu pulp, konjac jelly, oden, and hashed beef rice were all delicious...! Woo. I draw my manga with the support of all these people!

MOCHIZUKI'S MUSINGS

VOLUME 7

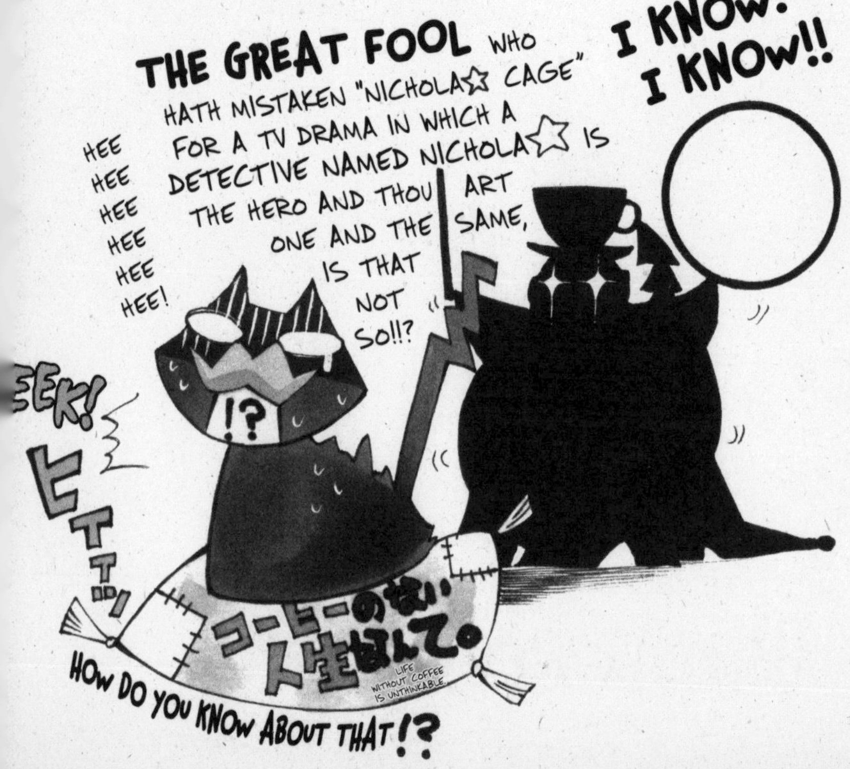
I KNOW. I KNOW!!
THE GREAT FOOL WHO HATH MISTAKEN "NICHOLA☆ CAGE" FOR A TV DRAMA IN WHICH A DETECTIVE NAMED NICHOLA☆ IS THE HERO AND THOU ART ONE AND THE SAME, IS THAT NOT SO!!?
HEE HEE HEE HEE HEE HEE!
EEK!
ヒィィィッ
コーヒーのない人生なんて。
LIFE WITHOUT COFFEE IS UNTHINKABLE.
HOW DO YOU KNOW ABOUT THAT!?